D0947135

ATLAS OF
THE SECOND
WORLD WAR

The CASSELL

ATLAS OF THE SECOND WORLD WAR

Edited by Brigadier Peter Young
Cartography by Richard Natkiel

CASSELL

Cassell
Wellington House, 125 Strand
London WC2R 0BB
www.cassell.co.uk

Text: Copyright © Weidenfeld & Nicolson
1973
Maps and diagrams: Copyright © Richard
Natkiel 1973

First published in Great Britain by
Weidenfeld & Nicolson 1973
This edition 1999

British Library Cataloguing-in-Publication
Data
A catalogue record for this book is available
from the British Library

ISBN 0-304-35286-1

Research for maps undertaken by Richard
Natkiel.
Text for map sections written by Christopher
Chant, Jonathan Martin, and Patrick
Scrivenor.

Designed by Rodney Josey

Printed and bound in Spain

Acknowledgements

The illustrations in this book are reproduced by kind permission of the following:
10: Imperial War Museum. 12/1: Ullstein. 13/1: Keystone. 13/2: Ullstein. 14: Camera Press. 15: Camera Press. 16: Ullstein. 17/1 and 2: Ullstein. 18/1: Camera Press. 18/2: Camera Press. 19/1: Novosti. 19/2: Camera Press. 20: Ullstein. 21/1: Ullstein. 21/2: Paul Popper. 22/1: Keystone. 22/2: Camera Press. 22/3: Keystone. 24: Ullstein. 25: Ullstein. 26: Keystone. 27: Ullstein. 28: Keystone. 29/1: I W M. 29/2: Süddeutscher Verlag. 30/1: I W M. 30/2: Süddeutscher Verlag. 33/1 Süddeutscher Verlag. 33/2: Camera Press. 34: Süddeutscher Verlag. 36/1: Süddeutscher Verlag. 36/2: Süddeutscher Verlag. 36/3: Ullstein. 37: Keystone. 38/1: Ullstein. 38/2: Ullstein. 39/1: Keystone. 39/2: Keystone. 40/1: Sado. 40/2: Sado. 41: Süddeutscher Verlag. 42: Camera Press. 44: Keystone. 45/1: Ullstein. 45/2: Camera Press. 46: I W M/Ballantine Books Photographic Library. 48/1: Ullstein. 48/2: I W M. 19: I W M. 50: Camera Press. 51: I W M. 52: Camera Press. 53: I W M. 54: Ullstein. 55/1: I W M 55/2: Ullstein. 56/1: Ullstein. 56/2: Camera Press. 57: Ullstein. 58: I W M. 59: Camera Press. 60/1: Ullstein. 60/2: Ullstein. 62: I W M. 63: I W M. 64/1: Associated Press. 64/2: Ullstein. 65: Ullstein. 66/1: Ullstein. 66/2: I W M. 67: I W M. 68/1: Camera Press. 68/2: I W M. 69: I W M. 70: Associated Press. 71: I W M. 72: I W M. 73: Keystone. 74: Camera Press. 75: Keystone. 76/1: Paul Popper. 76/2: I W M. 77: Keystone. 78: Keystone. 80: Ullstein. 82/1: Novosti. 82/2: Novosti. 83: Camera Press. 85: Süddeutscher Verlag. 86/1: Ullstein. 86/2: Ullstein. 88: Süddeutscher Verlag. 89: Novosti. 90: Süddeutscher Verlag. 93/1: Novosti. 93/2: Novosti. 94: Associated Press. 96: Camera Press. 97/1: Keystone. 97/2: Camera Press. 99: Paul Popper. 101/1: U S Navy/B P C Library. 101/2: Camera Press. 102: Paul Popper. 103/1: Camera Press. 103/2: Paul Popper. 104: I W M/Robert Hunt Library. 105/1: Camera Press. 105/2: Camera Press. 106: U S Navy/B P C Library. 108: B P C Library. 109: Associated Press. 111/1: Paul Popper. 111/2: Sado/BPC. 112/1: Paul Popper. 112/2: Camera Press. 113: Keystone. 114: Camera Press. 116/1: I W M. 116/2: Keystone. 117: Keystone. 118: Camera Press. 120: Keystone. 123/1: Keystone. 123/2: Keystone. 125: Camera Press. 126: Camera Press. 127: Keystone. 128: Keystone. 129: Keystone. 130: Keystone. 131: Keystone. 132: Associated Press. 134/1: I W M. 134/2: Associated Press. 135/1: Camera Press. 135/2: Camera Press. 136: I W M/B P C. 137: Paul Popper. 139: I W M. 141/1: U S Navy/B P C. 141/2: U S Marine Corps/B P C. 144: Associated Press. 146: Robert Hunt Library. 147: Paul Popper. 149: Keystone/Robert Hunt Library. 152: Keystone. 154: B P C. 155: Paul Popper. 156: I W M. 157: I W M. 158: Ballantine Books Photographic Library. 159: Robert Hunt Library. 161: Robert Hunt Library. 162: I W M. 164: U S Marine Corps/B P C. 165/1: Keystone. 165/2: Keystone. 166: Camera Press. 167/1: Camera Press. 167/2: Keystone. 168: I W M/Robert Hunt Library. 170: Camera Press. 172/1: Camera Press. 172/2: I W M. 173/1: I W M. 173/2: Camera Press. 174: I W M. 175: I W M. 176: I W M. 177/1: I W M. 177/2: I W M. 178/1: I W M. 178/2: I W M. 181: Camera Press. 182: Keystone. 183: Keystone. 184/1: I W M. 184/2: Paul Popper. 185: I W M. 186: Keystone. 188: Ullstein. 190/1: I W M. 190/2: Novosti. 191/1: Novosti. 191/2: Novosti. 193/1: Camera Press. 193/2: Camera Press. 194: Ullstein. 195: Ullstein. 196/1: Ullstein. 196/2: Ullstein.

198: Ullstein. 199: Ullstein. 200: Camera Press. 201/1: I W M. 201/2: Camera Press. 202–209: Novosti. 210: Ullstein. 211: Camera Press. 213/1: Novosti. 213/2: Keystone. 214/1: Ullstein. 214/2: I W M. 217/1: Ullstein. 217/2: Novosti. 218: Ullstein. 219: Ullstein. 220/1: Ullstein. 221: Ullstein. 224: Ullstein. 226/1: Camera Press. 226/2: Roger Viollet. 227/1: Keystone. 227/2: Roger Viollet. 228: Keystone. 229: Camera Press. 234: Paul Popper. 235: Keystone. 236: Roger Viollet. 237: Camera Press. 239/1: Roger Viollet. 239/2: Keystone. 240: Keystone. 241: Keystone. 242: Camera Press. 243: I W M. 244: I W M. 246: Keystone. 248: Süddeutscher Verlag. 250: I W M. 252/1: I W M/Robert Hunt Library. 252/2: Ullstein. 253/1: I W M/Robert Hunt Library. 253/2: Camera Press. 254: I W M. 257: Ullstein. 258/1: Süddeutscher Verlag. 258/2: I W M. 259: I W M. 261/1 and 2: Camera Press. 262: Ullstein. 263: Ullstein. 264: I W M. 265: Paul Popper. 267/1: I W M. 267/2: I W M. 268: Süddeutscher Verlag. 269: I W M. 270: I W M. 271: Paul Popper. 274: Robert Hunt Library. 280: I W M/B P C Picture Library.

CONTENTS

Germany Strikes in the West 11

The Rise of Germany 14

The Polish Campaign 16

The Finnish Campaign 18

The Invasion of Norway 20

Military Balance in the West 22

The German Assault in the West 24

Dunkirk and the Fall of France 26

Operation Sealion 28

The Battle of Britain 30

Actions in the French Overseas Empire 32

The War in the Mediterranean 35

The Italian Attack on Greece 38

The Invasion of Yugoslavia 40

The Invasion of Greece 42

The Attack on Crete 44

The North African Campaign 47

Wavell's Opening Offensive 50

The Ethiopian Campaign 52

Rommel's First Offensive 54

Operation Brevity 56

Operation Battleaxe 57

The Crusader Battles 58

Rommel's Drive to Gazala 60

The Fall of Tobruk 62

The German Advance to El Alamein 63

The First Battle at El Alamein 64

The Battle of Alam Halfa 66

The Battle of El Alamein 68

Operation Torch 70

The Advance of Eighth Army 72

The Battle of Kasserine 74

Breaking the Mareth Line 76

The End in Africa 78

Operation Barbarossa   81
The Military Balance on the Eastern Front   84
The German Assault   86
The Finnish Attacks   88
The Attack on Leningrad   89
The Battle for Moscow 1   90
The Battle for Moscow 2   92

The Japanese Offensive   95
The Situation in the Pacific   99
Pearl Harbor   100
The Invasion of Malaya   102
The Fall of Hong Kong   104
The Sinking of Force Z   105
The Fall of the Philippines   106
The Conquest of Bataan   108
The Fall of Dutch East Indies   110
The Fall of Burma   112

The Italian Campaign   115
The Invasion of Sicily   118
The Landings in Italy   120
The Drive to the Gustav Line   122
The Cassino Battles   124
Anzio and the Drive to Rome   126
Breaking the Gothic Line   128
The End in Italy   130

The Pacific War   133
The Battle of the Coral Sea   136
The Battle of Midway   138
Guadalcanal   140
The Solomon Island Naval Battles   142
The Naval Actions off Guadalcanal   144
New Guinea   146
Planning the US Counteroffensive   149
The Battle for the Solomons   150
Clearing the Marshalls   152

Clearing the Marianas 154
The Battle of the Philippine Sea 156
The Battle of Leyte Gulf 1 158
The Battle of Leyte Gulf 2 160
Clearing the Philippines 162
Iwo Jima 164
Okinawa 166
The End in the Pacific 168

The Burma Campaign 171
The Arakan Battles 174
The Chindit Operations 176
The Japanese Advance to Kohima and Imphal 178
The Battle at Kohima and Imphal 180
The Advance to Mandalay and Meiktila 182
The Capture of Rangoon 184
The War in Northern Burma 186
The War in China 187

Russia fights back 189
The Red Army Attacks in the South 192
The Drive to the Volga 194
The Assault on Stalingrad 196
The Russian Counterattacks 198
The End at Stalingrad 200
The Advance to Kharkov 202
The Battle of Kursk 204
The Dniepr and Smolensk Battles 206
The Relief of Leningrad 208
The Battles in the Ukraine 210
The Thrust into Poland 212
Clearing the Baltic States 214
Clearing the Balkans 216
The Drive to the Oder 218
The Invasions of Austria and Hungary 220
The Drive into Czechoslovakia 221
The Battle of Berlin 222

The War in North-west Europe 225
Preparation for D-Day 228
D-Day 230
The Battle of the Build-Up 233
The Battle for Normandy 234
The Anvil Landings 236
The Breakout 238
The Drive to the Rhine 240
The Arnhem Operation 242
The Battle of the Ardennes 244
Crossing the Rhine 246
The Drive into Germany 248

The Naval War 251
The Battle of the River Plate 254
The Raiders 256
The Naval War in the Mediterranean 258
Hunting the *Bismarck* 260
The Channel Dash 262
The Malta Convoys 264
The Arctic Convoys 266
Surface Battles of the Barents Sea 268
The Early Commando Raids 270
The Raid on St Nazaire 272
The Dieppe Operation 273

The War in the Air 275
The Bomber Offensive on Germany 278
The Bomber Offensive on Japan 280
Index 282

INTRODUCTION

THE MILITARY ATLAS is a reference book for the student and historian which provides detailed maps of the military side of the Second World War. It is divided into sections corresponding to the major theatres or campaigns of the war; and within these, the individual battles or phases of battles each have a double-page spread with a selection of maps. Accompanying these are a short explanatory text and illustrations. The introduction to each section has been written to fill in the background to the specific campaign, giving details about the forces and commanders involved, and the particular tactical, geographical and logistical problems with which they were faced.

GERMANY STRIKES IN THE WEST

This is not Peace. It is an Armistice for twenty years.
Marshal Foch on the Treaty of Versailles

In many ways the European armies
which went to war in 1939 were still
very like those of 1918, in which the
majority of the company commanders,
and all the more senior officers had
served. The most old-fashioned of
Germany's opponents was Poland,
whose army, for all its gallantry, was
completely outclassed by the new
Wehrmacht. Polish strategy, designed
to protect every yard of the frontiers,
was to say the least unrealistic. Even
so the legacy of the First World War
lay heaviest upon the French army.
The long slogging match on the Western
Front influenced the military thinking
of both sides, but more especially the
Allies: the Germans who had fought in
Rumania and Russia as well as France
and Belgium were by no means as
committed to ideas of trench warfare.
They knew far more about deep
penetration and the war of movement.
The French, though they had spent a
great deal of money on defence, had
devoted comparatively little to the air
force, and an inordinate amount to
their static – and incomplete – defences
in the Maginot Line, a system devised
for a new Verdun, which the Germans,
as it happened, had no intention of
fighting. The French actually had
rather more tanks than the Germans,
but they looked upon them as close
support for their infantry, rather than
a mobile arm. To a great extent the
French army still owed what mobility
it had to the horse. But this was true too
of the great mass of the German army.
The only motorized army on either side
was the British Expeditionary Force,
which as late as May 1940 had only
some fifteen divisions, three of them
incomplete, and only one armoured –
and that had only two brigades.

At the highest strategic level the
French commander General Gamelin,
Joffre's staff officer of 1914, attempted
to control events from a headquarters
so woefully deficient of communications
equipment, that he might as well have
ensconced himself in a monastery. His
plans, moreover, left him no *masse de*

manoeuvre, no reserve, a deficiency
which Churchill was to discover when
attempting to inspire the French
command into launching a
counterattack. Controversy will long
rage as to the merits of Gamelin and
Weygand. Would Gamelin, if left in
command, have counterattacked,
cutting the exposed lines of
communications of the German
panzer divisions? Was Weygand too
old, and too shattered by what he saw
of the German *blitzkrieg* to take
effective control? All one can say is that
in the fighting *after* Dunkirk, during
June 1940, the time when Weygand,
now gravely outnumbered, was in
command, the French army seems to
have inflicted far heavier casualties on
the Germans than it did in May.

As for the British the 'miracle' of
Dunkirk left them a nucleus for the
armies that were to conquer North
Africa and play their part from
Normandy to the Baltic. Had these
troops been destroyed at Dunkirk
there would have been little left of the
British army. It owed its survival as
much as anything to the fact that it was
motorized: it was so very much more
mobile than von Bock's army which
was following it up, even if it was
outclassed by von Rundstedt's armour
that was cutting it off. The miracle of
Dunkirk was that the BEF – despite a
steadfast rearguard action by the
Cavalry Club – went to France in 1939
without a single horse.

The geographical conditions under
which the campaign was fought were
more or less familiar to the commanders
on both sides of the rank of major and
above since, with the exception of the
Dutch, they had for the most part seen
fighting on the Western Front during the
First World War. But if the tactical
importance of Arras, or Kemmel, or
Mont des Cats was well-enough
remembered, experience was not
always a sure guide. The Ardennes
where the French had suffered so heavily
in August 1914 were now, on very
slender grounds, deemed to be well-

nigh impassable to armoured formations.

The French planners depended to a
great extent on their fortifications,
especially on the right of their line,
between Switzerland and Sedan. To
do them justice the Maginot
fortresses, for all the faults in their
organization, held out without difficulty
until the French field armies
surrendered. The modern Belgian
fortress of Eben Emael, guarding the
Meuse and Albert Canal bridges,
proof, no doubt, against the techniques
which had crushed the Liège fortresses
in 1914, succumbed to an airborne
coup de main. The Dutch depended on
the defence of inundations and,
everywhere, as the campaign
developed the Allies tended to form
successive defensive positions along
the lines of rivers and canals: there were
battles on the Dyle, the Scheldt, the
canals round Dunkirk, and the Somme,
to name but a few.

The armies of 1940 were armed and
organized very much like those of
1918, and, with the exception of the
British, they depended in the main upon
the horse for their mobility. Both sides
were adequately equipped with field
and medium artillery, though the
Germans by using the Stuka dive-
bomber as a form of mobile artillery
had the advantage here. It seems also
that they were rather better provided
with mortars than the Allies. The
latter were also short of anti-tank
guns, and the majority being 2-pounders
were too small to be certain of knocking
out a German tank.

With the lessons of 1914–18 both
sides had armed their infantry with
large numbers of machine guns. The
British with the Vickers MMG, the
Bren LMG, and a first-class rifle, the
Mark III Lee-Enfield, were well-
equipped, but unlike the Germans they
had as yet no sub-machine gun.

The Allies outnumbered the Germans
in tanks, but the latter were greatly
superior in their tactical handling.
The British, who put very few tanks in
the field suffered greatly from lack of

transporters. Travelling long distances
and with no time for maintenance,
they lost numbers of vehicles through
breakdowns. By 21 May, 1 Army Tank
Brigade had only seventy-four tanks.
Of these fifty-eight were Mark I and
sixteen Mark II. The former had
heavy armour, one 7·9-mm machine
gun and was very slow. The latter was
much bigger and had, in addition to
the machine gun, a 2-pounder gun.

Opposite above: German assault troops during
the invasion of Norway

Above: The BEF arrives in France in 1939

Right: German troops parade past the Arc
de Triomphe

13

THE RISE OF GERMANY

The Nazi party came to power in Germany in January 1933 pledged to tear up the Treaty of Versailles which had drastically cut down the size of Germany. The country would be restored to its 'rightful' place as the most powerful in Europe and all those Germans living in areas outside the Reich would be incorporated into the 'Greater Germany'. The treaty had limited Germany's armed forces to a 100,000-man army with no tanks, a small navy, and no airforce. But, under General Hans von Seeckt, the army was organized as a highly-trained, professional framework for a much larger force which could one day be raised by conscription. Development of tanks and military aircraft went ahead under various disguises – much of it undertaken in the Soviet Union – and civilian flying schools built up a pool of trained pilots. Thus in the spring of 1935, Hitler was able to announce that Germany repudiated the Treaty of Versailles, that she now had an airforce, and that conscription would be introduced to bring the army up to 300,000 men.

The Western democracies, Britain and France, made no effective protest and this convinced Hitler that they had lost the will to act decisively. In March 1936 he openly proved this by reoccupying the Rhineland – against the advice of his generals who knew that the army was still undertrained, underequipped, and far smaller than that of France.

In March 1938, with the apparent approval of the bulk of her population, Austria was annexed to the Reich. Once again, Britain and France made no effort to prevent it. Despite warnings, their governments were determined to avoid war and preferred to give way to Hitler rather than run any risks. But in the autumn of 1938 the Führer made his first overt move against an independent state, when he demanded that the Sudetenland – the western border of Czechoslovakia – with its 3,000,000 Germans should be annexed to the Reich, because its inhabitants were being maltreated by the native population. Czechoslovakia was a model democracy, prosperous and socially advanced, with large well-equipped armed forces and defences which would have proved a difficult opponent for the Germans. The government prepared to resist, but, as Hitler had foreseen, under pressure from Britain and France an 'honourable' solution was found guaranteeing 'peace in our time'. The Sudetenland with all of the Czech frontier defences was handed over to Germany. Hitler had removed a potentially difficult threat on his southern flank and was further convinced that he had nothing to fear from France and Britain. In March 1939 he completed the occupation of Czechoslovakia, but now at last the Western democracies had realized the true nature of his plans and begun to rearm. However, it would take time to redress the years of inactivity and the German forces were now more than equal in strength to their probable opponents. Hitler was ready to turn on his next victim – Poland – where the Danzig corridor cutting off East Prussia from the Reich presented an inviting excuse for intervention.

Left: Troops marching past Hitler during a Nazi rally in Nuremberg in 1936

August 1939

German expansion in Europe

THE POLISH CAMPAIGN

German troop carriers cross
the Polish frontier

Hitler's forces conquered Poland in eighteen days. It was not Polish morale that failed, they were simply not strong enough. Against nine armoured divisions the Poles could pit a dozen cavalry brigades and a handful of light tanks. Even in artillery and infantry the Germans outnumbered the Poles by at least three to two. In any case the defending army was not given time to complete its mobilization and the German fleet commanded the Baltic as effectively as the Luftwaffe did the sky. In addition the Germans had a new concept of war – blitzkrieg.

The basis of the blitzkrieg was surprise, speed and terror. Armoured forces were used to break through the enemies' defences and then to drive deep into his rear surrounding large pockets of troops, ignoring and by-passing stubborn defences, and disrupting communications. The German plan (**Map 1**) aimed for two massive pincer movements from north and south, which would break up the Polish armies, forcing them to fight individual survival battles rather than a co-ordinated defence.

At dawn on 1 September 1939 the Germans launched their invasion (**Map 2**). Two army groups swept across the borders supported by a massive air offensive which destroyed the bulk of the Polish airforce within two days. The Poles were unable to contain the armoured thrusts, and by 8 September the Germans were in the outskirts of Warsaw. General Kutrzeba, whose forces at Kutno had been by-passed, drew in troops from Torun and Lodz and boldly counterattacked the main German advance towards Warsaw with twelve divisions (**Map 3**). But by the 19th the battle of the Bzura was over.

Meanwhile the battle of the Vistula was being fought out. Lemberg fell on the 12th and on the 17th the German pincers closed near Brest-Litovsk. The Russians had crossed the eastern frontier on the 17th, taking Vilnyus the next day. The Polish government fled to Rumania but Warsaw held out till the 27th. On 28 September the victors arranged a fifth partition of Poland (**Map 4**). The Russians annexed 77,000 square miles, leaving the other 73,000 with most of the manufacturing areas under the 'protection' of the Reich.

October 1939

German expansion in Europe

Right: General von Blaskowitz negotiating the terms of Polish surrender

Below: A squadron of Stukas in flight. German control of the air enabled them to devastate the Polish defences

17

THE FINNISH CAMPAIGN

On 30 November, Russia invaded Finland. The troops of five armies crossed the frontier on four main fronts (**Map 1**) but soon found themselves bogged down in the deep snow and wooded terrain. Tanks and transports were forced to stick to the forest roads, and were ideal targets for Finnish ski troops who harassed the flanks, shot up convoys, and cut off formations. By the end of January, the Russians had made deep penetrations in the north of the country but on the Karelian Isthmus they had been unable to breach the Mannerheim Line. At the beginning of February, they launched a major assault (**Map 2**) preceded by a massive bombardment. By the middle of the month a breakthrough had been achieved and Finland was forced to surrender, ceding the Karelian Isthmus and considerable territory in the north. The Russian losses were about 200,000 men killed, about 1,600 tanks and 684 aircraft destroyed. The Finns lost 24,923 men killed and sixty-one aircraft.

Below: German specialists installed these obstacles on the Soviet–Finnish border

Below right: Finnish soldiers on the northern front

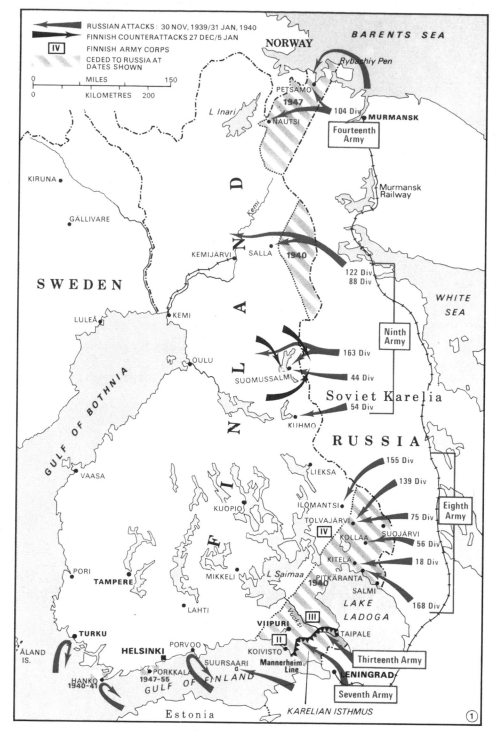

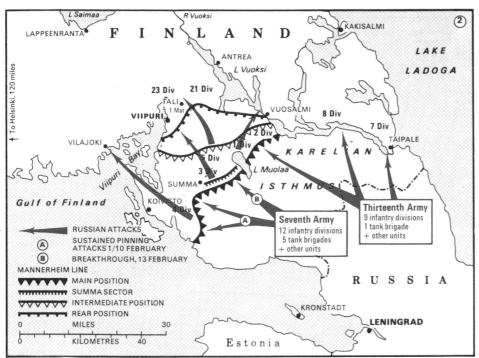

Above: Russian troops fighting on the Karelian Isthmus

Below: Finnish soldiers with a captured Russian tank

THE INVASION OF NORWAY

The German invasions of Denmark and Norway began on 9 April 1940. Denmark was swiftly overrun and a ceasefire agreed by the evening. German naval landings took place at five points on the Norwegian coast and two parachute drops were made. The naval force attacking Oslo was fired on by shore batteries and the cruiser *Blücher* sunk and the pocket battleship *Lützow* damaged. The expedition was forced to land on the east bank of the fjord and move overland to the capital, but their attack combined with that of six companies of paratroops swiftly captured the city. Kristiansand, Stavanger, Bergen, Trondheim, and Narvik all fell with only minor fighting.

The Allied reaction was hampered by lack of reserves trained for landing. British, French, and Polish forces landed at Harstad and Bodö to recapture Narvik and further south at Namsos and Åndalsnes to attack Trondheim. However, the southern forces soon found themselves under heavy German attack and had to be evacuated in two weeks. The northern forces captured Narvik on 28 May, but events in France made it necessary to withdraw them in June.

German soldiers practising advance over rocky terrain in preparation for the invasion of Norway

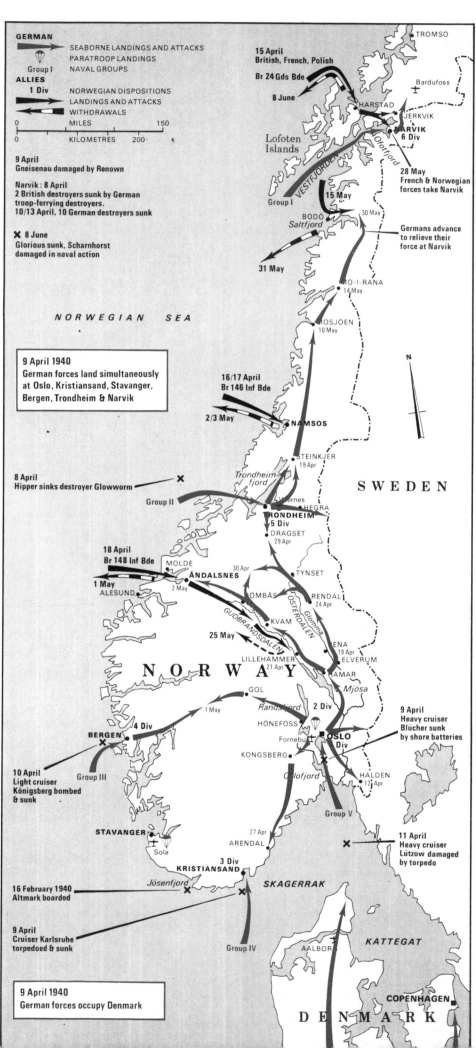

GERMAN
SEABORNE LANDINGS AND ATTACKS
PARATROOP LANDINGS
Group I   NAVAL GROUPS
ALLIES
1 Div   NORWEGIAN DISPOSITIONS
LANDINGS AND ATTACKS
WITHDRAWALS

MILES   150
0
KILOMETRES   200

9 April
Gneisenau damaged by Renown

Narvik : 8 April
2 British destroyers sunk by German troop-ferrying destroyers.
10/13 April, 10 German destroyers sunk

X 8 June
Glorious sunk, Scharnhorst damaged in naval action

9 April 1940
German forces land simultaneously at Oslo, Kristiansand, Stavanger, Bergen, Trondheim & Narvik

8 April
Hipper sinks destroyer Glowworm

18 April
Br 148 Inf Bde

10 April
Light cruiser Königsberg bombed & sunk

16 February 1940
Altmark boarded

9 April
Cruiser Karlsruhe torpedoed & sunk

9 April 1940
German forces occupy Denmark

TROMSÖ
15 April
British, French, Polish
Br 24 Gds Bde
8 June
Bardufoss
HARSTAD
JERKVIK
NARVIK
6 Div
Lofoten Islands
28 May
French & Norwegian forces take Narvik
Group I
15 May
30 May
BODÖ
Saltfjord
Germans advance to relieve their force at Narvik
31 May
MO-I-RANA
14 May
NORWEGIAN SEA
MOSJOEN
10 May
16/17 April
Br 146 Inf Bde
2/3 May
NAMSOS
STEINKJER
19 Apr
Trondheim-fjord
SWEDEN
Group II
Vaernes
HEGRA
TRONDHEIM
5 Div
DRAGSET
29 Apr
MOLDE
30 Apr
ÅNDALSNES
TYNSET
1 May
ALESUND
2 May
OMBÅS
RENDAL
24 Apr
GUDBRANDSDALEN
ÖSTERDALEN
KVAM
Glomma
25 May
ENA
19 Apr
ELVERUM
LILLEHAMMER
21 Apr
HAMAR
NORWAY
L. Mjösa
GOL
2 Div
Randsfjord
1 May
HONEFOSS
9 April
Heavy cruiser Blücher sunk by shore batteries
4 Div
Fornebu
OSLO
Div
BERGEN
X
KONGSBERG
Group III
Oslofjord
HALDEN
12 Apr
Group V
STAVANGER
27 Apr
ARENDAL
11 April
Heavy cruiser Lützow damaged by torpedo
Sola
X
3 Div
KRISTIANSAND
Jösenfjord
SKAGERRAK
X
X
KATTEGAT
Group IV
AALBORG
COPENHAGEN
DENMARK

German expansion in Europe

Right: German troops in a burning Norwegian village

Below: HMS *Glowworm* photographed from the bridge of the *Hipper* shortly before she was sunk

MILITARY BALANCE IN THE WEST

For six months after the fall of Poland, the armies on the Western Front remained practically motionless; the Allies waiting for the Germans to move, and Germans regrouping after their Polish victory. The key to Allied strategy was the Maginot Line which was still uncompleted as it only reached to the Belgian border. They were thus painfully aware of the gap and mesmerized by their memories of the Schlieffen Plan of 1914 – the massive sweeping thrust through Belgium which aimed towards Paris, and their Dyle Plan was designed to counter such an attack by pivoting forward into Belgium with their right flank hinged on Sedan and the hilly Ardennes (small map). Unfortunately, the Germans' leading planner, General Manstein had foreseen this reaction; and had realized that the Ardennes were certainly not impassable. His plan relied on an attack on the Low Countries to draw the Allies forward, and then a thrust through the Ardennes, breaking the Allied hinge near Sedan, aiming for the sea near Calais and cutting off the troops who had moved forward into Belgium.

Theoretically, the two sides were fairly equally matched (main map): the Allies had a total of 149 divisions facing 136 German divisions, and about 3,000 armoured vehicles against approximately 2,700. But the Allies were still wedded to outmoded ideas of positional warfare, their armour was assigned to the infantry divisions and spread out along the front. General Gamelin only maintained a small reserve. In contrast, the German armour was organized as a virtually independent Panzer Group, and was assigned to von Rundstedt's Army Group A which would have the job of making the vital thrust through the centre of the Allied line. The Germans also had a massive superiority in the air – more than 2,000 bombers against the Allied 800 and 4,000 fighters against 2,500.

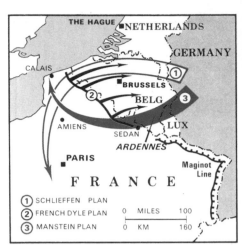

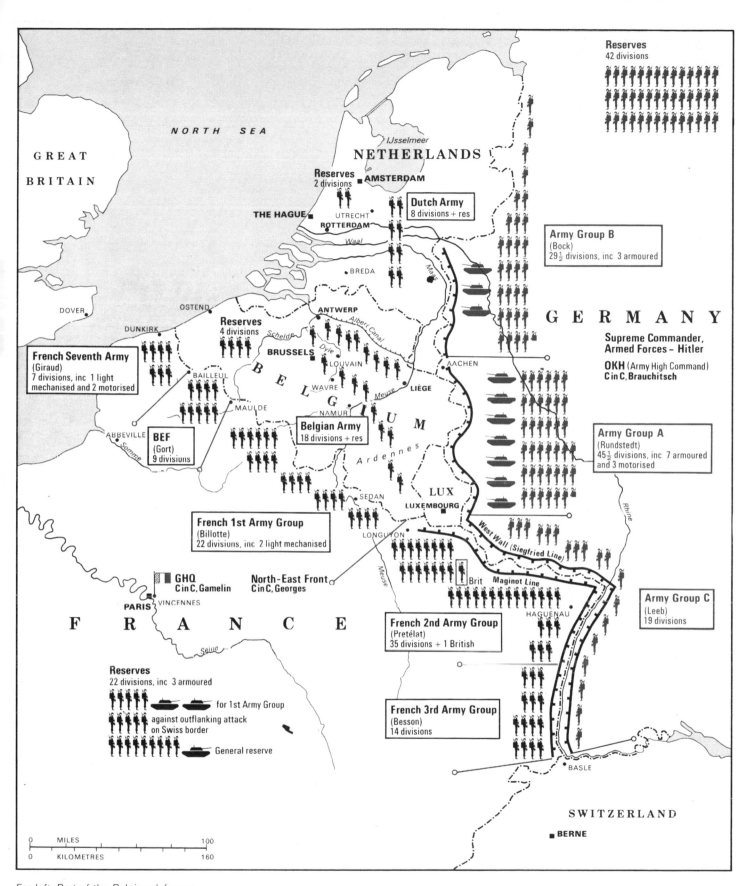

Reserves
42 divisions

NORTH SEA

GREAT BRITAIN

IJsselmeer

NETHERLANDS

Reserves
2 divisions

AMSTERDAM

Dutch Army
8 divisions + res

THE HAGUE
UTRECHT
ROTTERDAM

Waal

Army Group B
(Bock)
29½ divisions, inc 3 armoured

BREDA

Maas

GERMANY

DOVER

OSTEND

ANTWERP

Albert Canal

Scheldt

Reserves
4 divisions

DUNKIRK

AACHEN

**Supreme Commander,
Armed Forces – Hitler**

OKH (Army High Command)
C in C, Brauchitsch

French Seventh Army
(Giraud)
7 divisions, inc 1 light
mechanised and 2 motorised

B

E

BRUSSELS

Dyle

BAILLEUL

LOUVAIN

WAVRE

MEUSE

LIÈGE

L

G

MAULDE

NAMUR

I

U

ABBEVILLE

Somme

BEF
(Gort)
9 divisions

Belgian Army
18 divisions + res

M

Ardennes

Army Group A
(Rundstedt)
45½ divisions, inc 7 armoured
and 3 motorised

SEDAN

LUX
LUXEMBOURG

Rhine

French 1st Army Group
(Billotte)
22 divisions, inc 2 light mechanised

LONGUYON

West Wall (Siegfried Line)

GHQ
C in C, Gamelin

North-East Front
C in C, Georges

Meuse

Brit
Maginot Line

Army Group C
(Leeb)
19 divisions

PARIS
VINCENNES

FRANCE

Seine

HAGUENAU

French 2nd Army Group
(Pretélat)
35 divisions + 1 British

Reserves
22 divisions, inc 3 armoured

for 1st Army Group

against outflanking attack
on Swiss border

General reserve

French 3rd Army Group
(Besson)
14 divisions

BASLE

MILES   100

KILOMETRES   160

SWITZERLAND

BERNE

Far left: Part of the Belgian defences
along the German frontier

Above left: French troops moving forward
heavy artillery. Much of French equipment
dated from the First World War

Below left: A French lookout waits for
the enemy

THE GERMAN ASSAULT IN THE WEST

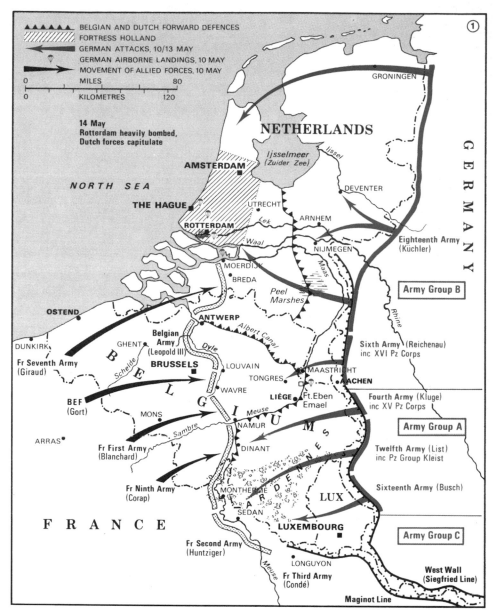

The campaign in the West falls neatly into two parts: the battle of the Low Countries and the battle of France. The first began abruptly on the morning of 10 May 1940 when the Germans struck with air attacks and parachute landings on Dutch airfields and bridges (**Map 1**) and their troops moved into Holland and Belgium. Both countries called for help from France and Britain, and the Allied army began its planned move forward to cover Brussels. The Dutch, however, despite flooding and demolitions were swiftly forced back into 'Fortress Holland'; on the 14th Rotterdam was blitzed and the Dutch forces surrendered after suffering 25 per cent casualties.

Meanwhile, the Germans had captured Fort Eben Emael on the 11th, and their Panzer divisions had thrust through the 'impassable' Ardennes (**Map 2**) to reach the Meuse. The first three bridgeheads were secured by the morning of 14 May, and were not counterattacked; a 50-mile breach was appearing at the hinge of the Allied line between Sedan and Dinant. After a brief disagreement between Kleist and Guderian as to whether to stop and consolidate, the Panzers again moved forward on the night of 15/16 May, heading behind the BEF and the French First and Ninth Armies which were forced to fall back from Belgium (**Map 3**). By the 20th the German tanks had reached the sea at Noyelles and established a corridor between the Allied forces. On the 21st the Allies made a vain attempt to cut this corridor near Arras, but this failed, and on the 22nd the Germans turned north to drive towards the Channel ports but, partly thanks to Hitler and partly to von Rundstedt, halted the next day and did not move forward until the 25th. The Allies fell back around Dunkirk, and after Boulogne had fallen on the 25th and Calais on the 27th, the decision was taken to evacuate as many Allied troops as possible by sea.

Right: German troops in action at the Aisne, 1940

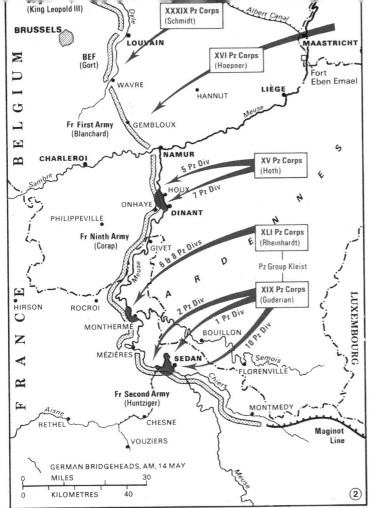

German soldiers fire
a howitzer in May 1940

Map 2 labels:

(King Leopold III)

XXXIX Pz Corps (Schmidt)

XVI Pz Corps (Hoepner)

BRUSSELS

LOUVAIN

BEF (Gort)

WAVRE

MAASTRICHT

Fort Eben Emael

HANNUT

LIÈGE

Fr First Army (Blanchard)

GEMBLOUX

NAMUR

CHARLEROI

XV Pz Corps (Hoth)

5 Pz Div

HOUX

7 Pz Div

PHILIPPEVILLE

ONHAYE

DINANT

Fr Ninth Army (Corap)

GIVET

XLI Pz Corps (Rheinhardt)

Pz Group Kleist

6 & 8 Pz Divs

HIRSON

ROCROI

XIX Pz Corps (Guderian)

MONTHERMÉ

2 Pz Div

MÉZIÈRES

1 Pz Div

BOUILLON

10 Pz Div

SEDAN

Semois

FLORENVILLE

Fr Second Army (Huntziger)

Chiers

LUXEMBOURG

MONTMEDY

Aisne

RETHEL

CHESNE

VOUZIERS

Maginot Line

Meuse

GERMAN BRIDGEHEADS, AM, 14 MAY

MILES 30

KILOMETRES 40

BELGIUM

FRANCE

ARDENNES

Map 3 labels:

XVI Pz Corps (Hoepner)

Belgian Army

BEF

BELGIUM

NAMUR

Meuse

DUNKIRK

COURTRAI

Lys

Escaut

MARCHE

YPRES

ROUBAIX

TOURNAI

3 Pz Div

CHARLEROI

DINANT

XV Pz Corps (Hoth)

CALAIS

ARMENTIÈRES

LILLE

MONS

4 Pz Div

Sambre

5 Pz Div

14 May

ONHAYE

ST OMER

ST AMAND

MAUBEUGE

PHILIPPEVILLE

GIVET

BOULOGNE
25 May

BÉTHUNE

Fr First Army

DOUAI

VALENCIENNES

7 Pz Div

NEUFCHÂTE

ÉTAPLES

21 May British armour attempts breakthrough

ST POL

ARRAS

CAMBRAI
18 May

LE CATEAU

AVESNES

XLI Pz Corps (Rheinhardt)

MONTHERMÉ

BOUILLON

MONTREUIL

FRANCE

8 Pz Div

ROCROI

15 May

MÉZIÈRES

XIX Pz Corps (Guderian)

DOULLENS

Fr Ninth Army

Oise

HIRSON

6 Pz Div

2 Pz Div

SEDAN
14 May

Meuse

NOYELLES
20 May

ALBERT

PÉRONNE 18 May

GUISE

VERVINS

1 Pz Div

Ardennes Canal

ST QUENTIN

MONTCORNET
15 May

10 Pz Div

RETHEL

MONT

ABBEVILLE
20 May

Somme

Weygand's plan to link up Allied forces

CRÉCY

MARLE

VOUZIERS

SENUC

VER

AMIENS

LA FÈRE

LAON

17/19 May De Gaulle's armour counterattacks

Aisne

Fr Second Army

Fr Tenth Army

MONTDIDIER

Oise

Serre

Fr Seventh Army

BEAUVAIS

Fr Sixth Army

REIMS

ENGLISH CHANNEL

FRONT LINE, 21 MAY

MILES 50

KILOMETRES 80

COMPIÈGNE

SOISSON

25

DUNKIRK AND THE FALL OF FRANCE

The failure of the Germans to close in on the Channel ports and the determined defence of Calais till 27 May (**Map 1**) enabled the Royal Navy to begin the evacuation of the BEF from Dunkirk (**Map 2**). In the nine days before 4 June, 338,226 men, including 120,000 French, were rescued. The Luftwaffe attempted to annihilate the operation but the intervention of the RAF, which shot down 179 aircraft for the loss of 29 between 27 and 30 May, limited the destruction to six destroyers sunk and nineteen seriously damaged as well as numerous smaller craft.

Dunkirk gave the French in the south some respite. General Weygand now attempted to organize a system of defence on the Somme and the Aisne, but the majority of the French army had lost all confidence in their leaders and themselves. Nor were the remaining Allied forces in any condition to help them. The 51 Highland Division surrendered at St Valery-en-Caux on 12 June. The 52 Division and 1 Canadian Division had to be evacuated.

The Germans were across the Seine by 10 June (**Map 3**) and on that day Mussolini declared war and Italian troops moved a short way into France, meeting stubborn resistance. On the 12th the French government declared Paris an open city and moved to Bordeaux. Churchill's offer of union between Britain and France was rejected. Reynaud resigned and his successor, Marshal Pétain, accepted the German terms on 22 June.

All France north and west of a line from the Swiss frontier at Geneva, via Bourges to St Jean Pied de Port was to be occupied (**Map 4**). The French government set up its capital at Vichy in the unoccupied zone. General de Gaulle arrived in London and established the Free French forces.

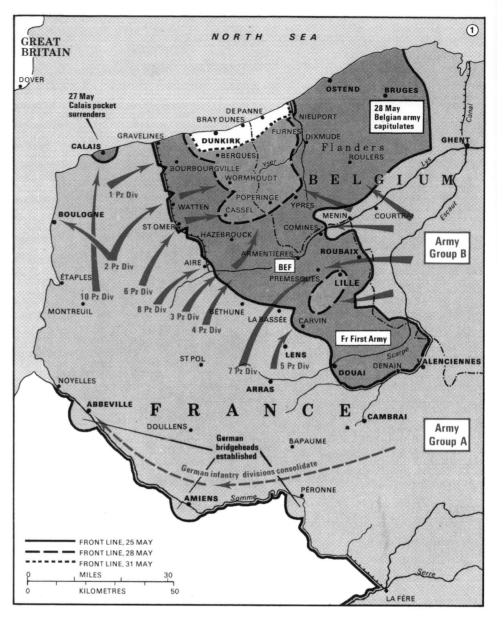

Below: A German flame-thrower team in action during the capture of the Maginot Line

Below right: The fall of Paris

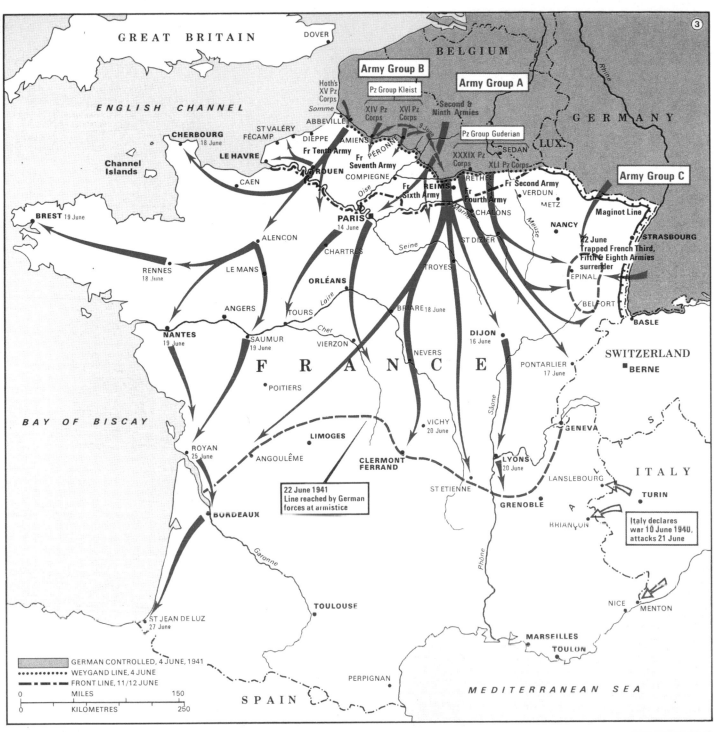

GREAT BRITAIN

DOVER

BELGIUM

Army Group B

Hoth's
XV Pz
Corps

Somme

Pz Group Kleist

XIV Pz
Corps

XVI Pz
Corps

Army Group A

Second &
Ninth Armies

GERMANY

Pz Group Guderian

LUX.

ENGLISH CHANNEL

ABBEVILLE

ST VALÉRY
FÉCAMP

DIEPPE

AMIENS

PÉRONNE

SEDAN

CHERBOURG
18 June

Fr Tenth Army

XXXIX Pz
Corps

XLI Pz Corps

Army Group C

Channel
Islands

LE HAVRE

ROUEN

CAEN

Fr
Seventh Army

COMPIEGNE

Oise

Fr
Sixth Army

REIMS

RETHEL

Fr Second Army

VERDUN

METZ

Maginot Line

Fr
Fourth Army

CHALONS

Marne

NANCY

STRASBOURG

BREST 19 June

PARIS
14 June

ALENCON

Seine

ST DIZIER

Meuse

22 June
Trapped French Third,
Fifth & Eighth Armies
surrender

EPINAL

RENNES
18 June

CHARTRES

LE MANS

ORLÉANS

TROYES

BELFORT

BASLE

ANGERS

Loire

TOURS

BRIARE 18 June

NEVERS

DIJON
16 June

PONTARLIER
17 June

SWITZERLAND

BERNE

NANTES
19 June

SAUMUR
19 June

Cher

VIERZON

BAY OF BISCAY

POITIERS

Sâone

VICHY
20 June

LYONS
20 June

GENEVA

LANSLEBOURG

ITALY

TURIN

ROYAN
25 June

LIMOGES

ANGOULÊME

CLERMONT
FERRAND

ST ETIENNE

22 June 1941
Line reached by German
forces at armistice

Rhône

GRENOBLE

BRIANÇON

Italy declares
war 10 June 1940,
attacks 21 June

BORDEAUX

Garonne

F R A N C E

NICE

MENTON

TOULOUSE

ST JEAN DE LUZ
27 June

MARSEILLES

TOULON

GERMAN CONTROLLED, 4 JUNE, 1941

· · · · · · WEYGAND LINE, 4 JUNE

— · — · FRONT LINE, 11/12 JUNE

PERPIGNAN

MEDITERRANEAN SEA

MILES   150

KILOMETRES   250

SPAIN

③

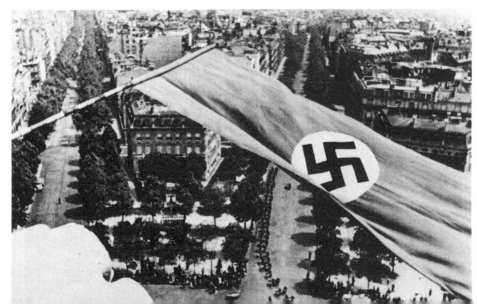

BRITAIN

BELGIUM

GERMANY

PARIS

FRANCE
(German occupied)

SWITZ

VICHY

(Vichy)

ITALY

BORDEAUX

MARSEILLES

SPAIN

④

27

OPERATION SEALION

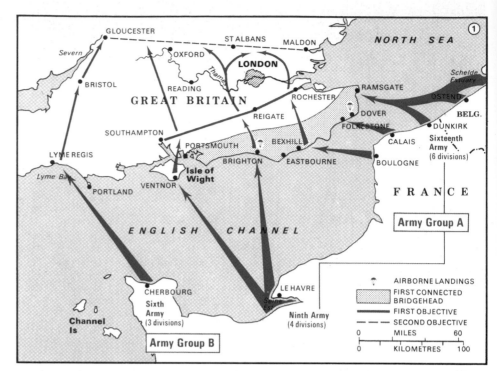

The German High Command was convinced that after the fall of France Britain would sue for peace. When no peace initiative was forthcoming Hitler planned a seaborne invasion, Operation Sealion.

The Germans set aside an army of some twenty divisions for the operation, the safe arrival of which depended on the Luftwaffe rather than the small German navy. If Göring's men could destroy the RAF and drive the Royal Navy out of the English Channel, the invaders had a good chance of landing without unacceptable casualties. Once ashore, they would have had to deal with some twenty-five divisions, woefully short of modern weapons, transport, and tanks, spread out from Kent to Cromarty, with no certainty of where the enemy would land.

The Germans collected a fleet of barges and steamers in the Channel ports; many of these were hurriedly adapted for beach landings and troops were trained in the techniques which would be required. But throughout August and the beginning of September they waited at ten days' readiness to sail while the Luftwaffe fought to gain control of the skies over the Channel. By the middle of September the date of the invasion had already been postponed three times, and on 2 October the invasion troops were stood down. On 12 October, when it was obvious that the Luftwaffe had failed, the operation was postponed until 1941, and the troops began moving away from their embarkation points.

June 1940

German expansion in Europe

Above: London Home Guards on parade as Britain prepares to meet a German invasion

Opposite above: Marshal Göring and his staff look across the narrow channel at the white cliffs of Dover

Opposite below: German troops practising with assault boats for Operation Sealion

THE BATTLE OF BRITAIN

German airpower was now at its height with eleven fighter groups, two fighter-bomber groups and ten bomber groups, 2,830 planes in all flying from bases in northern France and the Low Countries. Against these forces Fighter Command had on 8 August between 6–700 fighters, organized in fifty-five operational squadrons and directed by the newly-established radar chains.

The Battle of Britain began on 10 July when German bombers attacked merchant convoys in the Channel. On 16 July Hitler issued his instructions for Operation Sealion, to be completed by the middle of August. Barges were assembled in the Channel ports and the Luftwaffe turned its attention to the airfields of south-east England. In the first ten days of their August campaign the Luftwaffe lost several times the RAF loss of 153 planes. By 5 September casualties were beginning to make the Germans lose sight of their true objective, the destruction of the RAF. Had they persevered against the airfields their greater numbers must eventually have worn down the slender reserves of Fighter Command but at the crucial moment their targets were shifted. On 7 September came the first mass attack on London and the opening of the campaign against British towns and civilian morale. German casualties continued to mount and the bombers stopped coming over in the daytime on about 5 October. On 12 October Hitler cancelled Operation Sealion. The Blitz continued by night until the Luftwaffe was sent east to Russia, but the threat of invasion had passed.

Above: A Dornier bomber shot down over southern England

Right: Air crew walking out to their Spitfires

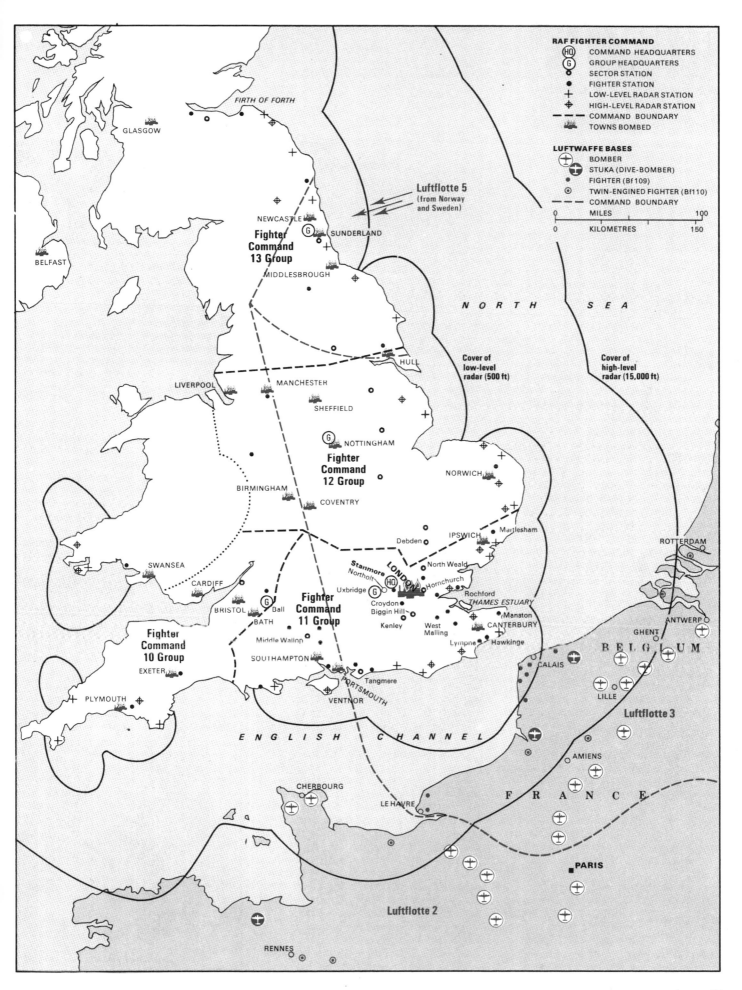

RAF FIGHTER COMMAND
- (HQ) COMMAND HEADQUARTERS
- (G) GROUP HEADQUARTERS
- ⊙ SECTOR STATION
- ● FIGHTER STATION
- + LOW-LEVEL RADAR STATION
- ✛ HIGH-LEVEL RADAR STATION
- − − − COMMAND BOUNDARY
- TOWNS BOMBED

LUFTWAFFE BASES
- ⊕ BOMBER
- ⊕ STUKA (DIVE-BOMBER)
- ● FIGHTER (Bf 109)
- ⊙ TWIN-ENGINED FIGHTER (Bf 110)
- − − − COMMAND BOUNDARY

MILES 0 — 100
KILOMETRES 0 — 150

Luftflotte 5
(from Norway
and Sweden)

N O R T H   S E A

Cover of
low-level
radar (500 ft)

Cover of
high-level
radar (15,000 ft)

GLASGOW
FIRTH OF FORTH
BELFAST
NEWCASTLE
**Fighter
Command
13 Group**
SUNDERLAND
MIDDLESBROUGH
HULL
LIVERPOOL
MANCHESTER
SHEFFIELD
NOTTINGHAM
**Fighter
Command
12 Group**
NORWICH
BIRMINGHAM
COVENTRY
Debden
IPSWICH
Martlesham
ROTTERDAM
SWANSEA
CARDIFF
Stanmore
Northolt
LONDON
North Weald
Hornchurch
Rochford
THAMES ESTUARY
ANTWERP
B E L G I U M
GHENT
BRISTOL
Ball
BATH
Uxbridge
Croydon
Biggin Hill
Kenley
West
Malling
CANTERBURY
Manston
CALAIS
LILLE
**Fighter
Command
10 Group**
Middle Wallop
SOUTHAMPTON
Lympne
Hawkinge
**Fighter
Command
11 Group**
EXETER
Tangmere
PORTSMOUTH
VENTNOR
Luftflotte 3
PLYMOUTH
E N G L I S H   C H A N N E L
AMIENS
CHERBOURG
LE HAVRE
F R A N C E
PARIS
Luftflotte 2
RENNES

31

ACTIONS IN THE FRENCH OVERSEAS EMPIRE

After the surrender of France, a major question-mark hung over the fate of her powerful and well-equipped navy. In June 1940, the French had six battleships, with one more nearing completion, and two battle-cruisers. Two of the battleships were in British ports and one was at Alexandria. Of the remainder, two battleships and the battle-cruisers were at Mers El Kebir near Oran, while the new battleship, *Richelieu*, was at Dakar. Her uncompleted sister ship, *Jean Bart*, had left her dock at St Nazaire the day before the Germans arrived and reached Casablanca safely. It was essential for the British that these ships should not fall into German hands for they would more than double German naval strength making up for her losses in the Norwegian campaign. They therefore demanded that the French ships should sail to British harbours, but when the armistice negotiations were completed it was laid down that the French fleet should be disarmed in home waters under German supervision.

Although Admiral Darlan, the French minister of marine, issued instructions that no ship should be allowed to fall intact into German hands, the British were disinclined to risk the possibility that the Germans might try to ignore the armistice regulations and seize the fleet. On 27 June 1940 it was decided that the French ships must be prevented from returning to their home ports. The next day, Vice-Admiral Sir James Somerville was given command of Force H – the battle-cruiser *Hood*, two battleships, and an aircraft-carrier – based on Gibraltar, and on 1 July he was instructed to obtain the surrender or destruction of the French naval units at Mers El Kebir.

Force H arrived off Oran on the morning of 3 July (**Map 1**), and an ultimatum was presented to the French commander, Admiral Gensoul, to join the British, demilitarize his ships, or scuttle them where they lay. He refused to reply, but radioed the message to

Darlan, prepared his ships for action, and called on all other French units for help. After the time limit for acceptance had been extended, the British opened fire at 1800 hours. Within fifteen minutes the battleship *Bretagne* had blown up, the *Provence* had been beached, and the battle-cruiser *Dunkerque* disabled. The battle-cruiser *Strasbourg* managed to escape to sea, and although the British gave chase she reached Toulon safely. No action was taken against the unarmed *Jean Bart* at Casablanca, but the *Richelieu* at Dakar was torpedoed and immobilized on 8 July by aircraft from HMS *Hermes*.

However, Vichy occupation of Dakar still seemed to pose a threat to Allied communications in the mid-Atlantic, and so it was decided to send Free French troops – Force M under General De Gaulle – to occupy Dakar and then take over the rest of the French West African territories. This sailed from England on 31 August (**Map 1**), and, after refuelling at Freetown, arrived off Dakar on 23 September. It had been hoped that the Vichy forces would not resist, but they opened fire on the British ships, and a three-day bombardment ensued in which the British battleship *Resolution* was badly damaged. When it became obvious that an unopposed landing could not be made, the operation was abandoned.

Another area still held by Vichy forces which posed a direct threat to the Allies was the French mandate territory of Syria and Lebanon. In April 1941, a nationalist revolt in Iran had led the British to intervene to protect the oilfields, and it was thought that German infiltration of neighbouring Syria might not only rekindle this but could lead to unrest in Egypt. After the fall of Greece and Crete it was decided that Vichy control in the area must be broken. On 8 June a force under General Sir Henry Maitland-Wilson consisting of 7 Australian Division, 4 Indian Brigade, and the Free French Division invaded

the area from Palestine and Trans-Jordan (**Map 2**). it was outnumbered by Vichy forces and it was only after fairly heavy fighting that Damascus was taken on 21 June (**Map 3**). As the Allied troops pushed on north further British forces from Iraq moved in to link up with them, and on 11 July an armistice was signed which placed Syria and Lebanon in Free French hands.

Opposite above: The French fleet under fire at Mers El Kebir

Opposite below: British troops crossing the Lebanese border

THE WAR
IN THE
MEDITERRANEAN

Opposite: An s s motorised column in
the streets of a Yugoslav town

It took the Axis powers no more than seven months to overrun the Balkans, a necessary preliminary not only to the invasion of Russia, but to the control of the Eastern Mediterranean.

Rumania and Bulgaria, so far from offering any resistance, joined the Axis camp. Greece and Yugoslavia had the courage to defend themselves, and Winston Churchill, the embodiment of pugnacity, was not slow to support them. General Sir Alan Brooke, Chief of the Imperial General Staff, was appalled by the risks the British courted by frittering away their resources. 'Are we', he asked in his diary, 'to have "Salonika supporters" as in the last war? Why will politicians never learn the simple principle of concentration of force at the vital point and the avoidance of dispersal of effort?' But Churchill's policy had powerful advocates in Anthony Eden, the war minister, and General Archibald Wavell, the Commander-in-Chief in the Middle East. The latter, with his profound interest in military history, seems to have imagined that the Balkans might prove in Hitler's day to be a theatre of war comparable with Spain and Portugal during the Peninsular War (1808–14). In such an inhospitable country even the most formidable army of modern times might lose its momentum.

On the face of it the Allies could put a substantial army of fifty-one divisions in the field: twenty-eight Yugoslav, twenty Greek, and three British. It may be recalled, for purposes of comparison, that in 1940 the Allies on the Western Front had a total of 146 divisions. That great host had been notably ill-co-ordinated, but, though they were not deployed to advantage, it had not lacked tanks. Its air cover had been thin except where it was within striking distance of England. The Allies in the Balkans had no overall headquarters, they were not well provided with either tanks or aircraft and their infantry divisions, for the most part, were armed with obsolescent

weapons and depended upon horse-drawn transport.

At sea they enjoyed some advantages. With Alexandria, Suda Bay (Crete), and Benghazi in their hands the Allies had firm strategic control of the eastern Mediterranean, and in combat with the British the Royal Italian Navy had no advantage save numbers; for in Admiral Sir Andrew Cunningham the British had a naval commander of the first rank. Only when compelled to operate within the range of shore-based German aircraft were the British warships at a disadvantage.

On 28 October 1940 Mussolini's ambassador in Athens presented an ultimatum. Without awaiting a reply the Italian army in Albania, 162,000 men in ten divisions under General Sebastiano Visconti-Prasca, was launched on the invasion of Greece. Mussolini hoped for a victory, and a cheap one at that. Generally speaking, he reasoned, a nation of forty-five million could be counted on to crush one of some seven million. Moreover, the Greek defences, the Metaxas Line, was constructed to meet an attack from Bulgaria, not Albania.

Great Britain reacted promptly with promises of support, but beyond establishing RAF bases in Crete there was little she could do to help.

November is the beginning of the rainy season in Greece, and it was scarcely prudent of Mussolini to launch his attack at that time of year. But, of course, the weather was equally inclement to both sides.

The Italian plan was to cut off the Greeks in Macedonia and in Thessaly from those in the Epirus. This they hoped to achieve by advancing up the valley of the Vijosë and the capture of Metsova. Despite initial progress it did not work. The Greek army, some 150,000 strong under General Alexander Papagos fought with real tenacity. In one action, armed with the obsolescent Boys anti-tank rifle, a weapon designed for the conditions of 1918, a consignment of which had been

flown in by the RAF, the Greeks succeeded in knocking out nine tanks.

One of the better Italian divisions (3 Alpini) was trapped in the Pindus gorges and lost 5,000 men. On the Albanian front the Greeks seized the initiative and astounded the invaders by capturing Koritsa and a vast amount of sorely needed arms and equipment. By the end of December a quarter of Albania was in Greek hands, and the RAF was bombing Valona and Brindisi. Marshal Pietro Badoglio, the Italian Chief-of-Staff, resigned.

Nothing daunted Mussolini replaced Visconti-Prasca with General Ubaldo Soddu (9 November) and declared 'We'll break the backs of the Greeks, and we don't need any help'.

His friend Hitler thought otherwise and on 13 December issued Directive No. 20 for 'Undertaking Marita' in which he stated that: 'In the light of the threatening situation in Albania it is doubly important to frustrate English efforts to establish, behind the protection of a Balkan front, an air base which would threaten Italy in the first place and, incidentally, the Rumanian oilfields.'

It was his intention to concentrate some twenty-four divisions, under Field-Marshal List, in southern Rumania. When the weather improved, probably in March, this force would move across Bulgaria and overrun the northern coast of the Aegean, and if necessary the whole mainland of Greece. Airborne troops would seize English bases in the islands.

Once the British had been denied their foothold in Europe the force would be switched to 'new employment'.

By January 1941 the German X Air Corps, operating from Sicily, was attacking British naval forces in the Mediterranean. Operations to save Tripoli and Albania were planned, but though Mussolini was prepared to accept the support of the *Afrika Korps* he could not stomach the idea of being deprived of his Albanian triumph, and at a conference on 19 and 20 January

induced the Führer to modify his orders.

In March Germany compelled Bulgaria to join the Tripartite Pact, which Germany, Italy, and Japan had signed on 27 September 1940. In addition on the 24th the Yugoslavs were forced to join the Pact, but public opinion rebelled against this affront and on 26 March a *coup* led by General Simovitch overthrew the régime of Prince Paul, the young King's uncle. Britain welcomed this brave attempt with enthusiasm, while the relentless Germans resolved to fell both Greece and Yugoslavia at a blow.

On 6 April 1941 they struck and by 1 June the campaign had ended in disaster for the Allies. There are those, General Guderian among them, who thought that British intervention in Greece had the effect of delaying the German invasion of Russia (22 June). Others have argued that any delay was due to the weather. But upon reflection there really seems no reason why operations in Russia should not have been opened at least as early as 15 May, the original date set for 'Barbarossa'. If that could be proved it would follow that the British intervention, however costly, was not only justified, but decisive. On balance it seems that the pugnacity of Mr Churchill, and the optimism of Mr Eden and General Wavell, is to be commended and that General Brooke's more rigid interpretation of the principles of war was somewhat unimaginative.

Opposite above: Luftwaffe aircrew at a forward airfield in Yugoslavia

Above right: Wrecked British tanks left behind in a Greek town

Above left: A German anti-tank gun in action in Yugoslavia

Bottom left: German troops in the Greek town of Larissa

THE ITALIAN ATTACK ON GREECE

In August 1940 Mussolini demanded that Greece should renounce the guarantee of her independence which had been made by Great Britain in 1939. When this was refused, he accused her of 'un-neutral' attitudes, and began to concentrate 162,000 men in Albania on the Greek frontier. To this array the Greeks could oppose no more than 75,000 men.

On 28 October an ultimatum was presented and before it had expired, Italian troops had crossed the border. The Italian plan was to push down the valleys of the Vijosë and the Thyamis to capture Metsova and cut off the Greek forces in Thessaly and Macedonia from those in the Epirus. At first progress was rapid but the Greeks mobilized swiftly, and between 8 and 10 November they turned back 3 Alpini Division in the Pindus mountains and advanced on Koritsa which they retook on 22 November. Thereafter they pushed on until by the beginning of March the front had stabilized with almost half Albania in Greek hands.

The Germans felt obliged to come to the help of their allies but their original plan to leave Albania to the Italians and to attack Greece after persuading Bulgaria and Yugoslavia to allow free passage of troops, was thwarted by a coup in Yugoslavia which overthrew the Regency. The Germans now decided to invade both Yugoslavia and Greece, and there was some delay while the new campaign was mounted. Meanwhile a British force of 56,657 men was being landed in Greece.

Above: Italian troops landing in an Albanian harbour

Below: Italian infantry in action on the Greek border

Above: Italian artillery fighting in the mountains of Albania

Below: Italian officers captured by the Greeks are taken away for questioning

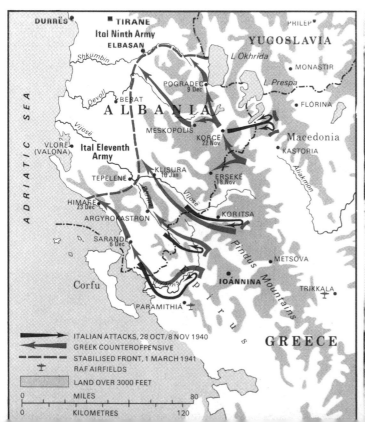

DURRËS
TIRANE
Ital Ninth Army
ELBASAN
PRILEP
YUGOSLAVIA
L Okhrida
MONASTIR
POGRADEC
9 Dec
L Prespa
FLÓRINA
BERAT
ALBANIA
Devoll
Shkumbin
ADRIATIC SEA
Vijosë
MESKOPOLIS
KORCE
22 Nov
Macedonia
VLORË
(VALONA)
Ital Eleventh
Army
KASTORIA
KLISURA
10 Jan
TEPELENE
ERSEKE
18 Nov
Aliakmon
HIMARE
23 Dec
ARGYROKASTRON
KORITSA
Vijosë
SARANDE
6 Dec
METSOVA
Corfu
Pindus Mountains
IOÁNNINA
TRIKKALA
PARAMITHIA
GREECE

ITALIAN ATTACKS, 28 OCT/8 NOV 1940
GREEK COUNTEROFFENSIVE
STABILISED FRONT, 1 MARCH 1941
RAF AIRFIELDS
LAND OVER 3000 FEET

0   MILES   80
0   KILOMETRES   120

THE INVASION OF YUGOSLAVIA

On 6 April 1941, the Germans invaded Yugoslavia with 33 divisions, six of them armoured. The Yugoslavs had 28 divisions, three armoured, strung out along the border with only one in reserve. The German plan was that the Twelfth Army in Bulgaria would thrust towards Skopje and Monastir to cut off the Yugoslavs from Greek help. Two days later, von Kleist's First Panzergroup was to advance towards Nis and Belgrade, and on 12 April, Second Army from Austria and Hungary and XLI Motorised Corps from Rumania would invade towards Belgrade. The attack began with heavy bombing of Belgrade, lasting two days, and on the Yugoslav airforce which was almost totally destroyed. On the ground the advance went as planned: in the south Twelfth Army swiftly reached its objectives, and the Yugoslavs were still unready when Kleist's Panzers thrust towards Nis which was reached on the first day. By 12 April the German columns had converged on Belgrade, which surrendered that evening. The Italians had advanced into Yugoslavia on the 11th, and worked their way down the coast to Dubrovnik. Yugoslavia sued for peace on 14 April and the capitulation was signed on 17 April.

Opposite above: Armour of Kleist's First Panzergroup advancing towards Belgrade

Above: German infantry support guns in action against a Yugoslav strongpoint

Right: German tanks passing obstacles on the Yugoslav border

40

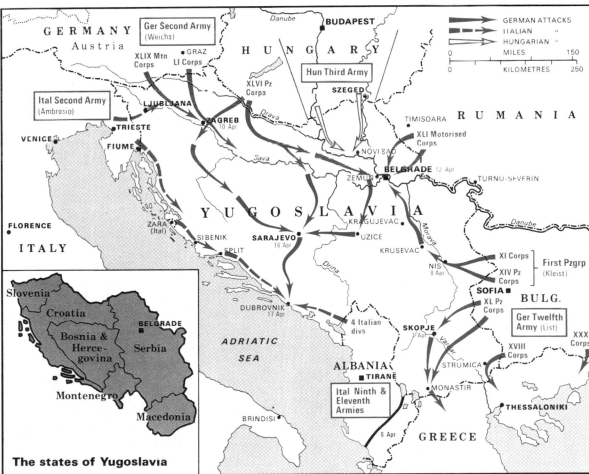

The states of Yugoslavia

GERMANY
Austria

XLIX Mtn Corps
LI Corps
GRAZ

Ger Second Army (Weichs)

Danube

BUDAPEST

H U N G A R Y

XLVI Pz Corps

SZEGED

Hun Third Army

Drava

RUMANIA

TIMISOARA

Ital Second Army (Ambrosio)

LJUBLJANA

ZAGREB
10 Apr

Sava

NOVI SAD

XLI Motorised Corps

VENICE

TRIESTE

FIUME

Y U G O S L A V I A

ZEMUN

BELGRADE 12 Apr

TURNU-SEVERIN

Danube

FLORENCE

ZARA (Ital)

SIBENIK

SPLIT

SARAJEVO
16 Apr

KRAGUJEVAC

UZICE

Morava

ITALY

Drina

KRUSEVAC

NIS
8 Apr

XI Corps

First Pzgrp (Kleist)

XIV Pz Corps

SOFIA

BULG.

DUBROVNIK
17 Apr

4 Italian divs

XL Pz Corps

Ger Twelfth Army (List)

ADRIATIC SEA

SKOPJE
7 Apr

Vardar

XVIII Corps

XXX Corps

ALBANIA

TIRANE

STRUMICA

Ital Ninth & Eleventh Armies

MONASTIR

THESSALONIKI

BRINDISI

6 Apr

G R E E C E

GERMAN ATTACKS
ITALIAN "
HUNGARIAN "

MILES 150
KILOMETRES 250

Slovenia
Croatia
Bosnia & Hercegovina
BELGRADE
Serbia
Montenegro
Macedonia

41

THE INVASION OF GREECE

At the beginning of April 1941, the main part of the Greek army, fourteen divisions, was facing the Italians in Albania. The British force of four divisions and a Polish brigade, and four Greek divisions were deployed to cover the Aliákmon line and the Monastir Gap (see map), while three and a half Greek divisions guarded the Metaxas Line further north covering Macedonia and the Rupel Pass.

The German aim was to cut the Allies in two by piercing the centre and isolating the army in Albania. At the same time an attack through the Rupel Pass to breach the Metaxas Line would cut off Greek forces in Thrace, while another attack from Strumica round the end of the line would capture Thessaloniki from the north-east.

The German invasion began on 6 April, the same day as that of Yugoslavia. The XXX Corps moved into Thrace, three divisions attacked the Metaxas Line frontally, and 2 Panzer Division made a successful thrust to Strumica. The rapid collapse of the Yugoslavs unhinged the position of the Allied forces holding the Metaxas Line for 2 Panzer Division now advanced towards Thessaloniki which was reached on 9 April. Meanwhile, the German XL Panzer Corps had reached Monastir and was heading towards the Gap. The Allies fell back to an intermediate position on the Aliàkmon – Klissoura river line, aiming to hold the German advance on the Aliákmon–Venetikos river line. On 10 April XL Panzer Corps advanced through the Monastir Gap but was held north of the Aliákmon for two days. However, its pressure was too great, and the Allied Command prepared to defend the Servia and Olympus Passes and the coast road. The Germans were harassed as they advanced on these new positions, but their control of the air, and the speed of their armour meant that they were only temporarily delayed. Their main attacks on the Servia Pass began on 16 April and by the next day they were through and aiming for Thermopylai where the Allies were planning their last major defence line while an evacuation from the Peloponnese was begun.

The Germans were delayed by supply problems and it was not until 22 April that they began to reach the position. On the morning of 24 April the Allied evacuation got under way while the main German attack on Thermopylai was launched. This was held during the day and on the night of 24/25 April the Allied defenders were moved back through the last line at Thebes. The Germans reached this on the 26th and were halted by heavy artillery fire, but that evening the defenders fell back to Rafina and Porto Rafti where they were evacuated on 28 April.

Meanwhile, the Germans had captured the Corinth bridge by a parachute assault on 26 April. Although the bridge was subsequently blown up, their forces were soon fanning out across the Peloponnese. The British managed to evacuate some 43,000 men before the German capture of Kalamata on 28 April closed the last embarkation port. But they left behind all their heavy *matériel* and 11,000 men.

Below: British troops being evacuated from the Peloponnese

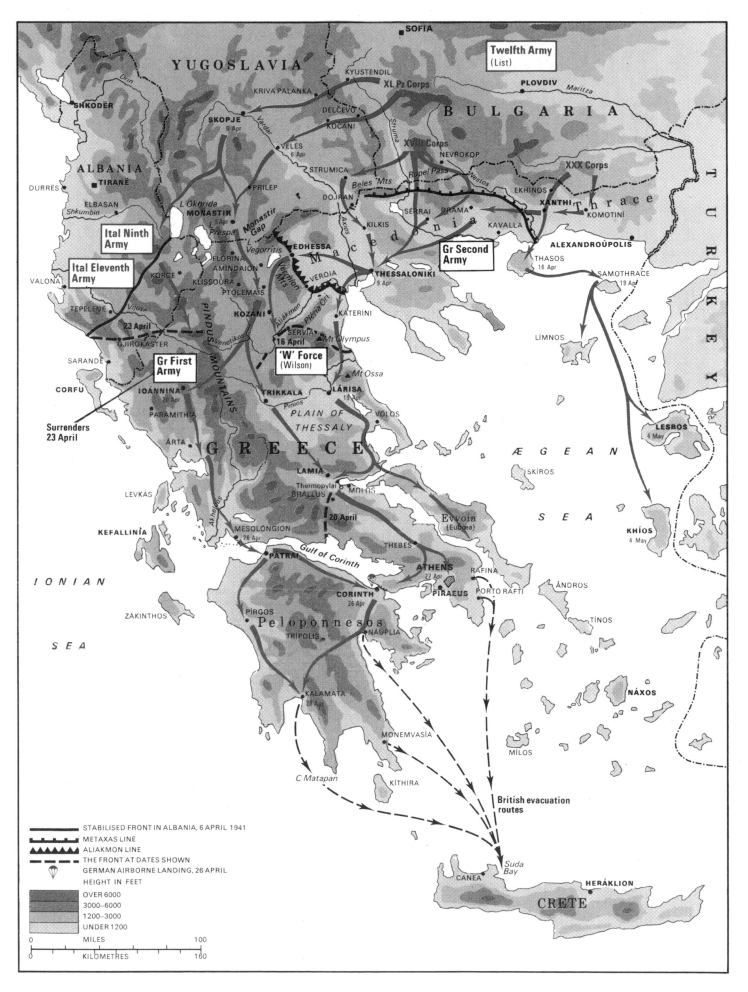

SOFIA

YUGOSLAVIA

Twelfth Army
(List)

KYUSTENDIL

KRIVA PALANKA

DELČEVO

SKOPJE
8 Apr

KOCANI

VELES
6 Apr

STRUMICA

PRILEP

DOJRAN

KILKIS

MONASTIR

Monastir
Gap

EDHESSA

FLORINA

AMINDAION

VÉROIA

THESSALONIKI
9 Apr

KLISSOÚRA

PTOLEMAIS

KOZÁNI

KATERÍNI

SÉRVIA
16 April

Mt Olympus

TRIKKALA

LÁRISA
19 Apr

Mt Ossa

IOANNINA
20 Apr

PARAMITHIA

PLAIN OF
THESSALY

VÓLOS

ÁRTA

GREECE

LEVKÁS

LAMIA

Thermopylai
BRALLUS
MOLOS

20 April

KEFALLINÍA

MESOLÓNGION
26 Apr

Gulf of Corinth

THEBES

ATHENS
27 Apr

RAFINA

PÁTRAI

PORTO RAFTI

ZÁKINTHOS

PÍRGOS

Peloponnesos

CORINTH
26 Apr

PIRAEUS

TRÍPOLIS

NAÚPLIA

KALAMATA
28 Apr

MONEMVASÍA

C Matapan

KÍTHIRA

British evacuation
routes

ÍOS

Suda
Bay

CANEA

HERÁKLION

CRETE

DURRÉS

TIRANË

ALBANIA

ELBASAN

Shkumbin

L.Okhrida

MONASTIR

Ital Ninth
Army

L.Prespa

L.Vegorritis

VALONA

Ital Eleventh
Army

KORÇË

23 April

GJIROKASTER

TEPELENÉ

Vijosa

PINDUS MOUNTAINS

Venetikos

Gr First
Army

SARANDË

CORFU

Surrenders
23 April

'W' Force
(Wilson)

Drin

SHKODËR

BULGARIA

PLOVDIV

Maritza

XL Pz Corps

XVIII Corps

NEVROKOP

XXX Corps

Rupel Pass

Nestos

EKHÍNOS

Beles Mts

Strumica

Vardar

Struma

STRUMICA

SÉRRAI

DRAMA

XANTHI

Thrace

KOMOTINI

KAVALLA

ALEXANDROÚPOLIS

THASOS
16 Apr

SAMOTHRACE
19 Apr

Gr Second
Army

Macedonia

Vermion Mts

Piéria Órt

Aliakmon

Pinios

Axiós

LÍMNOS

ÆGEAN

SEA

SKÍROS

Evvoia
(Euboea)

LESBOS
4 May

KHÍOS
4 May

ÁNDROS

TÍNOS

NÁXOS

MÍLOS

IONIAN

SEA

ZÁKINTHOS

Akhelóos

TURKEY

STABILISED FRONT IN ALBANIA, 6 APRIL 1941
METAXAS LINE
ALIAKMON LINE
THE FRONT AT DATES SHOWN
GERMAN AIRBORNE LANDING, 26 APRIL
HEIGHT IN FEET

OVER 6000
3000–6000
1200–3000
UNDER 1200

0   MILES   100
0   KILOMETRES   160

13

THE ATTACK ON CRETE

Following the German invasion of Greece, Crete was of major strategic importance – from it the Allies could threaten the Balkans while the Axis could strike at shipping using the Suez Canal and at Allied bases in Egypt and Libya. On Crete the British had about 30,000 men commanded by Major-General Freyberg VC, supported by nine tanks and thirty-five aircraft. There were in addition two weak and ill-equipped Greek divisions.

Lacking naval control of the area, the Germans aimed to capture the island by airborne assault. Their airborne forces numbered 22,750 paratroops and glider-borne troops under the command of Fliegerkorps XI, and were supported by 280 bombers, 150 dive-bombers, and 180 fighters. The plan was to attack in two waves – the first, in the morning to capture Máleme airport, Caneá town, and Suda port, the second later in the day to take the towns and airports of Rétimo and Heráklion. The key to success was swift capture of an airport so that reinforcements could be flown in.

The landings began at first light on 20 May 1941: after heavy attacks, part of the assault regiment led by General Meindl landed around Máleme airfield in the 5 New Zealand Brigade area, and the remainder came down astride the Alikianou–Caneá road near Galatas to attack Caneá. Around Máleme the situation swiftly became confused and the New Zealanders were hindered in co-ordinating their defences by incessant air attacks and inadequate radio equipment. By the end of the day, despite the massive German casualties, 22 Battalion was forced to withdraw east away from the airfield towards 23 Battalion. Near Galatas the Germans had been held and the landings which took place at Rétimo and Heráklion also failed to capture their airfields.

However, the next day the Germans succeeded in clearing Máleme airfield

and were not immediately counter-attacked. When this did take place, it met very heavy opposition and failed to retake the airfield. The New Zealanders were withdrawn towards Platanias and the two German forces began to co-ordinate their attacks towards Caneá. The second phase of the battle was the Allied attempt to hold on to Suda Bay, while the Germans tried to outflank their positions. On 25 May Galatas was occupied, and on the 27th Freyberg realized that the Allied position was untenable and began to withdraw to the south. Meanwhile the Germans occupied Caneá and Suda and pressed on to relieve their forces at Rétimo and Heráklion. During 29–30 May a bridgehead was maintained around Sfakia to allow evacuation, but the Rétimo garrison was forced to surrender. The next day the last evacuations took place and the Germans entered Sfakia. Nearly 15,000 Allied troops had been saved, but 18,000 remained behind. The Germans suffered some 7,000 killed – nearly one-third their landing force – and were never again to mount an airborne operation on such a scale.

Right: German assault troops move away from their dropping zone

Opposite above: Paratroops advance through a village

Opposite below: Suda Bay with shipping burning after a Luftwarfe attack

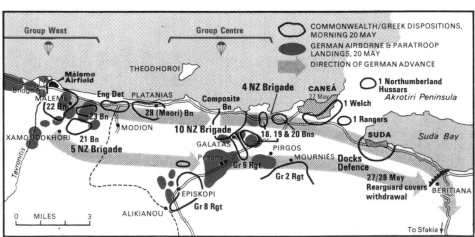

THE NORTH AFRICAN CAMPAIGN

The war in the desert presented conditions and problems all its own, for none of the combatants on either side were really prepared for desert warfare. Scorching days and bitter nights; lack of cover and tactical features which meant that places at which defensive positions could be prepared were few and far apart; navigational difficulties; unaccustomed ailments – all these contributed to the problems which each side were compelled to face. The Italians, although more or less accustomed to the climate had rearmed first of all the European powers and their weapons were already obsolescent in 1940. The British for their part were more or less acclimatized thanks to the fact that numbers of their regulars, officers and men, had seen a good deal of service in India, Palestine, and Egypt. Quite apart from the fact that they were used to the hot sun, there were eccentrics among them who had actually made long trips into the desert and had devised navigational aids. These flashes of private initiative were to be of great advantage when places like the Siwa Oasis, and units like the Long Range Desert Group, began to be of tactical importance. It was greatly to the credit of the methodical Germans that, with little previous experience of conditions in the Middle East, they were able to produce at short notice their admirable Afrika Korps.

However, the greatest of all the problems in the desert war, and the one which was eventually to prove crucial, was the age-old military essential of supply. The distance between the main Axis supply base at Tripoli, and the Allied bases around Alexandria was 1,500 miles of largely waterless and roadless desert with very few intermediate harbours at which new depots could be established. All essentials, petrol, water, ammunition, and food, had to be brought up along rough and highly vulnerable lines of communication.

This accentuated the basic military axiom that an advancing army becomes increasingly vulnerable as its supply lines stretch, and a retreating one becomes correspondingly stronger in proportion as it falls back on its basis. Twice the Axis and twice the Allied forces found that after huge advances they were so overextended that an enemy counterattack meant not a limited withdrawal to a defensive position, but a precipitate retreat across the bulge of Cyrenaica where every possible defensive position was vulnerable to outflanking moves.

Ultimately, the victor in the desert war would be the side which got the most and best supplies in the shortest time. On both occasions that Rommel began his great advances Axis domination of the centre of the Mediterranean had meant that his forces had received adequate fuel and equipment. But by the time the Afrika Korps reached El Alamein Eighth Army had never been better placed despite its apparently perilous position. Its supply lines were only 70 miles long and it was receiving petrol and equipment in unprecedented quantities. Rommel was now 370 miles from even his most forward base at Tobruk, and Allied domination of the sea and air meant that few supplies were even getting across the Mediterranean let alone forward to his troops.

Also, Rommel had an additional problem in that the enormous demands of the German armies fighting in Russia meant that little new material could be spared for what many at Supreme Headquarters increasingly saw as a sideshow – a successful but nonetheless basically peripheral campaign far away from the truly vital fronts. In contrast, the Western Allies had now accepted that their first major thrust against the Axis must come from the Mediterranean, and Eighth Army, as the means of clearing the North African shore, was receiving the pick of the new equipment available.

When the Allies broke through at El Alamein it was inevitable that Rommel would have to fall back at least as far as El Agheila where Eighth Army had twice been halted. But the Allied landings in Algeria and their advance into Tunisia introduced a new factor – not just Rommel's lines of communication but his very bases were directly threatened. He had to fall right back to protect them, and it is a measure of the supply difficulties that they encountered that Eighth's Army's pursuit was so slow and tentative.

The war in North Africa fell into three distinct phases. In the first Wavell, though against desperately long odds, had very much the better of the Italians. Major-General O'Connor's brilliant offensive, the first series of Allied victories, had a very important moral effect.

The second phase was the Rommel era, whose opening coincided with Wavell's ill-starred, but unavoidable campaign in Greece. It was a phase when the British had important successes, but when, on the whole, the Axis succeeded in baffling their opponents, and delivering telling blows such as the capture of Tobruk. British generals of real distinction, Wavell, Cunningham, and Auchinleck were unable to master the redoubtable Rommel.

Rommel was a very stylish corps

commander with splendid qualities of leadership. Of Bir Hacheim he writes: 'I frequently took over command of the assault forces myself and seldom in Africa was I given such a hard-fought struggle.' The fact is that he was still the ardent platoon and company commander who had so greatly distinguished himself in the First World War. In most armies a corps commander who exposed himself in such fashion would be roundly condemned by the pundits.

In phase three, with Alexander as commander-in-chief in the Middle East and Montgomery in command of Eighth Army, the tide quickly changed against the Axis. The defensive battle of Alam Halfa, followed, when he was ready, by the battle from which Viscount Montgomery took his title, marked the turn of the tide. As Winston Churchill put it – not without a measure of exaggeration – 'Before Alamein we never had a victory. After Alamein we never had a defeat.' But the end in Africa did not come quickly. Despite the landings in North Africa, Operation Torch, which began only four days after the successful conclusion of El Alamein, the Germans and Italians succeeded in holding out until May 1943.

Once Montgomery had taken over, Eighth Army changed its style

completely. Its new commander was swift to detect its strengths and weaknesses, and was severely critical of its state of training. 'Most commanders,' he thought, 'had come to the fore by skill in fighting and because no better were available: many were above their ceiling, and few were good trainers . . . The Eighth Army had suffered some eighty thousand casualties since it was formed, and little time had been spent in training the replacements.' When one recalls that O'Connor had begun his offensive with but 30,000 men one can appreciate the magnitude of the problem. Battle experience is in itself a form of training, and Eighth Army had seen plenty of fighting. On the other hand no battle is like the one before, and soldiers are all too prone to draw general tactical rules from their own particular experiences. That can be a dangerous snare for the unwary, for the truth is that every military problem whether strategical, or logistical, must be treated on its own merits, the factors analysed, and the plan made regardless of preconceived ideas and prejudices.

Compared with Rommel Montgomery, was altogether less of a paladin: more the professional. General Eisenhower, who knew him better than most wrote: 'General Montgomery had no superior in two most important characteristics. He quickly develops among British enlisted men an intense devotion and admiration – the greatest personal asset a commander can possess. Montgomery's other outstanding characteristic is his tactical ability in what might be called the "prepared" battle . . . He is careful, meticulous and certain.' The British soldiers who fought under Montgomery soon came to believe that, whilst they served under him, they simply could not be beaten. It was not that they considered themselves supermen. It was just that they credited him with knowing everything, caring for their welfare, and, thanks to expert co-ordination of the various arms

and services, reducing their casualties to the minimum.

In July 1943 Hitler gave it as his opinion that the protracted defence of Tunisia postponed the invasion of Europe by six months and kept Italy in the Axis. It cost the Axis 250,415 men, counting only prisoners of war. It was Hitler's view that, without the prolonged resistance in North Africa, the Allies would have been able to land in Italy unopposed and push forward to the Brenner, at a time when Germany as a result of Stalingrad 'would not have had a single man available to put there'. His argument is totally unconvincing. The men and tanks he lost in Tunisia could have been deployed to very much greater advantage for the defence of Sicily and Italy.

The campaign in North Africa ended in a triumph for the Allies, and not least for the Americans who emerged with an army greatly improved in tactical efficiency. By fighting in North Africa, where they could not deploy anything like their full strength, the Germans presented the Allies with a substantial victory, at a time when they were building up their forces for the invasion of Europe. Beyond question the experience won in North Africa was a pearl of great price for the British and for the Americans. To have attempted the invasion of Italy or Normandy in the teeth of the Wehrmacht, with inexperienced troops and commanders whose latest campaign – if any – had been Dunkirk, would have been to court disaster. The Allied armies which invaded Europe in 1943 or 1944 would have been raw indeed without the veterans of Africa.

Opposite above: Men of the Afrika Korps at El Agheila

Centre: A 25-pounder in action during the Battle of El Alamein

Above: German armour heads towards Mersa Bregha

WAVELL'S OPENING OFFENSIVE

In June 1940, the Italian forces in North Africa consisted of nine regular divisions, three 'Blackshirt' divisions, and two native divisions, a total of 250,000 men commanded by Marshal Graziani. Facing them the British had 36,000 men in Egypt and 27,000 in Palestine, under the overall command of General Sir Archibald Wavell. The force on the Egyptian border named Western Desert Force, consisted of 7 Armoured Division, 4 Indian Division, and the New Zealand Division, and was commanded by Major-General Richard O'Connor. As soon as war was declared, Western Desert Force began a series of raids which led the Italians to overestimate grossly the force facing them.

In September they moved cautiously over the border and occupied Sidi Barrani, but instead of continuing their advance they began to build a series of fortified camps south of the town (**Map 1**). The British plans for a counterattack were aided by the arrival of a major convoy with more than fifty infantry tanks. Wavell and General Wilson who commanded the forces in Egypt aimed for a limited attack to recapture Sidi Barrani. If successful, this could be extended to capture Tobruk and then to advance deeper into Libya.

The two fronts were separated by some 70 miles, and Western Desert Force began its approach on the night of 6 December, laagered in the desert on the 7th, and on the afternoon of the 8th reached 'Piccadilly'. The 7 Armoured Division then swung behind the Italian camps to cut the coast road at Buq Buq, while 4 Indian Division and 7 Royal Tank Regiment attacked Nibeiwa camp early on 9 December. This fell swiftly and by the evening Tummar West had also been taken. Meanwhile an independent column, Selby Force, had advanced along the coast road towards Sidi Barrani, and this was attacked and taken on the 10th with 38,000 Italian prisoners. Wavell now had to withdraw 4 Indian Division for service in the Sudan, and there was a delay while it was replaced by 6 Australian Division. This division began the next stage of the advance by capturing Bardia and another 38,000 Italians on 3 January 1941 (**Map 2**). The Italians had now lost almost eight divisions and were in full retreat, but the British supply lines were becoming over-stretched, and Wavell was being warned that he would soon have to withdraw troops to be sent to Greece However, Tobruk was taken on 22 January, Derna was abandoned by the Italians on the 29th and occupied the next day, and by 9 February the British reached El Agheila where they were halted. Despite the fact that there was no apparent resistance further west, forces now had to be withdrawn to Greece, and a thin covering force was left to guard the new territories.

Below: Italians surrendering during the capture of Tobruk

Opposite: A British tank passes destroyed Italian aircraft at El Adem

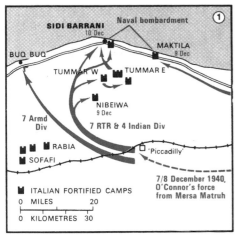

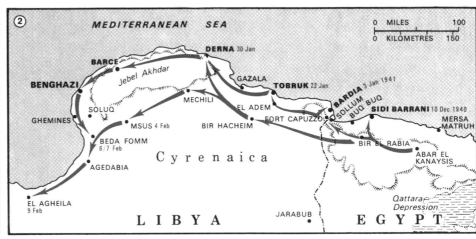

THE ETHIOPIAN CAMPAIGN

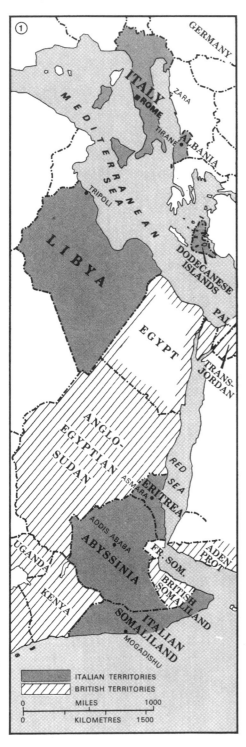

With France out of the war, it seemed possible that Mussolini would use his African armies to expel Britain from her African territories and achieve complete control over the Mediterranean and Suez route to the Far East (**Map 1**). On paper his forces were impressive: in addition to the army in Libya there were 350,000 men in Ethiopia faced by 9,000 British in the Sudan, 8,500 in Kenya, 2,500 in Aden, and 1,500 in British Somaliland, a total of but 21,500. The campaigns in East Africa began with the conquest of British and French Somaliland (**Map 2**), which enabled the Italians to tighten their control of the southern entrance to the Red Sea. The small British garrison was swiftly overwhelmed, its survivors being evacuated from Berbera on 19 August On 2 December, General Wavell assigned the task of retaking Ethiopia to Lieutenant-Generals Sir William Platt, commanding the forces in the Sudan, and Sir Alan Cunningham, commanding those in Kenya. The Italians had overestimated British strength in the Sudan and failed to move against Khartoum. Border raids induced them to evacuate Kassala, and General Platt's offensive began earlier than planned on 19 January 1941 with an advance into Eritrea which forced the Italians back to the well-nigh impregnable fortress of Keren. This eventually fell on 27 March after severe fighting in which the British lost 4,000 men and the Italians 3,000. This defeat broke Italian resistance in Eritrea, and Asmara and Massawa were swiftly occupied.

Meanwhile Cunningham had begun his advance on 10 February, crossing the Juba river to occupy Kismaya on 16 February. The 275-mile advance to Mogadishu was made in less than three days against negligible resistance, and Cunningham asked for permission to advance on Harar via Jijiga – 774 miles overland. He moved off on 1 March and made his first contact with the Italians midway between Gorrahei and Jijiga before capturing the latter on 17 March. A small force from Aden retook Berbera on 16 March and pushed forward to link up with the main force. Addis Ababa was abandoned by the Italians on 4 April, and the British now thrust north-west towards Dessie to link up with an advance south from Eritrea. The remnants of the Italian army were entrenched at Amba Alagi and after two weeks of stubborn resistance the Duke of Aosta surrendered with the honours of war. The final operations were expeditions towards Jimma and Ghimbi south and west of Addis Ababa, and towards Gondar where the last Italian resistance ended on 27 November.

Below: Abyssinian guerrillas firing on an Italian fort

Opposite above: South African troops cross the Juba river

②

GULF OF ADEN

ADEN

FR SOMALILAND

DJIBOUTI

ZEILA
5 Aug

ERIGAVO

BERBERA
19 Aug

BURAO

Tug Argan Pass

HARGEISA
5 Aug

BRITISH
SOMALILAND

HARAR

**3 August 1940,
Italians attack**

ABYSSINIA

ITALIAN
SOMALILAND

MILES	200
KILOMETRES	300

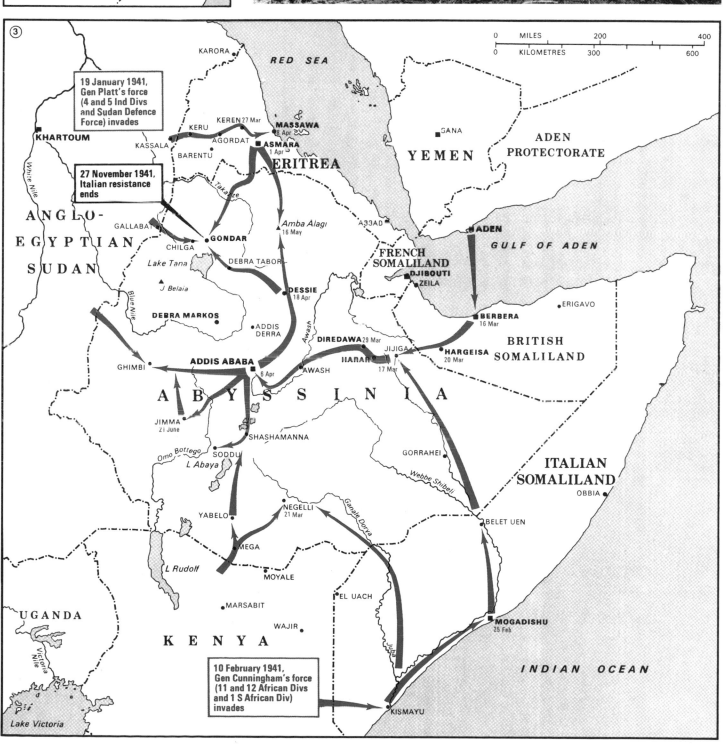

③

	MILES	200	400
	KILOMETRES	300	600

RED SEA

KARORA

KHARTOUM

**19 January 1941,
Gen Platt's force
(4 and 5 Ind Divs
and Sudan Defence
Force) invades**

KERU

KEREN 27 Mar

MASSAWA
8 Apr

SANA

ADEN
PROTECTORATE

KASSALA

AGORDAT

ASMARA
1 Apr

YEMEN

BARENTU

ERITREA

**27 November 1941,
Italian resistance
ends**

Takazze

ANGLO-
EGYPTIAN
SUDAN

GALLABAT

Amba Alagi
16 May

ASSAB

ADEN

GULF OF ADEN

CHILGA

GONDAR

FRENCH
SOMALILAND

DJIBOUTI

ZEILA

Lake Tana

DEBRA TABOR

J Belaia

DESSIE
18 Apr

BERBERA
16 Mar

ERIGAVO

White Nile

Blue Nile

DEBRA MARKOS

ADDIS
DERRA

DIREDAWA 29 Mar

Awash

HARAR
9

JIJIGA
17 Mar

HARGEISA
20 Mar

BRITISH
SOMALILAND

GHIMBI

ADDIS ABABA
6 Apr

AWASH

A B Y S S I N I A

JIMMA
21 June

SHASHAMANNA

Omo *Bottego*

SODDU

GORRAHEI

Webbe Shibeli

ITALIAN
SOMALILAND

OBBIA

L Abaya

YABELO

NEGELLI
21 Mar

Ganale Dorya

BELET UEN

MEGA

MOYALE

L Rudolf

EL UACH

Juba

UGANDA

MARSABIT

WAJIR

MOGADISHU
25 Feb

*Victoria
Nile*

K E N Y A

INDIAN OCEAN

Lake Victoria

**10 February 1941,
Gen Cunningham's force
(11 and 12 African Divs
and 1 S African Div)
invades**

KISMAYU

ROMMEL'S FIRST OFFENSIVE

Above: General Rommel meets his Italian opposite number General Gariboldi

General Erwin Rommel arrived in Tripoli on 12 February 1941, and the first German troops began landing on 14 February. At the end of the month their patrols were clashing with the British near Sirte, and by the middle of March, Rommel had realized that not only had the British no further plans for attack, but that they were actually depleting their forces. All O'Connor's forces had been withdrawn and General Philip Neame VC was left to hold Libya with a two-brigade, 2 Armoured Division, 9 Australian Division, and an Indian motorised brigade at El Adem. Although a concerted attack by the Germans was not expected he had orders to fall back if necessary as no reinforcements were available.

Rommel struck on 24 March (**Map 1**) capturing El Agheila with almost no resistance. His 5 Light Division went on to attack the British 2 Armoured Division at Mersa Brega, and after fierce fighting was halted. But the British failed to counterattack and were then forced to pull back. By 2 April the Germans were at Agedabia with the choice of going north to Benghazi, north-east to Msus and Mechili, or east to Tengeder to threaten British supply lines. Wavell had first taken over direct command himself, and then brought in O'Connor to act as Neame's adviser.

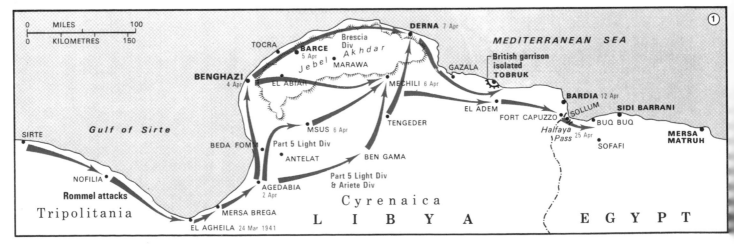

On 4 April Rommel attacked in all three directions meeting little resistance since 2 Armoured Division had fallen back. The swiftest Axis formation was that in the south which reached Tengeder on 5 April and Mechili the next day although it was too weak to attack 3 Indian Brigade which had moved forward to occupy the place. The appearance of this German force threatened to cut the British supply lines, and 9 Australian Division began to withdraw from Derna to which it had already retreated from Benghazi. On 8 April the remnant of 2 Armoured Division, which had lost most of its tanks through mechanical failure, and 3 Indian Brigade were overwhelmed at Mechili.

Meanwhile the British were reinforcing Tobruk with the 7 Australian Division. The first German units arrived piecemeal on 10/11 April and an improvised attack on the 11th was driven off. It was not until 14 April that 5 Light Division made a major assault from the south (**Map 2**) but their initial penetration ran into heavy artillery fire and counterattacks and by the afternoon the Germans were forced to retreat. The situation now stabilized with Italians replacing the German units which were preparing to cross the Egyptian frontier. On 25 April the Germans struck at Halfaya Pass and by the next day had pushed the British back to the line Buq-Buq/Sofafi. On 30 April Rommel made a full-scale attempt to capture Tobruk, but though a salient was pushed into the western sector, after four days fighting it was contained.

Above: A British patrol moves through the barbed wire of the Tobruk perimeter

Below: Armoured cars of the Afrika Korps during the swift German advance through Libya

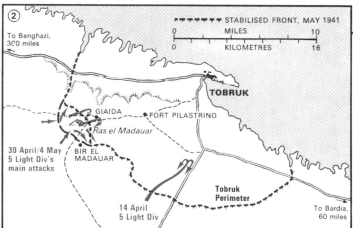

55

OPERATION BREVITY

After the occupation of Halfaya Pass by the Germans on 25 April, the situation stabilized while both sides concentrated on building up their forces. Wavell knew that without Halfaya he could not hope to mount any major operations to relieve Tobruk, and when he learned that a large convoy, 'Tiger', was bringing him additional tanks and aircraft, he gave Brigadier Gott the task of mounting an operation, 'Brevity', to recapture Halfaya. The attack was launched on 15 May against three points: the pass itself; Sollum and Fort Capuzzo; and the left flank. Halfaya Pass was swiftly taken and Fort Capuzzo seized after heavy fighting. Rommel thought that Brevity was the beginning of a major advance and sent in an immediate counterattack which recaptured Capuzzo, but when the Germans probed forward to find 7 Armoured Brigade they discovered that the British had withdrawn to Halfaya. Ten days later 8 Panzer Division recaptured Halfaya Pass by outflanking the British positions and compelling their defenders to fall back.

Below: German infantry advance through the sand dunes

Right: Italian artillery bombarding Tobruk, the eventual goal of Operation Brevity

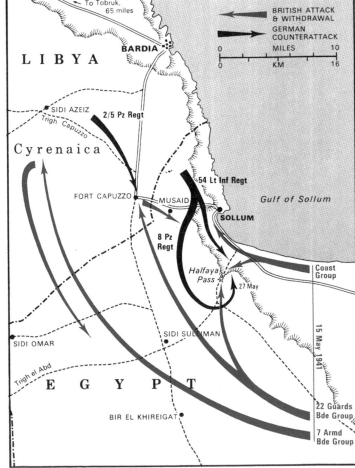

OPERATION BATTLEAXE

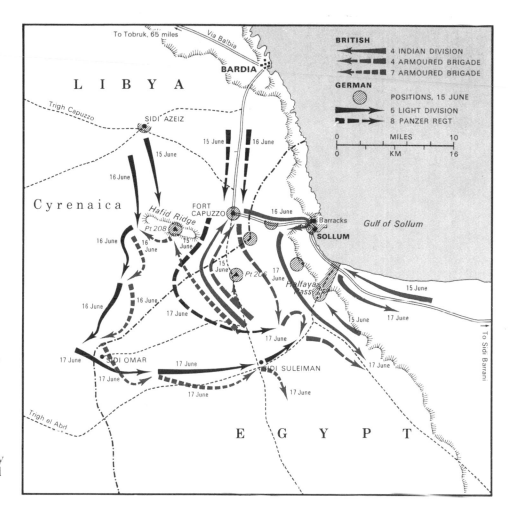

Despite the abandonment of 'Brevity', the arrival of the 'Tiger' convoy with 238 tanks on 12 May, enabled Wavell to mount another offensive. On the German side a new Panzer division – 15 – had begun to arrive. The British plan was to attack Halfaya frontally while 4 Armoured Brigade and part of 4 Indian Division swung round the desert flank of Capuzzo and Sollum, and 7 Armoured Brigade moved forward to occupy Hafid Ridge. Rommel, forbidden by the Axis Supreme Command to attack and lacking sufficient strength due to supply problems, had dug his troops in behind the 88-mm anti-aircraft guns – which were to prove fatal to tanks – and fortified Points 206 and 208 (on Hafid Ridge) to protect Capuzzo. The 15 Panzer Division was in reserve south of Bardia. The British attack began on 15 June and attempts to break through at Halfaya were soon halted by artillery. In the centre, Point 206 was taken by the evening and Capuzzo captured by 4 Armoured Brigade shortly after midday, and 22 Guards Brigade dug itself in. The 7 Armoured Division was heavily engaged on Hafid Ridge but had established a foothold by the evening. Rommel allowed his defensive positions to break up the British attacks and moved 5 Light Division around the west of Hafid Ridge towards Sidi Omar in an attempt to outflank the whole British force. Throughout 16 June they were fought by 7 Armoured Brigade which lost almost all its tanks through battle damage or mechanical failure. Meanwhile 4 Armoured Brigade was withdrawing south to link up with 7 Armoured and protect the left flank. But this was upset early on the 17th when 8 Panzer Regiment disengaged from Capuzzo and swung south and east to join 5 Light Division in a major attack towards Halfaya. The British then had to retreat swiftly so that by the afternoon Rommel had relieved the defenders of Halfaya Pass.

Below: The German 88-mm anti-aircraft gun which proved lethal to British armour during Operation Battleaxe

THE CRUSADER BATTLES

After the failure of Battleaxe, Wavell was removed from command and replaced by General Auchinleck with General Cunningham commanding Eighth Army. Both sides were short of supplies but Churchill pressed Auchinleck to mount an immediate offensive. The tactical concept behind Operation Crusader was that XIII Corps should contain Halfaya Pass and outflank it to strike towards Capuzzo while XXX Corps advanced to Gabr Saleh and engaged the enemy armour. The attack began well on 18 November with 7 Armoured Brigade reaching Gabr Saleh virtually unopposed (**Map 1**). The next day it continued its advance on Sidi Rezegh, but on the flanks 22 Armoured Brigade met unexpectedly heavy resistance at Bir El Gubi from the Ariete Division, and 4 Armoured Brigade moving north to protect the XIII Corps flank was heavily attacked by a group from 21 Panzer Division (the renamed 5 Light Division). Rommel had mistaken the British attack for a reconnaissance, and it was General Cruewell commanding Afrika Korps (the two German Panzer divisions) who made the first countermoves (**Map 2**), striking east to Sidi Azeiz on 19 April under the false impression that a major British force had reached that area. Realizing his error he turned south-west and on 20 November attacked 4 Armoured Brigade. To meet the threat 22 Armoured Brigade was moved from Bir El Gubi to Gabr Saleh. Rommel now ordered Cruewell to strike towards Sidi Rezegh on the morning of 21 November. He was followed by 4 and 22 Armoured Brigades, while the Tobruk garrison began its breakout to meet up with 7 Armoured. But since this had to turn to face Cruewell's attack the attempt was halted and 7 Armoured Brigade in fighting off the Panzer attack lost 113 of its 141 tanks. On the right, the New Zealand Division struck past the German frontier positions and moved up to Sidi Azeiz. On 22 November the fighting continued around Sidi Rezegh with 5 South African Brigade and 21 Panzer Division both suffering heavy losses. During the night 15 Panzer Division making a wide encircling movement to support 21 Panzer ran into 4 Armoured Brigade and virtually destroyed it.

Confused fighting in the Bir El Gubi/Sidi Rezegh area continued on 23 November with the British suffering such losses that Rommel became convinced that their tank strength must now be totally eroded. This idea led him to take the Afrika Korps on a dash for the frontier, designed to relieve the Halfaya garrison and cut off Eighth Army (**Map 3**). But the New Zealanders continued their advance towards Tobruk and Rommel had to turn north and then west on 28 November to follow them. There was a shortlived relief of Tobruk but by 1 December the Germans had cut the link. Rommel was now being threatened from the Bir El Gubi area by XXX Corps which had been recovering there: his deteriorating supply situation and the exhaustion of his troops induced him to pull back first to Gazala (**Map 4**), and then, unwilling to risk being cut off in the Benghazi bulge,

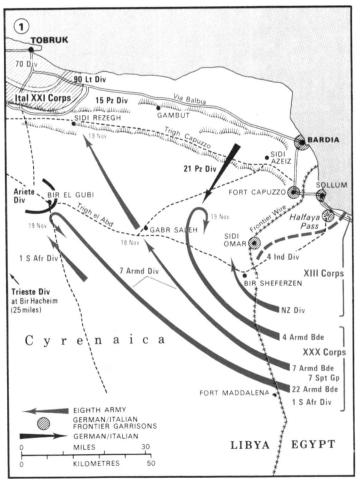

58

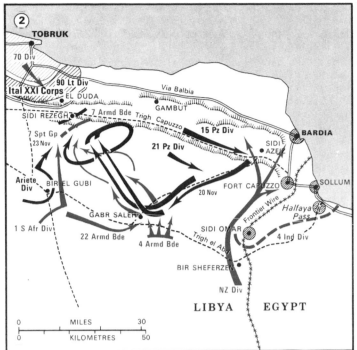

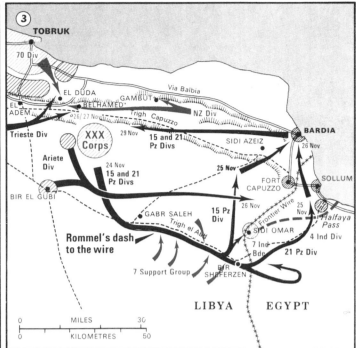

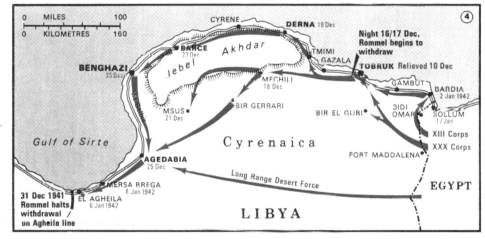

to El Agheila. In the battle the Axis forces had suffered about 30,000 casualties as against the British 18,000 and lost 300 tanks against 278.

Opposite: German prisoners being taken near Bardia

Below: Advancing British infantry take cover during a German bombardment

ROMMEL'S DRIVE TO GAZALA

When the British had followed Rommel back to the El Agheila area, they estimated that he would be unable to react for some time, and dispersed their units in order to refit. In reality, heavy air attacks on Malta had eased the Axis supply lines across the Mediterranean, and his forces were quickly rebuilt. Rommel decided not to await Eighth Army's next move, and on 21 January 1942 his forces advanced, pushing Eighth Army back towards Agedabia (**Map 1**). When DAK found Agedabia only lightly held, with the British obviously surprised by their advance, Rommel pushed on to

Antelat, and then to Msus. After a short halt there for supplies, 90 Light Division and Italian XX Corps struck north towards Benghazi, while a DAK task force moved to Er Regima to cut British communications. The threat of encirclement forced the British out of Benghazi and for the next eight days they were continually in retreat until the Axis forces halted close to the Gazala defensive position behind which Eighth Army had retired. The Gazala line consisted of minefields running south to Bir Hacheim with a series of fortified 'keeps' each containing a brigade group from XIII Corps (**Map 2**). These were designed to break up an Axis attack while the armour of XXX Corps intercepted any outflanking move and counterattacked. Rommel indeed aimed to outflank the line around Bir Hacheim – and to strike north towards Achoma. He hoped to open supply lines down Trigh Capuzzo and Trigh El Abd, but had failed to identify 150 Brigade's keep which lay astride these. The British had 849 tanks to the Axis 560, but only 320 aircraft against 704.

Holding attacks by Force Cruewell began in the afternoon of 26 May, and by night the main Axis force swung round Bir Hacheim. Trieste Division got lost and blundered into 150 Brigade, but by the morning of the 27th, 4 Indian Motor Brigade, 7 Motor Brigade, and 4 Armoured Brigade had been pushed back. However, as the Germans moved north across Sidra Ridge, they were attacked on both flanks, had lost about one-third of their armour, and were running short of water and fuel. For two days DAK was

Below: A German 88 in action against British armour

Above: A Stuka banks over advancing German tanks

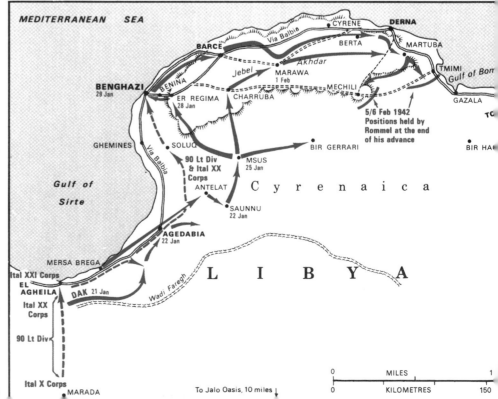

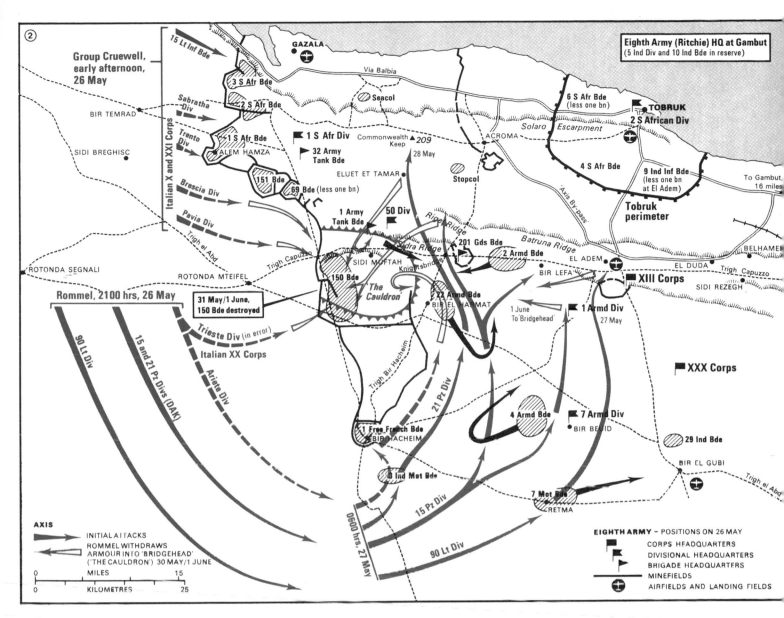

Map 2

② Group Cruewell, early afternoon, 26 May

15 Lt Inf Bde

GAZALA

Eighth Army (Ritchie) HQ at Gambut
(5 Ind Div and 10 Ind Bde in reserve)

Via Balbia

3 S Afr Bde

2 S Afr Bde

Seacol

6 S Afr Bde
(less one bn)

TOBRUK

2 S African Div

Sabratha Div

BIR TEMRAD

1 S Afr Bde

Commonwealth Keep 209

ACROMA

Solaro Escarpment

4 S Afr Bde

Trento Div

SIDI BREGHISC

ALEM HAMZA

1 S Afr Div

28 May

Stopcol

9 Ind Inf Bde
(less one bn
at El Adem)

To Gambut
16 miles

Italian X and XXI Corps

Brescia Div

151 Bde

ELUET ET TAMAR

32 Army
Tank Bde

Tobruk
perimeter

69 Bde (less one bn)

1 Army
Tank Bde

50 Div

Rigel Ridge

Pavia Div

Trigh el Abd

Sidra Ridge

201 Gds Bde

Batruna Ridge

BELHAME

ROTONDA SEGNALI

ROTONDA MTEIFEL

Trigh Capuzzo

SIDI MUFTAH

Knightsbridge

150 Bde

The Cauldron

2 Armd Bde

BIR LEFA

Axis By-pass

EL ADEM

EL DUDA

Trigh Capuzzo

XIII Corps

SIDI REZEGH

Rommel, 2100 hrs, 26 May

31 May/1 June,
150 Bde destroyed

22 Armd Bde
BIR EL HARMAT

1 June
To 'Bridgehead'

1 Armd Div

27 May

90 Lt Div

15 and 21 Pz Divs (DAK)

Trieste Div (in error)

Italian XX Corps

Ariete Div

21 Pz Div

4 Armd Bde

7 Armd Div
BIR BEUID

XXX Corps

29 Ind Bde

BIR EL GUBI

Trigh el Abd

Trigh Bir Hacheim

1 Free French Bde
BIR HACHEIM

3 Ind Mot Bde

15 Pz Div

7 Mot Bde
RETMA

0600 hrs, 27 May

90 Lt Div

AXIS
— INITIAL ATTACKS
← ROMMEL WITHDRAWS
◁ ARMOUR INTO 'BRIDGEHEAD' ('THE CAULDRON') 30 MAY/1 JUNE

MILES 0 ___ 15
KILOMETRES 0 ___ 25

EIGHTH ARMY – POSITIONS ON 26 MAY
⚑ CORPS HEADQUARTERS
⚑ DIVISIONAL HEADQUARTERS
⚐ BRIGADE HEADQUARTERS
— MINEFIELDS
⊕ AIRFIELDS AND LANDING FIELDS

held up, unable to push a supply line through the British minefields, until on 30 May Rommel abandoned his move north, and moved all his armour into the 'Cauldron' with its back to the British minefield to await Eighth Army's counterattack.

In the next four days, 150 Brigade was overwhelmed, and at last a supply line was opened through to DAK. Inexplicably the British attack did not come until 5/6 June and was easily beaten off with heavy losses. On the night of 10/11 June after fierce fighting the defenders of Bir Hacheim were forced to retreat, and the next day DAK burst out of the Cauldron (**Map 3**) swinging south and east. Piecemeal British counterattacks were beaten off by superior firepower and Eighth Army was forced to abandon the Gazala position and fall back to Tobruk and beyond. By 18 June the Axis forces had surrounded Tobruk

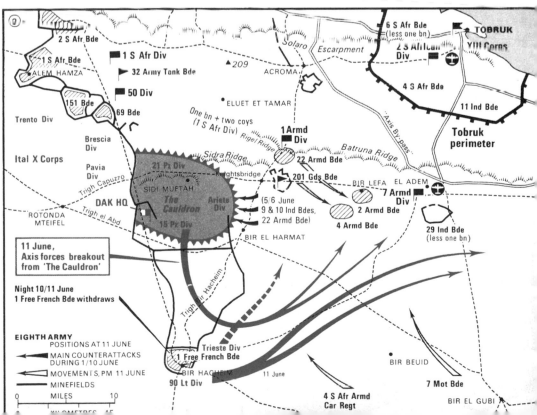

③ 2 S Afr Bde

1 S Afr Bde

ALEM HAMZA

1 S Afr Div

32 Army Tank Bde

50 Div

6 S Afr Bde
(less one bn)

TOBRUK

XIII Corps

2 S African Div

Solaro Escarpment

209

ACROMA

4 S Afr Bde

Trento Div

151 Bde

69 Bde

ELUET ET TAMAR

One bn + two coys
(1 S Afr Div)

Rigel Ridge

1 Armd Div

11 Ind Bde

Brescia Div

Ital X Corps

Pavia Div

Trigh Capuzzo

21 Pz Div

SIDI MUFTAH

Sidra Ridge

Knightsbridge

22 Armd Bde

Batruna Ridge

Tobruk
perimeter

DAK HQ

The Cauldron

Ariete Div

201 Gds Bde

BIR LEFA

EL ADEM

7 Armd Div

ROTONDA MTEIFEL

Trigh el Abd

15 Pz Div

(5/6 June
9 & 10 Ind Bdes,
22 Armd Bde)

4 Armd Bde

2 Armd Bde

29 Ind Bde
(less one bn)

BIR EL HARMAT

11 June,
Axis forces breakout
from 'The Cauldron'

Trigh Bir Hacheim

Night 10/11 June
1 Free French Bde withdraws

EIGHTH ARMY
POSITIONS AT 11 JUNE
← MAIN COUNTERATTACKS DURING 1/10 JUNE
◁ MOVEMENTS, PM 11 JUNE
— MINEFIELDS

MILES 0 ___ 10
KILOMETRES

Trieste Div

1 Free French Bde
BIR HACHEIM

90 Lt Div

11 June

4 S Afr Armd
Car Regt

BIR BEUID

7 Mot Bde

BIR EL GUBI

THE FALL OF TOBRUK

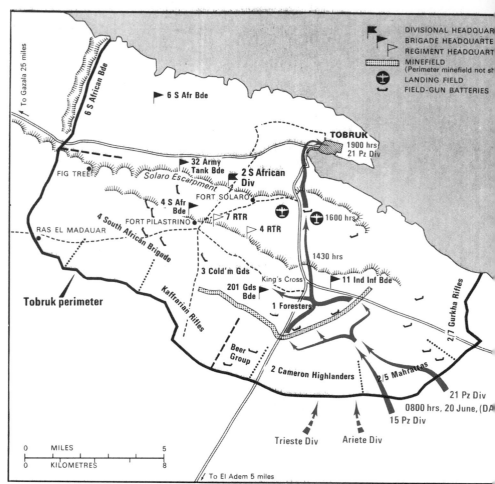

Rommel's attack on Tobruk began at first light on 20 June 1942 in the same south-eastern sector that O'Connor had selected in 1941. After heavy dive-bomber attacks, DAK pushed through the perimeter defences and by mid-morning had reached the minefields. At 1600 hours the airfields had been overrun, and three hours later, 21 Panzer Division moved into Tobruk. Isolated fighting continued during the night, but at 0800 hours on 21 June, General Klopper, the South African commander of the garrison, surrendered and during the rest of the day all remaining resistance was overcome.

Below: German troops in the main square of Tobruk

THE GERMAN ADVANCE TO EL ALAMEIN

As Tobruk fell, Eighth Army was attempting to re-form on the Egyptian frontier, and on 23 June it was authorized to withdraw to Matruh. Over 50,000 men had been lost as against 3,360 Germans, and the armour of XXX Corps was almost totally destroyed. On 25 June Auchinleck sent General Ritchie on leave, took over personal command of Eighth Army, and prepared to hold the Matruh position. Ritchie had intended to hold the area between Sidi Hamza and the sea with X Corps while striking at any outflanking attacks with the remains of XXX Corps, but Auchinleck saw that both corps were widely dispersed with an alarming gap south of 'Charing Cross', and so he decided that Eighth Army should withdraw as the enemy advanced to the more easily defensible El Alamein position. On 26 June although still weak (DAK had only sixty tanks left running and about 1,500 infantry), the Axis forces attacked astride the southern escarpment (**Map 1**). By the afternoon of the 27th, 90 Light Division had reached a position from which it could strike towards the coast, and 21 Panzer and 2 New Zealand Divisions were heavily engaged while 1 Armoured was holding 15 Panzer. But during the evening XXX Corps Headquarters ordered its divisions to fall back, and 90 Light Division cut the coast road. The X Corps was now surrounded and the next day its units broke out of Mersa Matruh in small parties while Eighth Army fell back on El Alamein (**Map 2**).

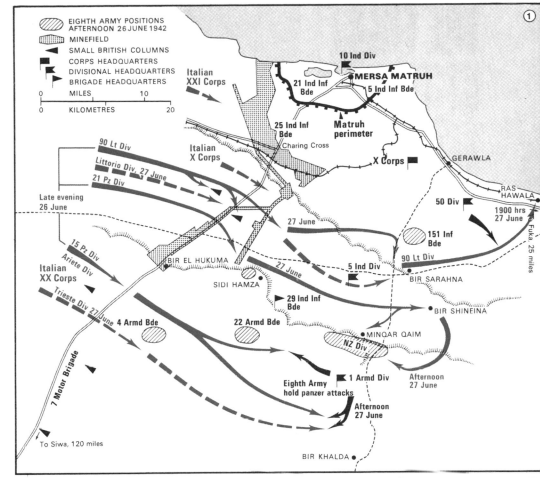

Right: A German supply column during the advance to El Alamein

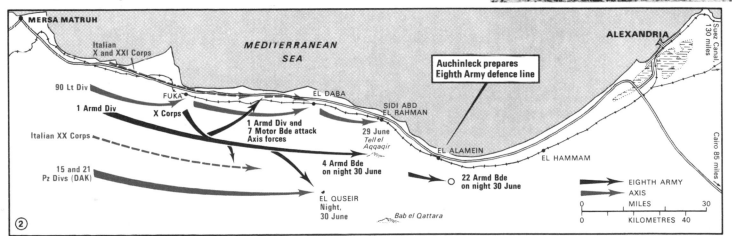

THE FIRST BATTLE AT EL ALAMEIN

Above: British units under artillery bombardment near El Alamein

Below: A German patrol returns from probing the British positions

With only two fully operational infantry divisions and a still-unorganized armoured division Auchinleck set about holding the El Alamein position. He aimed to rely on a fluid defence south of El Alamein based on the Ruweisat Ridge and Bab el Qattara. Although DAK was still seriously understrength, Rommel was confident that he could break through, bypass and surround El Alamein, and strike for the Delta. His forces moved off on 1 July, with 90 Light Division moving along the El Alamein perimeter closely behind the retiring 4 Armoured Brigade until halted near Alam el Onsol. DAK overran Deir el Shein, but was held near Point 64 on the Ruweisat Ridge. For two days, fighting continued here without the Germans making any headway while a southward move by the Ariete Division was shattered by 2 New Zealand Division. The Axis forces were now held in an arc from the sea to south of the Ruweisat Ridge, and Auchinleck decided to pull XIII Corps back northwards while preparing a counterattack by XXX Corps in the north against the Italians who were covering from the sea to the ridge. When he learned of XIII Corps withdrawal, Rommel was convinced that he had achieved a breakthrough and prepared to exploit it. But an attack by 9 Australian Division on Tell el Eisa during the night of 10/11 July compelled him to send his last reserves north to bolster the collapsing Sabratha Division, and two British attacks along the Ruweisat Ridge on 14/15 July and 21/22 July caused DAK such losses that Rommel had to abandon the operation and regroup. Auchinleck was determined to concentrate on building up his forces and his refusal to consider a further attack before mid-September caused Churchill to replace him by General Harold Alexander as Commander-in-Chief, Near East, and General Bernard Montgomery as commander of Eighth Army.

Above: Units of the Afrika Korps preparing
to attack El Alamein

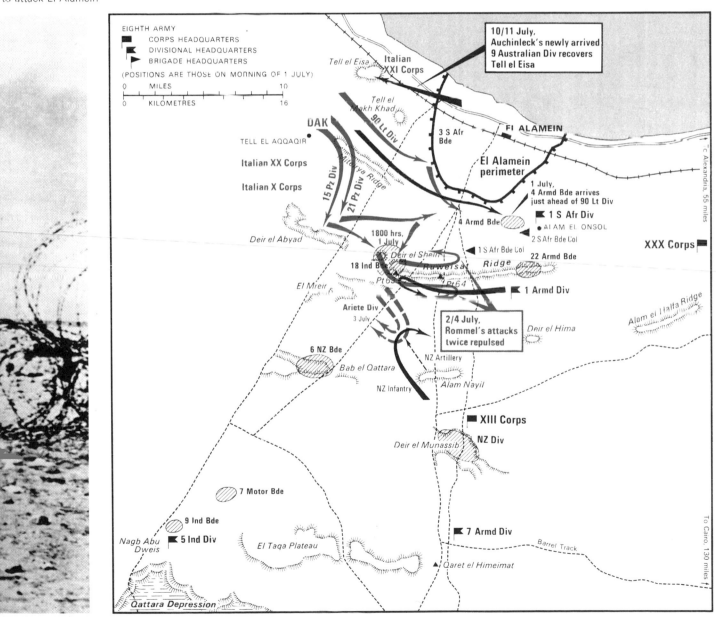

EIGHT ARMY

CORPS HEADQUARTERS
DIVISIONAL HEADQUARTERS
BRIGADE HEADQUARTERS

(POSITIONS ARE THOSE ON MORNING OF 1 JULY)

0   MILES   10
0   KILOMETRES   16

10/11 July,
Auchinleck's newly arrived
9 Australian Div recovers
Tell el Eisa

Tell el Eisa

Italian
XXI Corps

Tell el
Makh Khad

90 Lt Div

DAK

TELL EL AQQAQIR

Italian XX Corps

Italian X Corps

15 Pz Div

21 Pz Div

Miteirya Ridge

3 S Afr
Bde

EL ALAMEIN

El Alamein
perimeter

1 July,
4 Armd Bde arrives
just ahead of 90 Lt Div

4 Armd Bde

1 S Afr Div

ALAM EL ONSOL

2 S Afr Bde Col

Deir el Abyad

1800 hrs,
1 July

Deir el Sheff

18 Ind Bde

Nuweisat   Ridge

1 S Afr Bde Col

22 Armd Bde

XXX Corps

El Mreir

Pt 63

Pt 64

1 Armd Div

Ariete Div

3 July

2/4 July,
Rommel's attacks
twice repulsed

Deir el Hima

Alam el Halfa Ridge

6 NZ Bde

Bab el Qattara

NZ Artillery

NZ Infantry

Alam Nayil

XIII Corps

Deir el Munassib

NZ Div

7 Motor Bde

9 Ind Bde

Nagb Abu
Dweis

5 Ind Div

El Taqa Plateau

7 Armd Div

Barrel Track

Qaret el Himeimat

To Cairo, 130 miles

To Alexandria, 55 miles

Qattara Depression

65

THE BATTLE OF ALAM HALFA

Above: Italian troops advancing for a diversionary attack

Within seventeen days of his arrival, Montgomery had to face Rommel's last attempt to break through the El Alamein position. His defensive plan, broadly inherited from Auchinleck, was to defend the Alam Halfa Ridge and threaten any German offensive in the south with 7 Armoured Division. Rommel tried the tactics which had served him so well in the past – covering attacks in the north with his main attack swinging south of the British positions to come round east of Alam Halfa and surround Eighth Army. But in the event, the threat of 7 Armoured Division on the right flank forced Rommel to swing north earlier than he had intended; DAK was unable to break through the Alam Halfa position, and shortage of fuel forced it to halt. An attempt by 15 Panzer Division to outflank 22 Armoured Brigade on 1 September was prevented and on the 2nd Rommel ordered his forces to pull back to the line El Taqa/Bab el Qattara. On the night of 3/4 September, 2 New Zealand Division attacked south-west but was withdrawn after two days of heavy fighting.

The Axis forces now dug in and began to prepare a defensive position of great depth between the sea and the Qattara Depression. Rommel realized that if they were driven out of this line, they would be overwhelmed for lack of vehicles and the fuel to withdraw or fight a mobile battle. Thus he planned to hold each piece of ground at all costs halting each British attack with an immediate counterattack.

Right: German artillery bombards the British positions

Above: A British fieldgun in action against German vehicles

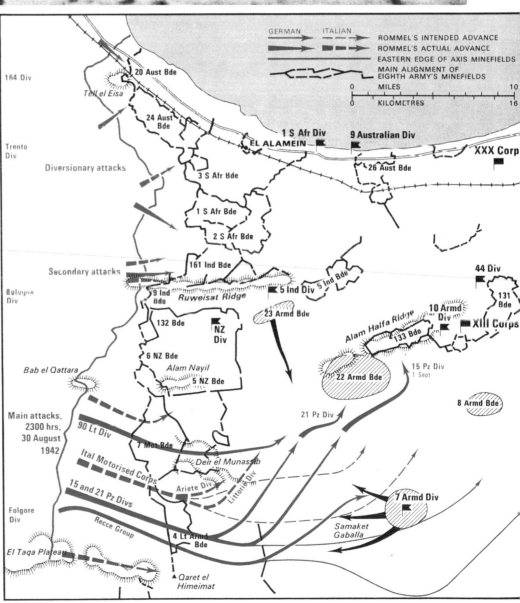

THE BATTLE OF EL ALAMEIN

Montgomery was determined not to attack until he had massive superiority, particularly in the air and in armour (see diagram). The Sherman tank was at last proving a match for the German Mark IV. Montgomery was faced with a heavily defended position whose flanks resting on the sea and the Qattara Depression could not be turned. His plan (**Map 1**) was to attack north of the Miteirya Ridge, with the infantry of XXX Corps pushing forward to the line 'Oxalic' and opening corridors in the minefields through which the armour of X Corps would pass. The XXX Corps would then form a screen at 'Pierson' while the infantry broke down the enemy defences before the final move to 'Skinflint' destroyed the Axis armour. The Germans had split their tanks to cover north and south of the line while the Italians provided the main static defences. Rommel was in hospital in Germany, leaving General Stumme in command, and did not return until 25 October.

Above left: British troops advance through a smoke screen

Left: A German sentry observes British positions before the battle

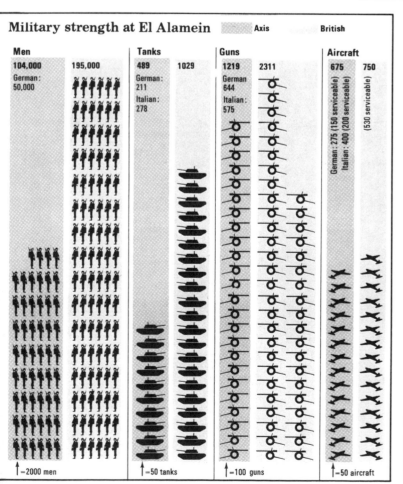

Military strength at El Alamein

Axis / British

	Men		Tanks		Guns		Aircraft	
	104,000	195,000	489	1029	1219	2311	675	750
	German: 50,000		German: 211 Italian: 278		German: 644 Italian: 575		German: 275 (150 serviceable) Italian: 400 (200 serviceable)	(530 serviceable)

↑ =2000 men   ↑ =50 tanks   ↑ =100 guns   ↑ =50 aircraft

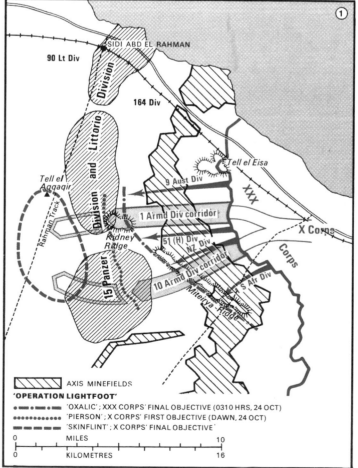

AXIS MINEFIELDS

'OPERATION LIGHTFOOT'

- ·—·—·—· 'OXALIC'; XXX CORPS' FINAL OBJECTIVE (0310 HRS, 24 OCT)
- ●●●●●● 'PIERSON'; X CORPS' FIRST OBJECTIVE (DAWN, 24 OCT)
- − − − − 'SKINFLINT'; X CORPS' FINAL OBJECTIVE

MILES	
0	10
0	16
KILOMETRES	

The battle began at 2130 hours on 24 October with a massive artillery bombardment, and at 2200 hours XXX Corps began its advance while XIII Corps mounted divisionary attacks in the south (**Map 2**). By dawn most units of XXX Corps had reached their 'Oxalic' positions but the armour of X Corps had not been able to clear the minefields. Axis reaction was hesitant, not knowing which was the main attack, and General Stumme died of a heart attack during the afternoon. By the evening 1 Armoured Division had got some units out, but 10 Armoured Division was still held up in its corridor. The XIII Corps was holding 21 Panzer Division in the south. Early in the morning of 25 October, congestion in the southern corridor reached a dangerous level, but Montgomery confirmed that the attempt to break through must continue. The New Zealand Division cleared the minefield and began to attack south-west, fighting off counterattacks by 15 Panzer Division. At midday Montgomery decided to switch the axis of attack sending 9 Australian Division to strike north covered by 1 Armoured Division. This attack began on 26 October, and compelled the Germans to commit their reserves in the north. Montgomery now decided to regroup, pulling out 2 New Zealand Division and moving 1 South African and 4 Indian Divisions north.

By this stage the Axis fuel problem was acute for two tankers had been sunk in Tobruk harbour. Rommel ordered 21 Panzer Division north and on the 27th DAK launched a series of unsuccessful attacks on 1 Armoured Division. On the evening of the 28th further attacks by 9 Australian Division had almost reached the coast road, and Montgomery began to prepare for a final breakout using X Corps. His first intention to attack in the far north was amended because German 90 Light Division had moved forward, and at 0200 on 2 November infantry assaulted the Italian positions further south and the armour began to break through. Although at the outset the attacks were contained by German counterattacks, by the evening Rommel had decided to pull back. This was delayed for twenty-four hours because Hitler forbade any withdrawal, but on the 4th, the British armour finally reached open ground.

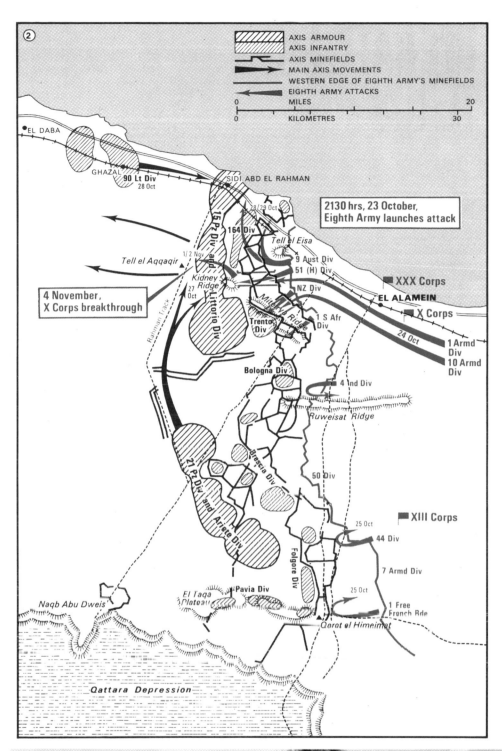

Right: British troops pinned down by Axis fire during the fighting in the corridors

OPERATION TORCH

On 8 November 1942, four days after Rommel started to retreat from El Alamein, American and British forces began landing in French North Africa (**Map 1**). The Western and Centre Task forces were American and the Eastern British. It had been hoped to arrange that French forces would not resist, but there was sporadic opposition – landing difficulties delayed the attacks on Casablanca and Mehdia, there was considerable fighting at Oran, and two destroyers were lost at Algiers. A ceasefire was arranged on 9 November. The weak point of the Allied plan was that Tunisia could not be occupied in the first landings; German troops began to arrive there on 9 November in order to protect Rommel's rear, and pushed out to form a defensive perimeter. The British made seaborne landings at Bougie on 11 November while airborne troops occupied Bône on the 12th only minutes ahead of German paratroops. The Allies now

began to push forward overland towards Tunisia and fresh parachute drops were made on 15 November by the Americans at Youks les Bains, and British at Souk el Arba on the 16th (**Map 2**). The British force had advanced to Beja by the evening, and the next day pushed forward to Sidi Nsir. On 18 November they made contact with the first German patrols. Heavy fighting developed in an attempt to seize Medjez el Bab, but on the 26th the Germans withdrew. The advance of First Army was now being held by a series of German strongpoints in the hilly terrain, and an attack on Djedeida was repulsed after the town had been occupied for a short time. The British 2 Parachute Battalion landed at Depienne and marched on Oudna, but ground forces were unable to break through to it, and it had to retire. The Germans now began to edge forward to meet the Allies until a front was established running from Bou Arada through Medjez and west of Sedjenane.

Above: American paratroops after their landing at Youks les Bains

Opposite above: British troops coming ashore east of Algiers

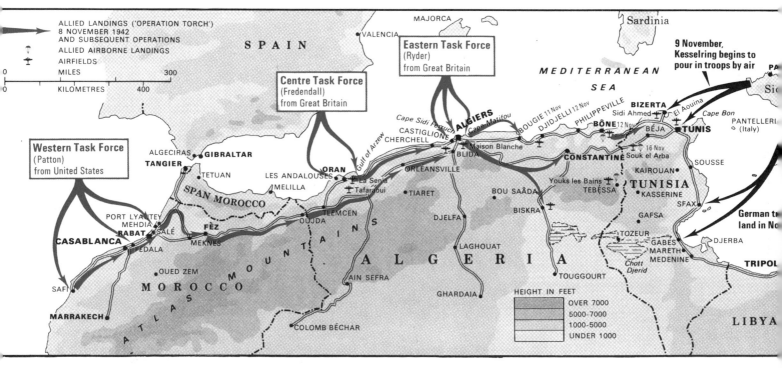

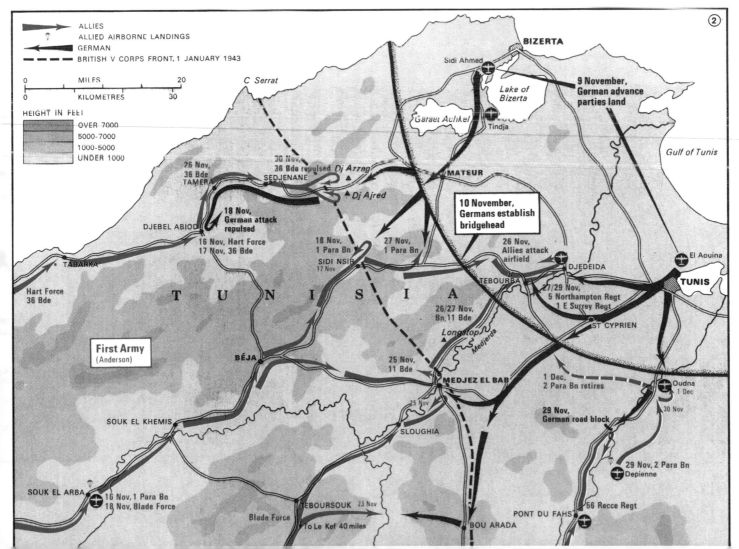

② ALLIES
ALLIED AIRBORNE LANDINGS
GERMAN
BRITISH V CORPS FRONT, 1 JANUARY 1943

0 MILES 20
0 KILOMETRES 30

HEIGHT IN FEET
OVER 7000
5000-7000
1000-5000
UNDER 1000

C Serrat

BIZERTA
Sidi Ahmed

**9 November,
German advance
parties land**

Lake of
Bizerta

Garaet Achkel

Tindja

Gulf of Tunis

26 Nov,
36 Bde
TAMERA

30 Nov,
36 Bde repulsed Dj Azzag
SEDJENANE

▲ Dj Ajred

MATEUR

**10 November,
Germans establish
bridgehead**

18 Nov,
German attack
repulsed

DJEBEL ABIOD

16 Nov, Hart Force
17 Nov, 36 Bde

18 Nov,
1 Para Bn
SIDI NSIR
17 Nov

27 Nov,
1 Para Bn

26 Nov,
Allies attack
airfield

DJEDEIDA

El Aouina

TABARKA

TEBOURBA

TUNIS

Hart Force
36 Bde

T U N I S I A

26/27 Nov,
Bn, 11 Bde

27/29 Nov,
5 Northampton Regt
1 E Surrey Regt

ST CYPRIEN

Longstop
▲

Medjerda

First Army
(Anderson)

BÉJA

25 Nov,
11 Bde

1 Dec,
2 Para Bn retires

Oudna
1 Dec

MEDJEZ EL BAB

30 Nov

29 Nov,
German road block

SOUK EL KHEMIS

25 Nov

SLOUGHIA

29 Nov, 2 Para Bn
Depienne

SOUK EL ARBA

16 Nov, 1 Para Bn
18 Nov, Blade Force

TEBOURSOUK   23 Nov

To Le Kef 40 miles

Blade Force

PONT DU FAHS

56 Recce Regt

BOU ARADA

THE ADVANCE OF EIGHTH ARMY

For the first three weeks of its advance from El Alamein, although hampered by heavy rains which had fallen on 6 November, Eighth Army met little opposition, for Rommel's forces were too disorganized to counterattack. Temporary defence lines at Fuka and Mersah Matruh were abandoned as soon as pressure built up, and news of the 'Torch' landings convinced Rommel that Halfaya could not be held. His main objective was to gain time in which to prepare defences at El Agheila and in this he was aided by the weather which had delayed Eighth Army's pursuit and supply problems which permitted Montgomery to keep only three divisions forward. By 23 November Eighth Army had reached Agedabia where it halted to reorganize, so that it was not until 12 December that Mersa Brega was attacked. The place was evacuated the next day and Eighth Army closed up to the El Agheila defences. On 14 December Montgomery sent 2 New Zealand Division deep into the desert to outflank the line and by the 16th it was threatening Axis supply lines so that Rommel had to complete his evacuation of El Agheila. The Germans left a delaying force at Sirte, while they fell back to Buerat. This line was both attacked frontally and outflanked on 15 January, and the second Axis position, Homs-Tarhuna, was swiftly breached and Tunis occupied on 23 January. Here supply problems again forced Eighth Army to halt, and it was not until 4 February that the first units crossed into Tunisia. The capture of Medenine on the 16th brought Eighth Army up towards the Mareth Line which was reached on 24 February.

Left: Axis prisoners outside Bardia

Opposite: Armour of Eighth Army entering Ben Gardane

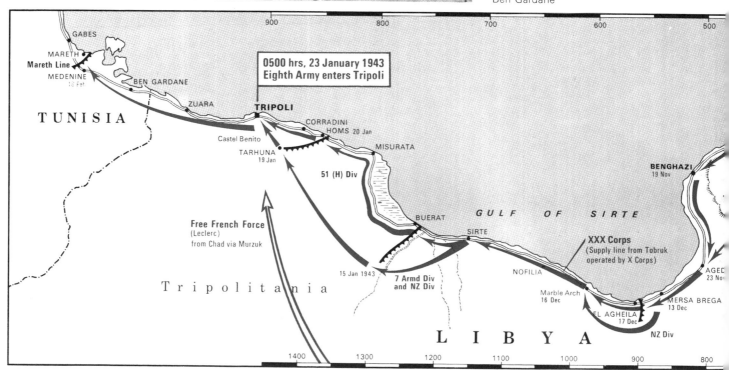

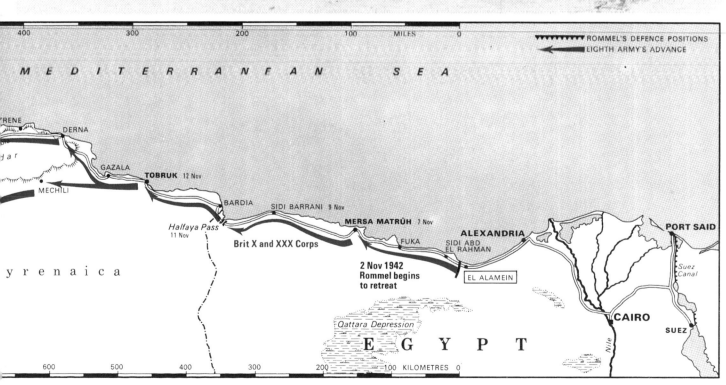

THE BATTLE OF KASSERINE

By the beginning of February 1943, with the bulk of Rommel's forces back behind the Mareth Line, and the Eighth Army so stretched as to pose no immediate threat, the Axis Supreme Command in North Africa accepted Rommel's proposal that a determined assault should be made on the Allied First Army so as to relieve pressure on Tunisia. The Allies were now lying along the Eastern Dorsale (**Map 2**) and had been pushed back from their most forward positions by limited counterattacks launched during January by General von Arnim. Rommel's plan (**Map 1**) was to strike between the American and French sectors towards Kasserine and Tebéssa and if the Allies began to fall back, to push towards Bône and Constantine. The major flaw in Axis planning was that although parts of von Arnim's and Rommel's forces were to be involved, neither had overall command. Von Arnim was more concerned with limited improvements in the Axis defensive positions than any spectacular breakthrough. General Anderson commanding the Allied First Army knew that his forward positions were still too weak, and had instructed his commanders to fall back where necessary to the Western Dorsale.

The Axis attack began at 0400 on 14 February, with twin thrusts which captured Sidi Bou Zid, and isolated the US forces on Djebels Lessouda and Ksaira. A counterattack by US 1 Armoured Division on 15 February failed to recapture Sidi Bou Zid, while a second Axis thrust captured Gafsa. During the night the US troops on Djebel Lessouda withdrew successfully, and the next day Axis troops began thrusting towards Fériana and Sbeitla. By 18 February both were in Axis hands and their forces were pressing up to Kasserine. Rommel was now urging an immediate thrust towards Tebéssa, but at the same time von Arnim was pulling 10 Panzer Division out of Sbeitla to move into a defensive position further north.

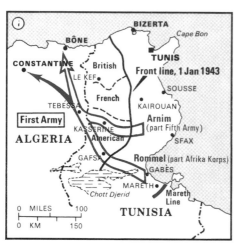

Below: Allied Shermans during the return to Kasserine

However, Rommel was now authorized to attack towards Le Kef, and this he did on 19 February with attacks towards Sbiba by 21 Panzer Division and towards Thala by 10 Panzer Division which had been recalled. A diversionary thrust by DAK units towards Tebéssa was held by US 1 Armoured Division. Meanwhile, General Alexander, who had taken command of the Allied armies, ordered that there should be no further retreat from the Western Dorsale, and began sending units of British 6 Armoured Division down to buttress the defences at Thala and Sbiba. These they reached just as Axis pressure was threatening a breakthrough. By the afternoon of 22 February Rommel had decided to call off the attacks and pull back. The Allies retook Kasserine on 25 February. They had suffered 10,000 casualties, 6,500 from US II Corps, as against only 2,000 Axis troops.

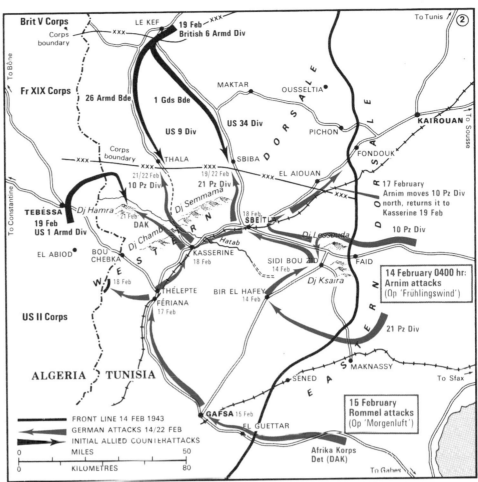

Below. American troops lifting mines after the recapture of Gafsa

BREAKING THE MARETH LINE

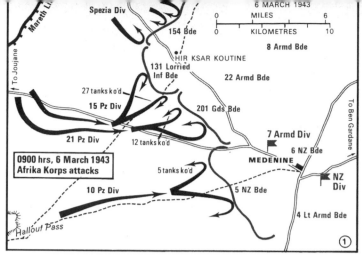

0900 hrs, 6 March 1943
Afrika Korps attacks

With the ending of the Kasserine battle, Rommel turned back to face Eighth Army which was now preparing to assault the Mareth Line. As soon as 15 and 21 Panzer Divisions were spotted moving south again, Montgomery reinforced his units in the forward positions around Medenine, and dug in his troops behind minefields and strong anti-tank defences. His tactical method was to break up any German attacks with artillery and not to involve his armour unless there was actual danger of a breakthrough. On 6 March Rommel put in attacks on a wide front, the main pressure being in the centre where the line was held by the British 131 Lorried Infantry Brigade and 201 Guards Brigade (**Map 1**). Both this and 10 Panzer Division's attack further south were successfully halted by anti-tank fire and by mid-morning the Axis units had pulled back. A second assault in the afternoon was equally unsuccessful, and the Germans fell back with the loss of 50 of their 150 tanks.

Montgomery's plan for breaking the Mareth Line was to send 2 New Zealand Division and 8 Armoured Brigade (now called New Zealand Corps) deep around the left flank through the Matmata Hills and north to the Tebaga Gap from which they could menace the El Hamma plain. The XXX Corps would then attack the Mareth Line frontally and form a bridgehead through which X Corps' armour could strike towards Gafsa and Sfax. The hazardous New Zealand Corps' move was made successfully, and by evening on 20 February it had closed up to the Tebaga Gap while German 164 Light Division began to pull back from the Mareth Line to ward off the threat (**Map 3**). During the night of the 20th, 50 Division supported by a tremendous barrage, launched the main attack and although a foothold had been formed by morning it was thrown back on the 22nd (**Map 2**). The German 21 Panzer and 164 Light Divisions were holding

the New Zealanders at the Tebaga Gap, and on 22 February 15 Panzer Division launched a major counter-attack on the bridgehead which severely mauled 50 Division.

Montgomery now altered his original plan completely by sending 1 Armoured Division and X Corps headquarters (General Horrocks) round via the Tebaga Gap, while 4 Indian Division made a short hook around the Mareth Line. Traffic congestion delayed the moves, but by 26 February 1 Armoured Division had reached Tebaga, and the next day it burst through the Gap, rolling up the Axis defences. However the Germans

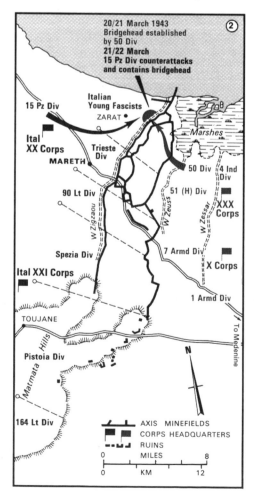

20/21 March 1943
Bridgehead established by 50 Div
21/22 March
15 Pz Div counterattacks and contains bridgehead

improvised a defence line at El Hamma, and due to Horrocks' determination to destroy this before moving on to Gabes they were able to pull back most of their forces to the Wadi Akarit. This was assaulted by Eighth Army during the night of 5/6 April. By morning 4 Indian Division had captured Point 275 and Djebel Mjerda and turned the Line. But there was no attempt to exploit this breakthrough, and, after counterattacks, the Axis forces were again able to disengage and retreat north. The fighting between these two experienced armies had been extremely severe. None the less Mareth

must be regarded as one of Montgomery's most skilful tactical battles. This was Rommel's last battle in Africa, for he was ordered home to Germany a few days later.

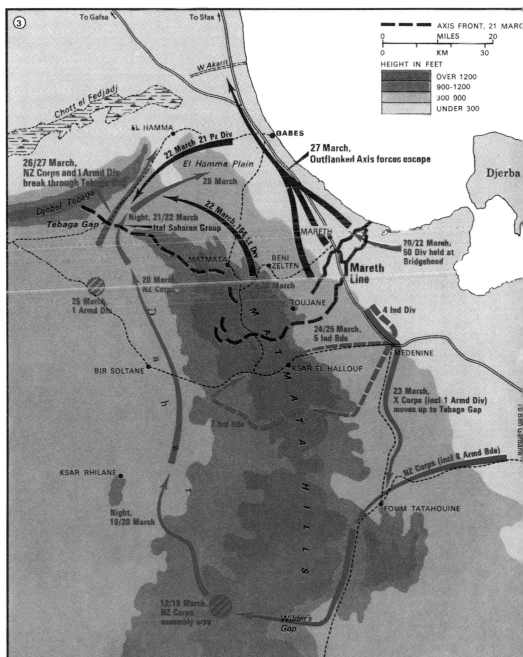

Above: A British 17-pounder in action against German armour at Medenine

Right: Italian troops digging defences at Wadi Akarit

Below: Units of the New Zealand Corps during the advance to the Tebaga Gap

THE END IN AFRICA

By the middle of April 1943, the Axis forces had been pressed into a tight perimeter based on the last hills before the coastal plain around Bizerta and Tunis (**Map 2**). Determined defence of these hills had halted the Allied First Army, but Eighth Army had now pushed up to a position just south of Enfidaville. The nineteen Allied divisions had some 1,200 tanks and 1,500 guns, against thirteen understrength Axis divisions with 500 guns but only 130 tanks. Allied airpower was now predominant. Alexander gave Eighth Army the first attempt to break through in the south, but their attack was contained and made little progress (**Map 1**). A German assault between Goubellat and Medjez el Bab on 20/21 April was also held, and on 22 April the First Army launched a series of assaults designed to capture the main remaining hills – particularly Hill 609 which dominated the valley which had been nicknamed the 'Mousetrap' through which the Americans could reach the plain, and those hills around 'Longstop' and 'Peter's Corner' which commanded the Medjerda Valley. By 29 April, US II Corps had made progress towards controlling the Mousetrap, but the other attacks had been halted. Alexander decided to regroup, and

transferred 4 Indian Division and 6 and 7 Armoured Divisions north from Eighth Army to IX Corps. He intended that once V Corps had captured Djebel Bou Aoukaz and opened the Medjerda Valley, IX Corps (now commanded by Lieutenant General Horrocks in place of Lieutenant-General Crocker who had been injured) would burst through. While this was taking place, US 9 Division had broken through in the north, and on 1 May was threatening Mateur and the German positions around the Mousetrap. On the same day, Hill 609 was taken, but US 1 Armoured Division's progress was held until the 3rd when it broke through to Mateur where the Germans had formed a new defence line and were still fighting with determination. On the evening of 5 May, Djebel Bou Aoukaz was taken, and early on the 6th, 6 and 7 Armoured Divisions supported by very heavy bombing pushed through into the plain. Their advance was enterprising for though the Axis communications had broken down, their forces were more or less intact. Tunis fell on 7 May, by which time US II Corps had broken through in the north and taken Bizerta. The coastal strip and Cap Bon were occupied, and by

Below: British infantry moving up for an attack on Longstop Hill

11 May all resistance had ceased.

The Italian, Marshal Messe, surrendered on 13 May. The moonlight advance of 6 Armoured Division from Hamman Lif to Hammamet (8 May) was one of the strangest, yet most impressive operations of the war. Without stopping to mop up they drove to the heart of the Axis position, stampeding the enemy into wholesale surrender. This exploit was the brain-child of General Alexander. By 12 May 250,415 German and Italian troops laid down their arms.

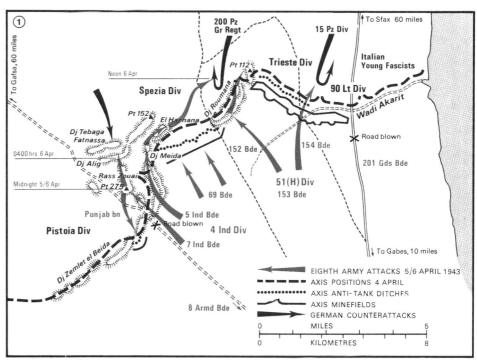

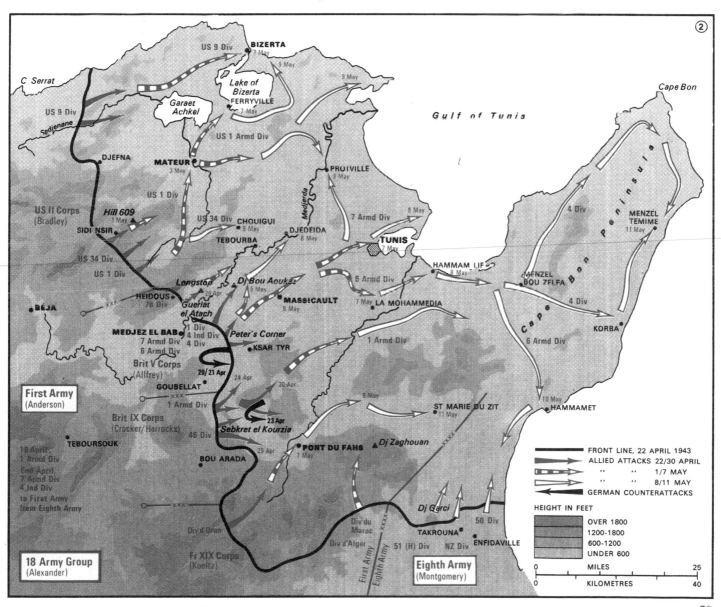

OPERATION BARBAROSSA

'When Barbarossa begins, the world will hold its breath.'

Adolf Hitler

Opposite: A Panzer column moves at night past burning buildings during the opening days of Barbarossa

Whatever the rest of the world may have felt when on 22 June 1941 Hitler's armies invaded Russia, the general opinion in Britain was that his final defeat was now inevitable. The British had never felt that they would lose the war, but so far it had not been exactly easy to see how they were going to win it. Now, like Charles XII of Sweden and Napoleon I, Hitler seemed doomed. Churchill, with his sure instinct for the mood of the moment, lost no time in declaring Britain's full and loyal support for the somewhat unlikely ally now thrust upon him.

But though the invasion of Russia unquestionably raised British morale there was in fact no solid ground for this optimism. The German onslaught had been carefully planned, wrought immense havoc, and came within an ace of capturing Moscow itself. The Russian army which had not shown to much advantage in Finland had been gravely weakened by Stalin's purges of the officer corps in 1937. At the outset Russian strategy was inept. By trying to hold too far forward all along the frontier they contrived, despite their enormous numbers, to be weak everywhere. The Russian soldier was courageous, robust, and frugal and he showed a remarkable skill at digging himself in. But lacking education he also lacked initiative, and from the first, being deployed to little advantage, suffered cruel losses in killed and wounded and staggering numbers of prisoners. Only time, it seemed, was against the Wehrmacht and for this Wavell's abortive Balkan campaign may perhaps be accorded some credit.

Hitler's attack on Russia was no sudden inspiration. It was part of his political philosophy to give the German people *Lebensraum*. The black-soil region of south Russia and east Europe had long figured on his map of the Greater Germany: his grand design. Nevertheless it seems that early in 1941 Hitler had come to recognize that he could not defeat England, and that he must, therefore, change his line of

operations. In Berlin on 14 June 1941 the Führer explained this concept to an assembly of his generals, including Guderian, the great armoured warfare expert, who is our authority for what Hitler said. Under the circumstances only a decisive victory on the Continent could bring the war to a successful conclusion. To ensure Germany's position the defeat of Russia was essential. Most of his audience knew enough military history to depart with heavy hearts. As for Guderian himself his opinion was clear: 'So long as the war in the West was still undecided, any new undertaking must result in a war on two fronts; and Adolf Hitler's Germany was even less capable of fighting such a war than had been the Germany of 1914.' Even so Adolf Hitler could dispose of 205 divisions: 145 of them on the Eastern Front. Of these last, nineteen were armoured and twelve motorized, but the rest like Napoleon's *Grande Armée* before them depended for their transport, their mobility, upon the horse. It is difficult a generation later to realize that of the great armies of the Second World War only the British and the American were genuinely motorized throughout. Nevertheless it is a factor that goes far to explain their eventual triumph.

Despite the lessons of history, Hitler, sustained by the opinions of his experts, was confident of a swift victory in Russia. General Halder (Chief of the Army General Staff) reckoned that eight to ten weeks would suffice. The Luftwaffe and the *Waffen-SS* prudently provided winter clothing for their men, but it was not until the end of August that the army recognized that it might be useful – yet 1812 was part of the folk memory of the European peoples and not least of the Germans who had formed at least a third of Napoleon's polyglot host.

Had Hitler not been supremely confident he could easily have built up his 'Russian' army by another ten divisions drawn from the thirty-eight in

the West and the twelve in Norway. But on 22 June 1941 it seemed to him quite unnecessary to add to the mighty host that was about to pass the Niemen – the river that Napoleon had crossed exactly 129 years ago. Hitler was superstitious, but since 22 June was the first anniversary of the Armistice he had imposed on the French in the Forest of Compiègne, he could afford to ignore Napoleonic memories.

In the summer of 1941 Stalin was very far from wishing to antagonize the Germans. He had honoured the agreement of January 1941 and delivered both food and raw materials to the Germans. He had ignored numerous violations of Soviet air space. and, it seems, had managed to persuade himself that there was nothing sinister about them.

It is not easy to say with any real exactitude how strong the Russians were in 1941. It may be that she had as many as 12,000,000 men under arms, including reserves. She had perhaps 160 infantry and 30 cavalry divisions, with, in addition, 35 armoured or motorized brigades. This mighty host had relatively little motor transport and was not trained for the *Blitzkrieg*. Traditional Russian assets were what they depended upon: plenty of room for manoeuvre – that is to say withdrawal; scorched earth; guerillas or partisans to operate in the enemy's rear; unmetalled roads; and those two celebrated generals Janvier and Février. It may be that the Russians had 7,500 aircraft, but they were quite outclassed by the Luftwaffe. They had no proper network of airfields and were seriously short of trained pilots. The Germans claimed that they destroyed 3,000 aircraft in the first week of the campaign. However that may be, Lieutenant-General Kopels of the Russian Military Air Power committed suicide on the second day, when he had already lost 600 planes and could not claim more than a dozen Germans shot down.

The Russians may have had as many

Far left: Soviet anti-tank guns in action

Left: Soviet cavalry advancing during the winter counteroffensive

Right: Gas holders are carried through Leningrad during the siege

as 20,000 tanks, but of this formidable number many were obsolescent. The KV and T-34s were only just coming into production. The Germans for their part, although they were now producing 1,000 tanks a year, were reduced to using French tanks in their new tanks division. The Panzer IV was neither as heavy nor as effective as the Russian T-34, which first went into action in July 1941. The German Army Ordnance Office had had the temerity to ignore Hitler's personal order to provide the Panzer III with a 50-mm cannon!

The first weeks of the campaign were weeks of triumph for the Germans. The spoils included 1,200 tanks, 600 guns, and 150,000 prisoners. By 10 July the Germans, having covered 400 miles in eighteen days, were before Smolensk. Moscow lay but 200 miles ahead. But now at last Russian resistance began to stiffen. A few more modern aircraft began to put in an appearance; the celebrated Katyusha mortar came into service (15 July); and generals alleged to have failed, like G. D. Pavlov, commander of the Western Front, were court-martialled and condemned to death.

Thus far the Germans had done pretty well – so well indeed that the Führer felt the time was ripe for a display of his skill as a commander. He informed his generals that events in France had proved that large-scale envelopments were not justified. According to Guderian Hitler 'preferred an alternative plan by which small enemy forces were to be encircled and destroyed piecemeal and the enemy thus bled to death.' In the opinion of his officers 'these manoeuvres on our part simply gave the Russians time to set up new formations and to use their inexhaustible man-power for the creation of fresh defensive lines in the rear area; even more important, we were sure that this strategy would not result in the urgently necessary, rapid conclusion of the campaign.'

As late as 4 August Hitler was still uncertain as to his objectives. On that day he held a conference at Novy Borissov, the HQ of Army Group Centre, and gave the industrial area round Leningrad as his first objective. He had not yet quite made up his mind whether to strike after that at Moscow or the Ukraine, but for various reasons the latter seemed to him the more favourable. Army Group South seemed to be poised for victory there; Germany needed the resources of the area and Hitler saw in the Crimea 'a Soviet aircraft-carrier operating against the Rumanian oil-fields . . .' In any case he hoped to have Moscow and Kharkov before winter.

By 21 August when he gave out his orders for the capture of Kiev Hitler had decided that: 'Of primary importance before the outbreak of winter is not the capture of Moscow but rather the occupation of the Crimea, of the industrial and coalmining area of the Donetz basin, the cutting of the Russian supply routes from the Caucasian oilfields, and, in the north, the investment of Leningrad and the establishment of contact with the Finns. . . . The capture of the Crimean peninsula is of extreme importance for safeguarding our oil supplies from Rumania.' It was a strategy of dispersal, but nevertheless in the short term it brought a dazzling success. On 18 September Kiev fell and by the 26th the Russians had lost 665,000 prisoners in the battle.

Early in October the Germans began their final advance on Moscow. 'Today', declared Hitler on 2 October, 'begins the last great decisive battle of the year!' At first all went well, and three weeks later von Bock's armour was within 30 miles of the capital. Meanwhile von Rundstedt had overrun the Crimea where only Sevastopol held out. The Soviet government and the *corps diplomatique* departed to Kubyshev, but Stalin stayed on in the Kremlin where on 7 November he galvanized his countrymen with his Holy Russia speech, in which he inspired them with the examples of their heroic ancestors, Alexander Nevsky, Dimitri Donskoi, Minin, and Pozharsky, Alexander Suvorov, Michael Kutuzov, and Lenin. Nor did he fail to mention the material aid, aircraft, tanks, and dollars, which Mr Harriman and Lord Beaverbrook had promised during the recent Moscow Conference. 'All this shows that the coalition between the three countries is a very real thing which will go on growing in the common cause of liberation.'

By mid-October, as in 1812, the weather broke. The 'Napoleon weather' which had broken the morale of the *Grande Armée* now brought the Germans to a standstill. First it was the mud, and then bitter cold. But Hitler had not finished, and it was as late as 15 November that he compelled his frost-bitten host to make another great offensive towards Moscow. It carried them into the suburbs, but by 6 December it had run out of steam. By that time their successes had cost the Germans 750,000 casualties on the Russian Front, including 8,000 officers and nearly 200,000 men killed. 'I would never have believed,' wrote Guderian, 'that a really brilliant military position could be so b . . . . d up in two months.' The story of the Russian campaign, with its occasional triumphs and its frequent disasters, would henceforth be influenced at every turn by the strategic inspirations and the will-power of Adolf Hitler. Halted before Moscow in the bitter cold his generals urged withdrawal. But Hitler insisted that they hang on. When in February the great Russian winter counteroffensive lost its momentum, and German Army Group Centre, despite dire sufferings, was saved, he could boast that it was thanks to his rejecting the advice of his staff-trained generals. From this time the Führer was his own commander-in-chief. Despite his occasional flashes of strategic insight and tactical skill, this was to prove very much to the advantage of the Allies.

THE MILITARY BALANCE ON THE EASTERN FRONT

Hitler ordered the preparation of an attack on Russia as early as 21 July 1940. The first plans of OKH (*Oberkommando des Heeres*/Army High Command) envisaged two major thrusts to Moscow and Kiev with a covering thrust in the north (**Map 1**). This was altered after war games, to include a major attack in the north, the main objective still being Moscow (**Map 2**). However, at planning conferences early in December Hitler directed that Leningrad was the most urgent target, and that part of the central thrust might be diverted after the capture of Smolensk to support this plan (**Map 3**). It was on this general idea that 'Barbarossa', the final plan was drawn up. The Germans aimed for a rapid campaign with deep armoured penetrations to surround and smash the Red Army well before winter. They had allotted 138 divisions, including 48 Panzer divisions, to the task. They estimated Russian strength at about 155 divisions. This proved an underestimate, for, of a total of some 230 divisions, the Red Army had 170 within operational distance of its Western front: but in no other way was it ready for war in 1941. The leadership had not recovered from the 1937 purges; a major reorganization and re-equipment programme put in hand after the Finnish War was not yet completed; units in the west were far too close to the frontiers; and the building up of a strong reserve to meet any deep penetrations had only just begun.

The front was divided into two separate halves by the Pripet marshes, and the bulk of German strength lay in the north (**Map 4**). Von Leeb's Army Group North with Leningrad as its objective was faced by an almost equal number of Russian divisions but these were deployed so far forward that they were vulnerable to being pushed back against the coast by a deep thrust towards Riga and beyond. Von Bock's Army Group Centre, with two Panzer armies, was the strongest. The Red Army West Front facing it was not only considerably weaker, but had a complete army lying invitingly in the salient around Bialystock. This the Germans planned to surround by striking from both flanks – the Panzer armies aiming to meet at Minsk while

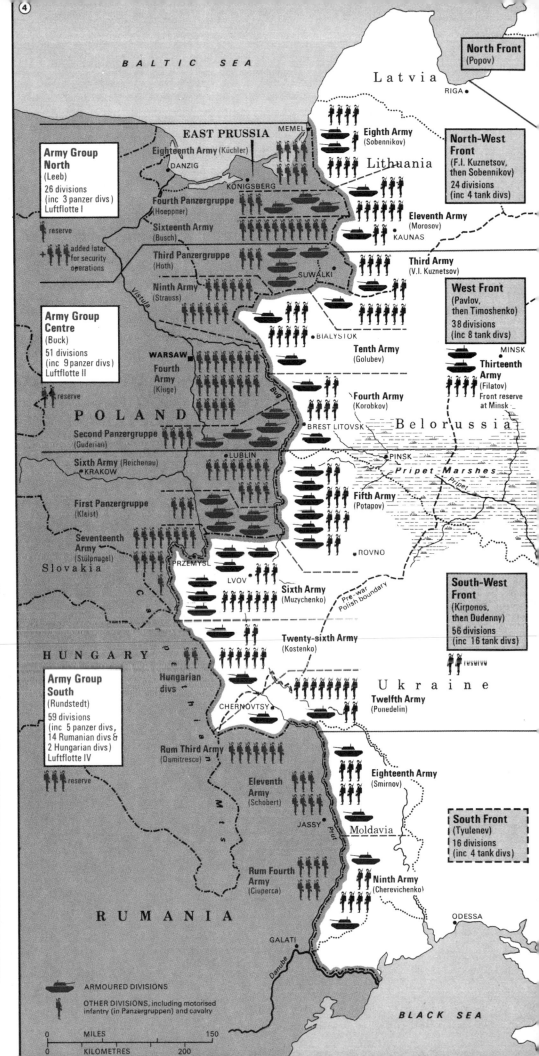

the infantry closed in to the east of Bialystok. The bulk of the Red Army lay south of the Pripet marshes defending the agricultural and industrial wealth of the Ukraine. Once again the Red Army's dispositions made it vulnerable to a south-easterly thrust by the bulk of von Rundstedt's Army Group South.

The massive German build-up had, of course, been observed by the Russians, but Stalin was so determined not to give Hitler any excuse to attack that in June 1941 the Red Army was still on a peacetime footing with most units widely scattered for summer training.

Below: A sentry guarding the Channel coast after Axis interest had moved east

④

North Front
(Popov)

BALTIC SEA

Latvia

RIGA

Eighth Army
(Sobennikov)

EAST PRUSSIA   MEMEL

North-West Front
(F.I. Kuznetsov, then Sobennikov)
24 divisions
(inc 4 tank divs)

Eighteenth Army (Küchler)
DANZIG

Lithuania

Army Group North
(Leeb)
26 divisions
(inc 3 panzer divs)
Luftflotte I

KÖNIGSBERG

Fourth Panzergruppe
(Hoeppner)

Sixteenth Army
(Busch)

Eleventh Army
(Morosov)
KAUNAS

reserve

Third Panzergruppe
(Hoth)

Third Army
(V.I. Kuznetsov)

added later
for security
operations

SUWALKI

Vistula

Ninth Army
(Strauss)

West Front
(Pavlov, then Timoshenko)
38 divisions
(inc 8 tank divs)

• BIALYSTOK

MINSK

Army Group Centre
(Bock)
51 divisions
(inc 9 panzer divs)
Luftflotte II

Tenth Army
(Golubev)

Thirteenth Army
(Filatov)
Front reserve at Minsk

WARSAW

Fourth Army
(Kluge)

Bug

Fourth Army
(Korobkov)

reserve

B e l o r u s s i a

P O L A N D

Second Panzergruppe
(Guderian)

BREST LITOVSK

Sixth Army (Reichenau)
• KRAKOW

• LUBLIN

PINSK

Pripet-Marshes

Pripet

First Panzergruppe
(Kleist)

Fifth Army
(Potapov)

Seventeenth Army
(Stülpnagel)

Slovakia

PRZEMYSL

• ROVNO

LVOV

Sixth Army
(Muzychenko)

Pre-war Polish boundary

South-West Front
(Kirponos, then Budenny)
56 divisions
(inc 16 tank divs)

reserve

Twenty-sixth Army
(Kostenko)

U k r a i n e

HUNGARY

Hungarian divs

Twelfth Army
(Ponedelin)

Army Group South
(Rundstedt)
59 divisions
(inc 5 panzer divs,
14 Rumanian divs &
2 Hungarian divs)
Luftflotte IV

CHERNOVTSY

Rum Third Army
(Dumitrescu)

Eighteenth Army
(Smirnov)

Eleventh Army
(Schobert)

Moldavia

reserve

South Front
(Tyulenev)
16 divisions
(inc 4 tank divs)

JASSY   Prut

Rum Fourth Army
(Ciuperca)

Ninth Army
(Cherevichenko)

ODESSA

R U M A N I A

GALATI

Danube

BLACK SEA

ARMOURED DIVISIONS

OTHER DIVISIONS, including motorised
infantry (in Panzergruppen) and cavalry

0   MILES   150

0   KILOMETRES   200

THE GERMAN ASSAULT

German forces invaded Soviet territory at 0300 hours on 22 June 1941, achieving almost total tactical surprise. In the north Fourth Panzergroup took Daugavpils by 26 June and began establishing bridgeheads across the River Dvina. Ostrov was reached by 4 July, and the Luga river by the 14th.

Army Group Centre began sealing off the Russian forces facing it around Bialystok and Gorodishche, and Second and Third Panzergroups met west of Minsk on 29 June. By 9 July all resistance in the pockets had ended with the Red Army losing some 300,000 prisoners and 2,500 tanks. Meanwhile the Panzers had pushed on across the Berezina on 1 July. On 3 July the two groups were merged into Fourth Panzer Army and the units of Fourth Army were renamed Second Army. Fourth Panzer was given the task of breaking through to Smolensk, and its units began crossing the rivers Dvina and Dniepr on 9 July. Smolensk was reached on 16 July but Russian counterattacks halted any further advance and prevented the Soviet forces near the city from being completely surrounded.

Army Group South had experienced the toughest resistance. A successful initial breakthrough by First Panzergroup was counterattacked on 10 July from the north near Korosten by the Russian Fifth Army and from the south near Kazatin. These were fought off but though the Panzers had pushed on to within ten miles of Kiev by 11 July they were unable to assault the city. The Soviet Fifth Army pulled back but continued to threaten the northern flank of the German advance.

It was now that Hitler began to envisage halting Army Group Centre and concentrating on capturing the Ukraine. On 19 July OKW (*Oberkommando der Wehrmacht*/Supreme High Command) directed that after the destruction of the Russian forces near Smolensk, Second Panzergroup and Second Army should swing south to destroy the Russian Fifth Army and

surrounded Kiev by linking up with units from First Panzergroup which would strike north.

Guderian, commanding Second Panzergroup, objected strongly to abandoning the Moscow offensive, but used the opportunity to strike south-east on 1 August to break up Russian forces strengthening his flank from Roslavl. The ring around the Russian forces at Smolensk had been closed on 27 July, and by 5 August these had been destroyed. Meanwhile First Panzergroup had struck towards Pervomaisk on 30 July linking up with units of Seventeenth Army on 3 August. Russian resistance in the pocket near Uman ended on 8 August, and Army Group South pushed on to reach Dnepropetrovsk and form a bridgehead at Kremenchug.

On 23 August Second Panzergroup and Second Army began moving south through Gomel and Starodub. The Russians had been reinforcing their South-West Front and on 30 August they launched a counteroffensive north of Gomel which was turned back, however, without halting the German advance. On 12 September First Panzergroup struck north from Kremenchug, and on the 15th the two pincers met at Lokhvitsa. During the next two days the Russian Fifth and Thirty-Seventh Armies were totally destroyed and about 500,000 men lost.

In the north, Army Group North had reached Novgorod by 16 August, and was poised to close in on Leningrad.

Above right: German motorized units pursue the Russians

Right: Engineers repairing a bridge over the Dniepr

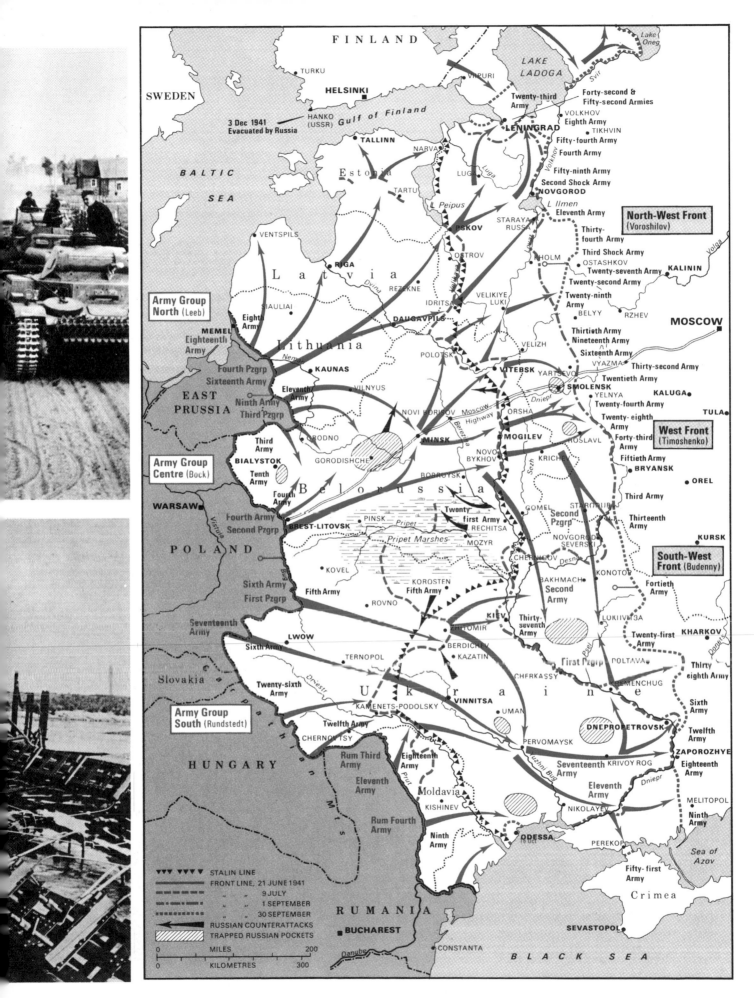

FINLAND

SWEDEN

TURKU

HELSINKI

HANKO
(USSR)
3 Dec 1941
Evacuated by Russia

Gulf of Finland

VIIPURI

*LAKE
LADOGA*

Twenty-third
Army

Forty-second &
Fifty-second Armies

Svir

*Lake
Oneg*

VOLKHOV
Eighth Army

LENINGRAD

*BALTIC

SEA*

TALLINN

Estonia

NARVA

L. Peipus

TARTU

Luga

Fifty-fourth Army

Volkhov

Fourth Army

Fifty-ninth Army

Second Shock Army

NOVGOROD

L Ilmen

Eleventh Army

North-West Front
(Voroshilov)

VENTSPILS

PSKOV

OSTROV

STARAYA
RUSSA

Thirty-
fourth Army

Volga

RIGA

L a t v i a

Dvina

REZEKNE

Third Shock Army

KHOLM

OSTASHKOV

KALININ

Twenty-seventh Army

Twenty-second Army

VELIKIYE
LUKI

Twenty-ninth
Army

BELYY

RZHEV

MOSCOW

**Army Group
North** (Leeb)

SIAULIAI

L i t h u a n i a

IDRITSA

DAUGAVPILS

Eighth
Army

MEMEL

Eighteenth
Army

Nemen

POLOTSK

VELIZH

VITEBSK

Thirtieth Army

Nineteenth Army

Sixteenth Army

VYAZMA

Thirty-second Army

**EAST
PRUSSIA**

Fourth Pzgrp
Sixteenth Army

KAUNAS

VILNYUS

NOVI BORISOV

ORSHA

Moscow

SMOLENSK

YARTSEVO

Twentieth Army

KALUGA

Ninth Army
Third Pzgrp

Eleventh
Army

Dnipr

MOGILEV

YELNYA

Twenty-fourth Army

GRODNO

Berezina

Highway

MINSK

TULA

Third
Army

BIALYSTOK

GORODISHCHE

NOVO
BYKHOV

ROSLAVL

KRICHEV

Twenty-eighth
Army

Forty-third
Army

West Front
(Timoshenko)

**Army Group
Centre** (Bock)

Tenth
Army

B e l o r u s s i a

BOBROYSK

Sozh

Fiftieth Army

BRYANSK

OREL

WARSAW

Fourth
Army

Twenty-
first Army

Second
Pzgrp

P O L A N D

Fourth Army
Second Pzgrp

BREST-LITOVSK

PINSK

Pripet

RECHITSA

GOMEL

STARODUB

Third Army

Vistula

Pripet Marshes

MOZYR

NOVGOROD
SEVERSKI

Thirteenth
Army

KURSK

Bug

KOVEL

KOROSTEN

CHERNIGOV

Desna

KONOTOP

**South-West
Front** (Budenny)

Sixth Army
First Pzgrp

Fifth Army

ROVNO

Fifth Army

BAKHMACH

Second
Army

LUKIIVITSA

Fortieth
Army

Seventeenth
Army

LWOW

Sixth Army

TERNOPOL

BERDICHEV

ZHITOMIR

KIEV

Thirty-
seventh
Army

Twenty-first
Army

KHARKOV

Slovakia

Orestr

KAZATIN

First Pzgrp

CHERKASSY

POLTAVA

Thirty-
eighth Army

Donest

Twenty-sixth
Army

U k r a i n e

KAMENETS-PODOLSKY

VINNITSA

Uzhni Bug

KREMENCHUG

Sixth
Army

**Army Group
South** (Rundstedt)

Twelfth Army

CHERNOVTSY

UMAN

PERVOMAYSK

DNEPROPETROVSK

Twelfth
Army

C a r p a t h i a n M t s

HUNGARY

Rum Third
Army

Eighteenth
Army

Prut

Seventeenth
Army

KRIVOY ROG

ZAPOROZHYE

Eighteenth
Army

Eleventh
Army

Moldavia

VINNITSA

Dniepr

MELITOPOL

Eleventh
Army

KISHINEV

NIKOLAYEV

Ninth
Army

Rum Fourth
Army

Ninth
Army

ODESSA

PEREKOP

*Sea of
Azov*

R U M A N I A

Fifty-first
Army

Crimea

Danube

BUCHAREST

SEVASTOPOL

▼▼▼ ▼▼▼▼ ▼ STALIN LINE
FRONT LINE, 21 JUNE 1941
9 JULY
1 SEPTEMBER
30 SEPTEMBER
RUSSIAN COUNTERATTACKS
TRAPPED RUSSIAN POCKETS

0 ——— MILES ——— 200
0 ——— KILOMETRES ——— 300

CONSTANTA

B L A C K   S E A

87

THE FINNISH ATTACKS

Finland's defeat by the Red Army in 1939/40 meant that Hitler had a ready ally for 'Barbarossa'. A co-ordinated attack by German troops from Norway in the far north and the Finnish army under Marshal Mannerheim in Karelia was planned to link up with Army Group North. The attacks began on 29 June, but by the beginning of September the three northern attacks had been halted. Further south Mannerheim's attacks north of Lake Ladoga had begun well with a breakthrough which reached the lake east of Sortavala on 16 July. But the Russians withdrew their outflanked forces by water, and fell back steadily so that by 1 September the Finns had reached a stop-line, close to the 1939 frontier. On the Isthmus an attack through Vuosalmi to outflank Viipuri began on 31 July and reached Vuosalmi on 16 August. But a chance to cut off the Russian forces at Viipuri was narrowly missed, and they were able to withdraw. By 1 September the Finns had reached the pre-1939 defences of Leningrad. Here they halted, for Mannerheim, having regained the territory lost in 1939–40, was reluctant to become more deeply involved in the attack on Russia.

The second stage of the offensive attacks north of Lake Ladoga to capture Petrozavodsk and cut the Murmansk railway began on 3 September and by the 8th the line had been cut at Lodeynoye Pele. Russian resistance was steadily increasing and Petrozavodsk was not taken until 1 October. For the next two months attacks continued in the area but once Medvezhegorsk was taken on 6 December the Finns went over to the defensive.

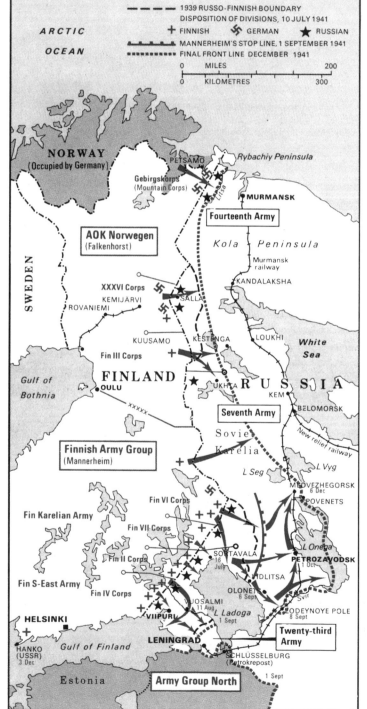

Below: Finnish troops advance through a ruined town in eastern Karelia

THE ATTACK ON LENINGRAD

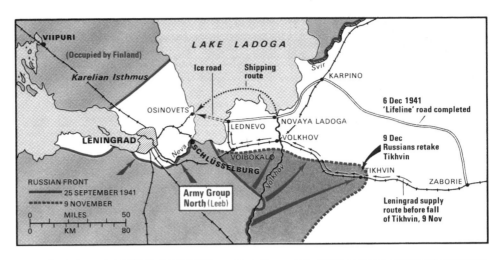

On 1 September 1941 the forces of Army Group North were close enough to begin the artillery bombardment of Leningrad. The Germans who had decided against storming the city strove to surround it and starve it into surrender. On 15 September, with the capture of Schlüsselburg, the city was completely cut off from overland communication with the rest of Russia. The food remaining in the city was sufficient, heavily rationed, for about one month, and starvation began to set in during October and November with 11,000 people dying in the latter month. A supply route from Tikhvin to Lednevo had been used to get some food across the lake in barges, but on 9 November the Germans took Tikhvin and in the middle of the month, ice on the lake – not yet thick enough to stand the weight of trucks – made navigation impossible. A new road from Zaborie via Karpino to Lednevo was opened on 6 December, but what with the weather and the difficult terrain trucks could scarcely do twenty miles a day on it. However, on 9 December, as part of the Red Army's great winter counteroffensive, Tikhvin was recaptured and the Germans were pushed back to the Volkhov river. The railway was repaired and an ice road opened across the lake allowing a proper supply line to the city. But the supply situation remained precarious; on 25 December, the day when it proved possible to increase the bread ration, 3,700 people died of starvation.

Right: A policeman looks at the corpses of civilians who had died of starvation in Leningrad

THE BATTLE FOR MOSCOW 1

With the ending of the Kiev battle, the Germans redeployed their forces for the assault on Moscow. Hoth's Third Panzergroup, brought down from Army Group North, and Fourth Panzergroup were to strike towards Vyazma while Guderian's Panzergroup further south aimed at Orel and Bryansk. The Germans had forty-four infantry divisions, eight motorized divisions, and fourteen Panzer divisions for the assault with a 2:1 superiority in men and tanks and about 3:1 in the air. Because of the greater distance to be covered Guderian's attack began on 30 September and the other on 2 October (**Map 1**). By 7 October large pockets of Russian troops had been cut off around Vyazma and Bryansk. But the next day heavy rains began and mud started to hinder the German mobile units which were now pushing towards Tula and Kaluga in the south and Rzhev and Kalinin in the north. The pocket at Vyazma was destroyed on 14 October and that at Bryansk on 20 October. However, increasingly stubborn Russian resistance along the Mozhaysk defence line and the weather meant that by 30 October the German attacks had halted between 45 and 75 miles short of Moscow. Now the freeze began to harden the roads again and the Germans prepared for the final thrusts to reach the Volga canal north of Moscow and the Moskva river to the south before undertaking the close encirclement of the city. The Germans had now virtually lost their superiority in men and tanks, and were finding it difficult to adapt to the extreme cold. The assault began on 15 November and by 27 November units of Third Panzergroup had reached the Volga canal within 19 miles of the centre of Moscow, while on the 25th units of Second Panzer Army reached Kashira but had to fall back for lack of support. The Germans were now unable to make any further progress and on 5 December it was decided to pull Third Panzergroup back to the Istra/Klin line and Second Panzergroup back to the Don/Ulla line and to go over to the defensive.

Meanwhile, Army Group South had launched attacks to capture Kharkov and secure the Ukraine (**Map 2**). Von Kleist's First Panzergroup burst across the Dniepr and Samara on 30 September, swinging south behind the Russian Eighteenth and Ninth Armies to reach Berdyansk on 6 October. More than 100,000 prisoners were captured in this pocket, but rain and mud were now slowing the German advance, and the Russians were no longer trying to hold the Germans with linear defences but were pulling back gradually towards the Donets while building up a new army – the Thirty-seventh – in the Krasnodon area to threaten the flank of any attack on Rostov. Kharkov was occupied by the Germans on 24 October and on 1 November First Panzergroup began its thrust towards Rostov. This reached the Tuslov river on 14 November, but the threat of Thirty-seventh Army on the flank forced the Germans to abandon plans to outflank Rostov, and the city was taken by frontal attack on 20 November. On 29 November Thirty-seventh Army and part of Second Army put in a counterattack which threatened to cut off the German units in the city. Von Rundstedt therefore ordered his forces to pull back to the Mius river, and resigned when Hitler tried to countermand the order.

Below: As the first snows arrive, German troops struggle to release an assault gun trapped by mud

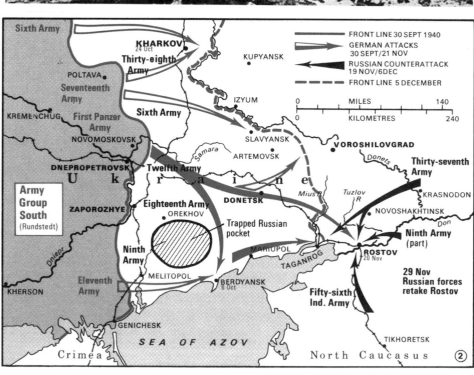

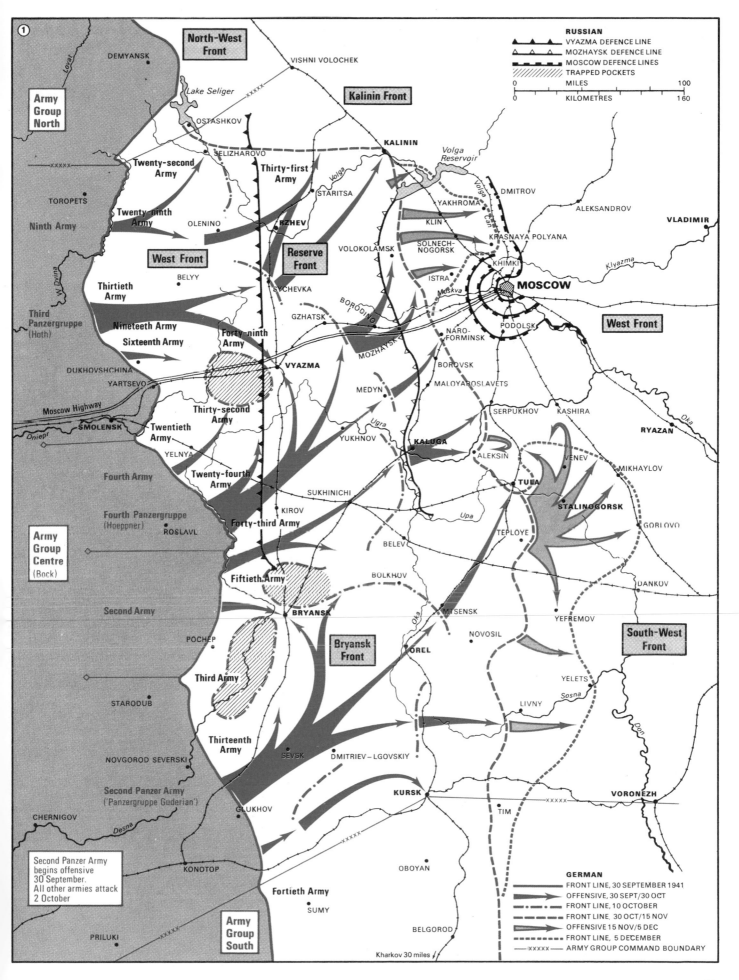

① North-West Front

DEMYANSK

Army Group North

Lake Seliger

VISHNI VOLOCHEK

Kalinin Front

OSTASHKOV

KALININ

Volga Reservoir

DMITROV

ALEKSANDROV

VLADIMIR

TOROPETS

SELIZHAROVO

Thirty-first Army

STARITSA

YAKHROMA

KLIN

KRASNAYA POLYANA

Klyazma

Ninth Army

Twenty-second Army

OLENINO

RZHEV

SOLNECH-NOGORSK

KHIMKI

Twenty-ninth Army

West Front

Reserve Front

VOLOKOLAMSK

ISTRA

Moskva

MOSCOW

Third Panzergruppe (Hoth)

Thirtieth Army

BELYY

SYCHEVKA

BORODINO

PODOLSK

West Front

W. Dvina

Nineteenth Army

Sixteenth Army

Forty-ninth Army

GZHATSK

MOZHAYSK

NARO-FORMINSK

DUKHOVSHCHINA

VYAZMA

MEDYN

BOROVSK

YARTSEVO

Thirty-second Army

Ugra

MALOYAROSLAVETS

SERPUKHOV

KASHIRA

Oka

Moscow Highway

SMOLENSK

Twentieth Army

YUKHNOV

KALUGA

ALEKSIN

VENEV

RYAZAN

Dniepr

YELNYA

Twenty-fourth Army

SUKHINICHI

MIKHAYLOV

Fourth Army

TULA

Fourth Panzergruppe (Hoeppner)

KIROV

Forty-third Army

BELEV

Upa

STALINOGORSK

GORLOVO

ROSLAVL

TEPLOYE

Army Group Centre (Bock)

Fiftieth Army

BOLKHOV

DANKOV

Second Army

BRYANSK

Oka

MTSENSK

YEFREMOV

POCHEP

Bryansk Front

NOVOSIL

South-West Front

Third Army

OREL

YELETS

STARODUB

Thirteenth Army

SEVSK

DMITRIEV – LGOVSKIY

LIVNY

Sosna

Don

NOVGOROD SEVERSKI

Second Panzer Army ('Panzergruppe Guderian')

GLUKHOV

KURSK

VORONEZH

CHERNIGOV

Desna

TIM

KONOTOP

Second Panzer Army begins offensive 30 September. All other armies attack 2 October

Fortieth Army

SUMY

OBOYAN

Army Group South

PRILUKI

BELGOROD

Kharkov 30 miles

RUSSIAN
▲▲▲ VYAZMA DEFENCE LINE
△△△ MOZHAYSK DEFENCE LINE
MOSCOW DEFENCE LINES
/// TRAPPED POCKETS

0   MILES   100
0   KILOMETRES   160

GERMAN
—— FRONT LINE, 30 SEPTEMBER 1941
➤ OFFENSIVE, 30 SEPT/30 OCT
—·—· FRONT LINE, 10 OCTOBER
—— FRONT LINE, 30 OCT/15 NOV
➤ OFFENSIVE 15 NOV/5 DEC
···· FRONT LINE, 5 DECEMBER
—xxxxx— ARMY GROUP COMMAND BOUNDARY

THE BATTLE FOR MOSCOW 2

On 5/6 December just as the Germans had decided to go over to the defensive, the Russian Kalinin, West, and South-West Fronts launched a counteroffensive. *Stavka* (The Soviet Supreme Command) had been bringing up fresh divisions from Siberia and had been planning the attacks from the last week in November. The main thrusts, spearheaded by First Shock Army to the north of Moscow and Tenth Army to the south, aimed to push back the Germans from their nearest penetrations to the city, and to threaten their supply lines from the south. The first week brought spectacular successes as disorganized German troops fell back swiftly and Stalin began to envisage a massive counteroffensive all along the front, which would relieve Leningrad and regain the Donbas region of the Ukraine, as well as cutting off the German Army Group Centre. *Stavka* and particularly General Zhukov, commanding West Front, advised against any widening of objectives which would weaken the existing thrusts and bring the Red Army up against prepared positions, but Stalin was insistent. Orders went out on

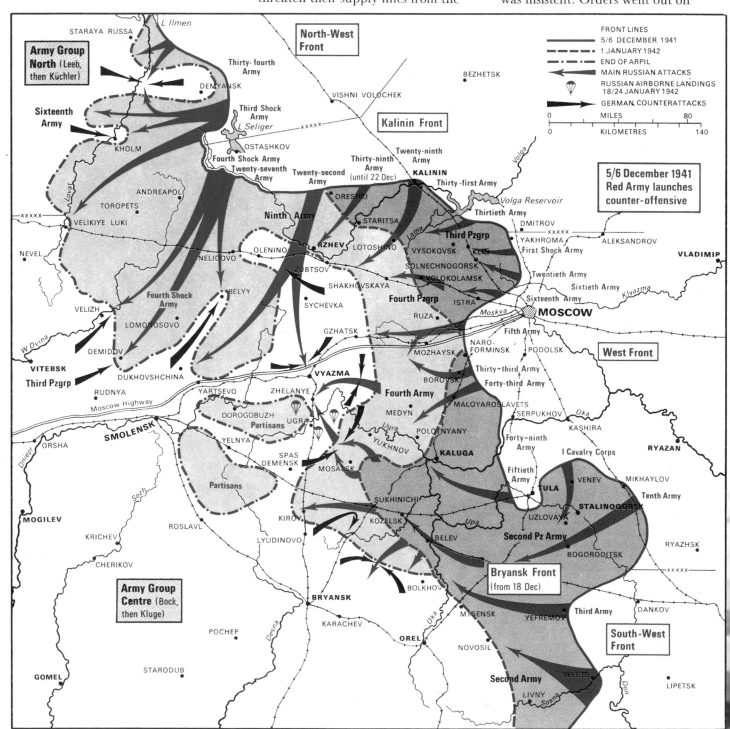

5 January and the new offensives began on the 7th.

In the north, Third Shock Army and Thirty-fourth Army struck west against Army Group North, while Fourth Shock Army thrust south towards Vitebsk aiming to cut the main supply lines of Army Group Centre. Kalinin Front pushed forward towards Rzhev, while Bryansk Front tried to cut behind the German Fourth Army and reach Bryansk. By late January the scale of the offensive had used up all Russian reserves and the Germans were beginning to counterattack. In the north seven divisions of German II Corps, surrounded near Demyansk, could not be destroyed and were eventually relieved. The southern attacks on Vyazma were being counterattacked from the flanks, and Twenty-ninth Army which had almost reached Vyazma from the north had its line of retreat cut south of Rzhev. For the next two months fighting continued, but the Germans, despite large-scale partisan activity behind their lines, were able to stabilize their front, holding on to the Rzhev/Gzhatsk/Vyazma triangle.

Above: Russian troops, well-equipped to withstand the extreme conditions, assault a German position

Below: Soviet tanks in attack. The Germans were shocked by the scale of the Russian operations

THE JAPANESE OFFENSIVE

On 7 December, without awaiting the declaration of war, the Japanese attacked the US Pacific Fleet in Pearl Harbor, taking it by surprise and inflicting heavy casualties. Many an Axis victory still lay ahead, but beyond question no event in the whole war equalled in importance the act which brought in the United States, with their wealth of resources, squarely on the Allied side. For Great Britain it was a turning point even more significant than the day nearly six months earlier, when the Germans invaded Russia.

No good American thought it possible that Japanese intentions could have been suspected in Washington, and when President Roosevelt denounced 7 December as 'a date which will live in infamy' his people readily accepted his declaration that the war was a single whole, comprising German and Italian enemies as well as Japanese. This too was of great advantage to the British, especially after it was agreed that the European war should take priority.

The Axis leaders were not unduly perturbed when their Japanese allies pushed the United States into the war, though Count Ciano, the Italian Foreign Minister, unlike his jubilant German counterpart, von Ribbentrop, had the wit to see that America would now enter the European conflict, which would be so long that she would be able to bring all her potential forces to bear. In this he proved absolutely right.

Japan had already been at war since 1937: against China. Like Hitler she was bent on obtaining *Lebensraum*, the so-called 'Greater East Asia Co-Prosperity Sphere'. In July 1941 the French government of Marshal Pétain, unable to protect Indo-China, had agreed to its occupation by Japan. Roosevelt, who had been financing and supplying the Chinese, immediately froze Japanese assets in the USA. Great Britain and the Netherlands followed suit. Major-General J. F. C. Fuller saw this as 'a declaration of economic war', and it may be that the Japanese were

persuaded that they had now to choose between war and economic ruin.

It is hard to conceive that General Tojo's government, which came to power in October 1941, can have hoped for complete victory over two such great maritime and industrial powers, as the USA and Great Britain, whose homelands were, practically speaking, beyond their reach. Rather the Japanese hoped by a swift onslaught to seize and consolidate a controlling position in the Pacific before the balance of forces should swing against them. In the short term they were in a strong position, whilst many Allied possessions were extremely vulnerable. Japan's main strength lay in her ten fast modern carriers, each of which carried some seventy-five aircraft. Japanese pilots were extremely well-trained and to a great extent Japan owed her initial successes to superiority at sea and in the air. In Malaya and the Philippines the Japanese did not owe their victory to any vast superiority in the strength of her land forces. The most important factor was that they had a balanced force, and the backing of numbers of efficient, modern aircraft. Their forces were, moreover, well-versed in the techniques of amphibious warfare. Their morale was excellent, and even at the end of the war it was rare indeed for them to lose more than a handful of prisoners. The men were hardy, frugal, and, it must be said, bloodthirsty. Tactically they were enterprising, never afraid to operate at night or in jungle, or to cut loose from their lines of communications. They had, moreover, four years of recent battle experience behind them.

A factor of some importance was that for the most part the indigenous inhabitants were not unduly disturbed at seeing their white rulers, however benevolent, ejected. And they had not all been benevolent.

It was ironical that by knocking out the American battleships at Pearl Harbor the Japanese had altered the nature of sea warfare, and practically

deprived their own numerous and expensive battleships of their *raison d'être*. In the decisive battles of the Pacific, battles between carriers, no ship on either side was to see an opposing capital ship. And as it turned out the Americans were rather quicker to master the new techniques of maritime warfare.

The first six months of the land fighting in the Far East was a period of practically unrelieved gloom. The splendid resistance of Major James Deveraux and his 500 United States Marines on Wake Island, and Lieutenant-General Jonathan Wainwright's dogged defence of Corregidor were practically the only bright spots, though General Douglas MacArthur emerged as a leader of real quality, and one who had prepared his command for war. In Malaya Lieutenant-General A. E. Percival had had only seven months in which to make ready, and what with the prevailing attitude of the white population and the lamentable state of training of his troops the task proved too much for him. Only one battalion, 2 Argyll and Sutherland Highlanders, is thought to have made any serious attempt to train for jungle warfare. Perceval still had some 85,000 British, Australian, and Indian troops when he surrendered – by far the biggest surrender in the annals of the British army. In Burma the British though gravely outnumbered, deployed too far forward and suffered a nasty setback in the Battle of the Sittang River, which led to the longest retreat any British force has ever made. Had it not been for the arrival of General Alexander and Lieutenant-General Slim Burma Corps might well have disintegrated. As it was the survivors lived to form the cadre of the Fourteenth Army, which was one day to reconquer the country.

Opposite above: A Japanese photograph of the US fleet under attack at Pearl Harbor

Above: Japanese troops advancing into Singapore under cover of a tank

Right: An Australian anti-tank gun in action outside Singapore

RUSSIA

Kamchatka

ULAN BATOR ■
MONGOLIA

MANCHURIA
HARBIN
(MANCHUKUO)
MUKDEN
VLADIVOSTOK

Sakhalin

Kurile Is
ETOROFU
Tankan Bay

Hokkaido

26 Nov 1941
Nagumo's fleet
sails

C H I N A

PEKING

KOREA
SEOUL

SEA OF
JAPAN

Honshu

TOKYO
JAPAN

7 Dec 1941

16 Dec
Part of fl
to Wake
support

CHUNGKING kiang
Yangtse

NEPAL
Ganges

DELHI ■

KARACHI ■

CHANGSHA
Burma Road
KUNMING

NANKING
HANKOW
SHANGHAI

NAGASAKI
KAGOSHIMA
Shikoku
Kyushu

BONIN IS

Shikoku

P   A   C

8 Dec
Wake I. at
23 Dec
surrendere
WAKE (USA)

CALCUTTA ■

LASHIO

I N D I A

MANDALAY

BOMBAY ■

BAY OF
BENGAL

MADRAS

ANDAMAN
IS

BURMA

RANGOON ■

THAI-
LAND

BANGKOK ■

HANOI

CANTON

PESCADORES
IS

Formosa
(Taiwan)

HONG KONG
(Brit.)

HAINAN

FRENCH
INDO-CHINA

IWO JIMA

Luzon

SAIPAN

Marianas
Islands

O   C

GUAM (USA)

ENIWETOK

KWAJALEIN

Ma
Isla

SAIGON

MANILA

PHILIPPINE
ISLANDS

Mindanao

YAP

TRINCOMALEE

COLOMBO ■

NICOBAR
IS

Ceylon

KHOTA BHARU

SOUTH CHINA
SEA

DAVAO

PALAU IS

TRUK

Maldive
Is

Equator

MALAYA

N BORNEO

SARAWAK

SINGAPORE ■

Sumatra

DUTCH   EAST   INDIES

BATAVIA ■

Borneo

Java

Celebes

FLORES

HALMAHERA

NAURU

New Guinea

NEW
BRITAIN

RABAUL

NEW IRELAND

BOUGAINVILLE

Caroline   Islands

TARAWA

NANU

OCE

Solomon Is

E

I   N   D   I   A   N

O   C   E   A   N

TIMOR

TIMOR SEA

ARAFURA SEA

DARWIN

PAPUA

PORT
MORESBY

NEW
GEORGIA

GUADALCANAL
SANTA
CRUZ IS

CORAL   SEA

CAIRNS

ESPIRITU-S

New
Hebrides

EFATE

Northern
Territory

Queensland

ROCKHAMPTON

New
Caledonia

NOUMEA

A   U   S   T   R   A   L   I   A

Western
Australia

South
Australia

New South
Wales

BRISBANE

NORFOLK

PERTH ■

ADELAIDE ■

Victoria

MELBOURNE ■

SYDNEY
CANBERRA ■

TASMAN

SEA

AUCKLAN

WELLINGTO

NEW ZEALAND

CHRISTCHURCH

JAPANESE EMPIRE, 1933
OCCUPIED BY JAPAN, JULY 1937/DECEMBER 1941
MILITARY BASES ESTABLISHED BY JAPAN, SEPTEMBER 1940
ABDA (American, British, Dutch, and Australian) COMMAND
MERCATOR'S PROJECTION

98

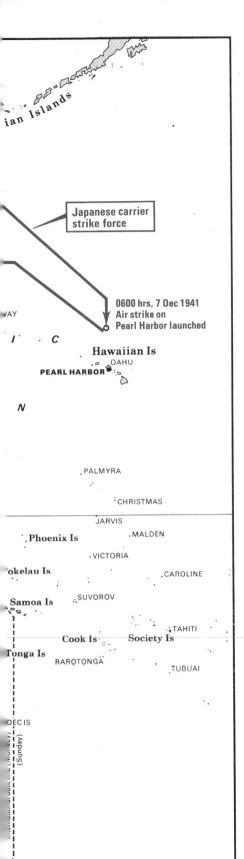

ian Islands

Japanese carrier
strike force

0600 hrs, 7 Dec 1941
Air strike on
Pearl Harbor launched

Hawaiian Is
OAHU
PEARL HARBOR

N

PALMYRA

CHRISTMAS

JARVIS

Phoenix Is   MALDEN

VICTORIA

okelau Is   CAROLINE

SUVOROV

Samoa Is

TAHITI

Cook Is   Society Is

Tonga Is
RAROTONGA

TUBUAI

DEC IS

(Sunday)

THE SITUATION IN THE PACIFIC

Japan had invaded China in 1937, and by 1941 had occupied about one-third of the country. But Chinese resistance was being bolstered financially by the United States and she was receiving supplies via the Burma Road and through the ports of French Indo-China. In August 1940 Japan persuaded the French to allow her airforce units to operate from northern Indo-China, and in July 1941 she presented an ultimatum demanding the use of bases throughout the country. America which had diplomatically opposed the steady growth of Japanese expansion, now reacted by freezing her assets and thus effectively cutting off her oil supplies.

It now seemed essential to the Japanese government that if Japan was to remain able to realize her long-term aim of ousting the colonial powers as the controllers of the Far East, she must strike decisively to seize the oil-rich Dutch East Indies and the British,

French, and American colonies astride the sea routes, before her supplies ran out. War plans were drawn up which envisaged first the invasions of Malaya and the Philippines and then the capture of the Dutch East Indies and Burma. The Japanese forces available were relatively modest – only eleven of the total fifty-one divisions could be spared from China and Manchuria – and they would be outnumbered in each theatre during the initial attacks. But they were well-supported in the air and had been trained in jungle warfare. The British and Dutch forces were depleted by two years of warfare elsewhere and the Americans had only just begun to build up the defences of the Philippines. At sea the Japanese fleet with six large and four smaller carriers, as well as eight battleships, outnumbered the US Pacific Fleet which had only four carriers and nine First World War battleships. The Japanese knew that they could not hope to win a long war but they were confident that they would achieve their aims within six months.

The attack was to begin with the destruction of the American fleet by a carrier-borne raid on Pearl Harbor at dawn on 7 December. Landings in Malaya would begin the same day and those on the Philippines two days later. Indo-China and Thailand would also be occupied during the first phase of the operation.

Below: Australian troops in the Malayan jungle before the Japanese attacks

PEARL HARBOR

The Japanese strike force to attack Pearl Harbor sailed on 26 November. It consisted of six fleet carriers escorted by two battleships and two heavy cruisers. It refuelled on 4 December and turned south-east on 6 December (see map on previous page) to reach the launch position at daybreak on the 7th. American monitoring of increased Japanese radio traffic during November had made it clear that some operation was planned and all forces in the Pacific had been alerted. But as the Japanese approached Pearl Harbor, the forces there were still on a peacetime – and weekend – footing: aircraft undispersed, ships anchored in lines with many of their crews ashore, and no extra reconnaissance flights being flown. The two carriers *Lexington* and *Saratoga* were away taking supplies to Wake Island, but eight battleships lay at anchor.

The Japanese strike force began launching its aircraft at 0600 hours.

The attack was to be made in two waves. The first wave was spotted at 0700 hours by a radar station; but its report was ignored. At 0740 the aircraft reached the north coast of Oahu and swung west around the island. A few minutes before 0800 the torpedo bombers went in to attack the harbour while fighters began to strafe the airfields. In the first attack five battleships – *West Virginia*, *Arizona*, *Nevada*, *Oklahoma*, *California*, and the target ship *Utah* were hit, and only *Maryland* and *Tennessee*, which were on inside berths, and *Pennsylvania*, which was in dock, were not struck by torpedoes. The dive bombers and high-level bombers then joined in so that by 0835 *West Virginia* was sinking, *Arizona* had settled on the bottom, *Oklahoma* and *Utah* had capsized, *Tennessee* was badly on fire, and *Oklahoma* mortally damaged. *Nevada* was under way for the harbour entrance, while almost all the US aircraft had been destroyed.

The second Japanese wave attacking a few minutes later damaged *Pennsylvania* and forced *Nevada* to beach herself. The Americans had reacted with remarkable speed and this wave was met with a more effective defence. The Japanese withdrew at 0945 hours, having lost only nine fighters, fifteen dive bombers, and five torpedo bombers, but their commander Vice-Admiral Nagumo refused to launch another attack which might have caught the aircraft carriers and completed destruction of the port facilities. The strike force withdrew, despatching some units to assist in

the subjection of Wake Island. This came under steady air and sea bombardment on 8 December. The US Marine Corps garrison succeeded in sinking two Japanese destroyers, and it was not until 23 December that the Japanese landed and overwhelmed it after a heroic defence.

Opposite above: The crew cheers as Japanese aircraft take off for the attack on Pearl Harbor

Opposite below: US sailors attempting to douse the flames on USS *West Virginia*

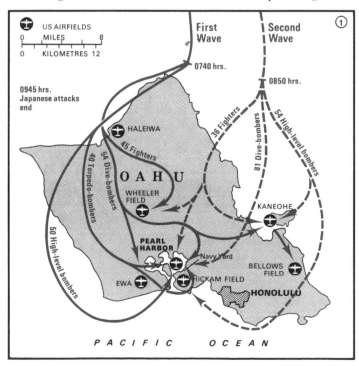

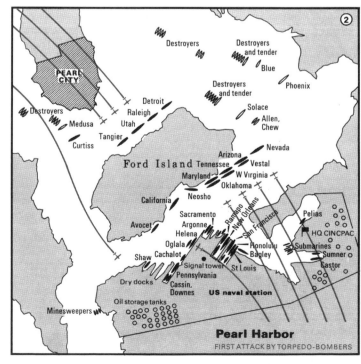

THE INVASION OF MALAYA

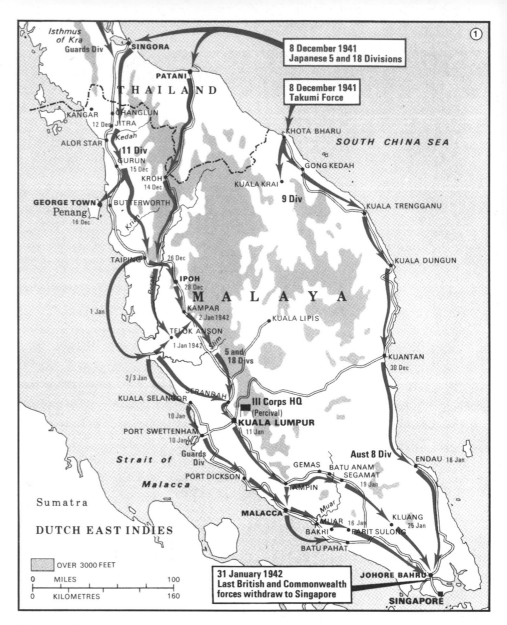

The invasion of Malaya had been assigned to the Japanese Twenty-fifth Army commanded by Lieutenant-General Yamashita. This consisted of three divisions – 5, 18, and Imperial Guards – supported by 600 aircraft. Against it Lieutenant-General A.E. Percival had two divisions supported by about 150 aircraft. Transports carrying Twenty-fifth Army left Indo-Chinese ports on 4 December, and at dawn on the 8th, while Fifteenth Army began the occupation of French Indo-China and Thailand, the 5 and 18 Divisions began landing at Singora and Patani on the Kra Peninsula just north of the Malay border, and 'Takumi Force', a regimental group, landed at Khota Baru (**Map 1**). The northern landings were unopposed, but Takumi Force had to fight its way ashore and was not secure until the evening. Meanwhile air attacks on RAF bases had reduced its strength to about fifty aircraft.

The Japanese 5 Division now led a double advance south, and the forward British force – 11 Indian Division – sited around Jitra was attacked on 11 December. After a series of Japanese breakthroughs it fell back in disorder to Alor Star on 12 December. Japanese momentum built up, and with the Guards Division keeping to the coast and 5 and 18 Divisions moving inland, they pushed back 11 Division, outflanking any attempts at defence. A defence line at Kampar was outflanked by sea, and the Slim River line forced by frontal attack. Kuala Lumpur was taken on 11 January by the Japanese 5 Division. The British had now brought forward the Australian 8 Division and 91 Indian Division to hold the Muar River line, but this again was outflanked by a seaborne operation and on 20 January the British forces began to withdraw to Singapore Island, the last units reaching there on 31 January. On 7 February the Japanese Guards Division launched a

feint landing on Pulau Ubin (**Map 2**) and the next evening 5 and 18 Divisions crossed in the north-west. By the evening of 9 February they had taken Tengah airfield, and on the 15th the British surrendered.

Opposite above: Japanese troops storm into Kuala Lumpur

Opposite below: General Percival and his staff on their way to surrender Singapore

Below: Australian forces training before the disaster

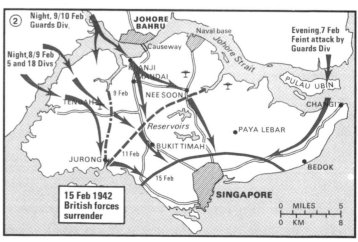

THE FALL OF HONG KONG

Hong Kong also was invaded on 8 December. Here the Japanese had a massive superiority over the defenders and had pushed them back to the Gindrinkers Line by the evening of 9 December. Once this had been breached by the capture of Shing Mun Redoubt the mainland had to be evacuated and this operation was completed on 13 December. On 18/19 December the Japanese crossed on a wide front and by evening they had captured more than half the island. Fierce fighting continued, but by 22 December most of the reservoirs had been taken and on 25 December the garrison surrendered.

Above right: Japanese officers parade through Hong Kong after the fall of the city

Opposite: HMS *Prince of Wales* in harbour at Singapore shortly before her last voyage

Opposite below: Survivors scramble from HMS *Prince of Wales* to an attendant destroyer

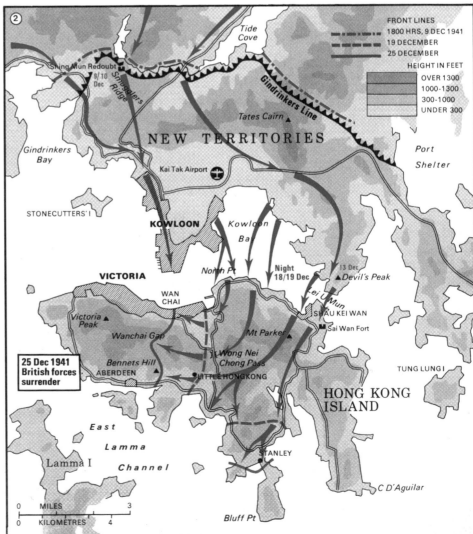

THE SINKING OF FORCE Z

As the likelihood of a Japanese attack on Malaya had increased, Churchill had despatched Force z – the battleship *Prince of Wales* and the battle-cruiser *Repulse* to Singapore, which they reached on 2 December. When Japanese landings were reported on the 8th, the force sailed to intercept the convoys, but was sighted on the afternoon of the next day and turned back to Singapore. Reported Japanese landings at Kuantan made the force head there and *en route* it was sighted by Japanese submarines. Finding nothing at Kuantan the force turned again for Singapore but was attacked by Japanese bombers at 1100 hours: by 1320 both ships were sunk.

THAILAND
BANGKOK

JAPANESE AIRBAS
MILES
KILOMETRES   30

8 Dec 1941
Jap Fifteenth Army
invades

FRENCH
INDO-CHINA

PRACHUAB

SAIGON

CHUMPHON

0905 hrs, 7 Dec
Japanese disperse
to landing points

Japanese
invasion fleet

From Hainan

BANDON   *Isthmus*

NAKHON   *of*

2015 hrs, 9 D
Force Z chang
course for
Singapore

Kra

Intended strike

SINGORA   PATANI

KHOTA BHARU
Japanese submarines
locate Force Z

3 Japanese
aircraft sigh

0200 hrs, 10 Dec

1340 hrs, 9 D

MALAYA

KUANTAN   10 Dec
Japanese aircraft
sink Repulse - 1233 hrs
& Prince of Wales -
1320 hrs

ANAMBA IS

Sumatra   SINGAPORE

1735 hrs, 8 Dec 1941
Force Z sails

THE FALL OF THE PHILIPPINES

In July 1941 the Philippines army was brought into the service of the United States, and General Douglas MacArthur became commander of US Forces in the Far East (USAFFE). He had some ten divisions consisting of 19,000 American troops and 160,000 Filippinos with about 200 aircraft. The bulk of his troops were underequipped and undertrained and the Japanese were confident that their Fourteenth Army with only two divisions supported by 500 aircraft could successfully conquer the islands.

The Japanese launched heavy air attacks on US air bases on 8 December (the same day as the attack on Pearl Harbor but dated one day later because of the International Date Line). Warned by Pearl Harbor, the USAFFE had flown its bombers off Clark Field in the morning, but by midday, when the Japanese attacked, they were back on the ground with their escorting fighters. More than fifty fighters and seventeen B-17s were destroyed and the attacks continued for the next two days so that US air power had ceased to exist when the Japanese made their first landings in the north of Luzon to capture the airfields at Vigan, Laoag, and Tuguegarao, and in the south to capture Legaspi as a base from which to threaten US seaborne reinforcements The airfields were captured with little resistance, while two other landings were made on Mindanao and Jolo, islands in the south of the Philippines group. The Japanese in the north then began moving south to meet the main landings which took place in Lingayen Bay on 22 December. There was little resistance and after delays due to rough seas a firm beachhead was formed by the 24th. The Japanese began to move out of this the next day (see inset map). Despite a determined stand by 26 Cavalry Regiment near Binalonan they were able to push down the major roads to Manila with little trouble. Realizing that his troops were unable to put up an effective resistance, MacArthur had announced his plan to withdraw to Bataan on 23 December, and on the 27th he declared Manila an open city.

By 2 January the Japanese had entered Manila, and come up to the Porac Line at the top of the Bataan peninsula. This they attempted to rush on 2 January but were halted by heavy artillery fire. The defenders then pulled back further along the peninsula.

Below: Japanese light tanks and infantry advance north of Manila

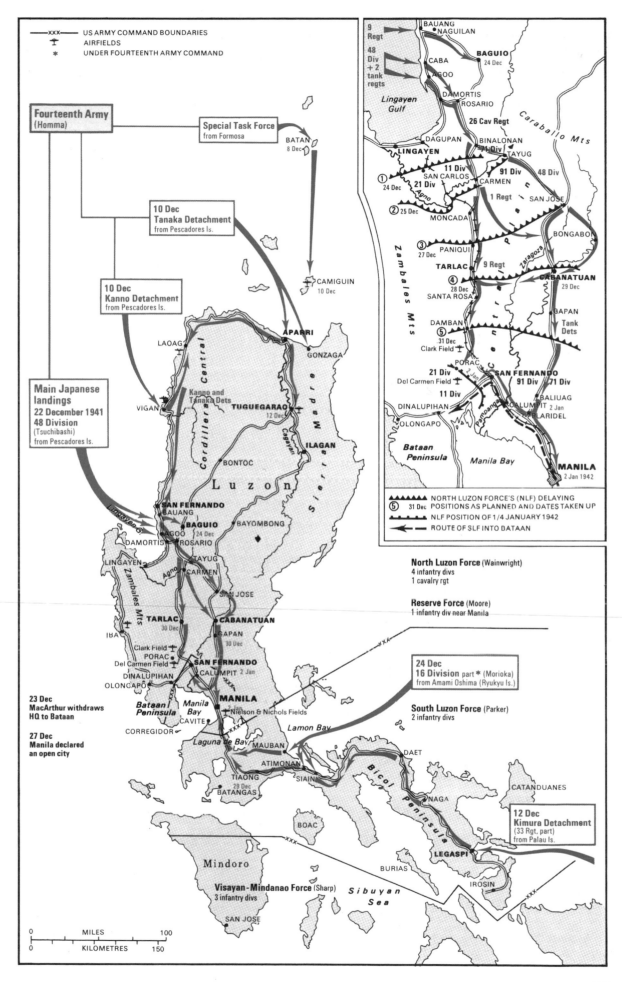

LEGEND (top left):

⊢——xxx——⊣ US ARMY COMMAND BOUNDARIES
✈ AIRFIELDS
✳ UNDER FOURTEENTH ARMY COMMAND

Fourteenth Army (Homma)

Special Task Force from Formosa
BATAN 8 Dec

10 Dec Tanaka Detachment from Pescadores Is.

10 Dec Kanno Detachment from Pescadores Is.

CAMIGUIN 10 Dec

Main Japanese landings 22 December 1941 48 Division (Tsuchibashi) from Pescadores Is.

Inset map (top right):

9 Regt
48 Div + 2 tank regts
BAUANG
NAGUILAN
BAGUIO 24 Dec
CABA
AGOO
DAMORTIS
ROSARIO
Lingayen Gulf
Caraballo Mts
26 Cav Regt
DAGUPAN
BINALONAN
LINGAYEN
71 Div
TAYUG
① 24 Dec
11 Div
SAN CARLOS
21 Div
91 Div
48 Div
Agno
CARMEN
1 Regt
SAN JOSE
② 25 Dec
MONCADA
Zambales Mts
BONGABON
③ 27 Dec
PANIQUI
Zaragoza
TARLAC
9 Regt
CABANATUAN 29 Dec
④ 28 Dec
SANTA ROSA
GAPAN
Tank Dets
DAMBAN
⑤ 31 Dec
Clark Field
PORAC
SAN FERNANDO
Del Carmen Field
2 Jan
91 Div 71 Div
21 Div
11 Div
BALIUAG
DINALUPIHAN
Pampanga
CALUMPIT 2 Jan
OLONGAPO
PLARIDEL
Bataan Peninsula
Manila Bay
MANILA 2 Jan 1942

▲▲▲ NORTH LUZON FORCE'S (NLF) DELAYING
⑤ 31 Dec POSITIONS AS PLANNED AND DATES TAKEN UP
NLF POSITION OF 1/4 JANUARY 1942
◄—— ROUTE OF SLF INTO BATAAN

North Luzon Force (Wainwright)
4 infantry divs
1 cavalry rgt

Reserve Force (Moore)
1 infantry div near Manila

24 Dec 16 Division part ✳ (Morioka) from Amami Oshima (Ryukyu Is.)

South Luzon Force (Parker)
2 infantry divs

12 Dec Kimura Detachment (33 Rgt, part) from Palau Is.

Main map labels:

LAOAG
APARRI
GONZAGA
Cordillera Central
VIGAN
Kanno and Tanaka Dets
TUGUEGARAO 12 Dec
ILAGAN
Cagayan
Sierra Madre
BONTOC
L u z o n
SAN FERNANDO
BAUANG
BAGUIO 24 Dec
BAYOMBONG
AGOO
DAMORTIS ROSARIO
Lingayen G.
LINGAYEN
TAYUG
Agno
CARMEN
Zambales Mts
SAN JOSE
IBA
TARLAC 30 Dec
CABANATUAN
Clark Field
GAPAN 30 Dec
PORAC
Del Carmen Field
SAN FERNANDO
DINALUPIHAN
CALUMPIT 2 Jan
OLONGAPO
Bataan Peninsula
Manila Bay
MANILA
Nielson & Nichols Fields
CAVITE
CORREGIDOR
Laguna de Bay
MAUBAN
Lamon Bay
ATIMONAN
DAET
SIAIN
TIAONG
BATANGAS 29 Dec
Bicol Peninsula
NAGA
CATANDUANES
BOAC
Mindoro
Visayan-Mindanao Force (Sharp) 3 infantry divs
BURIAS
Sibuyan Sea
LEGASPI
IROSIN
SAN JOSE

23 Dec MacArthur withdraws HQ to Bataan

27 Dec Manila declared an open city

Scale:
0 MILES 100
0 KILOMETRES 150

THE CONQUEST OF BATAAN

MacArthur's main defence line on Bataan ran down the sides of Mount Santa Rosa. This was taken up on 7 January as the defenders were forced back on to the peninsula. There were now about 80,000 troops and 26,000 civilians in the area. The Japanese began their attack on the main battle position on 9 January with a frontal assault following a heavy bombardment (**Map 1**). This was held after severe fighting, and an attempt on 11 January to outflank the line was thwarted after minor infiltration. But by 23 January, Japanese pressure on the eastern sector of the American line and the threat of an outflanking move forced II Corps to pull back to the reserve battle positions, swiftly followed by I Corps. The Japanese were now suffering from disease and the continual fighting and were unable to make any significant headway during the next two months. Meanwhile MacArthur was flown out on 12 March and Lieutenant-General Jonathan Wainwright took over command. Various attempts to establish seaborne beachheads behind the US lines were defeated and it was not until 3 April that the Japanese, reinforced with a fresh division, began their final offensive with a five-hour air and artillery bombardment. By the morning of 7 April a deep penetration had been achieved in the US II Corps sector and US I Corps was forced to fall back as well. During the next two days the Japanese pushed forward until on 9 April the decision was made to surrender.

The last US forces held out on Corregidor Island which had been under heavy bombardment since the beginning of January. By the end of April most of the defenders' artillery had been knocked out and on 5 May the Japanese launched their assault (**Map 2**). Their troops were to land in the Malinta Tunnel area, but strong tides swept them down to Cavalry Point. They were met by heavy fire, but were able to establish a beachhead.

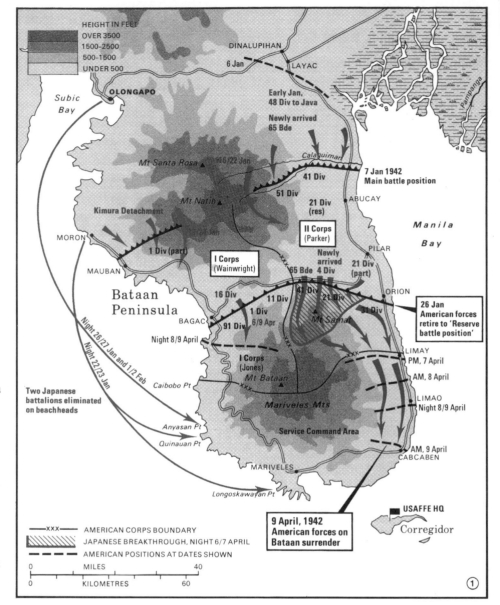

By 1030 on 6 May the US defences in the Malinta Tunnel area had been breached, and soon afterwards the island was compelled to surrender.

Below: Japanese troops coming ashore on Corregidor

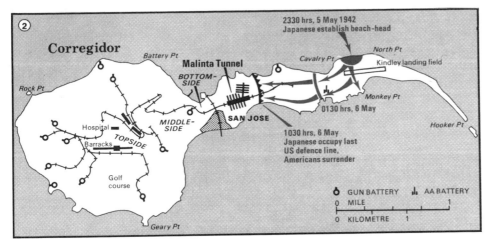

Corregidor

Rock Pt

Battery Pt

Malinta Tunnel

BOTTOM-SIDE

Hospital

MIDDLE-SIDE

Barracks
TOPSIDE

Golf course

Geary Pt

SAN JOSE

2330 hrs, 5 May 1942
Japanese establish beach-head

Cavalry Pt

North Pt

Kindley landing field

Monkey Pt

0130 hrs, 6 May

Hooker Pt

1030 hrs, 6 May
Japanese occupy last
US defence line,
Americans surrender

♦ GUN BATTERY   ⊥ AA BATTERY

0   MILE   1

0   KILOMETRE   1

Below: The artillery of Corregidor firing in support of the defenders of Bataan

THE FALL OF DUTCH EAST INDIES

By the beginning of 1942, with their campaigns in Malaya and the Philippines proceeding well, the Japanese could set about the occupation of the Dutch East Indies. This was to be undertaken by a three-pronged attack: Western Force from Indo-China and Sarawak, which had been taken during December 1941, would attack southern Sumatra, western Java, and North Borneo; Central Force from Davao would attack Borneo; and Eastern Force, also from Davao, would take the Celebes, Amboina, and then Timor, Bali, and eastern Java. The Allies in the South-West Pacific had set up a combined command – (ABDA:

American, British, Dutch, and Australian) – under General Sir Archibald Wavell, but this had few forces except a six-cruiser naval flotilla under the Dutch Rear-Admiral, Karel Doorman.

The first Japanese landings, by Central Force at Tarakan and Eastern Force at Manado and Kema, were made on 11 January. By the 13th all three places had been firmly occupied. The next attacks were at Balikpapan, where four US destroyers sank three Japanese transports before withdrawing, and Kendari, where an important airbase was swiftly captured. By 10 February the Japanese had complete control north of the Java and Flores Seas. On 14 February Western Force began landings on Sumatra and parachute landings were made at Palembang on the 16th. Both were successful, and on 20 February the Japanese landed on Timor and Bali. The invasion force for the latter was attacked in the Lombok Straits by the Allied naval force on the night of 18/19 February but managed to beat it off.

The final Japanese move was against western Java with units from Western and Eastern Forces. Once again the Allies sighted Eastern Force and Admiral Doorman attacked the convoy on the evening of 27 February. In the

Battle of the Java Sea both Dutch cruisers were sunk before they could damage the Japanese transports and in the aftermath HMS *Exeter* was also destroyed. The next day, HMAS *Perth* and USS *Houston* came upon the Japanese Western Force and were sunk after causing it considerable damage. Once the Japanese were ashore, there was little to stop them and hostilities ended on 8 March.

Right: Netherlands East Indies troops training

Opposite below: Japanese troops storm ashore during a landing in the Dutch East Indies

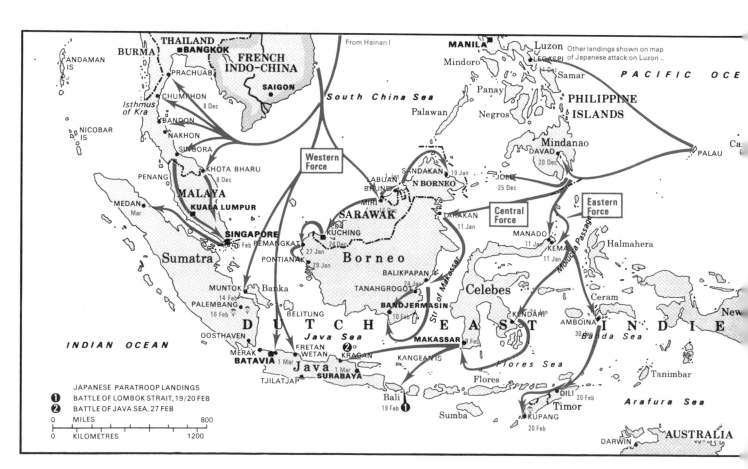

THE FALL OF BURMA

The Japanese invasion of Burma began on 15 January 1942 when a detachment of Fifteenth Army occupied Victoria Point before moving north to take Tavoy on 19 January. British defences in Burma had been seriously neglected and only one brigade of 17 Indian Division and a Burmese division under Lieutenant-General T. J. Hutton were available. The main Japanese advance began on 20 January, thrusting towards Moulmein. The British attempted to hold the town but were forced to retreat and fell back with the Japanese continually threatening to outflank them. Delaying actions were fought at the Salween and the Bilin rivers, and a stand was made on the Sittang. Once this had been forced on 21 February the Japanese pushed forward to Rangoon which they occupied on 8 March, only just missing cutting off the British garrison which pulled out hurriedly. General Hutton was now replaced by General Sir Harold Alexander, the British ground forces being placed under Lieutenant-General W. Slim.

Meanwhile the Chinese Fifth and Sixth Armies began to advance into Burma towards Taunggyi where they were attacked by the Japanese on 24 March. When this fell on 30 March the British at Prome had to fall back for fear of being outflanked. The Japanese then continued to pursue the British and Chinese northwards until by 15 May they had completed the conquest of Burma.

Opposite above: Japanese troops take cover while their aircraft bombard a Burmese town

Above: Equipment ablaze at the oilfield of Yenangyuang as the British prepare to retreat

Right: Japanese light tanks crossing an improvised bridge

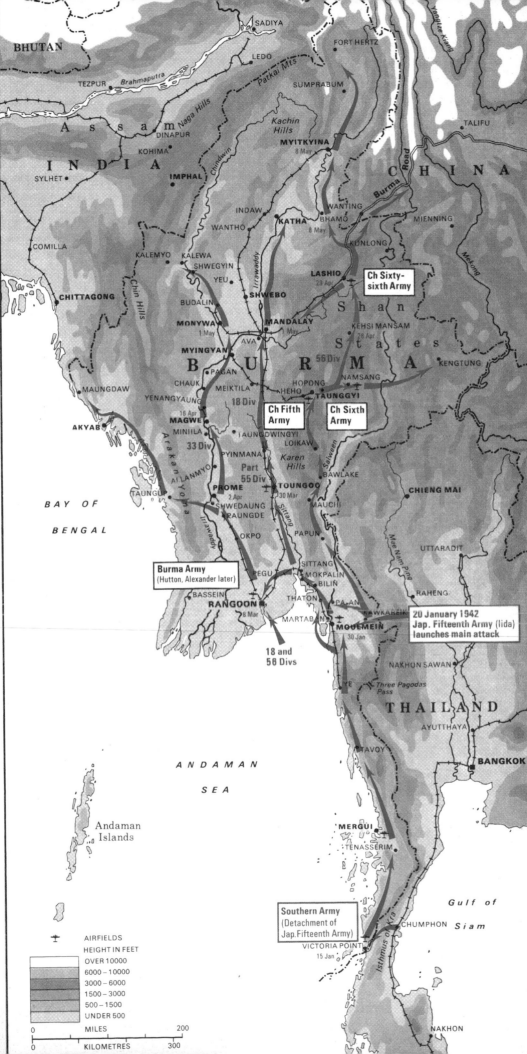

BHUTAN

TEZPUR *Brahmaputra*

SADIYA

LEDO

FORT HERTZ

Patkai Mts

SUMPRABUM

A s s a m

Naga Hills

DINAPUR

Kachin Hills

TALIFU

KOHIMA

I N D I A

SYLHET

IMPHAL

MYITKYINA
8 May

C H I N A

Chindwin

INDAW

WANTING

Burma Road

Appemein

WANTHO

KATHA

BHAMO
8 May

MIENNING

COMILLA

KALEMYO

KALEWA

SHWEGYIN

KUNLONG

CHITTAGONG

YEU

LASHIO
29 Apr

**Ch Sixty-
sixth Army**

Chin Hills

BUDALIN

SHWEBO

S h a n

MONYWA
1 May

MANDALAY
May

KEHSI MANSAM

MAUNGDAW

MYINGYAN

AVA

S t a t e s
28 Apr

B U R M A

PAGAN

56 Div

KENGTUNG

CHAUK

MEIKTILA

HOPONG

NAMSANG

YENANGYAUNG

18 Div

AHEHO

TAUNGGYI

AKYAB

MAGWE
18 Apr

**Ch Fifth
Army**

**Ch Sixth
Army**

MINILA

TAUNGDWINGYI

LOIKAW

Arakan Yoma

33 Div

PYINMANA

Karen Hills

Salween

ALANMYO

Part
55 Div

BAWLAKE

B A Y   O F

TAUNGU

PROME
2 Apr

TOUNGOO
30 Mar

CHIENG MAI

B E N G A L

SHWEDAUNG
RAUNGDE

MAUCII

Irrawaddy

OKPO

PAPUN

Mae Nam Ping

UTTARADIT

Sittang

SITTANG
MOKPALIN

Burma Army
(Hutton, Alexander later)

PEGU

BILIN

RAHENG

BASSEIN

THATON

PA-AN

RANGOON
8 Mar

MARTABAN

PAWKAREIK

20 January 1942
Jap. Fifteenth Army (Iida)
launches main attack

MOULMEIN
30 Jan

**18 and
56 Divs**

YE

*Three Pagodas
Pass*

NAKHON SAWAN

T H A I L A N D

AYUTTHAYA

A N D A M A N

TAVOY

S E A

BANGKOK

Andaman
Islands

MERGUI

TENASSERIM

Gulf of

Southern Army
(Detachment of
Jap.Fifteenth Army)

CHUMPHON *Siam*

VICTORIA POINT
15 Jan

Isthmus of Kra

✈ AIRFIELDS

HEIGHT IN FEET

	OVER 10000
	6000 – 10000
	3000 – 6000
	1500 – 3000
	500 – 1500
	UNDER 500

0 ———— MILES ———— 200

0 ———— KILOMETRES ———— 300

NAKHON

THE ITALIAN CAMPAIGN

The paramount task before us is, . . .
using the bases on the African shore,
to strike at the underbelly of the
Axis in effective strength and in the
shortest time.
Winston S. Churchill, January 1943

Opposite: Allied forces passing the Colosseum
after the capture of Rome

With the collapse of the Tunisian bridgehead (12 May 1943) Italy found herself in the front line. Her main ally, inextricably engaged in Russia, was not exactly forthcoming with offers of assistance. 'Can our country resist an invasion?' demanded General Guiseppe Castellano. 'The Italians do not lack patrotism, but it cannot be claimed that they will endure beyond a certain limit when their hopes of a final victory are fading day by day.' Already in March there had been serious strikes in the industrial towns of north Italy, and Mussolini had sacked his chief of police and the secretary of the Fascist party for failing to suppress this discontent. In a meeting with Hitler near Salzburg on 7 April Mussolini had utterly failed to persuade the Führer to patch up a truce with Russia and concentrate on the defence of the Mediterranean – a policy which had the support not only of Rumania and Hungary but of Japan.

The time was not yet ripe for an Allied invasion of northern France, but an assault on Sicily and Italy was calculated to bring about the disintegration of the Axis.

The invasion was not exactly a surprise to the Italian High Command or to their German colleagues in Rome. Strategic bombing – especially that of Pantelleria – and the concentration of shipping in North African ports, clearly indicated what lay ahead. But the Germans, deeply involved with the planning of Operation Citadel, the ill-fated battle of Kursk, had few troops to spare. At the same time they had few illusions as to the state of Italian morale. As General von Rintelen reported to Hitler on 5 May an Allied landing was likely to be followed by 'most unpleasant consequences' . . . 'in view of the prevailing atmosphere of fatalism'. He proved a true prophet. The Sicily landings (10 July) met with far less resistance than had been expected, and some Italian units surrendered *en masse*. Even so General Montgomery's rush to

take Catania failed, and the Axis forces, with the German General Hube virtually in command, reacted very creditably, ensconcing themselves in a formidable position around Mount Etna.

Hitler was furious at the poor performance of his allies in defence of their own soil. General Vittorio Ambrosio, Chief of the Italian General Staff, for his part had the hardihood to blame the Germans, and to point out that it was up to them to put things right. His memorandum of 4 July made it clear to Mussolini that they now faced the prospect of a Second Front on Italian soil. Italy herself lacked the land and air forces to meet such a situation. The Germans must remedy it even if that meant suspending operations in Russia. 'If we cannot prevent the setting up of such a front', he wrote, 'it will be up to the highest political authorities to consider whether it would not be more expedient to spare the country further horror and ruin, and to anticipate the end of the struggle, seeing the final result will undoubtedly be worse in one or more years.' Mussolini, now a sick man, did not contradict Ambrosio. On the other hand he did not dare to put his views to Hitler, though he did consider it. Instead on 21 July he assured von Rintelen that he was resolved to defend Sicily to the last man.

By this time the defeatism of the Italians had aroused the suspicions of Hitler's advisors. A conference at Feltre (19 July) between the two dictators was not a success. Hitler had been briefed by Warlimont to demand a unified command; Mussolini by Ambrosio to tell the Führer frankly that Italy could not go on with the war. Neither spoke to their brief, indeed Mussolini hardly spoke at all, except to read out, in a shaken voice, an announcement that Allied aircraft had just attacked Rome for the first time. Ambrosio was furious at the negative results of the conference, and soon afterwards was drawn into the

Above: Sherman tanks advancing near Cassino

Opposite above: Allied artillery bombarding Cassino

Below: An American anti-tank gun in action at Anzio

plot by which Marshal Badoglio and members of the Royal family were contriving to get rid of Mussolini, who, by his lack of moral courage at Feltre, had let slip his last chance to save himself. On 24 July the Fascist Grand Council, led by Count Grandi voted for the Crown to assume more power, and next day Mussolini was arrested, on Ambrosio's orders, as he emerged from an audience with the King. He was spirited away to the island of Ponza.

The news threw Hitler and his advisors into a turmoil of planning from which emerged Operation *Achse* (Axis) the first orders for which went out on 28 July. A new Army Group B, consisting of eight divisions mostly drawn from France, began to assemble under Rommel whose headquarters were at Munich. Kesselring, the German commander-in-chief in Italy was to conduct his relations with the Italian High Command in such a way that the penetration of German divisions into northern Italy would be unhindered. The Germans had to tread delicately for, whilst doing nothing to provoke Italian hostility or hasten her collapse, they had to be ready to deal with either.

On the very day (28 July) that the first orders for Operation Axis went out the Badoglio government decided to make overtures to the Allies and sent envoys to Lisbon and Tangier.

The Allies did not take the fullest advantage of this situation. For this there were various reasons. The chief was American insistence on Unconditional Surrender. Mr Roosevelt in a speech delivered on 28 July voiced this viewpoint. 'Our terms for Italy are still the same as our terms for Germany and Japan – Unconditional Surrender. We will have no truck with Fascism in any way, shape or manner. We will permit no vestige of Fascism to remain.' It was stirring stuff, but not very realistic at a time when patriotic senior officers like Ambrosio and Castellano had come to loathe their German allies. At a time when it was essential to enlist

Italian cooperation in support of the Salerno landing, it was not very sensible to offer the Italians no hope at all. It should not have been beyond the wit of man to foresee the collapse of Italy. It behoved the Allies, and especially the staff of their Foreign Offices, to work out and agree well in advance the terms upon which Italy should be allowed to withdraw from the – or change sides.

As it was the Italian surrender was arranged in such a way that chaos ensued. The royal family and most of the key figures of the High Command and the government managed to escape to Brindisi. But they left no orders, and the Italian army, not knowing how to behave under the circumstances, permitted itself to be disarmed practically without a shot. General Carboni made an attempt to organize the defence of Rome but in vain. The Germans, who had been planning for two months for just such a situation, were able to meet the Salerno landing practically undistracted by their luckless former allies.

Until the invasion of Normandy the campaign in Italy was, of course, the most important being waged by the Anglo-American Allies in Europe. It tied down, as it was to do until the end, a rather larger number of German divisions – about twenty-five – than the Allies themselves deployed there. By the capture of the Foggia airfields it brought heavy bombers within striking distance of targets in southern Germany. The advance up the Adriatic coast and the occupation of Vis enabled the Allies to support and encourage the partisans groups in the Balkans, and especially Yugoslavia, who themselves managed to occupy the attentions of a number of German divisions. But, after the battle of the Sangro, troops and landing-craft began to be drawn away to England in preparation for the Second Front: General Alexander's campaign now took second priority in the eyes of the Allied strategists. Still the very presence

of Allied troops in the peninsula was a continuing threat not only to Germany's position in the Balkans, but to her southern frontier. The long slog up Italy could have been immeasurably less lengthy and less costly had the Allies been more amply provided with landing-craft, for operations similar to the Termoli landing of 1943, might have 'unlocked' the successive river lines which the Germans held during the course of their long rearguard action.

In the opinion of the late Major-General J. F. C. Fuller the Italian campaign was one 'which for lack of strategic sense and tactical imagination is unique in military history'. He failed to take into account the extent to which the Allied commanders were handicapped by the continual withdrawals of divisions and of landing-craft, not only for Normandy, but for Operation Dragoon, the landing in the south of France – an operation of very doubtful value. The defence of Italy cost the Germans 556,000 casualties, and the Allies 312,000 killed and wounded. The twenty-one Allied divisions contained a total of something like fifty-five German divisions in the Mediterranean area, troops which might well have tipped the balance against the Allies in Russia or in France in the campaigns of 1944.

THE INVASION OF SICILY

With the surrender of the final Axis forces in Tunisia on 13 May, the whole of North Africa was in Allied hands. Where should these victorious Allied troops next be used? As there was still no possibility of a Second Front in north-west Europe, it was considered that the Mediterranean offered further opportunity, but where? Two major strategic opportunities were immediately apparent (**Map 1**): a 'left hook' through Sardinia into northern Italy and southern France, and a 'right hook' into Sicily and southern Italy. The latter alternative was adopted as it offered safer sea communications and allowed the western Allies to draw German forces further away from their supply bases in Germany and from the front in Russia. Moreover parts of Sicily were within range of fighter cover, based on Malta.

The Italian island fortress of Pantelleria lay between Tunis and Sicily, and had to be neutralized before the invasion went in. After an

Below: Unloading stores on the beach at Syracuse

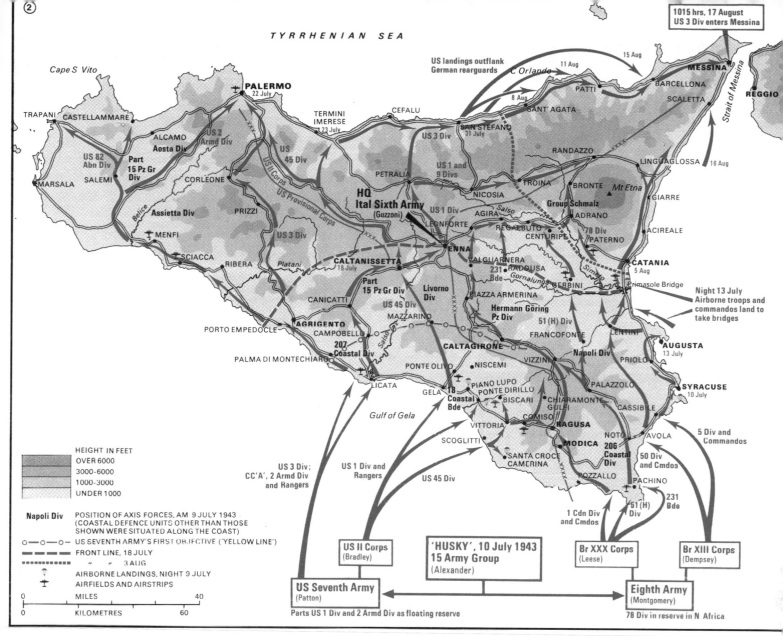

TYRRHENIAN SEA

1015 hrs, 17 August
US 3 Div enters Messina

US landings outflank
German rearguards

Cape S Vito

MESSINA

REGGIO

TRAPANI
CASTELLAMMARE

BARCELLONA
SCALETTA

Strait of Messina

PALERMO
22 July

CEFALU

SANT'AGATA
PATTI

15 Aug

11 Aug

8 Aug

MARSALA

ALCAMO
Aosta Div

US 2
Armd Div

Part
15 Pz Gr
Div

SALEMI

US 82
Abn Div

SAN STEFANO
31 July

US 3 Div

RANDAZZO

LINGUAGLOSSA

16 Aug

TERMINI
IMERESE
23 July

US
45 Div

US 3 Div

CORLEONE

PRIZZI

Assietta Div

MENFI

PETRALIA

US 1 and
9 Divs

NICOSIA

TROINA

BRONTE

Mt Etna

GIARRE

US II Corps

HQ
Ital Sixth Army
(Guzzoni)

US 1 Div

ENNA

LEONFORTE

AGIRA

Group Schmalz

ADRANO

ACIREALE

Salso

REGALBUTO

78 Div
PATERNO

CENTURIPE

SCIACCA

RIBERA

CALTANISSETTA
18 July

Platani

VALGUARNERA

231
Bde

RADDUSA

Gornalunga

CATANIA
5 Aug

Primosole Bridge

Night 13 July
Airborne troops and
commandos land to
take bridges

CANICATTI

Part
15 Pz Gr Div

Livorno
Div

US 45 Div

MAZZARINO

PIAZZA ARMERINA

Hermann Göring
Pz Div

GERBINI

Simeto

51 (H) Div

FRANCOFONTE

LENTINI

PORTO EMPEDOCLE

AGRIGENTO

CAMPOBELLO

Salso

207
Coastal Div

PALMA DI MONTECHIARO

LICATA

PONTE OLIVO

CALTAGIRONE

NISCEMI

Napoli Div

VIZZINI

PALAZZOLO

AUGUSTA
13 July

PRIOLO

GELA

18
Coastal
Bde

PIANO LUPO
PONTE DIRILLO

BISCARI

CHIARAMONTE
GULFI

SYRACUSE
10 July

CASSIBLE

Gulf of Gela

VITTORIA

COMISO

RAGUSA

NOTO

AVOLA

5 Div and
Commandos

SCOGLITTI

SANTA CROCE
CAMERINA

MODICA

206
Coastal
Div

50 Div
and Cmdos

US 3 Div;
CC'A', 2 Armd Div
and Rangers

US 1 Div and
Rangers

US 45 Div

POZZALLO

PACHINO

51 (H)
Div

231
Bde

1 Cdn Div
and Cmdos

HEIGHT IN FEET
OVER 6000
3000-6000
1000-3000
UNDER 1000

Napoli Div POSITION OF AXIS FORCES, AM 9 JULY 1943
(COASTAL DEFENCE UNITS OTHER THAN THOSE
SHOWN WERE SITUATED ALONG THE COAST)
o—o—o— US SEVENTH ARMY'S FIRST OBJECTIVE ('YELLOW LINE')
———— FRONT LINE, 18 JULY
.... " " 3 AUG
AIRBORNE LANDINGS, NIGHT 9 JULY
AIRFIELDS AND AIRSTRIPS

MILES 0 — 40
KILOMETRES 0 — 60

US II Corps
(Bradley)

'HUSKY', 10 July 1943
15 Army Group
(Alexander)

Br XXX Corps
(Leese)

Br XIII Corps
(Dempsey)

US Seventh Army
(Patton)

Eighth Army
(Montgomery)

Parts US 1 Div and 2 Armd Div as floating reserve

78 Div in reserve in N Africa

aerial bombardment lasting a week, the garrison surrendered on 11 June as an assault force was approaching the island. The way was now open for the invasion fleet for Sicily. Meanwhile, Allied air forces operating from North Africa continued their bombardment of Axis airfields and communications in Sicily, Sardinia, and southern Italy. This aerial bombardment was prosecuted with great vigour for a whole month up to the time of the actual invasion. The land forces for this comprised General George S. Patton's US Seventh Army and Montgomery's British Eighth Army, both from Alexander's 15 Army Group, and were transported to Sicily in some 3,000 vessels. The Axis defence was entrusted to General Alfredo Guzzoni's Italian Sixth Army, a mainly Italian force with powerful German strengthening.

The assault went in on 10 July, the Americans landing in the Gulf of Gela and the British in the Gulf of Syracuse

(**Map 2**). Allied airborne landings, intended to secure a preliminary beachhead and coastal communications, were not particularly successful as a result of rough weather and inexperience in this type of operation. The poor weather did, however, have one good effect, in that the Italians did not expect a landing and were therefore taken by surprise. Allied naval gunfire in support of the landings was particularly effective.

The landings were effected with little difficulty, though the Americans had to face vigorous counterattacks by German divisions on 11 and 12 July. Thereafter the forces of the two Allies advanced evenly against strengthening Axis resistance until 18 August, when Montgomery's progress was checked in front of Catania. Patton's forces, however, continued to sweep forward towards the north-west until they reached the north coast and turned east towards Messina. Western Sicily

had been cleared by 23 July. Resistance was now becoming more and more a German matter, and battlefield command was being exercised by a German, Colonel-General Hube. But with the aid of small amphibious operations along the north coast, Patton continued to advance on Messina, while Montgomery was able to speed up his progress again after 5 August. The Italians evacuated the island in some disorder between 3 and 16 August, leaving the Germans to fight an excellent rearguard campaign up to the 17th, when Patton occupied Messina.

THE LANDINGS IN ITALY

With the overthrow of Mussolini on 24 July and his replacement as head of government by Marshal Ugo Cavallero, secret talks were started with the Allies for an armistice for Italy. Hitler was ignorant of this, but, naturally suspicious, he started to send reinforcements into northern Italy to safeguard German communications. Meanwhile Field-Marshal Albert Kesselring, the German supreme commander in the south, reckoned that the Allied conquest of Sicily would soon be followed by a landing in Italy, in all probability on the Gulf of Salerno, just south of Naples.

The armistice with Italy, which was to be published and made effective on 8 September, was signed on 3 September, the day that the British Eighth Army made a landing on the toe of Italy, at Reggio di Calabria

Below: British troops come ashore from an American landing ship at Salerno

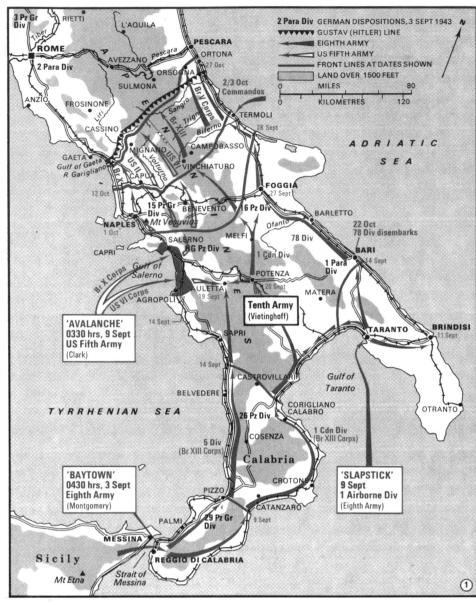

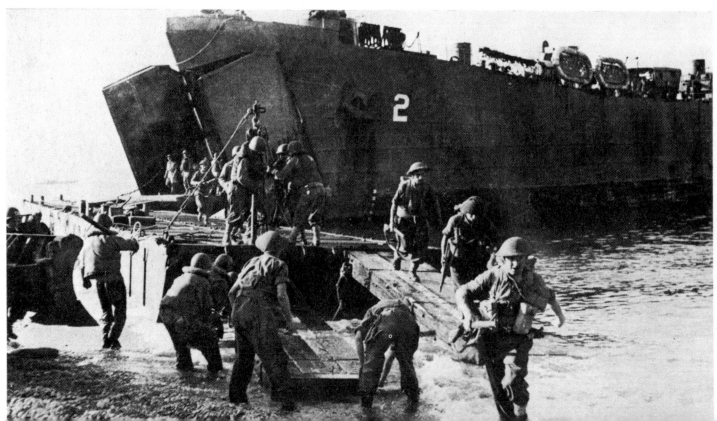

(**Map 1**). This was in fact a diversionary attack, designed to draw German reinforcements down from the Salerno area. Kesselring still thought that the main landing would be at Salerno, and so sent only minor forces to slow the British advance in the south.

The main landing in southern Italy was indeed to be at Salerno. Here, on 9 August, after the publication of the Italian armistice, landed General Mark Clark's US Fifth Army (**Map 2**). This was composed of the British X and the US VI Corps. The German defence was ready, however, and by nightfall the Allies had only secured four small beachheads. Further south, Montgomery was advancing through Calabria, and a British division had landed further east at Taranto.

At Salerno, the position was desperate. The Germans shelled the beachheads with great accuracy from the hills surrounding the gulf, and a powerful German attack on 12 September nearly cut the Allies in two. US artillery just managed to save the situation on the 13th. The Allies managed to hold on during the 14th, during which reinforcements reached them, and by 18 September had consolidated the beachhead. On the 16th Montgomery's advance units made contact with Fifth Army, and Kesselring began to withdraw cautiously north to his main defensive position, the Gustav Line running along the rivers Garigliano and Sangro.

The Allies pursued, Americans in the west and British in the east. By 8 October the Volturno/Termoli line had been reached, and here the Allies halted for four days to rest before assaulting the Gustav Line. The Americans resumed their advance in appalling conditions of weather and terrain on the 12th and the British on the 22nd.

Right: US troops beginning to move off the beachhead at Salerno

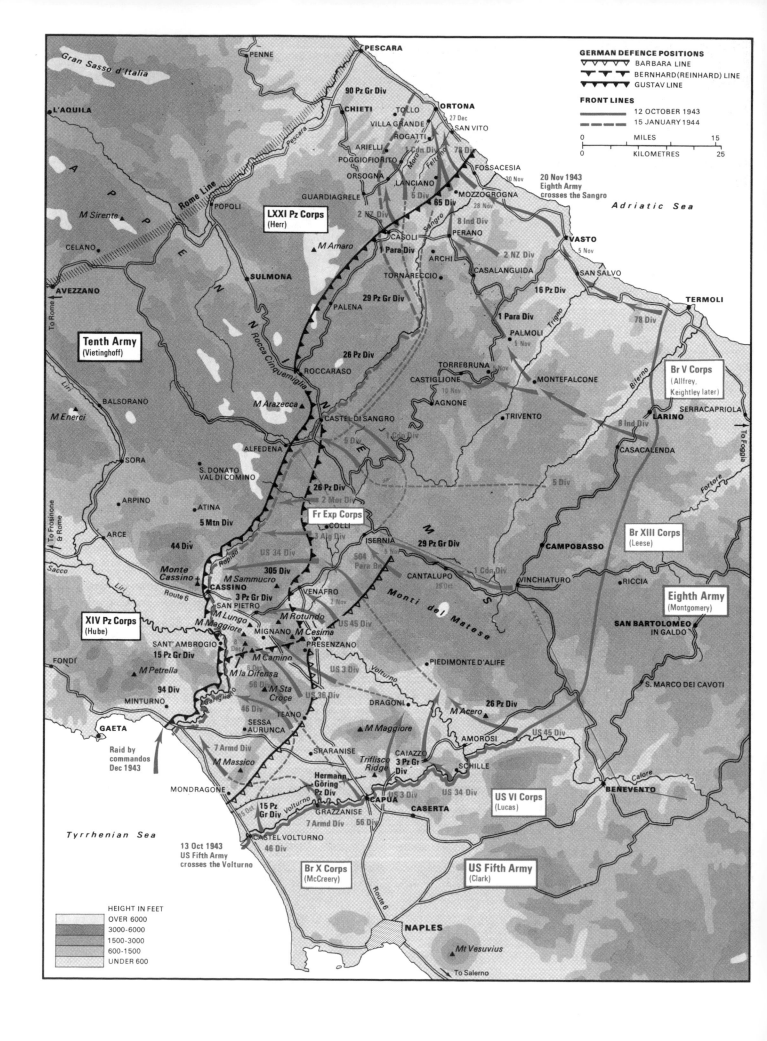

GERMAN DEFENCE POSITIONS
VVVVV BARBARA LINE
VVVVV BERNHARD (REINHARD) LINE
VVVVV GUSTAV LINE

FRONT LINES
━━━ 12 OCTOBER 1943
╌╌╌ 15 JANUARY 1944

MILES 0 — 15
KILOMETRES 0 — 25

Gran Sasso d'Italia

L'AQUILA

PENNE

PESCARA

90 Pz Gr Div

CHIETI   TOLLO   ORTONA
                              27 Dec
    VILLA GRANDE   SAN VITO
        ROGATTI
    ARIELLI   78 Div
POGGIOFIORITO   FOSSACESIA
    ORSOGNA   LANCIANO   30 Nov   20 Nov 1943
GUARDIAGRELE   1 Cdn Div   Eighth Army
                    5 Div   MOZZOGROGNA   crosses the Sangro
POPOLI   2 NZ Div   65 Div   28 Nov
                              8 Ind Div
M Sirente   LXXI Pz Corps   CASOLI   PERANO   *Adriatic Sea*
              (Herr)   1 Para Div
CELANO   2 NZ Div   VASTO
              M Amaro   ARCHI   5 Nov
AVEZZANO   TORNARECCIO   CASALANGUIDA   SAN SALVO
                                                              TERMOLI
              SULMONA   29 Pz Gr Div   16 Pz Div
Tenth Army   1 Para Div   78 Div
(Vietinghoff)   PALENA   PALMOLI
                                          5 Nov
              26 Pz Div   TORREBRUNA
                          CASTIGLIONE   MONTEFALCONE
BALSORANO   AGNONE   10 Nov   Br V Corps
M Enerci   ROCCARASO   TRIVENTO   (Allfrey,
                                                          Keightley later)
SORA   *M Arazecca*   CASTEL DI SANGRO   SERRACAPRIOLA
                                                          LARINO
ARPINO   S. DONATO   ALFEDENA   5 Div   1 Cdn Div
          VAL DI COMINO   5 Div   CASACALENDA
ATINA   26 Pz Div   To Foggia
ARCE   5 Mtn Div   2 Mor Div   Fr Exp Corps
                    COLLI   CAMPOBASSO   Br XIII Corps
          44 Div   3 Alg Div   ISERNIA   29 Pz Gr Div   (Leese)
                                5 Nov   VINCHIATURO
Monte   US 34 Div   504   CANTALUPO   RICCIA
Cassino   Para Bn   28 Oct   1 Cdn Div   Eighth Army
Route 6   305 Div   (Montgomery)
        CASSINO   M Sammucro   *Monti del Matese*   SAN BARTOLOMEO
        3 Pz Gr Div   VENAFRO   IN GALDO
XIV Pz Corps   SAN PIETRO   2 Nov   US 45 Div
(Hube)   M Lungo   M Rotundo   US 45 Div
        M Maggiore   MIGNANO   M Cesima
SANT'AMBROGIO   8 Dec   PRESENZANO   PIEDIMONTE D'ALIFE
15 Pz Gr Div   M Camino   S. MARCO DEI CAVOTI
FONDI   *M Petrella*   6 Dec   US 3 Div   *Volturno*
        M la Difensa   26 Pz Div
94 Div   56 Div   M Sta   US 36 Div   DRAGONI   *M Acero*
MINTURNO   46 Div   Croce   PIEDIMONTE
          Garigliano   TEANO   *M Maggiore*   AMOROSI
GAETA   SESSA   US 45 Div
        AURUNCA   SPARANISE   CAIAZZO
Raid by   7 Armd Div   Triflisco   3 Pz Gr   SCHILLE   BENEVENTO
commandos   *M Massico*   Ridge   Div   *Calore*
Dec 1943   Hermann   US 3 Div   US 34 Div
        MONDRAGONE   Göring   US VI Corps
                      Pz Div   CAPUA   CASERTA   (Lucas)
                  GRAZZANISE
Tyrrhenian Sea   15 Pz   *Volturno*
              Gr Div   7 Armd Div   56 Div
13 Oct 1943   CASTEL VOLTURNO
US Fifth Army   46 Div   Br X Corps   US Fifth Army
crosses the Volturno   (McCreery)   (Clark)
                          Route 6
HEIGHT IN FEET
    OVER 6000
    3000-6000
    1500-3000
    600-1500
    UNDER 600   NAPLES

                        Mt Vesuvius

                    To Salerno

THE DRIVE TO THE GUSTAV LINE

The major obstacle facing the US Fifth Army when it resumed its offensive on 12 October 1943 was the Volturno river, which was in spate with the autumn rain, and whose bridges the Germans had demolished. Clark managed to get both his corps across by the 15th, but then made appallingly slow progress over the roadless mountains north of the river.

On the other side of Italy, Montgomery's regrouped Eighth Army resumed the advance on 22 October and forced a passage over the Trigno river. On both sides of the central mountains, however, the Germans continued to slow the Allied advance with skilful delaying actions. On 15 November Alexander decided that his forces had had enough and halted the offensive. Kesselring, meanwhile, had been using the time won for him by his men to complete the Gustav Line. This magnificent defensive line, in places ten miles wide, ran along the line of the Garigliano and Rapido rivers, over the central mountains and then just north of the Sangro river to the Adriatic. The line was held by the German Tenth Army under General Heinrich von Vietinghoff. On the western end, the Gustav Line was particularly strong, backed up as it was by the mountains on either side of the Liri and by Cassino.

It was against this sector of the line that the US Fifth Army attacked on 20 November. Progress was made, but at enormous cost. At the end of the year, the Fifth Army had been brought to a halt in arctic conditions some five miles south of the Rapido. In the east the British had slightly better fortunes — switching two divisions from his left wing, Montgomery formed a powerful right and forced the Sangro on 15 November. The Eighth Army then broke through the Gustav Line east of Lanciano and took Ortona on 27 December.

Above: US artillery advancing
Below: Supplies being brought forward

THE CASSINO BATTLES

At the beginning of 1943, US Fifth Army had reached the Gustav Line along the Garigliano, but was still held in front of the Bernhard Line along the Rapido section of the Gustav Line. Alexander then ordered a head-on offensive which, coupled with the Anzio landings about to take place, would force Kesselring to evacuate the Gustav Line. The US VI Corps, aided by the French Expeditionary Corps, finally reached the Rapido and the frontal assault went in on 17 January (**Map 1**).

The British X Corps managed to secure a bridgehead across the Garigliano, while the US II Corps, which had replaced VI Corps, had mixed fortunes. Its 36 Division was repulsed with heavy losses, while 34 Division made slightly better progress and crossed the Rapido. The French Expeditionary Corps also made limited advances but suffered extremely heavy casualties. Further attacks, by the New Zealand Corps, were also unsuccessful between 15 and 18 February. Attempts to take Cassino by storm having failed, Alexander halted the offensive to rest and regroup. At Cassino there had been a six-week interval after the failure of the February offensive. During this period the Allies were considerably regrouped and reinforced for the next attempt, which started on 11 May 1944 (**Map 2**).

The renewed offensive was launched along a 20-mile front running from east of Cassino to the sea. The British managed to push over the Rapido, but the Germans succeeded in containing this attack. On the coast the Americans broke through the Gustav Line but were then held at Santa Maria Infante. On the Americans' right, however, the French Expeditionary Corps stormed over the Garigliano and advanced to cut the German communications. Kesselring realized that the position was lost and ordered a withdrawal on 17 May. Next day the Poles had the final honour of taking Cassino, or what

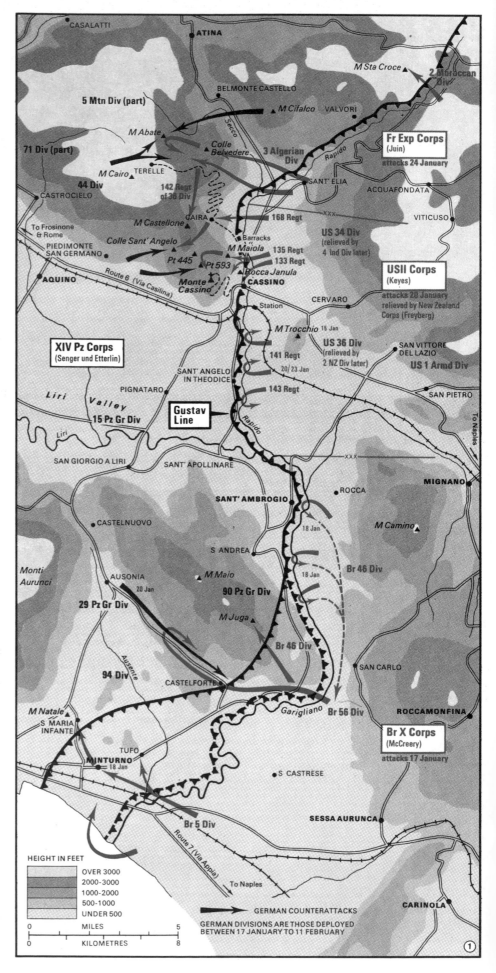

remained of it after the bombing and shelling.

At Anzio (see next page), VI Corps had been reinforced and broke out of its beachhead on 23 May. On the 25th advance units of the US II and VI Corps established contact.

Although the Anzio landing had been designed to lift pressure from Cassino, it was in fact the Allied success at Cassino that allowed the US VI Corps to break out of its beachhead. A point worth noting is that the Allied success at Cassino would not have been possible without the starvation of the German garrison of many essential supplies by Allied bombers and fighter bombers. This was a factor that was to become increasingly important as the Italian campaign progressed.

Right: A German paratrooper amid the ruins of the abbey at Monte Cassino

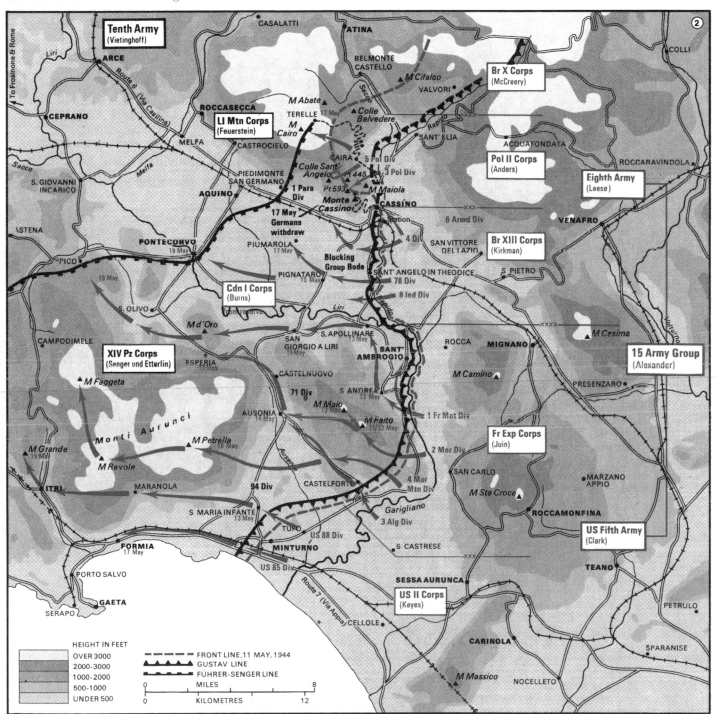

ANZIO AND THE DRIVE TO ROME

The plan behind the Anzio landing was for the US VI Corps under Major-General John Lucas to land behind the German lines at the same time that the frontal assault on Cassino was being launched in January 1944 (**Map 1**). Advancing rapidly inland,

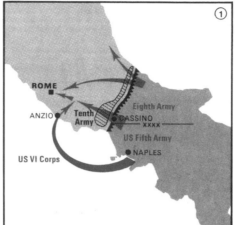

VI Corps was to cut German communications between Rome and Cassino, and either isolate the German Tenth Army or compel it to abandon the western end of the Gustav Line. Whatever happened, the Allies would soon find themselves across the Rapido and in possession of Cassino. Meanwhile, Eighth Army would continue its advance up the east coast.

The operation was a failure. The first landings took place on 22 January, most of the 50,000 troops were ashore within the next two days (**Map 2**). But instead of pressing inland Lucas decided to wait for his heavy artillery and tanks, and meanwhile dig in to consolidate the beachhead. Not so much as a reconnaissance in force did he venture.

The Germans, as usual, reacted swiftly, improvising the Fourteenth Army under General Hans Georg von Mackensen. This soon pinned down VI Corps in its beachhead until

Below: Supplies coming ashore at Anzio

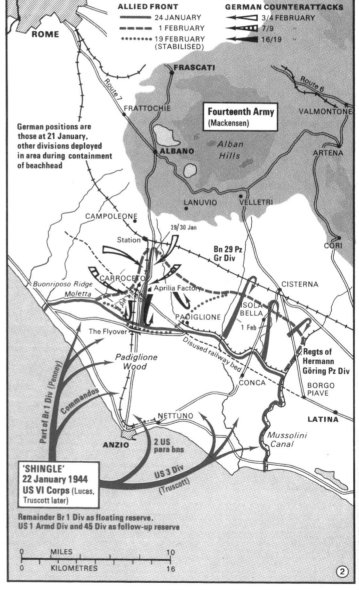

Mackensen had massed forces for a major counterattack. This went in on 16 February and had considerable initial success until halted on 19 February. Lucas was replaced by Major-General Lucius Truscott on the 23rd, but the position was past immediate redemption. Both sides then settled down to a siege, which lasted well into May.

With the final breaking of the Gustav Line at Cassino, the Allies could once more resume their advance northwards (**Map 3**). But instead of swinging his Fifth Army eastward, which would in all probability have trapped the German Tenth Army, Clark decided on the capture of Rome, which now had little strategic, but great propaganda, value. The Germans, yet again fighting skilful rearguard actions, checked the Americans at Velletri and Valmontone long enough to allow the complete escape of all the German forces in the area. Rome was entered on 4 June – two days before the Normandy landings.

Right: American troops advancing under cover of a Sherman tank into the suburbs of Rome

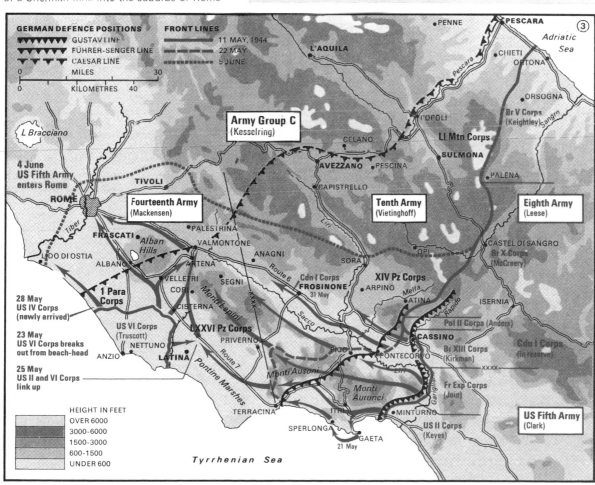

127

BREAKING THE GOTHIC LINE

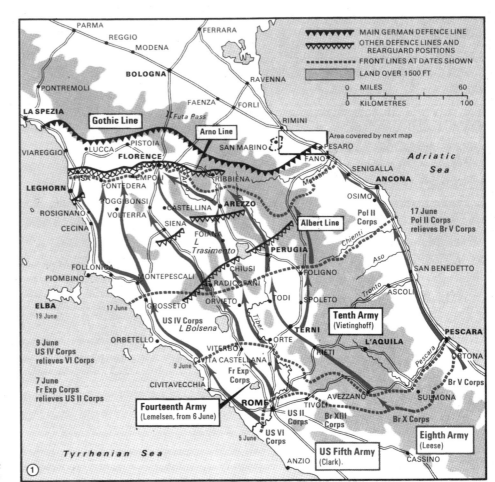

After the fall of Rome, the Allies pushed on northwards as fast as the summer weather would allow them, forcing the Germans back through the Albert and Arno Lines to their final defence, the redoubtable Gothic Line (**Map 1**). Reductions in troops, aircraft, and landing craft at a time when the Germans were being reinforced from the Balkans and Germany combined to slow down the Allied advance.

The first to reach the Gothic Line was the British Eighth Army under Lieutenant-General Sir Oliver Leese. Rather than attack on the coast, Leese decided to attack further inland, using

his V Corps and the left wing of the Canadian I Corps. The attack was launched on 30 August (**Map 2**), and contrary to expectations, the Gothic Line itself proved a relatively minor obstacle. Trouble lay ahead, however, in the form of the Gemmano and Coriano Ridges. Until these two commanding positions could be taken, the planned advance to Rimini could not take place. It was only after very heavy fighting, and some of the heaviest casualties of the whole campaign, that the Germans were driven off. The British advance was then resumed and Rimini fell on 21 September.

Meanwhile, the US Fifth Army had also broken through the Gustav Line, and by 25 September only a small portion on the coast between Leghorn and La Spezia remained in German hands. The weather was about to break, so Clark threw in all his reserves in a last attempt to reach Bologna before the winter (**Map 3**), but by 20 October his exhausted forces had still not reached their objective, and the Allied armies halted. A small advance was made in the winter, mostly by the British, who pushed their line forward to the Senio river.

As the armies settled down to wait for spring, there were wide-ranging changes in the Allied command structure: Alexander, promoted to Supreme Allied Commander in the Mediterranean, was succeeded as commander of 15 Army Group by Clark, who was in turn succeeded in Fifth Army by Truscott. At the same time Lieutenant-General Richard McCreery took over command of Eighth Army from Leese.

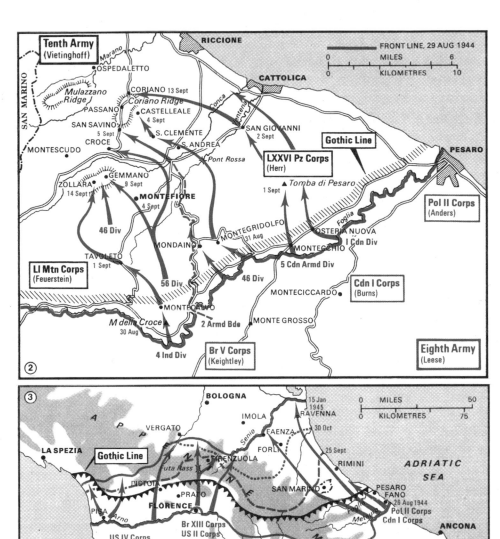

Opposite: An American M–18 tank destroyer in action near Firenzuola

Right: Shermans firing on the Gothic Line

THE END IN ITALY

The new year of 1945 brought no immediate action to the Italian theatre. Clark, who had received new equipment and reinforcements during the winter, was busy training his men for the final offensive, while Vietinghoff, who had succeeded Kesselring as commander of Army Group C (or South-West) on the latter's transfer to an army group in western Germany, was busy strengthening the defences along his front.

The plan put forward by Clark was for Eighth Army to drive forward on Ferrara, the Fifth Army starting its offensive a few days later, with Bologna as its objective. In this way, the aircraft available would be able to give massive support first to the British and then to the American offensive.

McCreery's forces started their assault on 9 April under cover of a great artillery bombardment (**Map 1**). The German Tenth Army, now under General Herr, had expected an attack on its centre and right, and was caught off balance when its left was enveloped by an amphibious operation across Lake Comacchio. It pulled back and opened the way for the British to move into the Argenta Gap, south-east of Ferrara.

Five days after McCreery's attack, Truscott's Fifth Army went over to the offensive. Lemelsen's German Fourteenth Army could do nothing to halt the advance, and the Americans quickly broke through to the Po valley on 20 April. Vietinghoff threw in his last reserves but these had practically no effect. The Germans, under enormous pressure from the Americans, pulled back to the left bank of the Po, abandoning all their heavy weapons and armour. On the American right wing, Bologna had fallen on 21 April. Further to the east again, 8 Indian Division of the Eighth Army by-passed Ferrara and pushed straight on to the Po.

It was now all up with the Axis forces in Italy. The Fifth and Eighth Armies continued to press on towards Austria and France, to meet American troops advancing the other way on 6 May, and French troops coming from France. The Fascist Ligurian Army had melted away completely.

General von Vietinghoff had already signed the surrender of the German forces in Italy on 29 April, and this became effective on 2 May.

Opposite below: America troops digging in during the winter lull

Below: An American armoured column halts before entering Milan

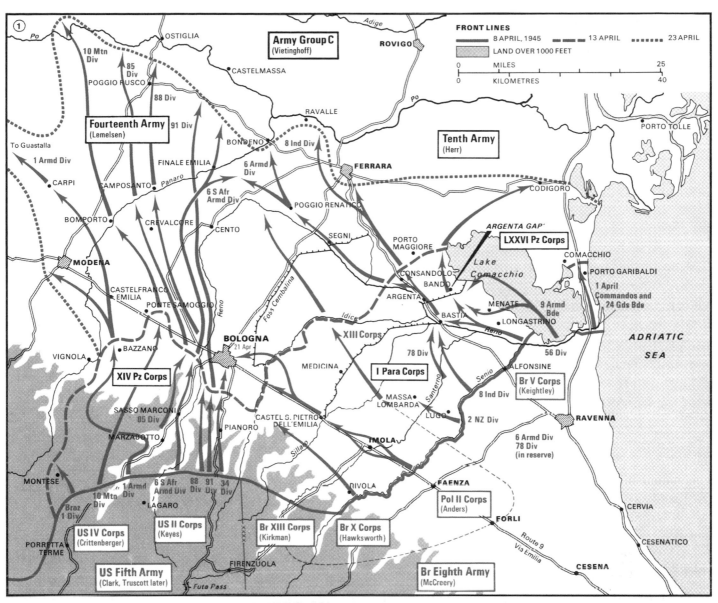

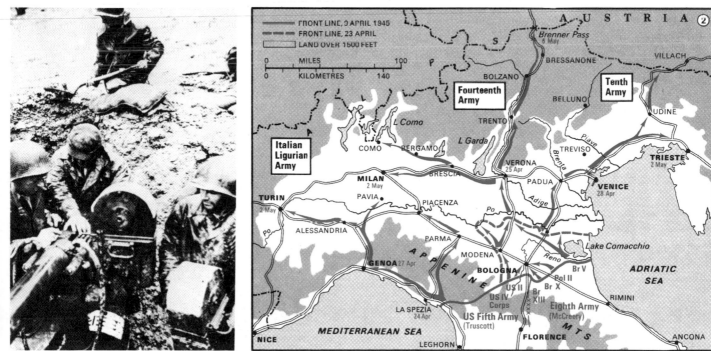

THE PACIFIC WAR

Success went to the heads of the Japanese. Imperial General Headquarters were now afflicted by what, after the war, one of their own admirals was to describe as 'Victory Disease'. It was understandable enough, but it led the Japanese to look farther afield than they had originally intended. They now planned to capture Tulagi in the Solomons and Port Moresby in Papua, in order to give their air force control of the Coral Sea. They would then follow this up by seeking out the US Pacific Fleet. A victory by their main fleet would, they hoped, give them Midway and the Western Aleutians. They saw, correctly, the importance of fighting the US Pacific Fleet before American war production could build it up. The Japanese strategists intended to follow up this operation by taking New Caledonia, Fiji, and Samoa, which would, in all probability, deprive Australia of American support.

By mid-April American Intelligence, thanks to breaking of the Japanese naval code, knew that they were planning a battle for the Coral Sea, and Admiral Chester W. Nimitz (CINCPAC) sent Rear-Admiral Fletcher there with Force 17, which included the carriers *Lexington* and *Yorktown*. A curious battle ensued, the first in which the main units on either side were carriers and in which no ship made visual contact with the enemy. Both sides were learning a new technique as the fighting developed.

The two forces were fairly evenly matched with the Japanese having two fleet and one light carriers with about 150 aircraft, and the Americans two fleet carriers with 122 aircraft. By the end of the battle one of the US carriers, the *Lexington*, had been sunk, and the other, *Yorktown*, was damaged. The Japanese had lost their light carrier, and one of the others had been damaged. In terms of losses inflicted, the battle was very even, but in reality the Japanese had suffered a major strategic defeat for the projected attack on Port Moresby, the key to New Guinea, was abandoned.

Both sides, not surprisingly in a battle of a kind the world had not previously seen, made serious blunders at every level particularly with regard to the identification and location of enemy forces. From the point of view of Allied morale it was a wonderful thing to have inflicted a serious defeat on the Japanese aggressors only six months after Pearl Harbor, and only two days after the fall of Corregidor. The Coral Sea is of particular interest to the military historian as an illustration of the way in which relatively minor events, such as the report of an inexperienced pilot failing to detail enemy ships correctly, or the presence of a rain squall which hid one of the Japanese carriers at a crucial moment, can influence the fate of a whole force.

The Americans were not slow to learn from their mistakes, and in the next big battle, Midway, they fought with great skill.

Nimitz with seventy-six ships had to face 162 warships and auxiliaries. Nagumo had four fleet carriers and three light carriers, whilst the Americans only had three. It is a remarkable tribute to American efficiency that one of these was *Yorktown*. Repairs which in peacetime could have taken ninety days had been effected at Pearl Harbor in *two* days! In contrast, neither *Shokaku* or *Zuikaku* which had also been damaged in the Coral Sea action were ready on the Japanese side.

In addition to his fleet Nimitz had an 'unsinkable aircraft carrier' in Midway Island itself, where there were 115 planes.

The Japanese were still not aware that the Americans had broken their naval cipher: knowing when and where they meant to attack Nimitz had a tactical advantage which few commanders have enjoyed in modern warfare.

Nagumo enjoyed no such advantage, and indeed the disaster that overtook him may be attributed to the fact that he did not expect to encounter American carriers and in consequence sent out too few reconnaissance flights. Had he

appreciated that there were enemy carriers within striking distance he ought probably to have sought them out *before* attacking Midway. When before sunrise on the 4 June he sent 108 aircraft to attack the island he kept a reserve of ninety-three aircraft, armed with bombs and torpedoes. His fatal and, as it proved, mistaken decision was made about 0700 hours when he heard from the commander of his striking force that Midway required further attention, and from his reconnaissance flights that they had seen nothing. The consequence was that he was caught with the decks of his carriers crowded with aircraft unable to take off.

Midway was not only one of the decisive battles of the Second World War but of modern history. The destruction of all Nagumo's carriers gave the United States the initiative in the Pacific War, and was a terrible blow to the Japanese navy. From now on the Japanese were on the defensive, and deprived of the means of supporting the outposts of the empire they had so swiftly seized. An unusual feature of the battle was that both Nagumo and Fletcher were compelled to change their flagships, the former from *Akagi* to *Nagara*, the latter from *Yorktown* to the cruiser *Astoria*.

Both Spruance and Fletcher deserve high praise for their performance in this battle, which does not alter the fact that, like Waterloo, it was 'a damned near run thing'. As Professor Morison puts it 'for about one hundred seconds the Japanese were certain they had won the Battle of Midway, and the war.' That moment came at about 1024 hours on 4 June when the third attack of the US torpedo-bombers ended without a single hit scored and most of the aircraft destroyed. From this time onwards the Japanese navy could scarcely face the

Above left: The hulk of a Japanese cruiser after a US air attack

Above right: US Marines on Eniwetok Atoll in the Marshall Islands

Americans by day, unless they were within range of the support of land-based aircraft.

The Coral Sea and Midway showed that the day of the battleship was done. Since the Japanese could not hope to keep up with the Americans in the construction of new carriers the balance of power had now swung decisively in favour of the latter.

Whilst the Allies, in general, were agreed that the first aim of Allied strategy must be the defeat of Germany, Admiral Ernest J. King, in particular, determined to prevent the Japanese consolidating their gains, had decided to wage a 'defensive-offensive' war in the Pacific. Aware that the Japanese were planning a second attempt on Port Moresby he determined to seize Tulagi and Guadalcanal in the Solomon Islands, using the 1 US Marine Division based on New Zealand. Thus began the determined fight for . . . 'an island that neither side really wanted, but which neither could afford to abandon to the enemy' (Morison).

The six months battle proved to the US Marines that they were superior to the Japanese in jungle warfare. Admiral Tanaka, a most capable and determined commander, attributed the defeat of his side to the lack of an overall plan of operations, to inferiority in the air, to forces being committed piecemeal, to bad communications, bad inter-service relations, and a tendency to underrate the enemy. 'We stumbled along from one error to another, while the enemy grew wise.' In fact the Japanese had fought bravely and though their losses on land exceeded those of the Americans, at sea things were pretty even since, oddly enough, each side lost twenty-four warships. The truth is that American superiority in numbers and equipment was beginning to tell.

From here on the Allied strategy was to work to within range of Japan, leapfrogging across the Pacific by means of a series of amphibious operations, by-passing countless Japanese island strongholds, whose garrisons soon

became as useless as if they had been in prisoner of war camps. 'This', wrote General Matsuichi Ino, 'was the type of strategy we hated most. The Americans attacked and seized, with minimum losses, a relatively weak area, constructed airfields, and then proceeded to cut the supply lines . . . Our strongpoints were gradually starved out. The Japanese army preferred direct assault after the German fashion, but the Americans flowed into our weaker points and submerged us, just as water seeks the weakest entry to sink a ship.' It was an amphibious application of the strategy of the indirect approach of which the late Captain Sir Basil Liddell-Hart was the exponent.

The Americans did not always get ashore scot free. At Tarawa for example they fought one of the costliest battles in their history (19/23 November 1943), in ratio to the number of troops engaged. The US Marines lost 3,000 casualties, and of 4,000 Japanese defenders only seventeen were taken. The Americans made an intensive study of the operation and learned by their mistakes, reaping the benefit during the rest of the war.

At the tactical level both sides fought with the most creditable determination. The Japanese with their spirit of 'no surrender' were always dangerous. The Americans were well-led at platoon and squad level, and accepted the fact that they were up against an enemy who had to be winkled out bunker by bunker, and cave by cave, with grenade and flame-thrower. Massive fire support, though available, was not in itself enough. The Japanese modified their tactics as time went by. At Peleliu, for example, they sited their main position well in rear of the beach, and kept a strong reserve for counterattack.

If the Americans were flexible tacticians, their strategy was to some extent bedevilled by the personal prejudices of their chiefs. King and Nimitz wished to take Formosa and assault Japan from bases on the China coast. MacArthur, yearning to liberate the Filipinos, wanted to make Luzon the

jumping off place. He may have been right for much of the China coast was in Japanese hands and Formosa was very strongly held.

To the end the Japanese resisted with fanaticism. Okinawa cost the Americans 12,513 killed and 36,600 wounded in the army and navy alone. But its capture besides giving an air base for the final assault on Japan, practically cut the sea communications of all Japanese positions to the southward. As Nimitz put it: 'It has made the Japanese situation in China, Burma, and the Dutch East Indies untenable and has forced withdrawals which are now being exploited by our forces in China.'

Effectively, the Japanese were now beaten. But the problem was to make them realize it. Plans went ahead for an invasion of the Japanese home islands, but the dropping of two atomic bombs made this unnecessary.

Above left: A US Marine on Okinawa

Above right: Landing craft massed on the beaches of Okinawa

THE BATTLE OF THE CORAL SEA

By April/May, 1942, the Japanese had enjoyed a run of unbroken victories, at less cost than even they had anticipated. For the loss of only twenty-three warships (none larger than a destroyer) and sixty-seven other vessels, they had overrun the Philippines, Malaya, Burma, the Dutch East Indies, and a number of the British Pacific Islands. These successes encouraged the Japanese planners to extend the defence perimeter of Greater East Asia, and they were strengthened in this resolve by the Doolittle Raid on Tokyo on 18 April. This carrier-borne raid, designed to raise American and Chinese morale, while it caused little damage, made the Japanese take the threat of the bombing of their homeland seriously. In extending the perimeter of their conquests two choices were open to them: to strike eastwards in the central Pacific to capture Midway, gain a base within striking distance of Hawaii, and eliminate the bombing threat; or to strike south and east from Rabaul, capture Port Moresby, extend their hold on the Solomon Islands, and isolate Australia from the United States. In the event they chose to do both.

The capture of Port Moresby, the primary strategic aim of the Coral Sea operations, was entrusted to Admiral Shigeyoshi Inouye, commanding at Rabaul. The forces available to him, designated Task Force MO, were divided into five groups (**see map**):

The Port Moresby Invasion Group, eleven transports screened by destroyers, was to make straight for Port Moresby round the tip of New Guinea through the Jomard Passage.

A smaller Tulagi Invasion Group was to make for the Southern Solomons, capture the island of Tulagi, and set up a seaplane base.

A small support group was to establish a base in the Louisiade Archipelago, close to the Jomard Passage.

A Covering Group, under Rear-Admiral Goto, comprising the aircraft carrier *Shoho*, four heavy cruisers and one destroyer was to cover the Tulagi landing and then turn north-west to protect the Port Moresby Invasion Group.

The Carrier Striking Force, under Vice-Admiral Takagi, containing the carriers *Shokaku* and *Zuikaku*, was to move south from the Central Pacific, enter the Coral Sea from the east, and cover the whole operation from United States' surface interference.

The complexity of this plan suggests that Inouye did not expect serious Allied opposition, and indeed he calculated that only one United States' carrier could be in the area at the time. However, Admiral Nimitz, C-in-C, US Pacific Fleet, knew of the Japanese plans and prepared a Task Force to meet the emergency. Task Force 17, under Admiral Fletcher, including the carrier *Yorktown*, was to be joined by Task Force 11 (Rear-Admiral Fitch), with the carrier *Lexington*. The final component of the Allies force was Task Force 44, a mixed group of Australian and US cruisers and destroyers under Rear-Admiral Crace, RN. These groups were due to rendezvous in the Coral Sea on 4 May.

But on 3 May the Japanese attack began. The island of Tulagi was occupied without opposition, and Goto, with the *Shoho* turned north-west. At 1900 hours Fletcher received news of this, and moved north. At 0630 hours on 4 May, aircraft from the *Yorktown* bombed the landings on Tulagi, registering hits on minor vessels. Shrewdly, Fletcher, resisting the temptation to follow up this success, moved south again to meet the two other Task Forces. Throughout 5 and 6 May the Japanese and US fleets searched for each other in vain. On the 5th, Takagi had entered the Coral Sea, but in perfect weather had missed the opportunity of locating Fletcher's force refuelling. Fletcher then detached the destroyer *Sims* and the tanker *Neosho* to sail south to his next fuelling rendezvous.

On 7 May at 0630 hours Fletcher detached Crace and Task Force 44 to attack the Japanese Port Moresby Invasion Group. Crace was spotted by Japanese aircraft at 0810, and Japanese land-based aircraft continued to attack him throughout the day, under the impression that he was the main Allied force. Miraculously he survived these attacks, at some cost to the attackers. At 0600 hours, Takagi had launched reconnaissance aircraft which had located the *Sims* and *Neosho*. These, as well, were attacked in mistake for the main Allied force, the *Sims* being sunk and the *Neosho* damaged.

These Japanese errors allowed Fletcher to operate undisturbed, and aircraft from the *Yorktown* and *Lexington* located Goto's Covering Group shortly after 1100 hours. Smothered by a three-wave attack, the *Shoho* sank at 1135 hours.

Early in the day, the Japanese had realized the threat to the invasion transports, and had ordered them to turn back, but by the end of the 7th, Fletcher's position was known and Takagi's force was still fresh. Despite the loss of the *Shoho* the Japanese chances still looked favourable. Takagi determined to launch a strike during the night of the 7/8th. This proved entirely abortive, and of the twenty-seven aircraft launched, only six survived.

At 0815 hours on the 8th, Takagi and Fletcher's reconnaissance aircraft located their opposite fleets more or less simultaneously, and by 0925 both sides had launched strikes. At 1057 hours the *Shokaku* was attacked and disabled, and at 1118 hours the *Yorktown* and *Lexington* came under attack. The *Lexington*, hit several times, was eventually abandoned, scuttled and sunk.

Tactically the Battle of the Coral Sea was a draw – the Japanese lost more aircraft, the US more ships. It was the first true carrier battle – no surface ship was ever in sight of an opposing one. Strategically it was a major US victory, halting the invasion of Port Moresby, and throwing the Japanese on the defensive.

Below: USS *Lexington* on fire after being hit in a Japanese attack

Opposite: A destroyer comes alongside the *Lexington* as her crew slide down ropes into the water

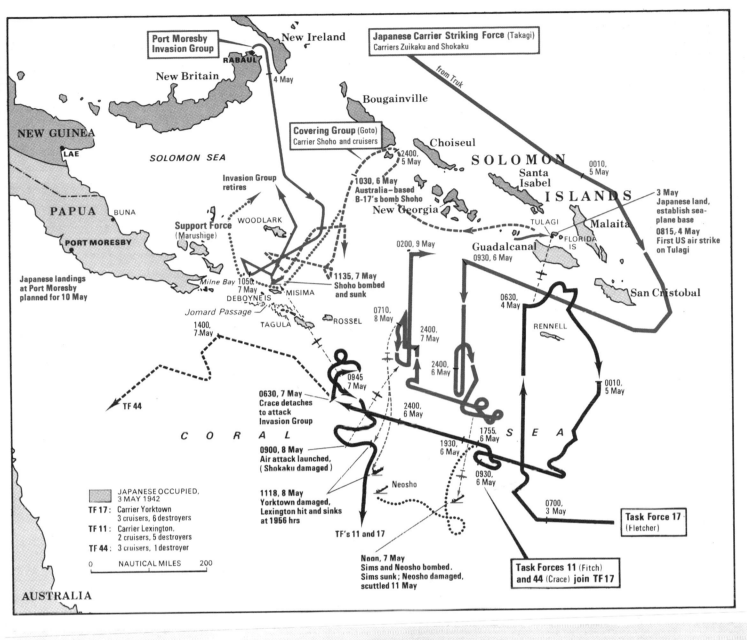

THE BATTLE OF MIDWAY

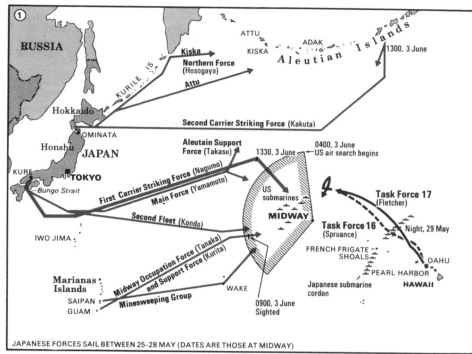

①

RUSSIA

ATTU ADAK

KISKA *Aleutian Islands* 1300, 3 June

Kiska

Northern Force (Hosogaya)

Attu

KURILE IS.

Hokkaido

Second Carrier Striking Force (Kakuta)

OMINATA

Honshu JAPAN

Aleutian Support Force (Takasu) 1330, 3 June 0400, 3 June ←US air search begins

KURE TOKYO

Bungo Strait First Carrier Striking Force (Nagumo) Main Force (Yamamoto) US submarines

MIDWAY Task Force 17 (Fletcher)

Second Fleet (Kondo) Task Force 16 (Spruance) Night, 29 May

IWO JIMA FRENCH FRIGATE SHOALS OAHU

Midway Occupation Force (Tanaka) and Support Force (Kurita) WAKE PEARL HARBOR

Marianas Islands Minesweeping Group Japanese submarine cordon HAWAII

SAIPAN 0900, 3 June Sighted

GUAM

JAPANESE FORCES SAIL BETWEEN 25-28 MAY (DATES ARE THOSE AT MIDWAY)

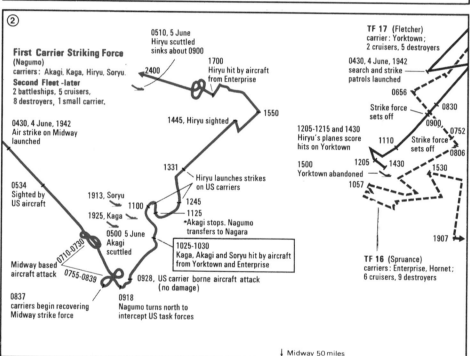

②

First Carrier Striking Force (Nagumo) carriers: Akagi, Kaga, Hiryu, Soryu. Second Fleet -later 2 battleships, 5 cruisers, 8 destroyers, 1 small carrier.

0510, 5 June Hiryu scuttled sinks about 0900

1700 Hiryu hit by aircraft from Enterprise

2400

1550

1445, Hiryu sighted

0430, 4 June, 1942 Air strike on Midway launched

1331

Hiryu launches strikes on US carriers

0534 Sighted by US aircraft

1913, Soryu 1245

1925, Kaga 1100 1125

0500 5 June Akagi scuttled •Akagi stops. Nagumo transfers to Nagara

0710-0730

Midway based aircraft attack 0755-0839

0837 carriers begin recovering Midway strike force

0918 Nagumo turns north to intercept US task forces

0928, US carrier borne aircraft attack (no damage)

1025-1030 Kaga, Akagi and Soryu hit by aircraft from Yorktown and Enterprise

TF 17 (Fletcher) carrier: Yorktown; 2 cruisers, 5 destroyers

0430, 4 June, 1942 search and strike patrols launched

0656

Strike force sets off 0830

0900 0752

1205-1215 and 1430 Hiryu's planes score hits on Yorktown 1110 Strike force sets off 0806

1500 Yorktown abandoned 1205 1430

1057 1530

1907

TF 16 (Spruance) carriers: Enterprise, Hornet; 6 cruisers, 9 destroyers

↓ Midway 50 miles

The clash at Midway, the most important naval battle of the war (and one of the decisive battles of history), was the result of Japan's determination to extend the perimeter of her conquests in the Central Pacific. Both strategically and tactically its outcome was the result of several disastrous misappreciations by the Japanese commanders.

After the Battle of the Coral Sea, Yamamoto, C-in-C of the Combined Japanese Fleet, erroneously believed both the carriers *Yorktown* and the *Lexington* to have been destroyed. In fact the *Yorktown* was still very much alive and, after a miraculously swift refitting at Pearl Harbor during the last week in May, she was ready again for service. This miscalculation was understandable, but Yamamoto further deduced that the two other US carriers, *Hornet* and *Enterprise*, which had raced to take part in the Coral Sea action, were still in the South Pacific. A strike against Midway during the first week in June, he concluded, could not be opposed by a US carrier force. Accordingly he laid his plans for the Midway operation. They were characteristically complex (**Map 1**), involving nearly the whole of Japan's surface fleet. A Northern Force under Vice-Admiral Hosogaya (two light carriers, seven cruisers, and twelve destroyers) was to launch diversionary attacks on the Aleutian Islands just before the main strike at Midway. The remainder of the fleet destined for Midway was organized in three separate forces: the First Carrier Strike Force, under Vice-Admiral Nagumo (carriers *Kaga, Akagi, Soryu,* and *Hiryu*); the Midway Occupation Force, comprising the Second Fleet (Vice-Admiral Kondo), the occupation and support forces, and a minesweeping group (in all one light carrier, two battleships, two seaplane carriers, seven cruisers, twenty-five destroyers, and twelve transports carrying 51,000 men); and Yamamoto's Main Force (one light carrier, seven battleships, four cruisers, and twelve destroyers). Lastly, a screen of eighteen submarines was to operate between

Pearl Harbor and Midway. These groups were independently organized and disposed in such a way that mutual co-operation in action could not be immediate. For the purposes of the opposing US admirals, therefore, there was, in this huge armada, one overridingly important target – Nagumo's First Carrier Strike Force.

Nimitz (US C-in-C Pacific Fleet) knew of these plans and had accurate intelligence of sailing dates and timings. At his disposal were three fleet carriers carrying 250 aircraft (about the same number as on Nagumo's four carriers). In addition the fortress of Midway itself could provide a further 109 aircraft.

No time was wasted. By the end of May (before the Japanese submarine screen was in position) Nimitz' forces were at sea. They comprised Task Force 17, with the carrier *Yorktown*, under Rear-Admiral Fletcher; and Task Force 16, with the carriers *Enterprise* and *Hornet*, under Rear-Admiral Spruance. Fletcher had overall command.

Between 3 and 7 June the Japanese Northern Force carried out successful attacks on the Aleutians and, had Nimitz not known these to be diversions, might have provoked the response intended. But on 4 June, at 0430 hours, Nagumo launched his first strike against Midway (**Map 2**) to soften up the defences preparatory to landing the invasion force. Only one such strike was thought to be needed. The second wave of aircraft on Nagumo's carriers was armed to meet naval contingencies; armed, that is, with torpedoes or armour-piercing bombs.

At the same time US land-based aircraft rose from Midway to attack the approaching bombers and the Japanese fleet itself. The US aircraft were hopelessly outclassed, and the majority were destroyed, but their courage and tenacity had one important result. The commander of the Japanese airstrike signalled to Nagumo that a further strike would be necessary to subdue the island. Nagumo received this message at 0700 hours and proceeded to rearm his waiting aircraft, stripping them of their naval armament, and replacing it with high explosive and fragmentation bombs. This was a lengthy task, an hour's work at least. It was half completed at 0728 hours when Nagumo was handed a message from a spotter plane reporting the presence of ten US ships 200 miles to the north-east. If this force contained no carriers it presented no immediate threat, and the message gave no indication of its composition. Not until 0758 hours did Nagumo receive a further message from the spotter plane stating that the ten ships were five cruisers and five

destroyers. He received this message with relief, for at the same moment his force came under attack from Midway-based US bombers. As it happened, this attack did no damage, but every available Zero fighter was sent up to repel it. Then, at 0820 hours, Nagumo received another message: 'Enemy force accompanied by what appears to be a carrier.'

Nagumo's dilemma was insoluble. A strike against the approaching US carrier force would require fighter cover, but now all his Zeros required refuelling and rearming, and the rearming of his strike aircraft was not complete. Also, at 0830, the Midway strike aircraft would be returning, almost out of fuel and demanding urgent recovery. Against advice, he decided to postpone the preparation of a strike until after the Midway force had been recovered, but, as a precautionary measure, altered course 90 degrees north-east to meet the new threat at 0918 hours.

At dawn the US carriers had launched search patrols and, at 0752, the first strike was launched against Nagumo from the *Enterprise* and *Hornet*. The *Yorktown*, over an hour to the north east, did not launch a strike until 0900 hours. Both these strikes comprised Dauntless dive bombers, Devastator torpedo bombers, and Wildcat fighters.

At 0930 hours the torpedo bombers located Nagumo's force. Lacking fighter cover the low-level Devastators were massacred by the Japanese Zeros and the anti-aircraft fire of the cordon of cruisers and destroyers. Nagumo, seeing this, assumed the attacking force to have been destroyed and feverishly continued the arming of his strike. At 1025 this was complete, and on all four Japanese carriers the flight decks were crowded with waiting aircraft. But the dive bombers of all three US carriers had located the Japanese force and, at this moment, they struck. Within five minutes the *Kaga*, *Akagi*, and *Soryu* had been sunk. Only the *Hiryu*, cruising separately, was undamaged, and she was able to launch counter-strikes against the US force. Between 1200 hours and 1430 hours these strikes located and hit the *Yorktown*, rendering her uncontrollable. Abandoned at 1500 hours she was subsequently sunk by a submarine while under tow.

But this was the *Hiryu*'s last action. Aircraft from the *Enterprise* continued to attack her during the afternoon, and by 1700 hours she was damaged beyond repair. Next day she was scuttled.

Without carriers the remainder of the Japanese force was powerless. Within one day, effectively within five minutes, Japanese mastery of the sea had been destroyed. During the remainder of 4 and 5 June Yamamoto made abortive attempts to bring the US force to action with his still vastly superior surface fleet, but these were correctly and wisely avoided. From this point on in the Pacific, both on the sea and in the air, the initiative belonged to the United States.

Left: The Japanese aircraft carrier *Hiryu* on fire after a US air attack

GUADALCANAL

MILES 0 — 10
KILOMETRES 0 — 20

Florida I

Savo I

**0740/1200,
2 Marine Regt plus 1 Para Bn
Strong resistance overcome** → TULAGI / GAVUTU

**1/7 Feb 1943,
Japanese forces
withdraw**

**7 August 1942
US 1 Marine Div
(Vandegrift)**

C Esperance

I R O N B O T T O M   S O U N D

TENARO

**October,
Japanese reserves
land**

**Night 7/8 Sept
Marine raiders
attack Jap base**

**0909,
5 Marine Regt lands
unopposed
1 Marine Regt follows**

Tassafaronga Pt

**PM, 8 Aug
Henderson Field
taken**

Aug
Sept
TAIVU

**17 Jan 1943,
Jap Seventeenth Army
begins withdrawal from
the Matanikau**

Lunga Pt
KUKUM

Koli Pt

TENARU

**23/26 Oct,
Maruyama's attacks
repulsed**

'Bloody Ridge'

**Night 20/21 Aug,
Ichiki's detachment
destroyed**

Matanikau

Mt Austen

**12/14 Sept,
Kawaguchi suffers
heavy losses at
'Bloody Ridge'**

Lunga

Tenaru

G u a d a l c a n a l

→ AMERICAN ATTACKS
→ JAPANESE COUNTERATTACKS AND WITHDRAWALS
▲▲▲ US DEFENCE PERIMETER 9 AUGUST
▬ US POSITIONS 23 OCTOBER

EARLY DECEMBER, 1 MARINE DIV RELIEVED BY 25 INF, 2 MARINE AND AMERICAL DIVS (XIV CORPS [PATCH])

The US victory at Midway made it imperative for the Japanese to build airfields to provide the air cover that their fleet could no longer supply. In July 1942 news of the construction of an airfield by the Japanese on the Solomon Island of Guadalcanal hastened the American plans to move into the southern Solomons, and an amphibious task force under Rear-Admiral Turner was prepared. Turner's force carried the 19,000 men of Major-General Vandegrift's 1 Marine Division, and it was supported by Fletcher's three-carrier naval task force. As at Midway, Fletcher had overall command of the expedition.

In spite of the hasty composition of this force, and its inexperience of combined operations, it achieved tactical surprise. On 7 August, elements of 1 Marine Division landed unopposed on Guadalcanal. Two smaller detachments landed on the islands of Tulagi and Gavutu, valuable for their harbours and potential airfields, and encountered determined opposition. By the end of 8 August all landings had been successfully completed, and the Marines had reached Henderson Field, the site of the Japanese airstrip, to find that the Japanese had fled.

During the night of 8/9 August a naval action was fought around Savo Island at the mouth of Ironbottom Sound (see following pages), and the threat of Japanese warships forced the transports to retire, taking with them much of the landing forces' equipment. The Marines were now left to themselves, short of equipment and surrounded by waters dominated by the Japanese navy.

Between 9 and 18 August the Marines on Guadalcanal were busy strengthening the perimeter around Henderson Field, and preparing the airfield itself. They were under constant attack by Japanese ships and aircraft, and on 18 August the first Japanese troop reinforcements landed

on Guadalcanal at Taivu, 20 miles to the east of Henderson Field – one regiment under Colonel Ichiki. Ichiki's regiment moved west and, on the 21st, launched an attack against Vandegrift's position at Henderson Field. By this time the Marines had received their first aircraft, on the 20th, and were no longer as powerless in the air as before. Throughout the 21st and 22nd, Ichiki continued to launch attacks against the Marines across the Tenaru river. They were all repulsed, and eventually, after the Marine reserve regiment had worked its way behind the Japanese position, Ichiki's force was driven into the sea and destroyed. Ichiki himself committed suicide.

During 23 and 24 August the Battle of the Eastern Solomons (following pages) was fought. The Japanese were forced to retire with the loss of one carrier. This, and the presence of aircraft at Henderson Field, reduced Japanese daytime mastery of the sea, but, with their superiority in cruisers and destroyers, they still dominated the sea at night. However, this did not prevent a party of Marine Raiders from attacking the Japanese base at Taivu on the night of 7/8 September. As well as destroying a large number of stores, the Raiders captured the details of further attacks to be

launched on Henderson Field.

On 12 September these attacks materialized. The Japanese 35 Brigade under General Kawaguchi, a far more formidable array than Ichiki's single regiment, attacked the Marine position from the east. Wave after wave was thrown in, and at one point the Japanese were within 1,000 yards of the airstrip. But they suffered appalling losses, and on the 14th Kawaguchi withdrew, leaving behind 1,200 dead and wounded.

Both sides now received reinforcements. Rushed down by sea under the cover of darkness the Japanese forces were landed night after night by the 'Tokyo Night Express' at Tenaro, to the west of Henderson Field. They comprised the headquarters of Seventeenth Army and 2 Division, about 20,000 men. Vandegrift's Marines were joined by US 7 Marines and 164 Infantry Regiment, bringing his force to 23,000.

On the night of 11/12 October another cruiser action took place off Cape Esperance (following pages), in which the US ships drove off the Japanese force, sinking a cruiser and destroyer. This upset Japanese reinforcement plants, and delayed the attack planned by the Japanese commander, General Maruyama.

By 23 October, however, Maruyama was ready. For two days he attacked Henderson Field from the south, but his forces were operating separately and lacked adequate communications. The Marines defeated each attack in detail, and by nightfall on the 26th, Maruyama broke off the engagement leaving 3,500 casualties.

It was time for the US forces to take the offensive, but the Marines on Guadalcanal were in no condition for this. Throughout November the exhausted Marines and Japanese watched each other, and not until December did the XIV Army Corps replace the Marines. The Japanese, at the same time, appalled by their losses, both at sea and on the land, decided to withdraw. Pursued by the fresh US forces, Maruyama's Seventeenth Army made its painful way west, and by 9 February the remaining 11,000 of the original 20,000 force had been evacuated from Guadalcanal.

For the Allies, the heroic Marine defence and seizure of Guadalcanal brought immense advantages. Australia and New Zealand were safe, and the Allies now stood on the flank of the outer cordon of Japan's conquests. The psychological effect of this repulse of the invincible Japanese army was incalculable.

Above right: Japanese sailors manning a machine gun on Guadalcanal

Right: US troops with tank support following the retreating Japanese

THE SOLOMON ISLANDS NAVAL BATTLES

The Marine landings on Guadalcanal brought the naval forces of each side into play. These naval clashes were related to the Guadalcanal fighting, but also had an importance of their own.

Map 1: Savo Island

A Japanese cruiser force under Vice-Admiral Mikawa was despatched on 8 August 1942, to attack the transports of the Guadalcanal landings. On the night of 8/9 August it encountered an Allied cruiser force under Rear-Admiral Crutchley. The Japanese were expertly trained and equipped for night fighting. The Allied force, being a composite one, was hampered by having no common doctrine or weapons system. Between 0100 hours and 0230 on the 9th, Mikawa's force treated the Allies, split into Northern and Southern Groups, to a dazzling display of night fighting. Avoiding the Allied destroyers *Blue* and *Ralph Talbot*, Mikawa pounced on the

cruisers *Chicago* and *Canberra*, damaging both, the *Canberra* beyond repair. Turning north-east at 0138 he encountered the cruisers *Vincennes*, *Quincy*, and *Astoria*. These, too, were disabled beyond hope. The Japanese force then retired leaving four cruisers sinking. But in spite of the skill shown in this action Mikawa had failed to achieve his objective – the destruction of the invasion transports.

Map 2: The Battle of the Eastern Solomons

On 23 August 1942, an attempt to run supplies to the Japanese forces on Guadalcanal was intercepted by Task Force 61 (carriers *Saratoga*, *Enterprise*, and *Wasp*) under Vice-Admiral Fletcher. The Japanese transports were supported by a diversionary group (carrier *Ryujo*) under Hara, and a Striking Force (carriers *Zuikaku* and *Shokaku*) under Nagumo.

A strike by Fletcher on the 23rd was avoided by reversing course, but on the 24th the *Ryujo* was sighted by US search planes. A strike was launched against her, but at that moment other spotter planes sighted the *Zuikaku* and *Shokaku*. Fletcher tried to divert the strike, but communication difficulties prevented this. Only a few aircraft from the *Enterprise* located and attacked the *Shokaku*, and the main strike hit the *Ryujo*, sinking her by 1550 hours. But by 1630 hours a strike from Nagumo's carriers had found the *Enterprise*, and by 1641 had hit her. Though disabled she could still recover her aircraft. At the end of the 24th both carrier forces retired, but the

Japanese Transport Group continued to head for its destination. On the 25th, Marine dive-bombers from Henderson Field discovered them, and hit the *Kinryu Maru* and the *Jintsu*. Later Flying Fortress bombers sunk the destroyer *Mutsuki*.

The Battle of the Eastern Solomons showed the Japanese the impossibility of daytime runs to reinforce Guadalcanal. The 'Tokyo Night Express' was resumed from Bougainville.

Map 3: The Battle of Cape Esperance

Another cruiser night action was fought on the night of 11/12 October 1942. An American force, under Rear-Admiral Scott, had orders to cover and escort a supply convoy to Guadalcanal, and also to ambush any Japanese naval forces approaching down the 'slot' (the narrow channel between the Eastern and Western Solomons). On the 11th Scott received news of a Japanese supply convoy moving down the slot, covered by Rear-Admiral Goto's cruiser squadron. He moved to intercept them and, at 2325 hours, the cruiser *Helena* made radar contact with the Japanese force at a range of about 14 miles. She failed to report this to Scott, who, assuming he had missed the enemy, decided to reverse course at 2332 hours. This manoeuvre dislocated his force, and at the same moment he learnt of Goto's approach. During the turn, the destroyer *Duncan* had made radar contact with the enemy and had attacked on her own initiative. At 2346 the *Helena* opened fire on the Japanese

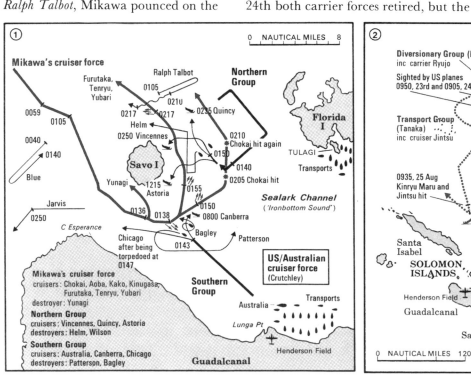

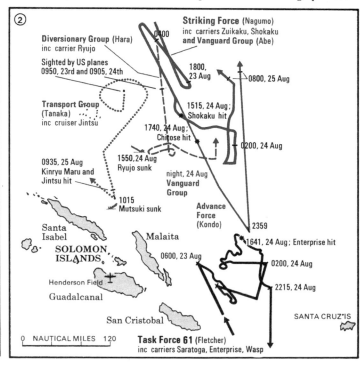

cruisers, quickly followed by the other US cruisers. Because the turn had placed destroyers between the cruisers' guns and the enemy, Scott ordered a ceasefire, but this order was ignored for long enough for the cruisers *Furutaka* and *Aoba* to be seriously hit, and for the destroyer *Fubuki* to be sunk. The Japanese cruiser *Kinugasa*, however, with her attendant destroyer *Hatsuyuki*, had turned to port on contact with the US squadron, avoiding the US cruisers' broadside. They encountered the lone *Duncan* and left her a burning hulk.

The Japanese force was now retreating, and Scott pursued them for another half hour. During the pursuit the US cruiser *Boise* was damaged by gunfire from the *Aoba*, and Scott broke off the pursuit at 0028 hours.

Cape Esperance left the Americans under the misapprehension that they had mastered the Japanese at night fighting. Goto's force had been unalert, and had failed to use their most potent weapon – the torpedo. The American tactical dispositions had been poor, but the most important aspect of Cape Esperance had been the surprise achieved by the US force – surprise made possible by the use of radar.

Map 4: The Battle of Santa Cruz

In October 1942 the Japanese launched an offensive under General Maruyama against the US Marines on Guadalcanal (see previous pages). To synchronize with this the Japanese combined fleet was to move to the north of Guadalcanal to fly aircraft to Henderson Field as soon as it was recaptured. The US Task Forces 16 and 17 (carriers *Hornet* and *Enterprise*) were ordered to sweep the area around the Santa Cruz islands, and to intercept any Japanese forces making for Guadalcanal.

At 1200 hours on 25 October an American flying-boat spotted two Japanese aircraft carriers, but a strike launched from the US carriers failed to find its target. On the 26th, however, both sides were alert. Nagumo, in command of the Japanese carrier group (the lessons of Midway still in his mind) launched his first strike at 0659 hours and immediately struck down the lifts to prepare the next strike. At this moment one of his carriers, the *Zuiho*, was attacked and put out of action by two of the *Enterprise* dive bombers. These had located the Japanese carriers at 0640 hours, and at 0730 a full strike was launched from both the *Hornet* and the *Enterprise*. Both US and Japanese strikes were in the air simultaneously, and, indeed, encountered each other on their way. At 0915 the first Japanese strike attacked the *Hornet*, hitting her with two torpedoes and six bombs. Meanwhile, at 0930 hours, the *Shokaku* was seriously hit, by US dive bombers. A second Japanese strike hit the *Enterprise*, damaging her flight deck and lift, but leaving her speed unimpaired.

With both his carriers hit, the US Admiral, Kinkaid, ordered a withdrawal, the *Hornet* abandoned and burning.

Undoubtedly a Japanese success, Santa Cruz was a Pyrrhic victory. The cost in irreplaceable air crews had been too high. Although unhit, the *Zuikaku* was virtually out of action through air crew losses. Over 100 experienced pilots had been lost.

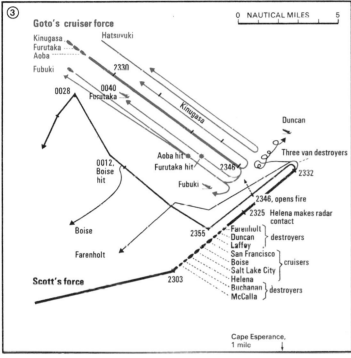

③ Goto's cruiser force

0 NAUTICAL MILES 5

Kinugasa
Furutaka
Aoba
Hatsuyuki
Fubuki
2330
0028
0040 Furutaka
0012, Boise hit
Kinugasa
Duncan
Three van destroyers
Aoba hit
Furutaka hit
2346
Fubuki
2332
2346, opens fire
2325 Helena makes radar contact
Boise
2355
Farenholt
Duncan } destroyers
Laffey
San Francisco
Boise } cruisers
Salt Lake City
Helena
Buchanan } destroyers
McCalla
Scott's force
2303

Cape Esperance, 1 mile

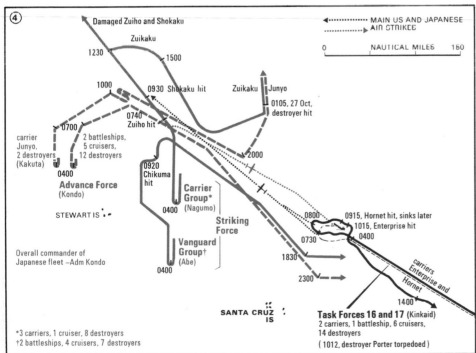

④ Damaged Zuiho and Shokaku

◀······· MAIN US AND JAPANESE
······▶ AIR STRIKES

Zuikaku
1230
1500
1000
0930 Shokaku hit
Zuikaku Junyo
0105, 27 Oct, destroyer hit
0740 Zuiho hit
0700
2 battleships, 5 cruisers, 12 destroyers
carrier Junyo, 2 destroyers (Kakuta)
0400
2000
Advance Force (Kondo)
STEWART IS
0920 Chikuma hit
0400
Carrier Group* (Nagumo)
Striking Force
Vanguard Group† (Abe)
0400
0800
0915, Hornet hit, sinks later
1015, Enterprise hit
0730
0400
Overall commander of Japanese fleet –Adm Kondo
1830
2300
carriers Enterprise and Hornet
1400

0 NAUTICAL MILES 160

SANTA CRUZ IS
Task Forces 16 and 17 (Kinkaid)
2 carriers, 1 battleship, 6 cruisers, 14 destroyers
(1012, destroyer Porter torpedoed)

*3 carriers, 1 cruiser, 8 destroyers
†2 battleships, 4 cruisers, 7 destroyers

143

THE NAVAL ACTIONS OFF GUADALCANAL

In November 1942, when both sides were reinforcing their ground troops on Guadalcanal, the covering naval forces again clashed. On 12 November, eleven destroyers under Admiral Tanaka accompanied eleven transports containing 13,000 men to Guadalcanal. To cover this operation a strong group under Vice-Admiral Abe (two battleships, two cruisers, and fourteen destroyers) was sent to shell Henderson Field. Meanwhile the main Japanese carrier force moved to the north of the Solomons to provide air cover. At the same time US reinforcements arrived at Guadalcanal escorted by five cruisers and eight destroyers under Rear-Admiral Callaghan.

Learning of the approach of Abe's group, Callaghan moved to intercept relying on surprise to offset his marked inferiority. The US carrier force (under Kinkaid) was too far to the south to support. Callaghan possessed radar, and should have achieved surprise with ease. However, this priceless asset was misused, and both forces blundered into each other in the darkness at 0141 hours. A confused and violent action followed (**Map 1**). After 36 minutes both sides broke off the engagement leaving the Japanese battleship *Hiei* helpless, two of their cruisers sunk (*Akatsuki* and *Yudachi*), and all the remaining Japanese vessels damaged. The Americans had lost two cruisers sunk (*Juneau* and *Atlanta*), four destroyers (*Cushing*, *Barton*, *Aaron Ward*, and *Laffey*), and all remaining ships save one were damaged. Callaghan was killed.

This costly action prevented the Japanese reinforcements from landing, and averted the bombardment of Henderson Field. The *Hiei* was sunk on the following morning by torpedo bombers from Kinkaid's carrier *Enterprise*.

On 13 November, air activity by both sides was intense. Tanaka again started south with his transports, and during the morning of the 14th seven of these were sunk by US aircraft, along with two accompanying cruisers under Admiral Mikawa. Tanaka persevered, however, and to cover him Admiral Kondo, with the battleship *Kirishima*, four cruisers, and nine destroyers, raced southwards.

To intercept Kondo the US Task Force 64 (two battleships and four destroyers under Admiral Lee) moved up to the sound between Savo Island and Guadalcanal (**Map 2**).

At 2210 hours on the 14th a Japanese scouting group under Hashimoto, sighted Task Force 64, and the cruiser *Sendai* shadowed it. At 2300 the radar of the US ships located the *Sendai*, and at 2316 the two US battleships, *Washington* and *South Dakota*, opened fire. In the ensuing exchange the US destroyers *Preston* and *Walke* were quickly sunk, and the remaining two damaged. Shortly afterwards the *South Dakota* was hit, causing a power failure, and successfully putting her out of action. It became a battle between the *Washington* and fourteen Japanese ships. Concentrating her radar controlled guns on the *Kirishima* the *Washington* quickly sank the Japanese ship along with her attendant destroyer. The *Washington* pursued the now retreating Japanese until 0035 hours, but inflicted no further damage.

Although with almost incredible persistence Tanaka had succeeded in putting ashore some reinforcements on Guadalcanal, this was the last serious Japanese attempt to reinforce the garrison. Control of the seas around Guadalcanal passed to the Americans. While the Japanese may have given up hope of reinforcing the Guadalcanal garrison, they had no intention of abandoning it. On 30 November Tanaka and the 'Tokyo Night Express' again made a supply run to Guadalcanal. The Japanese 2nd Destroyer Flotilla, eight destroyers under Tanaka, was encountered at the entrance of Ironbottom Sound by Rear-Admiral Wright with five cruisers and seven destroyers (**Map 3**). At 2306 hours on the 30th, Wright's force made radar contact with the Japanese. But Wright instead of allowing his leading destroyers to engage the unsuspecting Japanese with torpedoes, hesitated and allowed the opportunity to pass. Then he ordered his cruisers to engage the Japanese with gunfire. The flashes alerted the Japanese, and their expert crews made ready their battle stations while the whole force was turning to engage the Americans. During this turn the outlying destroyer *Takanami* was sunk by American gunfire. The turn complete the Japanese destroyers launched torpedoes against the American ships. One cruiser was sunk and three more seriously damaged, with the loss of 400 killed.

Tassafaronga was a resounding tribute to the Japanese superiority at night fighting, and illustrated that the Americans still had to master the tool that was eventually to give them complete tactical superiority – radar.

Below left: A US naval task force in the Solomons

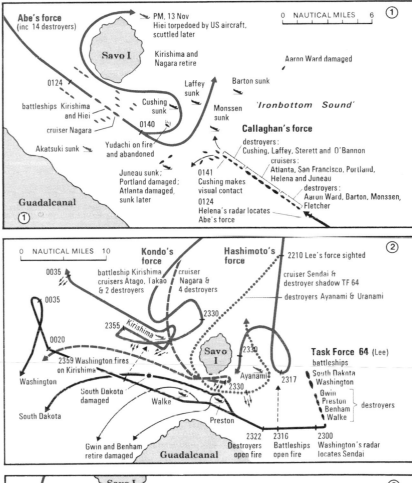

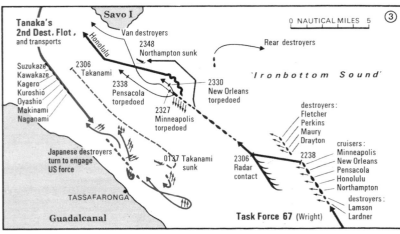

NEW GUINEA

The collapse of the Japanese attempt to capture Port Moresby from the sea (see Battle of the Coral Sea) forced them to attempt its capture overland. On the night of 21/22 July 1942, Japanese troops of the Eighteenth Army under Major-General Horii landed on the northern coast of Papua at Buna. Immediately they struck west over the Owen Stanley range by the Kokoda trail (**Map 1**). Fighting tenaciously, the Australian/US opposition, under Major-General Hering, was pushed back until, by 12 August, Horii had captured the main pass over the Owen Stanleys. Australian resistance increased, and by 26 September, although Horii was within 30 miles of Port Moresby, the efforts of Hering's men, and local Allied air superiority, brought the Japanese to a halt.

Partly under Allied pressure, and partly in response to orders from above, Horii began the long retreat over the Owen Stanleys, followed by an Australian division and a US division. By November Horii had fallen back on strong defensive positions in the Buna-Gona area, where he had landed. The Allied forces were racked by disease, exhausted, and, although learning fast, were untrained in jungle warfare. At first the Buna defences were too much for them, but on 9 December Gona was stormed by the Australians, and in January 1943, after an appalling fight, Buna too was captured.

The Allied success along the Kokoda trail left their forces in the New Guinea area in a position to form the left wing of a two-pronged encircling movement to isolate the Japanese at Rabaul. But first New Guinea itself had to be cleared. From January to December 1943, a series of small scale but brilliantly contrived combined operations were mounted against the Japanese in New Guinea (**Map 2**).

In January, 1943, a brigade of General Hering's New Guinea Force was airlifted to Wau, 30 miles west of Salamaua, and established a forward

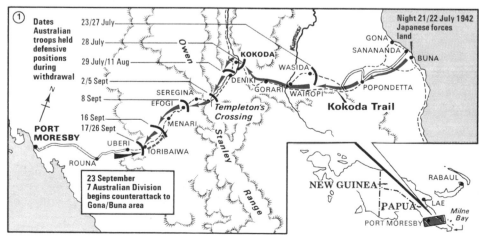

base to threaten the Japanese base there. Meanwhile General MacArthur, Allied C-in-C South West Pacific, built up his forces for an offensive.

By June the Allied forces were ready. An American amphibious landing on the 29/30th threatened Salamaua, which was simultaneously threatened from Wau by 17 Australian Brigade. These forces maintained their threatening posture in front of Salamaua until September when, on the 4th, 9 Australian Division landed to the east of Lae. At the same time US paratroops were dropped at Nadzab, and 7 Australian Division was airlifted to support them. All these forces made a converging attack on Lae, while the Allied troops investing Salamaua also took the offensive. Salamaua was taken on the 12th and Lae on the 16th.

During the rest of September and October, the new Allied commander of the New Guinea force, the Australian General Sir Thomas Blamey, thrust west and east to encircle the Huon Peninsula. With additional landings by US forces on the north coast of the peninsula, this encirclement was complete by April 1944.

The way was now clear to isolate, defeat, and most important to destroy the airfields of the remaining Japanese forces in New Guinea. From April to July 1944, the Hollandia operation was carried out, and it was among the most brilliant operations of the war. One after another the Japanese bases were isolated and destroyed. The fighting was never on a large scale, but co-operation between land, sea, and air on the Allied side was superb. By July 1944 an entire Japanese army in New Guinea had been isolated and neutralized.

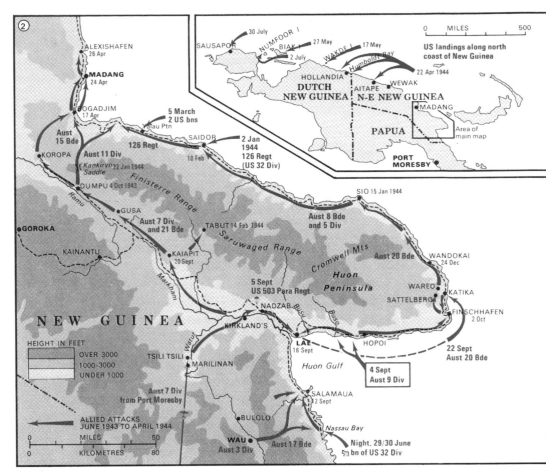

Opposite: Australian troops advance against a Japanese position

Right: US paratroops landing on Numfoor island

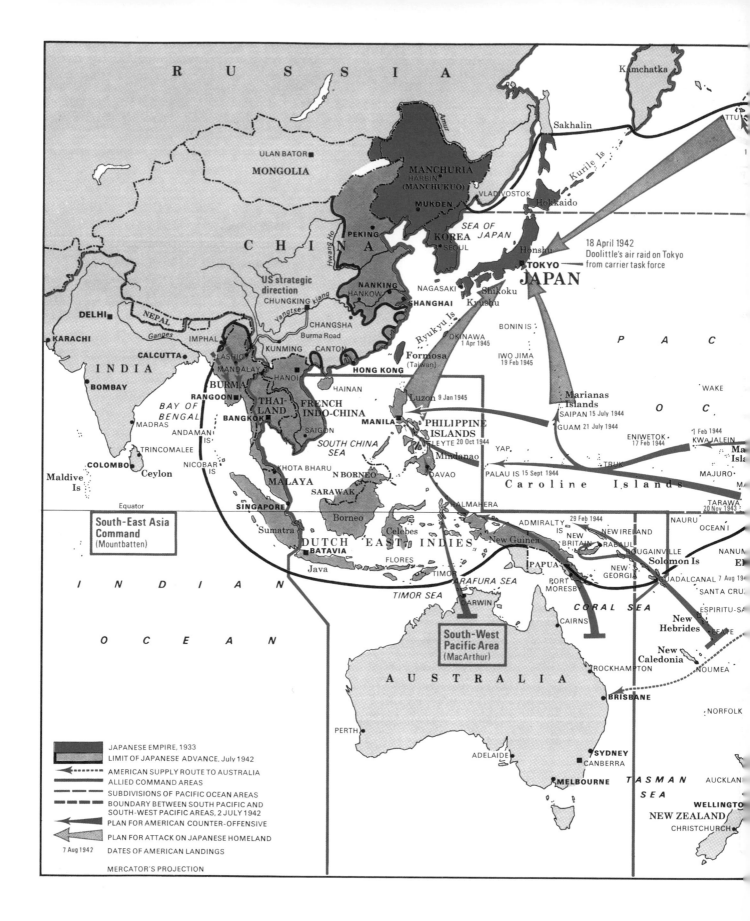

18 April 1942
Doolittle's air raid on Tokyo
from carrier task force

South-East Asia
Command
(Mountbatten)

South-West
Pacific Area
(MacArthur)

US strategic
direction

JAPANESE EMPIRE, 1933
LIMIT OF JAPANESE ADVANCE, July 1942
AMERICAN SUPPLY ROUTE TO AUSTRALIA
ALLIED COMMAND AREAS
SUBDIVISIONS OF PACIFIC OCEAN AREAS
BOUNDARY BETWEEN SOUTH PACIFIC AND
SOUTH-WEST PACIFIC AREAS, 2 JULY 1942
PLAN FOR AMERICAN COUNTER-OFFENSIVE
PLAN FOR ATTACK ON JAPANESE HOMELAND
7 Aug 1942   DATES OF AMERICAN LANDINGS

MERCATOR'S PROJECTION

Pacific Area

Pacific Ocean Areas
(Nimitz)

Hawaiian Is
OAHU
PEARL HARBOR
HAWAII

PALMYRA

CHRISTMAS

JARVIS
MALDEN
Phoenix Is
VICTORIA
okelau Is
CAROLINE
SUVOROV
Samoa Is
TAHITI
Cook Is
Society Is
onga Is
RAROTONGA
TUBUAI

Pacific Area
(ey, Halsey later)

DEC IS
(Sunda)

PLANNING THE US COUNTER OFFENSIVE

After the Allies had isolated Rabaul and cleared the south-west Pacific, a spirited argument developed as to where best to attack the Japanese next. At the back of the planners' minds was always the dread that, sooner or later, they would have to contemplate the invasion of the Japanese homelands themselves.

Two schools of thought arose. The first, supported by Admirals Nimitz and King, advocated a thrust straight at the weakest point of the Japanese conquests, the islands that linked Japan proper with South-East Asia – Formosa and the Ryukyus. Possession of these would place the Allies athwart the Japanese Empire, cutting it in half, and, most important of all, cutting off Japan proper from all its sources of raw materials, food, and fuel.

The second school of thought, led by General MacArthur, advocated a move up from the south-west, liberating the occupied territories as a major objective in themselves.

The dispute between these two views was not simply a straightforward service wrangle. If anything it was the outcome of intense personal rivalry between MacArthur and King. Strategically, the Formosa plan was unquestionably superior, and it speaks volumes for MacArthur's personality and tenacity that the compromise eventually arranged by President Roosevelt heavily favoured the MacArthur Philippine plan.

Whichever course was adopted, the price was going to be high. Japan's delusive hope was that the Allies, and particularly America, would expend their strength at great cost against the jungle-clad island fortresses on the perimeter of their empire, and, becoming discouraged, sue for a negotiated peace. No such considerations occurred to the Allies, however. Operations in the Far East and Pacific, while still to some extent held back by the 'Germany First' policy, were aimed at the defeat and unconditional surrender of Japan.

Right: Japanese troops patrolling on Guam before the US counterattack began

THE BATTLE FOR THE SOLOMONS

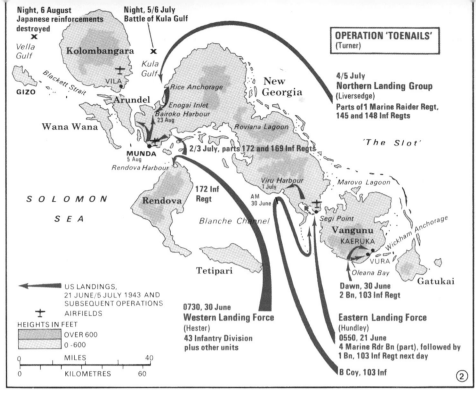

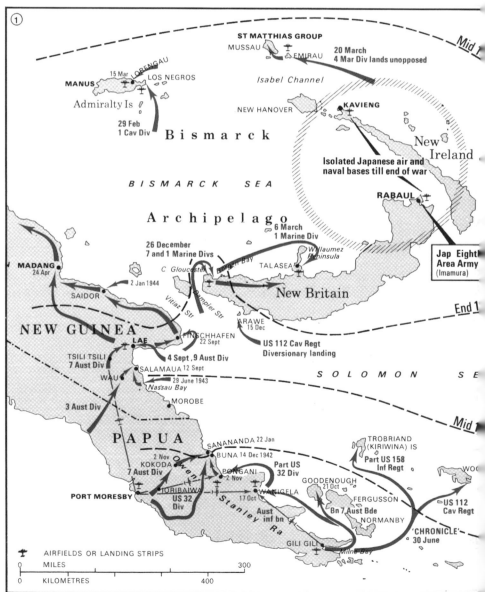

The drive through the Solomons was a preview of how the whole of the Pacific island war was to be waged (**Map 1**); a series of outflanking operations to secure the key airbases, followed by two or three month build-up for the next 'hop'. The inset map shows the Elkton Plan to surround and neutralize the Japanese forces in the Solomons and New Guinea. The advance up the Solomons was to form the right hand of its two pincers.

The two key islands to the Solomons campaign were New Georgia (**Map 2**) and Bougainville (**Map 3**). Successful landings on these would isolate the Japanese on the more northerly islands, and put commanding air bases into Allied hands.

Between February and June 1943, preparations were in hand for an attack on New Georgia. In February the Russell Islands were seized, and in June Rendova Island, within artillery range of New Georgia, was captured.

On 2 July, US 43 Division and part of 37, supported by a naval task force, landed at Munda on the western end of New Georgia. Other small units had already established footholds in the east. Under the command of Major-General Hester the US troops attacked the Japanese base at Munda, encountering savage opposition. On 25 July, US 25 Division was thrown into the fight, and the Allied force, now commanded by Major-General Griswold captured the airfield on 5 August. By the 25th all resistance in New Georgia was at an end.

Also during August a US combat team landed on Vella Lavella, north-west of New Georgia (**Map 1**), to establish a base there, outflanking the Japanese on Kolombangara. In mid-September New Zealand troops cleared the remainder of Vella Lavella and the Japanese were compelled to withdraw from Kolombangara.

By October the next stage of the Allied thrust was ready. On 27 October, a feint assault on the island of

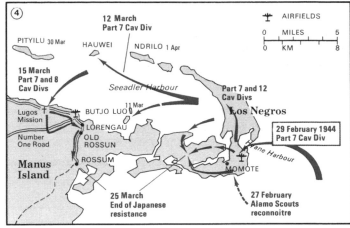

Map 3 (top left):

US BEACH-HEAD NIGHT, 1 NOVEMBER
FRONT LINES AT DATES SHOWN
AIRFIELDS UNDER CONSTRUCTION

MILES 4
KILOMETRES 6

③

Laruma
Numa Numa
Trail

Trails defended by
parts Jap 23 Inf Regt

26 Nov
Koromokina
Piva
Piva
Fields
'Hellzapoppin'
Ridge
East-West Trail
37 Div
7 Nov
1 Nov
3 Marine Div
5 Nov
Part Jap 23 Inf Regt
15 Dec
Torokina

0400/0600, 7 Nov
Part Jap 17 Div
from Rabaul.
Eliminated 8 Nov

PURUATA I

Cape Torokina
Opened
9 Dec

3 Raider Bn

0722, 1 November 1943
'CHERRYBLOSSOM'
3 Marine Div (Turnage)

Empress Augusta Bay

Map 4 (top right):

④

AIRFIELDS
MILES 0 5
KM 0 8

12 March
Part 7 Cav Div

PITYILU 30 Mar
HAUWEI
NDRILO 1 Apr

15 March
Part 7 and 8
Cav Divs

Seeadler Harbour

Part 7 and 12
Cav Divs

Los Negros

Lugos
Mission
11 Mar
BUTJO LUO
LORENGAU
OLD
ROSSUN
ROSSUM

29 February 1944
Part 7 Cav Div

Number
One Road

Manus
Island

MOMOTE

Jane Harbour

25 March
End of Japanese
resistance

27 February
Alamo Scouts
reconnoitre

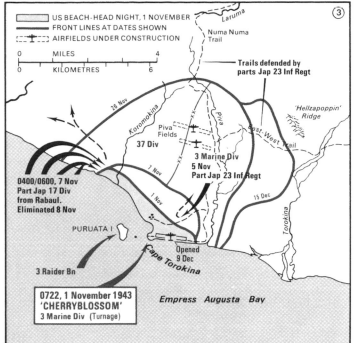

Map 2 (Elkton Plan):

KAVIENG
Operation 'CARTWHEEL'
RABAUL

NEW
GUINEA
PAPUA

SOLOMON ISLANDS
Jap Seventeenth
Army (Hyakutake)

LAE
Jap Eighteenth
Army (Adachi)

PORT
MORESBY

Command boundary

GUADALCANAL

Milne Bay

South-west
Pacific Area
(MacArthur)

South Pacific
Area
(Halsey)

AUSTRALIA

Final 'Elkton Plan' (26 April 1943)

Map 1 (Solomon Islands):

Bougainville
Tenekau
Kieta
Augusta
Bay
Kara
Kahlli
BIUN
SHORTLAND
IS
'LOSSOM'
iv

15 February
3 NZ Div
BUKA

'BLISSFUL' (diversion for 'Cherryblossom')
28 October
2 Mar Para Bn
(withdraws 3 Nov)
VOZA

PACIFIC OCEAN

SOLOMON
ISLANDS

FAURO
TREASURY IS

The Slot

Choiseul
SAGIGAI

'GOODTIME'
27 October
8 NZ Bde Group

VELLA
LAVELLA

KOLOMBANGARA
4 July
15 Aug
MUNDA
New
Georgia
13 Aug
VANGUNI

(New Georgia Sound)

Santa Isabel

RENDOVA

'TOENAILS'
30 June
US 43 Inf Div

RUSSELL IS
BANIKA
FLORIDA
IS

Malaita

PAVUVU
'CLEANSLATE'
21 February 1943
US assault bns

Henderson
Field

1942

Guadalcanal
7 Aug 1942/7 Feb 1943

San
Cristobal

Choiseul (Operation Blissful), obscured the real objective, Bougainville. On 27 October New Zealand troops had captured Treasury Island (**Map 1**).

On 1 November, US 3 Marine Division went ashore at Empress Augusta Bay (**Map 3**). By the end of the year, in spite of Japanese counterattacks, the Americans held a defensive perimeter ten miles wide and five miles deep, and had made Augusta Bay into a naval base with three operating airstrips. The eastern arm of the Elkton Plan was complete.

The western arm depended on the clearing of New Guinea and Papua (see New Guinea), and the occupation of the Admiralty and St Matthias groups. The New Guinea campaign in 1943 had captured and cleared the small islands of Trobriand and Woodlark in the Solomon Sea, and landings had been effected on the western tip of New Britain.

On 29 February 1944, a reconnaissance in force by US 1 Cavalry Division swiftly became an invasion of Los Negros in the Admiralty group (**Map 4**). Two more US divisions were landed during the first two weeks of March, and by 25 March all Japanese resistance was at an end. At the same time US 1 Marine Division had landed on the northern coast of New Britain, and units of Fortieth Army and 1 Marine Division moved along the coast to join up with them (**Map 1**).

Thus by the end of March 1944 the pincers of the Elkton Plan were complete. The Japanese bases on New Britain and New Ireland remained isolated till the end of the war.

CLEARING THE MARSHALLS

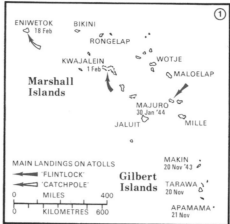

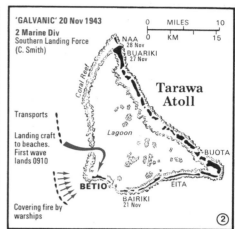

While MacArthur's forces in the South-West Pacific were completing the encirclement of Rabaul (previous pages), the drive against the Japanese in the West Central Pacific was proceeding under Admiral Nimitz.

Between January and October 1943, men, ships, and aircraft in enormous numbers began to assemble in Hawaii, the Fijis, and the New Hebrides. By October Nimitz could deploy the Fifth Fleet (Vice-Admiral Spruance) comprising seven battleships, seven heavy and three light cruisers, eight carriers, and thirty-four destroyers; the Fifth Amphibious Force (Turner) carrying more than 100,000 troops; and the V Amphibious Corps (Major-General 'Howling Mad' Smith). In addition to naval air cover, Nimitz could call on the Seventh Army Air Force (Major-General Hale) operating from the Ellice Islands. Also, after the completion of the Solomons operation, he had the naval and marine elements that had previously comprised Halsey's Third Fleet.

Nimitz's first target was the Gilbert Islands, to provide bases for the next step, the capture of the Marshall Islands (**Map 1**). Possession of these two atoll groups would put him in a position to threaten the Japanese naval base at Truk. In the Gilberts, the Japanese defences were based on the two largest atolls, Makin and Tarawa.

From 13–20 November Makin and Tarawa were thoroughly strafed by Army Air Force bombers, and then subjected to heavy naval gunfire. Between 20 and 23 November the atoll of Makin was cleared and occupied with little difficulty. The main US losses were, in fact, incurred at sea where the carrier *Liscombe Bay* was sunk by a Japanese submarine.

Tarawa, however, was another matter. The atoll was a roughly triangular string of small islands and coral reefs (**Map 2**). The main Japanese stronghold was Betio (**Map 3**), a flat, sandy 300-acre

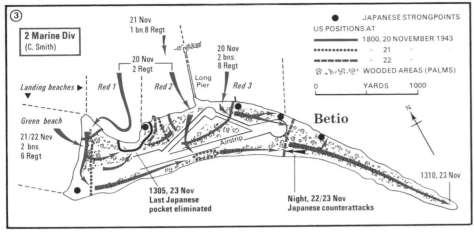

3

2 Marine Div
(C. Smith)

21 Nov
1 bn,8 Regt

20 Nov
2 Regt

20 Nov
2 bns,
8 Regt

◄ Landing beaches ▶ Red 1   Red 2   Long Pier   Red 3

Green beach

21/22 Nov
2 bns,
6 Regt

● JAPANESE STRONGPOINTS
US POSITIONS AT
——— 1800, 20 NOVEMBER 1943
•••••••••• 21 "
— — — 22 "
WOODED AREAS (PALMS)

0   YARDS   1000

N

Betio

Airstrip

1305, 23 Nov
Last Japanese
pocket eliminated

Night, 22/23 Nov
Japanese counterattacks

1310, 23 Nov

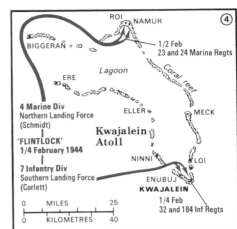

4

ROI   NAMUR

BIGGERAN

1/2 Feb
23 and 24 Marine Regts

ERE   Lagoon   Coral reef

4 Marine Div
Northern Landing Force
(Schmidt)   ELLER   MECK

'FLINTLOCK'
1/4 February 1944   Kwajalein
                              Atoll
7 Infantry Div
Southern Landing Force   NINNI   LOI
(Corlett)

                              ENUBUJ
                              KWAJALEIN
0   MILES   25   1/4 Feb
                              32 and 184 Inf Regts
0   KILOMETRES   40

island, honeycombed with underground shelters, pillboxes, and strong points. Insufficient US reconnaissance had failed to reveal that the inner coral reef of Betio itself was too shallow to allow landing craft to approach.

Despite the heavy preliminary bombardment, when the assault waves of 2 Marine Division went in on 20 November, they encountered intense resistance from the Japanese garrison under Rear-Admiral Shibasaki. Most of the landing craft grounded on the inner reef and the Marines were compelled to wade several hundred yards under intense criss-cross fire. By nightfall on the 20th, 1,500 of the 5,000 Marines put ashore were casualties. During the night, tanks, guns, and ammunition were landed, and, during the 21st and 22nd, inch-by-inch frontal assaults drove the Japanese back. Most of the defenders were killed in a suicidal counterattack on the night of the 22nd, and on the 23rd the last pocket of Japanese resistance on Betio was eliminated. Of the 4,700 Japanese on the island only 100 were taken prisoner (of these only 17 were combat troops). The rest were dead. The Marines lost nearly 1,000 dead and over 2,000 wounded.

Safely installed in the Gilberts, the US forces were, by February 1944, ready to tackle their next target, the Marshalls. Here the centre of the Japanese defences was Kwajalein Atoll (**Map 4**), a large, spread-out lagoon with small islands at its northern and southern ends. Operation Flintlock was carried out by 4 Marine Division under Schmidt, and 7 Infantry Division under Corlett. They were carried by Turner's Fifth Amphibious Force, and Admiral Mitscher's East Carrier Task Force swept ahead of them to neutralize Japanese air power in the Marshalls. On 1 and 2 February, 23 and 24 Marine Regiments landed on Roi and Namur at the north end of the lagoon. At the same time 32 and 184 Infantry

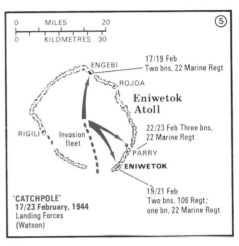

5

0   MILES   20
0   KILOMETRES   30

ENGEBI

17/19 Feb
Two bns, 22 Marine Regt

ROJOA

Eniwetok
Atoll

RIGILI   Invasion
         fleet   22/23 Feb Three bns,
                                  22 Marine Regt

                                  PARRY

'CATCHPOLE'   ENIWETOK
17/23 February, 1944
Landing Forces   19/21 Feb
(Watson)   Two bns, 106 Regt;
                                  one bn, 22 Marine Regt

Regiments tackled Kwajalein itself. The Japanese garrisons fought to the death in both places, but, learning from the lessons of Tarawa, the US forces were able to overrun them with relatively few losses (372 dead out of 41,000 landed). Of 8,000 Japanese troops 7,870 were killed.

The final step in the Marshalls campaign was the capture of Eniwetok Atoll, to the north-west of Kwajalein. Turner's Amphibious Force again put the Marines ashore. On 17 February, two battalions of the 22 Marine Regiment landed on Engebi (**Map 5**), encountering little opposition. But on 19 and 22 February, further battalions of 22 Regiment, and two battalions of 106 Infantry Regiment were landed on Eniwetok and Parry islands. The Japanese garrisons fought desperately and to the death. All 2,000 defenders were killed.

Left: US Marines in action in the jungle

CLEARING THE MARIANAS

Some 1,000 miles to the north-west of the Marshalls lay the next objective of Nimitz's trans-Pacific drive – the Mariana Islands. The main Japanese defences here rested on three large islands, Saipan and Tinian (**Map 1**), and Guam (**Map 2**). Again Turner's Fifth Amphibious Force, 530 warships and auxiliaries carrying over 127,000 troops of 'Howling Mad' Smith's V Amphibious Corps, rendezvoused off Eniwetok Atoll. Ahead of it, Mitscher's Task Force 58 had softened up the island defences of Saipan destroying 200 Japanese aircraft and twelve or more cargo ships.

On 15 June Turner's force arrived off Saipan. They faced the Japanese Thirty-first Army, under the overall command of Admiral Nagumo. Landings by 2 and 4 Marine Divisions on eight beaches were hotly contested, but by nightfall a beachhead had been established. Heavy resistance, however, compelled Smith to commit the 27 Infantry Division on the 17th, and the departure of his naval support on the 19th to take part in the Battle of the Philippine Sea hampered his operations still further. Not until 9 July did Japanese resistance end, after a Japanese counterattack on 7 July had been wiped out by 4 Marine Division.

Casualties on Saipan were high. 3,126 US dead, and 27,000 Japanese dead – virtually the whole garrison.

From 9 July to 24, 2 and 4 Marine Divisions reorganized themselves for the assault on Tinian. Again the Japanese fought furiously, expending enormous numbers on suicidal counter-attacks. By 31 July the island had been cleared from north to south.

On 21 July, 3 Marine and 77 Army Divisions landed on Guam, supplemented by 1 Marine Brigade. Two landings were made, north and south of the Orote Peninsula. After a struggle, costing 1,400 US killed and 10,000 Japanese killed, the island fell.

Opposite: Japanese dead and a wrecked tank on Saipan

Below: US Marines landing on the beach of Guam

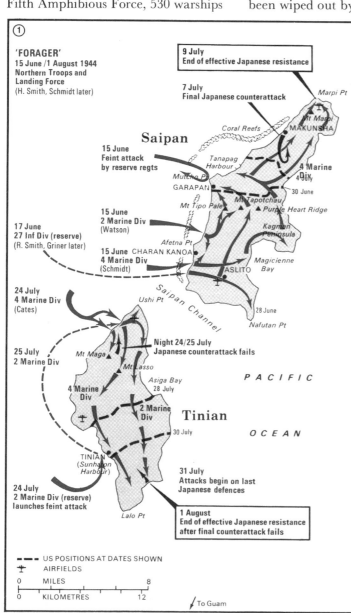

'FORAGER'
21 July/10 August 1944
Southern Troops and
Landing Force
(Geiger)

10 August
End of effective
Japanese resistance

ACIFIC OCEAN

0829, 21 July
3 Marine Div
(Turnage)

0830, 21 July
1 Prov Marine
Bde (Shepherd)
Followed later by
77 Inf Div (reserve)
(Bruce)

Mt Machanao

1 Marine Bde
FINAGUAYAC

Pati Pt

TAGUAC

UPI

LULOG

3 Marine
Div

6 Aug

Mt Santa Rosa

Tumon
Bay

DEDEDO

77 Inf Div

Asan Pt

Adelup Pt

Mt Barrigada

CABRAS I

ASAN

AGANA

1 Aug

Piti Navy Yard

Orote
Peninsula
29 July

Mt Chachao

Mt Alutom

Apra Harbour

Mt Tenjo

Guam

AGAT

Bangi Pt

Mt Alifan

Coral Reef

Mt Lamlan

MATA

INARAJAN

UMATAC

Aiavan
Pt

JAPANESE COUNTERATTACKS
ON NIGHT OF 25/26 JULY

AIRFIELD

0   MILES   10

0   KILOMETRES   15

Last Japanese soldier surrendered in 1972

THE BATTLE OF THE PHILIPPINE SEA

After the capture of the Marshalls, the next US objective was of such strategic importance that the Japanese could not let it go unchallenged. Possession of the Marianas would put the US in a position to cut the homeland of Japan off from the Philippines and her other South-East Asian possessions. When the US assault fell upon the Marianas (previous pages), the Japanese First Mobile Fleet under Ozawa, and a Southern Force under Ugaki, were sent to give battle. US submarines reported the rendezvous of these groups on 16 June, and the US Task Force 58, under Mitscher, was prepared to meet Ozawa (**Map 1**). The US force totalled seven heavy and eight light carriers, seven battleships, eight heavy and thirteen light cruisers, and sixty-nine destroyers. To oppose this the Japanese had only five heavy and four light carriers, five battleships, eleven heavy and two light cruisers, and twenty-eight destroyers.

Early on June 19, Ozawa's scouting planes spotted Mitscher's force and immediately, at 0830 hours, strike aircraft were launched (**Map 2**). Further strikes were launched at 0900 hours. However, the US radar gave warning of the approach of these aircraft, and fighters were sent up to intercept them fully 50 miles before they reached the US fleet. More than 200 aircraft were shot down, eliminating Ozawa's first strike. Meanwhile US submarines had located Ozawa's force and had attacked. At 0905 hours the carrier *Taiho* was torpedoed and sunk, and at 1220 hours the *Shokaku* was also hit,

sinking finally at 1624 hours. A second strike by Ozawa at 1400 hours was misdirected, and was intercepted by US fighters on its way to Guam. By nightfall the battle was over. So heavy had the Japanese air losses been that the US crewmen dubbed the battle 'The Great Marianas Turkey Shoot'. Two carriers and over 300 aircraft had been lost, against some thirty US aircraft and slight damage to a battleship.

On the 20th (**Map 3**) Mitscher pursued Ozawa's force, but did not make contact until the afternoon. At 1624 hours he launched a strike which, at 1844 hours, sunk the carrier *Hiyo* and two oilers. Twenty US aircraft were lost, and Ozawa lost a further sixty-five. Realizing the magnitude of his defeat, he retired hastily towards Okinawa.

The Battle of the Philippine Sea dealt irreparable damage to Japanese sea power. Not only the loss of carriers and aircraft, but the loss of over 460 irreplaceable trained aircrews, was crippling.

Opposite: A near miss on a US carrier during the Battle of the Philippine Sea

Below: US sailors watch a Japanese aircraft crash into the sea

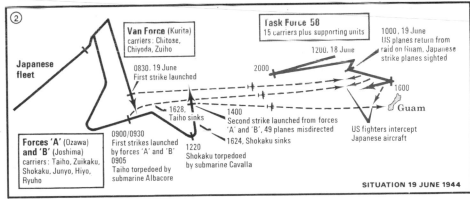

② Japanese fleet

Van Force (Kurita)
carriers: Chitose,
Chiyoda, Zuiho

Task Force 58
15 carriers plus supporting units

1000, 19 June
US planes return from
raid on Guam, Japanese
strike planes sighted

1200, 18 June

2000

0830, 19 June
First strike launched

1600

Guam

1628,
Taiho sinks

1400
Second strike launched from forces
'A' and 'B', 49 planes misdirected

US fighters intercept
Japanese aircraft

Forces 'A' (Ozawa)
and 'B' (Joshima)
carriers: Taiho, Zuikaku,
Shokaku, Junyo, Hiyo,
Ryuho

0900/0930
First strikes launched
by forces 'A' and 'B'
0905
Taiho torpedoed by
submarine Albacore

1220
Shokaku torpedoed
by submarine Cavalla

1624, Shokaku sinks

SITUATION 19 JUNE 1944

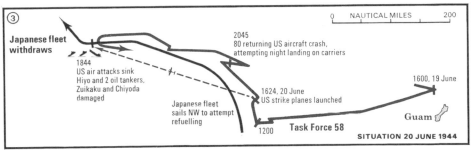

③ Japanese fleet
withdraws

0   NAUTICAL MILES   200

2045
80 returning US aircraft crash,
attempting night landing on carriers

1844
US air attacks sink
Hiyo and 2 oil tankers,
Zuikaku and Chiyoda
damaged

Japanese fleet
sails NW to attempt
refuelling

1624, 20 June
US strike planes launched

1600, 19 June

Guam

1200   **Task Force 58**

SITUATION 20 JUNE 1944

THE BATTLE OF LEYTE GULF 1

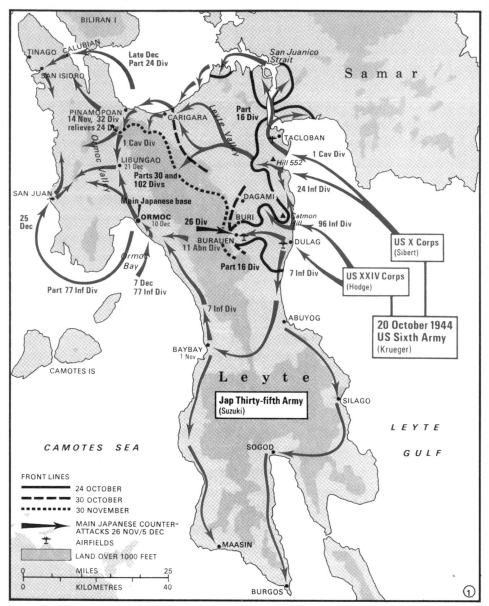

The capture of the Marianas and the completion of the Solomons/New Guinea operations prepared the way for the next move of the war. Nimitz favoured a drive against Formosa or China, but General MacArthur insisted on a move to free the Philippines, (not only for military and political reasons, but because he himself had vowed to return there). President Roosevelt favoured the MacArthur plan, and arrangements were made for a move by both MacArthur's and Nimitz's forces against the southern Philippine island of Leyte.

The force given this task was General Krueger's US Sixth Army. Following intensive bombardment by Admiral Olendorf's gun-fire-support group, Sibert's X Corps and Hodge's XXIV Corps landed, on 20 October, on the Eastern shore of Leyte (**Map 1**). By nightfall a beachhead was established, and 132,400 men had moved ashore. 200,000 tons of supplies had been landed.

These landings were lightly opposed by the Japanese 16 Division, while General Yamashita, Japanese C-in-C in the Philippines, reinforced Leyte from Luzon and the Visayas, building up the Japanese Thirty-fifth Army. However, by mid-December US aircraft had brought to a standstill all Japanese shipping in the Leyte waters. Throughout October and November the Sixth Army made slow progress. The X Corps, using overland and amphibious movements, thrust north of the beachhead to try to outflank Suzuki's Thirty-fifth Army from the north. XXIV Corps, having made a hook to the south, attacked Ormoc, the key to the Japanese defences. Then, in December the northern and southern 'hooks' converged, and, using amphibious landings for further outflanking movements, cut Suzuki off from his last remaining naval base. All organized resistance ended by Christmas day. Japanese casualties had been 70,000; American 15,584. In the

meantime Sibert's X Corps had also secured a foothold on Samar.

The Japanese, rightly appreciating that a successful US landing in the Philippines would cut their empire in two, severing the homeland from the Southern Resources Area with its supplies of food and fuel, decided to destroy the landings on the eastern coast of Leyte and their attendant naval escorts. The plan to achieve this, optimistically called the 'Sho' (victory) Plan, was put into operation in late October 1944 shortly after the US forces had begun landing on Leyte.

The whole of the Japanese Combined Fleet moved from widely scattered bases (**Map 2**). Ozawa's Northern Force, or Carrier 'Decoy' Force (the four remaining carriers, two battleships, four cruisers, and eight destroyers), steamed south from Japan to lure the US Third Fleet (eight heavy and eight light carriers, six battleships, three heavy and nine light cruisers, fifty-eight destroyers, and more than 1,000 planes), under Halsey away from the landings. Kurita's Force 'A' (two superbattleships, three other battleships, twelve cruisers, and fifteen destroyers), sailed east from Borneo to traverse the San Bernardino Strait and attack the landings from the north. A second force from Borneo, Force 'C' under Vice-Admiral Nishimura (two battleships, one heavy cruiser, and four destroyers), backed up by the Second Striking Force under Vice-Admiral Shima (two heavy and one light cruisers and four destroyers), was to pass through the Surigao Strait to attack the landings from the south (**Map 2**).

On 23 October the US submarines *Darter* and *Dace* spotted Kurita's First Striking Force. Not only did they send word to Halsey, but they sank two heavy cruisers *Atago* and *Maya*. Kurita, continuing into the Sibuyan Sea, was attacked by aircraft from Mitscher's Task Force 38 (the carrier element of Halsey's Third Fleet). After nearly two days of incessant bombardment the super-battleship *Musashi* was sunk at 1000 hours on the 24th. Late on the 24th Kurita turned and headed west again, and Halsey assumed that he was retreating. Meanwhile Japanese aircraft from Clark Field on Luzon attacked part of Task Force 38 and succeeded in sinking the light carrier *Princeton*. Unknown to Halsey, after dark, Kurita changed course again and headed for San Bernardino Strait.

Opposite: The crew of an escort carrier take cover from a Japanese dive bomber

Right: The US fleet under Japanese air attack during the invasion of Leyte

POSITIONS OF US CARRIER TASK GROUPS, 0600, 24 OCTOBER
TIMES ARE THOSE FOR 24 OCTOBER UNLESS OTHERWISE INDICATED

0   NAUTICAL MILES   300

Carrier 'Decoy' Force (Ozawa) 0100
0000, 25th
1140
0600, 25th
0822, 25th
Group 'A' (Matsuda) 2000
2241
Task Force 38 (Halsey's Third Fleet) steams north to engage Ozawa's force
2345
2000

C. Engaño

Luzon

Second Striking Force (Shima)

Clark Field

TG 38.3 (Sherman)
Princeton

0935 Carrier Princeton hit, sinks at 1630

MANILA

PHILIPPINE ISLANDS

TG 38.2 (Bogan)

1200, 23 Oct

Mindoro

Sibuyan

San Bernardino Str

0600, 25th

1026/1530 US air strikes. Battleship Musashi sinks at 1935, cruiser Myoko retires damaged

Sea

Masbate

Samar

TG 38.4 (Davison)

CALAMIAN GROUP

1000

1200, 23 Oct

Panay

0400, 25th

US Seventh Fleet (Kinkaid)

Force 'A' (Kurita)

Negros

Cebu

Leyte

Bohol

0632, 23 Oct US Submarines sink cruisers Atago and Maya, Takao retires damaged

Surigao Str

Palawan

1000

2000

2330

TG 38.1 (McCain) to Ulithi

0918

1000

Force 'C' (Nishimura)

1200, 23 Oct

Mindanao

Sulu Sea

First Striking Force (Kurita)

BRITISH NORTH BORNEO

Sails 22 Oct

BRUNEI

(2)

THE BATTLE OF LEYTE GULF 2

Warned of the approach of Nishimura and Shima from the south, Kinkaid, in command of the US Seventh Fleet at the landings, ordered Olendorf's gun-fire support group (Task Group 77) to intercept them. On the night of the 24th Olendorf drew up his battleships he deployed his approach of Nishimura's force. In front of his battleships he deployed his cruisers, and in front of them his destroyers (**Map 1**). Between 0300 hours and 0340 on the 25th destroyer attacks on Nishimura's flanks torpedoed the battleship *Fuso* and four destroyers. The remainder of Nishimura's force, in line ahead, ran into Olendorf's cruisers and battleships. Olendorf was in the classic naval position of having crossed his opponents' 'T'. In the ensuing forty minutes the whole of Nishimura's force, save one destroyer, had been wiped out. Nishimura went down with his flagship, *Yamashiro*.

Shima's force, bringing up the rear, had already suffered the loss of a cruiser, torpedoed by a PT boat. Attempting to retire, Shima's own flagship, the *Nachi*, collided with a crippled ship of Nishimura's force. One more cruiser was lost next day as Shima withdrew. Olendorf turned back after a short pursuit, knowing that he might well have to fight again to protect the landings.

Halsey, meanwhile, convinced that Kurita was permanently out of the fight, steamed north after Ozawa's Decoy Force, failing to inform Kinkaid of this. Early on 25 October, Kurita surprised Rear-Admiral Sprague commanding Taffy 3, an escort carrier group of Kinkaid's Seventh Fleet. With only six escort carriers, three destroyers, and four destroyer escorts, he found himself giving battle to four battleships, six heavy cruisers, and ten destroyers. His aircraft were armed for land operations, and were almost helpless against the Japanese ships. In an amazing two-hour running fight Sprague staved off disaster, using his destroyers skilfully to keep the Japanese

160

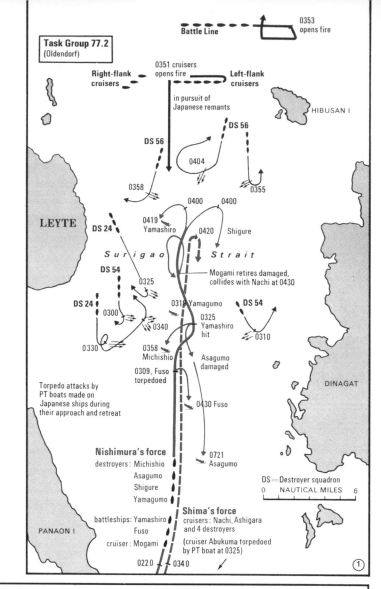

Task Group 77.2
(Oldendorf)

Battle Line — 0353 opens fire

Right-flank cruisers — 0351 cruisers opens fire — **Left-flank cruisers**

in pursuit of Japanese remnants

HIBUSAN I

DS 56

DS 56

0404

0358 — 0355

0400   0400

LEYTE

DS 24 — 0419 Yamashiro   0420   Shigure

Surigao   Strait

DS 54

0325   Mogami retires damaged, collides with Nachi at 0430

DS 24   0319 Yamagumo   DS 54

0300   0325 Yamashiro hit

0340   0310

0330   0358 Michishio   Asagumo damaged

0309, Fuso torpedoed

Torpedo attacks by PT boats made on Japanese ships during their approach and retreat

DINAGAT

0430 Fuso

0721 Asagumo

DS = Destroyer squadron
0   NAUTICAL MILES   6

Nishimura's force
destroyers: Michishio
Asagumo
Shigure
Yamagumo

battleships: Yamashiro
Fuso

cruiser: Mogami

Shima's force
cruisers: Nachi, Ashigara and 4 destroyers
(cruiser Abukuma torpedoed by PT boat at 0325)

PANAON I

0220   0340

①

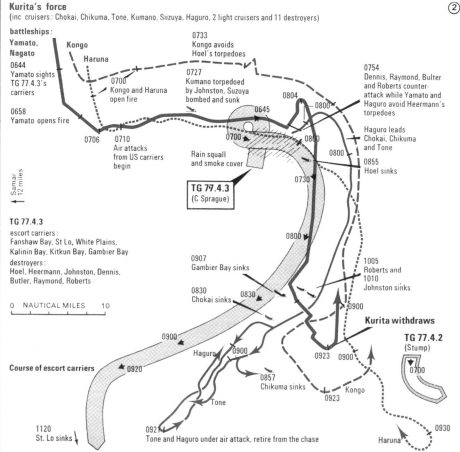

Kurita's force
(inc cruisers: Chokai, Chikuma, Tone, Kumano, Suzuya, Haguro, 2 light cruisers and 11 destroyers)

②

battleships:
Yamato, Nagato   Kongo   Haruna

0733 Kongo avoids Hoel's torpedoes

0644 Yamato sights TG 77.4.3's carriers

0700 Kongo and Haruna open fire

0727 Kumano torpedoed by Johnston, Suzuya bombed and sunk

0754 Dennis, Raymond, Bulter and Roberts counter-attack while Yamato and Haguro avoid Heermann's torpedoes

0804

0658 Yamato opens fire

0645

0800

0706   0710 Air attacks from US carriers begin   0700   Rain squall and smoke cover   0800   Haguro leads Chokai, Chikuma and Tone

0855 Hoel sinks

Samar 12 miles

TG 77.4.3
(C Sprague)

0730

TG 77.4.3
escort carriers:
Fanshaw Bay, St Lo, White Plains, Kalinin Bay, Kitkun Bay, Gambier Bay
destroyers:
Hoel, Heermann, Johnston, Dennis, Butler, Raymond, Roberts

0800

1005 Roberts and 1010 Johnston sinks

0907 Gambier Bay sinks

0   NAUTICAL MILES   10

Kurita withdraws

0830   0830 Chokai sinks

TG 77.4.2
(Stump)

0900   Haguro   0900   0923   0900   0700

Course of escort carriers   0920   0857 Chikuma sinks   Kongo

0923

1120 St. Lo sinks   0921   Tone   Tone and Haguro under air attack, retire from the chase   Haruna   0930

at their distance (**Map 2**). He was assisted by aircraft from other escort carrier groups, but nonetheless one carrier, *Gambier Bay*, and three destroyers were lost. Persistent and superb destroyer action by the US force succeeded in sinking three Japanese cruisers.

At 0923 hours, when Sprague's force could hardly have held out any longer, Kurita decided to withdraw. The aircraft from other escort carriers had misled him into supposing that he had engaged Task Force 38 which was in reality many miles away to the north. His decision was strengthened by reports that Nishimura's force had been destroyed. Within a few hours of success Kurita turned to make off homewards via the San Bernardino Strait.

Sprague's ordeal was not quite over, however. Returning southward he was attacked by Japanese land-based aircraft, including the first Kamikaze missions, and the carrier *St Lo* was sunk.

Halsey's headlong rush northwards to catch Ozawa paid off in the small hours of the morning of the 25th (**Map 3**). At 0220 hours Mitscher's search aircraft located Ozawa, and by 0845 hours the first of four strikes was on the way. Ozawa, most of whose few remaining aircraft had been put ashore to operate as land-based forces, had nothing to oppose these strikes. Throughout the day the strikes continued as Ozawa fled north. By nightfall all four Japanese carriers had been sunk, and five other ships. Only two battleships, two cruisers, and six destroyers escaped.

The four-phased Battle of Leyte Gulf shattered Japan's seapower for ever. Four carriers, three battleships, six heavy and four light cruisers, eleven destroyers and a submarine were sunk. Almost every other Japanese ship was in some way damaged. 500 aircraft and a total of 10,000 men were lost. These were casualties that could never be made good.

Right: The battleships of Task Group 77 in line ahead off Leyte

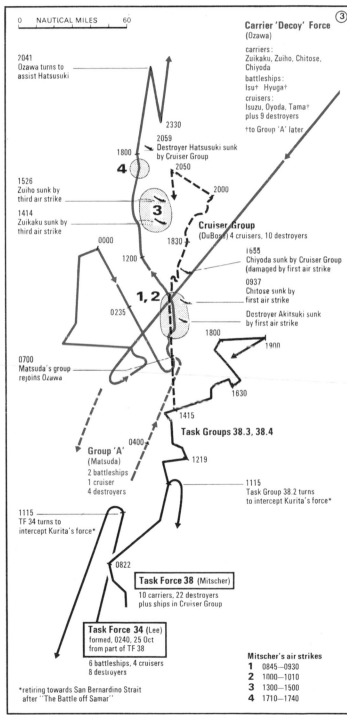

③

0 NAUTICAL MILES 60	

Carrier 'Decoy' Force (Ozawa)

carriers: Zuikaku, Zuiho, Chitose, Chiyoda
battleships: Ise† Hyuga†
cruisers: Isuzu, Oyoda, Tama† plus 9 destroyers

†to Group 'A' later

2041 Ozawa turns to assist Hatsusuki

2330

2059 Destroyer Hatsusuki sunk by Cruiser Group

1800   2050

4   2000

1526 Zuiho sunk by third air strike   **3**   1830

1414 Zuikaku sunk by third air strike

Cruiser Group (DuBose) 4 cruisers, 10 destroyers

0000   1200   1655 Chiyoda sunk by Cruiser Group (damaged by first air strike

0937 Chitose sunk by first air strike

1, 2   Destroyer Akitsuki sunk by first air strike

0235   1800

1900

0700 Matsuda's group rejoins Ozawa

1630

1415

Task Groups 38.3, 38.4

0400   1219

Group 'A' (Matsuda) 2 battleships 1 cruiser 4 destroyers

1115 Task Group 38.2 turns to intercept Kurita's force*

1115 TF 34 turns to intercept Kurita's force*

0822

Task Force 38 (Mitscher)
10 carriers, 22 destroyers plus ships in Cruiser Group

Task Force 34 (Lee) formed, 0240, 25 Oct from part of TF 38
6 battleships, 4 cruisers 8 destroyers

*retiring towards San Bernardino Strait after "The Battle off Samar"

Mitscher's air strikes
1 0845—0930
2 1000—1010
3 1300—1500
4 1710—1740

CLEARING THE PHILIPPINES

After the capture of Leyte in December 1944 the way was open for a US attack on the main Philippine Island, Luzon.

Between 2 and 8 January, the Sixth Army (General Krueger), moved from Leyte to Lingayen Gulf on Luzon, carried by the Seventh Fleet. The Japanese air bases on Formosa, that might have harassed the landings, were neutralized by aircraft from Halsey's carriers and by aircraft operating from China. Although US aircraft from Leyte and Mindoro tried to neutralize the aircraft on Luzon itself, Olendorf's gun-fire-support group lost heavily to Kamikaze pilots – both on the way

up, and during the preliminary bombardment. One carrier was sunk, and another damaged. The battleship *New Mexico*, one heavy, and four light cruisers, and several other ships were damaged. On 9 January the Sixth Army went ashore in Lingayen Gulf. The Japanese commander, General Yamashita, commanding the Japanese Fourteenth Army, decided not to contest the landing. The US forces landed on a two corps front, four divisions abreast. On the left, I Corps (General Swift); on the right XIV Corps (General Griswold). Griswold's corps pushed aside Japanese delaying

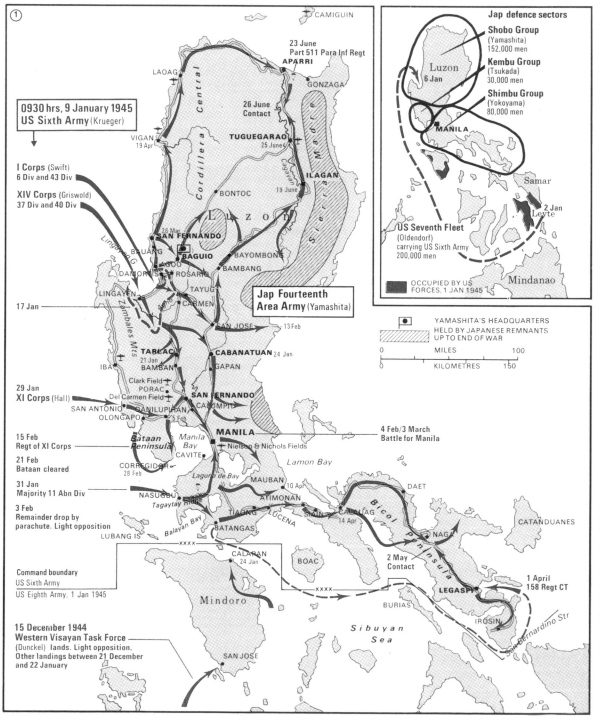

forces and pressed on to Clark Field, which he reached by 23 January.

On the left of the beachhead, however, Swift's I Corps had heavier going against the bulk of Yamashita's Shobo Group.

Between 29 January and 4 February, task forces from General Eichelberger's Eighth Army made landings on the north and south of Manila Bay. On the north XI Corps under General Hall landed at San Antonio and drove straight across the top of the Bataan Peninsula. To the south 11 Airborne Division landed at Nasugbu, to make straight for Manila itself. For a whole month, 3 February to 4 March, the Americans fought their way into Manila. Elements of Griswold's corps, approaching from the north, split. Part continued to attack Manila from the north, and part executed a flanking movement to link up with 11 Airborne Division in the south. By 22 February the Japanese had been driven back into the old walled city where, ignoring Yamashita's orders, they conducted a street by street defence. When the last resistance ended the city was rubble and 16,000 Japanese lay dead.

In the same month, Corregidor was captured. On 16 February paratroopers of 11 Airborne Division dropped on its tiny golf course, supported by an amphibious landing from Bataan. By the 27th the fortress was clear. US ships began to move into Manila bay, and on 13 April the bay's last fortification, Fort Drum, the 'Concrete Battleship', was overcome by pouring petrol down the ventilators and lighting it, cooking the garrison inside.

Between April and August the weight of Sixth Army turned east, north, and south in a series of assaults against Yamashita's mountain strongholds. When Yamashita surrendered at the end of the war, he still had organized forces of about 50,000 men.

Luzon was the largest single campaign undertaken by the Americans in the Pacific. Their losses were 7,933 killed and 32,732 wounded. The Japanese lost 192,000 killed.

At the same time as the Luzon campaign, Eichelberger's Eighth Army was tackling the remaining Philippine Islands garrisoned by elements of the Japanese Thirty-fifth Army, in all some 102,000 men, mainly concentrated on Mindanao. Between February and July, 1945, Eighth Army task forces conducted more than fifty amphibious operations. The pattern rarely varied. The landing would be followed by a Japanese withdrawal into the interior, US forces would secure the island, and mopping-up would be left to the active Filipino guerrilla units.

On Mindanao itself, however, Suzuki, having escaped from Leyte, put up a sterner resistance. Concentric landings from north, east, and south finally isolated his forces into two groups, in which they remained until the end of the war.

Left: US troops climbing into their landing craft before the landings in Lingayen Gulf

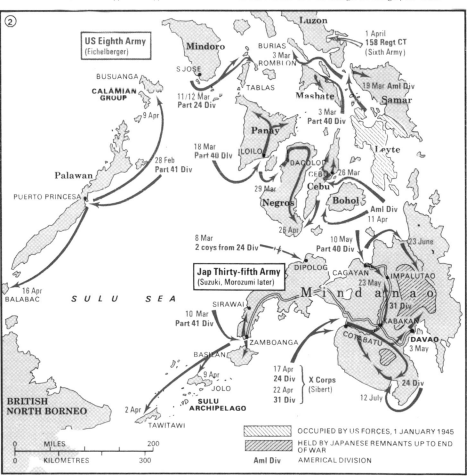

IWO JIMA

The seizure of Iwo Jima, so costly that it was to eclipse even Tarawa in US Marine Corps legend, was dictated by several considerations. First, although distant from Japan, it was a part of the Japanese homeland, and its capture would be a deep psychological shock to the Japanese, military and civilian alike. Second, it was within fighter range of Tokyo, and US bomber losses demanded that their raids enjoy fighter protection. Third, crippled or fuelless bombers would be able to make a landfall there.

Nobody pretended however, that Iwo Jima could be taken easily. A mere eight square miles, wholly devoid of cover, and dominated at one end by the sugar-loaf massif of Mount Suribachi, it was garrisoned by 22,000 Japanese army and navy troops under Major-General Kuribayashi. 'Honeycombed' is a cliché, but no other word can describe the complex of tunnels, gun emplacements, pillboxes, and caves that the Japanese had created on Iwo Jima.

On 19 February 1945, after the most prolonged and intense bombardment in the Pacific war (a 72-day softening up by B–24 and B–25 bombers, followed by a pre-assault barrage fired by the US navy for three days), 4 and 5 Marine Divisions, with the 3rd in reserve, were put ashore by Schmidt's V Amphibious Corps. For the first few minutes they encountered only sporadic resistance. Either the garrison had been overestimated, or the barrage had done its job more than well. After twenty minutes, however, the fire of all the defenders' weapons, artillery, mortars, and small arms, opened up on the exposed Marine positions. Brilliant though the co-ordination of this fireplan was, the Japanese had left it just too late. They had allowed the Marines to land with all the equipment they needed, and to establish a large enough beachhead to land more. By the end of the day 30,000 Marines had been landed, and had swarmed right

across the neck of the island. With them had come tanks, bulldozers, and artillery.

For the following three days the Marines fought for the control of Suribachi, and by the 23rd had achieved this with the historic raising of the Stars and Stripes on its summit. But the fall of Suribachi did not mean the fall of Iwo Jima. The north-east of the island remained to be conquered, and this was to take until 26 March. The maze of underground defences and the closeness of the opposing forces made the fighting of this phase more like the First World War than the Second. There was little room to manoeuvre round the defenders' flanks: every assault was a frontal attack, using the tactics of fire and movement to shoot the men forward. It was extremely costly.

Some 6,821 US Marines and sailors lost their lives on Iwo Jima, and almost all of the 22,000-man Japanese garrison was killed.

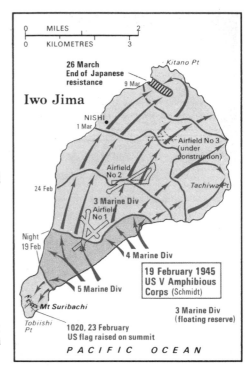

Below: Landing craft approaching Iwo Jima

Opposite above: Supplies being unloaded on the beachhead at Iwo Jima

Oppposite below: A rocket barrage on Japanese positions during the final stages of the advance

OKINAWA

The final preliminary to an invasion of Japan itself was the capture of Okinawa, the main island of the Ryukyu group, the southernmost islands of Japan. It was held by the 130,000 men of the Japanese Thirty-second Army, under Lieutenant-General Ushijima. Unlike the other Pacific islands (with the exception of some parts of the Philippines) Okinawa was quite densely populated, having a civilian population of about 450,000.

From 14 to 31 March preliminary air operations were undertaken to isolate and soften-up the target. Japanese air bases on Formosa and the islands surrounding Okinawa were attacked by US and British carrier forces, both of which paid a toll to Kamikaze pilots. But of the 196 Kamikaze attacks launched, 169 were destroyed before reaching their targets.

From 23 March onwards, Okinawa itself was subjected to a continuous air and artillery strafing. Neighbouring small islands were captured to provide fleet anchorages and bases. On 1 April, Operation Iceberg began. General Buckner's Tenth Army, one Army corps and one Marine corps, landed at the southern end of Okinawa. On the left, the Marine III Amphibious Corps was to push north and secure the whole northern end of the island in just over a fortnight. On the right, however, Hodge's XXIV Corps ran against formidable Japanese defences – the Shuri Line. Buckner was faced with a difficult decision. Should he attack the Shuri defences frontally, or outflank them with another amphibious landing in their rear? The frontal assault would be costly, but the amphibious operation might split his force in the presence of a formidable enemy. In the event he did both, but in the meantime, on 3/4 May, the Japanese had obliged him with one of their now inevitable suicidal counterattacks. It was repulsed with the loss of 5,000 Japanese, and the hitherto concealed Japanese positions on the Shuri Line were given away. From 11 to 21 May Buckner's forces tore at the Japanese defences in appalling weather conditions. They broke through, and Ushijima, disengaging, retreated to the hill masses of the southern tip of the island. A massive two-pronged attack overwhelmed the final resistance by 21 June.

Japanese losses on Okinawa were staggering. The known dead totalled 107,500 and probably a further 20,000 died sealed in their cave hideouts. About 4,000 Japanese aircraft were lost in combat, and an equal number from other causes. But for the first time Japanese soldiers had surrendered in appreciable numbers – 7,400 prisoners were taken.

The US Tenth Army lost 7,613 killed, including Lieutenant-General Buckner, and 31,800 wounded. The US Navy's casualties were 4,900 killed and 4,800 wounded. In addition, thirty-four ships and aircraft were sunk and 368 damaged.

Below: Marines assault a Japanese strongpoint

Opposite above: Part of the preliminary bombardment before the landings on Okinawa

Opposite below: Men of 6 Marine Division advancing into Naha, the capital of Okinawa

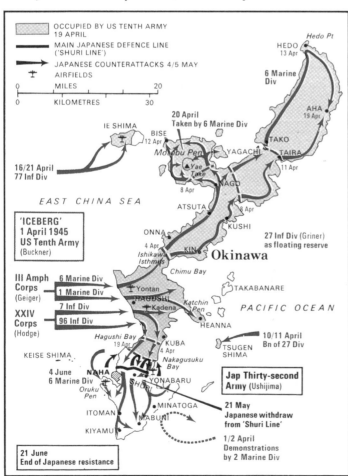

THE END IN THE PACIFIC

With the invasion of Okinawa, the American forces were now faced with their last and greatest challenge – the invasion of the home islands of Japan (opposite). The fanatical resistance which had been encountered at every stage of the Pacific War gave the American planners no reason to hope or expect that a surrender would be forthcoming, and the combined staffs of General MacArthur and Admiral Nimitz began to prepare for an eventual invasion. Landings on southern Kyushu were to be made on 1 November 1945 in Operation Olympic and on Honshu on 1 March 1946 in Operation Coronet. The operations were then to be extended and pushed ahead until all Japanese resistance had been overcome.

The forces to be assembled for these two operations would have been the largest amphibious assault force ever raised. While the earlier landings would use forces already in the Pacific, the second landings would utilize men and equipment redeployed from Europe. It was assumed that the landings would be resolutely opposed by the still-powerful forces remaining on the Japanese islands, and the planners were pessimistic about the likely casualty rate which the operation would entail.

It was against this background that President Truman was presented with the decision as to whether to use the atomic bomb to force the Japanese surrender. He decided that the immediate advantage in saving lives outweighed the disadvantages of unleashing a new and unthinkably powerful form of warfare on the world, and on 6 August 1945 the Superfortress 'Enola Gay' dropped the first atomic bomb on Hiroshima. In one minute more than 78,500 people died and many more were to be struck down in the weeks which followed, but a surrender ultimatum to Japan was ignored. On 9 August a second bomb was dropped at Nagasaki, and Japan surrendered. The war in the Pacific was over.

The Russian attack on Manchuria was a nine-day wonder of logistics, staff work, and planning. This was almost the only occasion in the war when the Japanese did not put up a stiff resistance. The campaign was the result of Russia's need to get her foot into the Far Eastern door before peace shut it. It had been long planned, and long delayed, but the atomic bombing of Hiroshima and Nagasaki prompted Russia to speed into action.

Manchuria was garrisoned by nearly one million Japanese troops of the Kwantung Army under General Yamada. On 8 August Russia declared war on Japan, and on 9 August Marshal Malinovsky's Trans-Baikal Front moved into Manchuria from the north, west, and east. The Kwantung Army was no match for the armoured and motorized units under Malinovsky's command. By 18 August the whole of Manchuria had been overrun.

Right: Smoke billowing 20,000 feet over Nagasaki after the second atomic raid

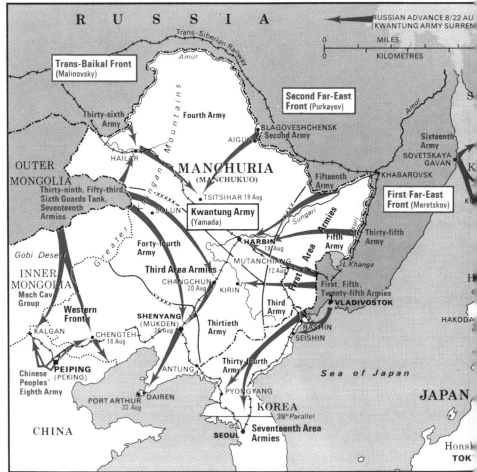

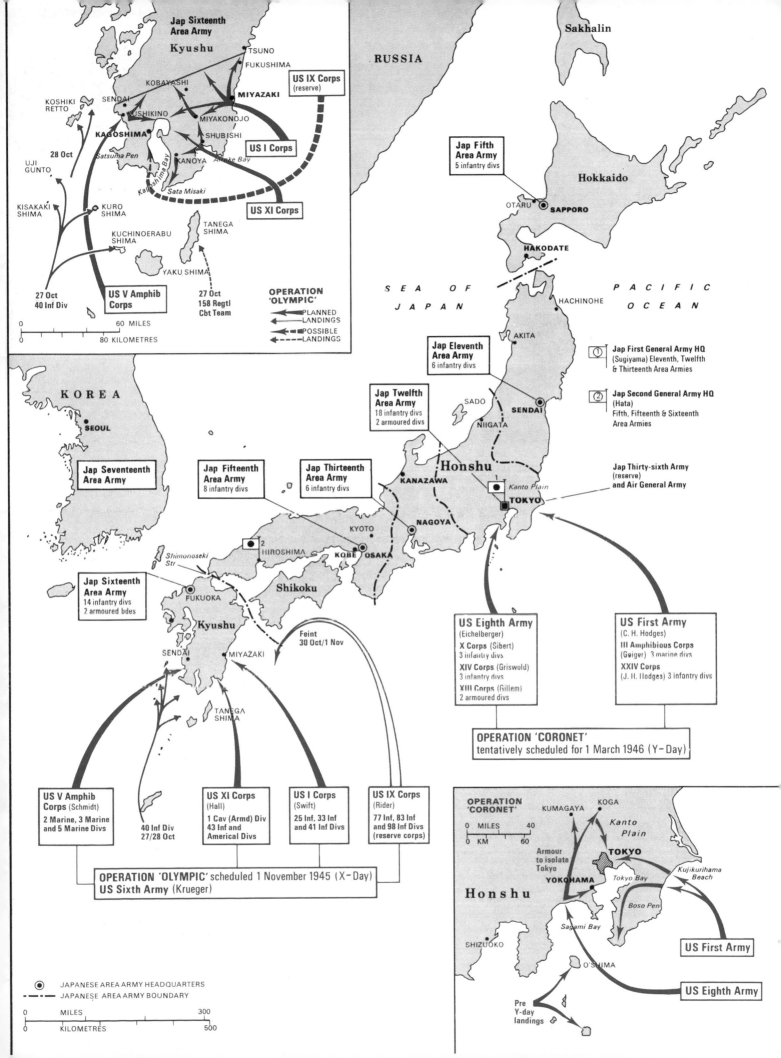

Jap Sixteenth Area Army
Kyushu

TSUNO
FUKUSHIMA
KOBAYASHI
SENDAI
KUSHIKINO
MIYAZAKI
MIYAKONOJO
KAGOSHIMA
SHUBISHI
KOSHIKI RETTO
Satsuma Pen
KANOYA
Ariake Bay

US IX Corps (reserve)

US I Corps

US XI Corps

28 Oct
UJI GUNTO
Kagoshima Bay
Sata Misaki

KISAKAKI SHIMA
KURO SHIMA
KUCHINOERABU SHIMA
TANEGA SHIMA
YAKU SHIMA

27 Oct
40 Inf Div

US V Amphib Corps

27 Oct
158 Regtl Cbt Team

OPERATION 'OLYMPIC'

→ PLANNED LANDINGS
⇢ POSSIBLE LANDINGS
⇠ LANDINGS

0 ___ 60 MILES
0 ___ 80 KILOMETRES

Sakhalin

RUSSIA

Jap Fifth Area Army
5 infantry divs

Hokkaido

OTARU ● SAPPORO

HAKODATE

SEA OF JAPAN

PACIFIC OCEAN

HACHINOHE

AKITA

Jap Eleventh Area Army
6 infantry divs

① **Jap First General Army HQ**
(Sugiyama) Eleventh, Twelfth & Thirteenth Area Armies

② **Jap Second General Army HQ**
(Hata) Fifth, Fifteenth & Sixteenth Area Armies

Jap Twelfth Area Army
18 infantry divs
2 armoured divs

SADO
SENDAI ●
NIIGATA

Honshu

KANAZAWA

Jap Thirty-sixth Army (reserve) and Air General Army

KOREA

SEOUL

Jap Seventeenth Area Army

Jap Fifteenth Area Army
8 infantry divs

Jap Thirteenth Area Army
6 infantry divs

Kanto Plain
■ **TOKYO**

KYOTO
NAGOYA

■ 2 HIROSHIMA
KOBE OSAKA

Shimonoseki Str

Jap Sixteenth Area Army
14 infantry divs
2 armoured bdes

Shikoku

FUKUOKA ●

Kyushu

SENDAI
MIYAZAKI

Feint
30 Oct/1 Nov

TANEGA SHIMA

US Eighth Army
(Eichelberger)
X Corps (Sibert)
3 infantry divs
XIV Corps (Griswold)
3 infantry divs
XIII Corps (Gillem)
2 armoured divs

US First Army
(C. H. Hodges)
III Amphibious Corps
(Geiger) 3 marine divs
XXIV Corps
(J. H. Hodges) 3 infantry divs

OPERATION 'CORONET'
tentatively scheduled for 1 March 1946 (Y-Day)

US V Amphib Corps (Schmidt)
2 Marine, 3 Marine and 5 Marine Divs

40 Inf Div
27/28 Oct

US XI Corps (Hall)
1 Cav (Armd) Div
43 Inf and
Americal Divs

US I Corps (Swift)
25 Inf, 33 Inf
and 41 Inf Divs

US IX Corps (Rider)
77 Inf, 83 Inf
and 98 Inf Divs
(reserve corps)

OPERATION 'OLYMPIC' scheduled 1 November 1945 (X-Day)
US Sixth Army (Krueger)

● JAPANESE AREA ARMY HEADQUARTERS
–·– JAPANESE AREA ARMY BOUNDARY

0 ___ MILES ___ 300
0 ___ KILOMETRES ___ 500

OPERATION 'CORONET'

0 ___ MILES ___ 40
0 ___ KM ___ 60

KUMAGAYA
KOGA
Kanto Plain

Armour to isolate Tokyo
TOKYO
YOKOHAMA
Tokyo Bay
Kujikurihama Beach

Sagami Bay
Boso Pen

Honshu

SHIZUOKA

O'SHIMA

Pre Y-day landings

US First Army

US Eighth Army

THE BURMA CAMPAIGN

'If the armies and government of
Generalissimo Chiang Kai-shek had
been finally defeated, Japan would
have been left free to exploit the
tremendous resources of China
without harassment. It might have
made it possible when the United
States and Britain had finished
the job in Europe, and assaulted the
Japanese home islands, for the
government to flee to China, and
continue the war on a great and
rich land mass.'

General George C. Marshall

Opposite: Japanese officers laying down
their swords in surrender

One does not lightly differ from the strategic opinions of so distinguished a soldier as General Marshall, and it may, therefore be some consolation to the veterans of the Fourteenth Army that without their efforts China could not have been kept in the fight. Even after the Burma Road was cut at Lashio on 29 April 1942 the Allies had continued to fly supplies to the Chinese over 'the Hump', a flight which meant clearing the Himalayas at an altitude of 23,000 feet. At first these supplies amounted to about 10,000 tons a month.

The Allies, in the words of Lieutenant-General Joseph W. Stilwell – *alias* 'Vinegar Joe' – had taken 'a hell of a beating' in the first Burma campaign. Even so by the end of 1942 the British had begun to think of going over to the offensive. Early in 1943 they made a thrust down the Arakan coast with the object of recapturing Akyab and its airfield, but this proved a costly failure. The truth is that morale was low at this time. The Japanese soldier had come to be regarded as a kind of Superman. A high sick rate is usually an indication of low morale. In 1942 for every man wounded 120 were being sent back sick. At the end of the year one division, 17,000 strong, had 5,000 sick. Malaria, dysentery, mite typhus, and skin diseases all took their toll.

It was at this time that Brigadier Orde Wingate appeared on the scene. Experience of guerilla warfare in Palestine and Abyssinia had led him to conceive the idea of long-range penetration, and this he had contrived to 'sell' to Winston Churchill, who was often receptive to unorthodox ideas and willing to encourage a commander who wanted to fight. Wingate was allowed to raise a 'private army', the Chindits, and with this force he waged war beyond the Chindwin from February to May 1943. His men cut the Mandalay–Myitkyina railway in seventy-five places – exploits which generally speaking left the Japanese unimpressed, for, unlike the Germans, they were not particularly sensitive about being raided. But, thanks

to the Press, the morale effect on the Allies was quite different. Although the Chindits had endured terrible hardships and had been compelled to abandon many of their sick and wounded, they had shown that they could take on the Japanese in the jungle. The myth of the Japanese Superman began to dissolve. Wingate had moreover demonstrated the value of air supply. He himself enjoyed in the eyes of the British public a reputation akin to that of T. E. Lawrence in the First World War, and, despite his eccentricities, he was clearly a very talented soldier. At the same time he was unscrupulous about getting his own way, and having direct access to the Prime Minister, an unwarrantable by-passing of the normal military channels – was now able, at the expense of Fourteenth Army, to build his brigade into a division.

In August 1943 another young and brilliant commander came on the scene. This was Lord Louis Mountbatten, a member of the British Royal Family. At the beginning of the war he had been a dashing destroyer captain. Later he had scored notable successes as Chief of Combined Operations. Now at the early age of forty-three he was made Supreme Commander of the newly created South-East-Asia Command (SEAC). It would be wrong to underrate Mountbatten as a strategist, but his great asset was that he had an inspiring personality. His brand of leadership appealed to the men of his command, and his tireless visits to every kind of unit were a very real factor in raising morale. In this sphere he was as effective as Montgomery himself. But morale is not only a question of enthusiasm, but of discipline. The improvement in Fourteenth Army was partly a question of improving its health, and to some extent this was simply a matter of discipline. The strictest health precautions were needed, for example in seeing that every man took his daily mepacrine tablet to prevent malaria.

Mountbatten's immediate object was to reopen land communications

with China. To this end American engineers, with coolie labour, had been building the Ledo road, begun in December 1942 and eventually completed in January 1945. This was to be extended so as to join the old Burma Road at Mongyu near Lashio. Fuel pipelines were to be built from Calcutta to Assam, and parallel to the Ledo road. Supplies over the Hump were to be increased to 20,000 tons a month.

The key to the reconquest of Burma was air supply. As Admiral Mountbatten himself pointed out:

'It was not just a question of auxiliary air supply, because 96 per cent of our supplies to the Fourteenth Army went by air. In the course of this campaign we lifted 615,000 tons of supplies to the armies, three quarters of it by the US Air Force and one quarter by the Royal Air Force; 315,000 reinforcements were flown in, . . . 110,000 casualties were flown out, . . . in our best month – March 1945 – we actually lifted 94,300 tons. During that time the American Air Transport Command were building up their 'Hump' traffic, so that by July they had reached their peak of 77,500 tons per month.'

Despite this administrative effort and backing the motto of the Fourteenth Army was 'God helps those who help themselves'. The feat of improvisation which brought into being the flotilla that made possible the Irrawaddy crossing is a classic example.

No amount of administrative skill will win wars without soldiers prepared to fight with the skill and determination of the men who defended Imphal and Kohima. But stout-hearted soldiers will still be defeated if they are not well commanded. In Sir William Slim the Fourteenth Army had a general of the highest calibre.

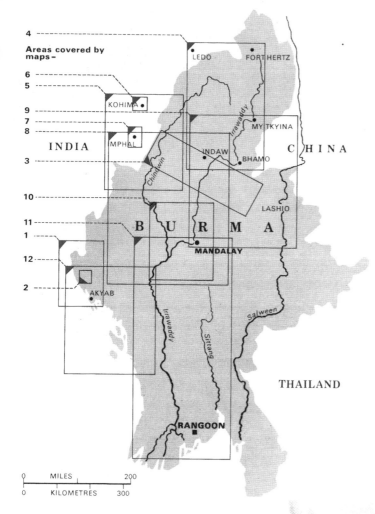

Opposite left: Japanese representatives being marched to sign surrender terms in Hong Kong

Opposite right: Troops boarding landing craft for the seaborne attack on Ramree Island

Right: A British officer searches a Japanese after the surrender

Above right: A Bren-gun carrier during the advance to Mandalay

THE ARAKAN BATTLES

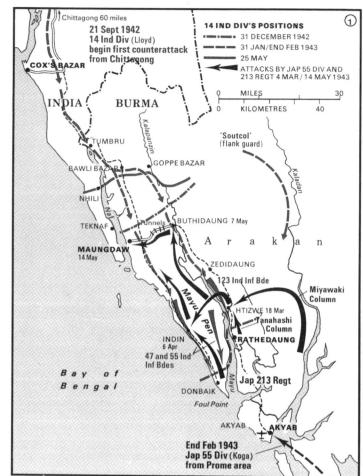

After the series of reverses during 1942 that drove the British first into surrender at Singapore and then headlong defeat in Burma, General Wavell, commanding the Allied forces in India, realized that a counter-invasion of Burma was out of the question until late 1943 at the very earliest, but wished to raise the morale of his men by success in small scale, carefully planned operations. These were to have the additional benefit of providing up to date experience on combat with the Japanese. For the first of these small offensives, Wavell chose the Arakan, operations being directed against the island post of Akyab, from which the Japanese could bomb Chittagong and Calcutta.

The 14 Indian Division advanced carefully from its base at Chittagong to the forward base at Cox's Bazar by sea and overland along a very poor road (**Map 1**). From Cox's Bazar onwards, the only means of advance was fair weather tracks. The British advance continued cautiously against skilful Japanese delaying tactics, but gave the Japanese commander in Burma, General Iida, time to move up his 55 Division in time to halt 14 Indian Division in front of Donbaik and Rathedaung.

After a stalemate lasting from January to March 1943 the Japanese counterattacked, both frontally and over the mountains to the east that the British had considered more or less impassable. The 14 Indian Division retreated in some disorder, leaving the Japanese still holding the Arakan, and the British troops further impressed by Japanese fighting abilities.

In December 1943 the British, in the form of Christison's XV Corps, once again tried to advance on Akyab (**Map 2**). The Japanese, who were starting to plan an invasion of eastern India by Mutaguchi's Fifteenth Army, soon halted the British along the line Maungdaw–Buthidaung and prepared a counterstroke. While the Doi Column pinned down the 5 and

7 Indian Divisions, the Sakurai Column moved through the 'impassable' eastern flank jungle and mountains and cut off the two Indian divisions. General Slim, commanding Allied forces operating against Burma from India, refused to contemplate a withdrawal and decided to supply the encircled divisions by air. After bitter fighting, the two surrounded divisions made contact with each other on 24 February and in turn cut off part of the Japanese 55 Division. Between March and April XV Corps finally broke through the Japanese defence and began the advance on Akyab again, only to be halted by the need to send reinforcements to Imphal.

Above: Gurkha troops at a camp on the Arakan

Opposite: Indian gunners in action during the offensive in the Arakan

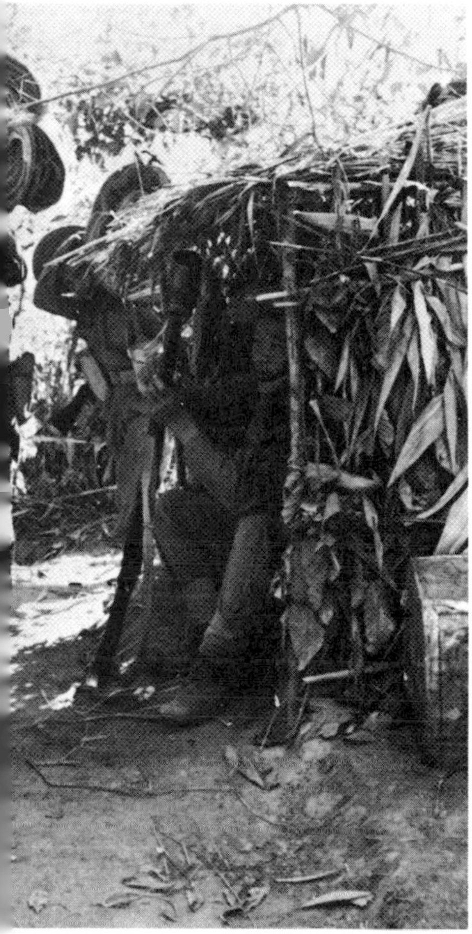

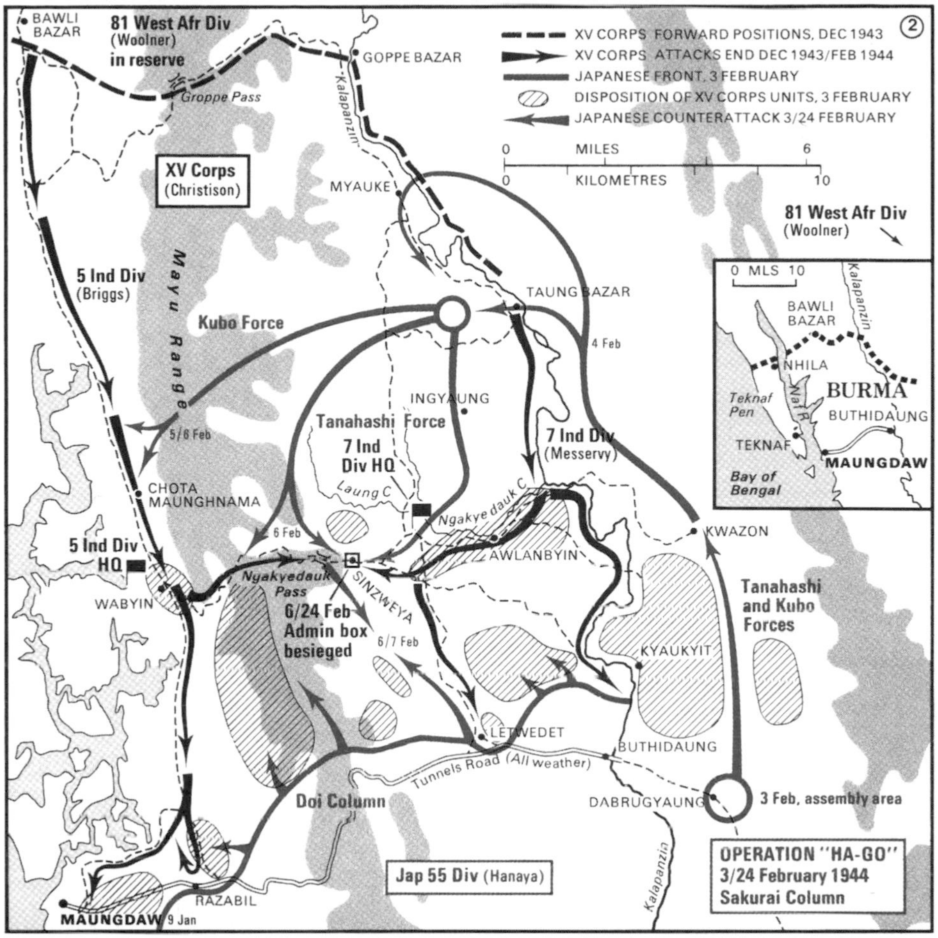
2
XV CORPS FORWARD POSITIONS, DEC 1943
XV CORPS ATTACKS END DEC 1943/FEB 1944
JAPANESE FRONT, 3 FEBRUARY
DISPOSITION OF XV CORPS UNITS, 3 FEBRUARY
JAPANESE COUNTERATTACK 3/24 FEBRUARY
0 MILES 6
0 KILOMETRES 10
BAWLI BAZAR
81 West Afr Div (Woolner) in reserve
Groppe Pass
GOPPE BAZAR
Kalapanzin
XV Corps (Christison)
MYAUKE
81 West Afr Div (Woolner)
5 Ind Div (Briggs)
Mayu Range
TAUNG BAZAR
Kubo Force
4 Feb
INGYAUNG
Tanahashi Force
5/6 Feb
7 Ind Div HQ
7 Ind Div (Messervy)
CHOTA MAUNGHNAMA
Laung C
Ngakyedauk C
5 Ind Div HQ
6 Feb
AWLANBYIN
KWAZON
WABYIN
Ngakyedauk Pass
SINZWEYA
6/24 Feb Admin box besieged
6/7 Feb
Tanahashi and Kubo Forces
KYAUKYIT
LETWEDET
BUTHIDAUNG
Tunnels Road (All weather)
Doi Column
DABRUGYAUNG
3 Feb, assembly area
Jap 55 Div (Hanaya)
OPERATION "HA-GO" 3/24 February 1944 Sakurai Column
RAZABIL
MAUNGDAW 9 Jan
Kalapanzin
0 MLS 10
BAWLI BAZAR
NHILA
BURMA
Teknaf Pen
Naf R
BUTHIDAUNG
TEKNAF
MAUNGDAW
Bay of Bengal

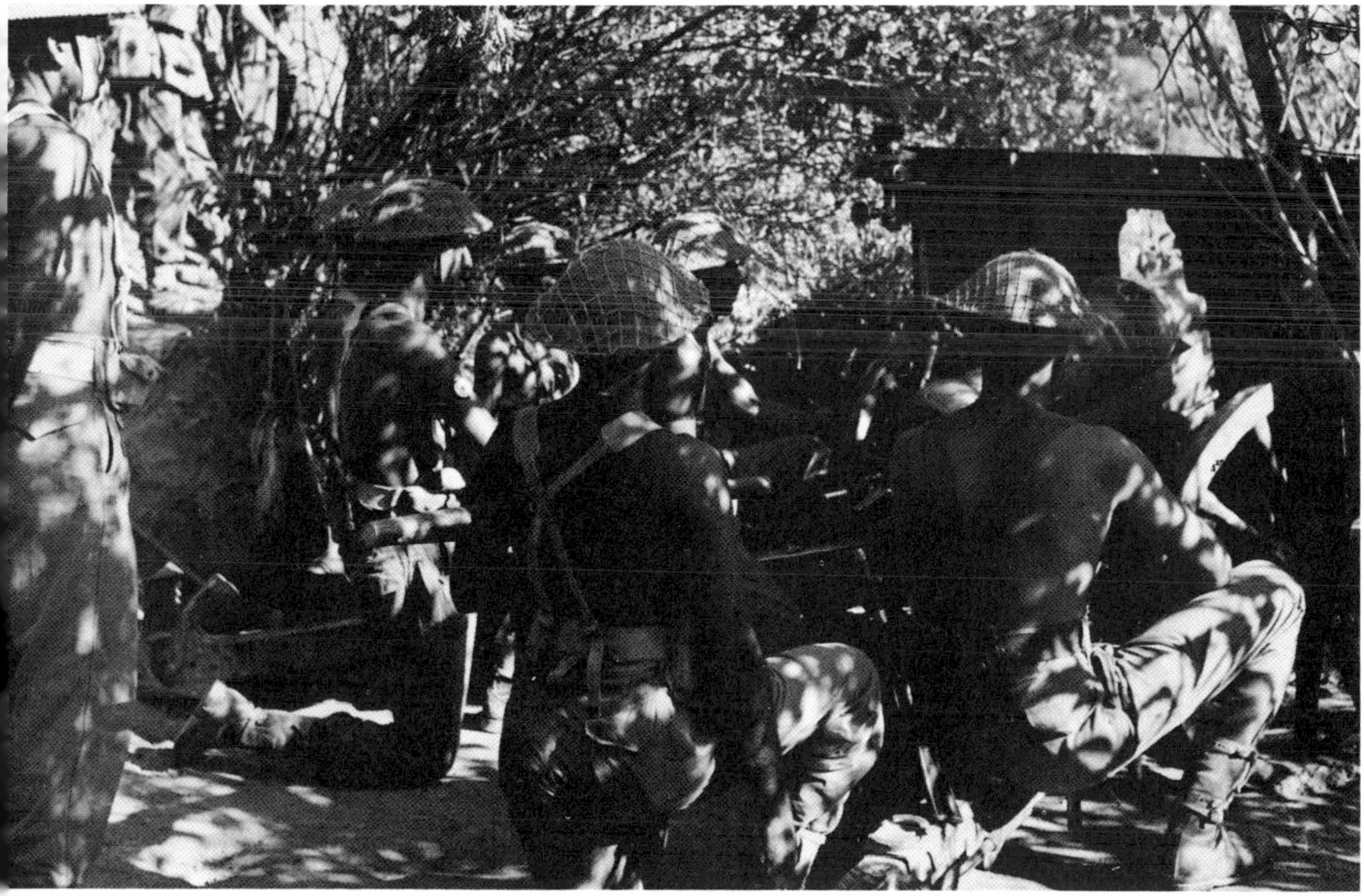

THE CHINDIT OPERATIONS

At the same time as he initiated the first venture into the Arakan, Wavell also gave permission for a second operation that might bolster Allied morale – Wingate's first 'Chindit' operation by 77 Indian Brigade. The aim of the brigade was to operate for lengthy periods behind the Japanese lines, cutting communications, gathering Intelligence, and causing confusion, relying on air supply for essentials before finally pulling back through the Japanese lines. Above all the idea was to demonstrate that British, Indian, and Ghurka troops could take on and beat the Japanese.

The brigade was split into two groups, the Southern one crossing the Chindwin first as a diversion for the larger Northern Group (**Map 1**). Both then advanced in a easterly direction, causing as much damage as they could to Japanese communications. Supply caused difficulty at first as it was not realized that drops could be made in jungle, and much time was wasted in finding open dropping zones. Little damage was caused as the groups advanced to the Irrawaddy, but the Japanese were massing forces against the Chindits, and the advance became very difficult after the Irrawaddy had been crossed. The remains of the two Groups joined up on 24 March, the day Wingate was ordered to return to India. Wingate's last plan to cut the Mandalay–Lashio railway had to be abandoned. The various columns made their way back during late March and April.

Losses were over 33 per cent, too high to justify the small amount of damage inflicted, but the operation was a definite propaganda and morale success, and many valuable lessons were learnt.

Meanwhile General Joseph Stilwell, commanding in the American and Chinese forces in southern China, disappointed by the fact that there was to be no major Allied offensive in Burma in 1943, and fearing a Japanese thrust into north-eastern India, where the vital supply road from Ledo to China was being built, decided to advance on Myitkyina (**Map 2**). Japanese resistance was tough in the Hukawng Valley, but Stilwell was able to resume his advance after a

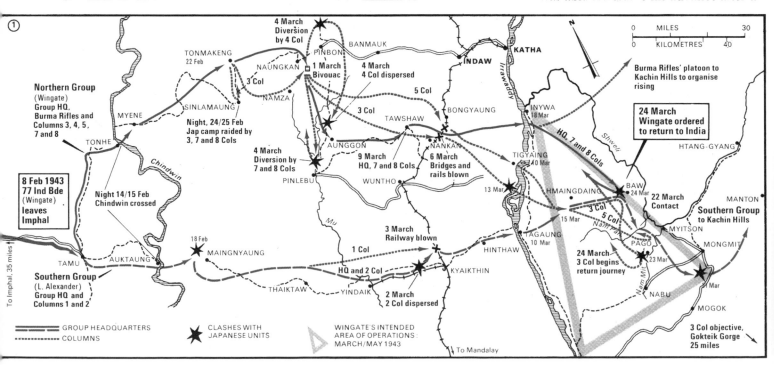

month's delay on 24 December 1943.
But in January 1944 the Japanese
18 Division again halted the Chinese
advance until late February, when the
US 5307 Provisional Regiment under
Brigadier-General F. Merrill arrived.
This allowed the development of the
tactics that led to renewed advances:
Chinese pinning attacks combined
with American flanking movements.

To complement Stilwell's advance,
a second Chindit operation was
mounted. The main force was flown
in by glider and later by transport
aircraft to the area indicated, while
another brigade marched from Ledo.
The Chindits were to harass Japanese
communications by establishing
'blocking points' such as 'White City'
and preventing supplies being moved
up against Stilwell. Wingate was killed
in an air crash on 25 March and was
succeeded by Major-General
W. Lentaigne. Finally exhausted, most
of the Chindits were flown out from
Lake Indawgyi in June and July,
leaving 77 Brigade to take Mogaung
and 16 Brigade to co-operate as best it
could with the prickly Stilwell.

In May the exhausted and disease-
ridden Marauders, now commanded
by Colonel C. N. Hunter, failed to take
Myitkyina, but after the fall of
Mogaung, a combined Allied force
finally took the town on 3/4 August as
the Japanese evacuated it.

Opposite: Chindits prepare to blow up
a bridge

Above: A Chindit mortar crew in action
Below: A supply drop being made near
'White City'

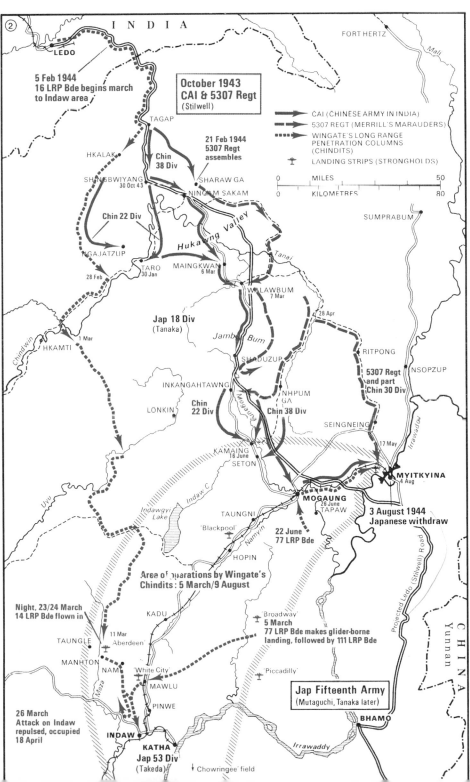

2

I N D I A

LEDO

5 Feb 1944
16 LRP Bde begins march
to Indaw area

TAGAP

October 1943
CAI & 5307 Regt
(Stilwell)

CAI (CHINESE ARMY IN INDIA)
5307 REGT (MERRILL'S MARAUDERS)
WINGATE'S LONG RANGE
PENETRATION COLUMNS
(CHINDITS)
LANDING STRIPS (STRONGHOLDS)

HKALAK

Chin
38 Div

21 Feb 1944
5307 Regt
assembles

SHINGBWIYANG
30 Oct 43

SHARAW GA
NINGAM SAKAM

0   MILES   50
0   KILOMETRES   80

Chin 22 Div

SUMPRABUM

Hukawng Valley

Tanai

NGAJATZUP

28 Feb

TARO
30 Jan

MAINGKWAN
6 Mar

WALAWBUM
7 Mar

28 Apr

FORT HERTZ

Mali

Chindwin

HKAMTI

1 Mar

Jap 18 Div
(Tanaka)

Jambu Bum

SHADUZUP

RITPONG

NSOPZUP

INKANGAHTAWNG

NHPUM
GA

5307 Regt
and part
Chin 30 Div

LONKIN

Chin
22 Div

Chin 38 Div

SEINGNEING

17 May

Irrawaddy

Uyu

KAMAING
16 June
SETON

MYITKYINA
4 Aug

Indaw C

MOGAUNG
26 June
TAPAW

3 August 1944
Japanese withdraw

Indawgyi
Lake

TAUNGNI

'Blackpool'

22 June
77 LRP Bde

Namyin

HOPIN

Area of operations by Wingate's
Chindits: 5 March/9 August

Night, 23/24 March
14 LRP Bde flown in

KADU

'Broadway'

5 March
77 LRP Bde makes glider-borne
landing, followed by 111 LRP Bde

TAUNGLE

11 Mar
Aberdeen

MANHTON

NAM

'White City'

'Piccadilly'

Projected Ledo (Stilwell) Road

C H I N A
Yunnan

Meza

MAWLU

26 March
Attack on Indaw
repulsed, occupied
18 April

PINWE

Jap Fifteenth Army
(Mutaguchi, Tanaka later)

BHAMO

INDAW

KATHA

Jap 53 Div
(Takeda)

Chowringee' field

Irrawaddy

THE JAPANESE ADVANCE TO KOHIMA AND IMPHAL

In Burma, the Japanese Burma Area Army (Lieutenant-General Shozo Kawabe) had ordered the Fifteenth Army (Lieutenant-General Renya Mutaguchi) to start the movement of the three of its four divisions that were to take part in the invasion of India (Operation 'U-GO') on 7/8 March 1944. This invasion, which had been long in the planning, was not a strategic offensive but rather a strategic defensive move, designed to safeguard the Japanese position in Burma by spoiling the Allied offensive that was clearly being prepared. Mutaguchi's offensive had two main objectives: the occupation of the plain on which lie Imphal and Kohima, in Manipur, which was the only practical jumping off point for an Allied invasion of central Burma from India, and the cutting of the single railway to Assam in north-east India, over which most of the supplies for China and Stilwell's forces operating against Burma were carried.

In line with the forces facing them, Scoones' XV Corps, the Japanese sent one division against Kohima, and two against the larger centre of Imphal. The British were expecting the offensive, but even so were taken by surprise by the sheer speed of the Japanese advance. Nevertheless, the British withdrew in good order, those units which were cut off mostly being able to fight their way back to their parent formations.

Kohima was cut off by the Japanese 31 Division on 4 April, and Imphal by the Japanese 15 and 33 Divisions a day later. Slim, though surprised, had his plans ready: the two garrisons were to hold out, being supplied by air, while XXXIII Corps, which was to relieve them, finished assembling at Dimapur.

Above right: A British soldier keeps watch on a Japanese supply track

Right: Searching for snipers in the Kohima area

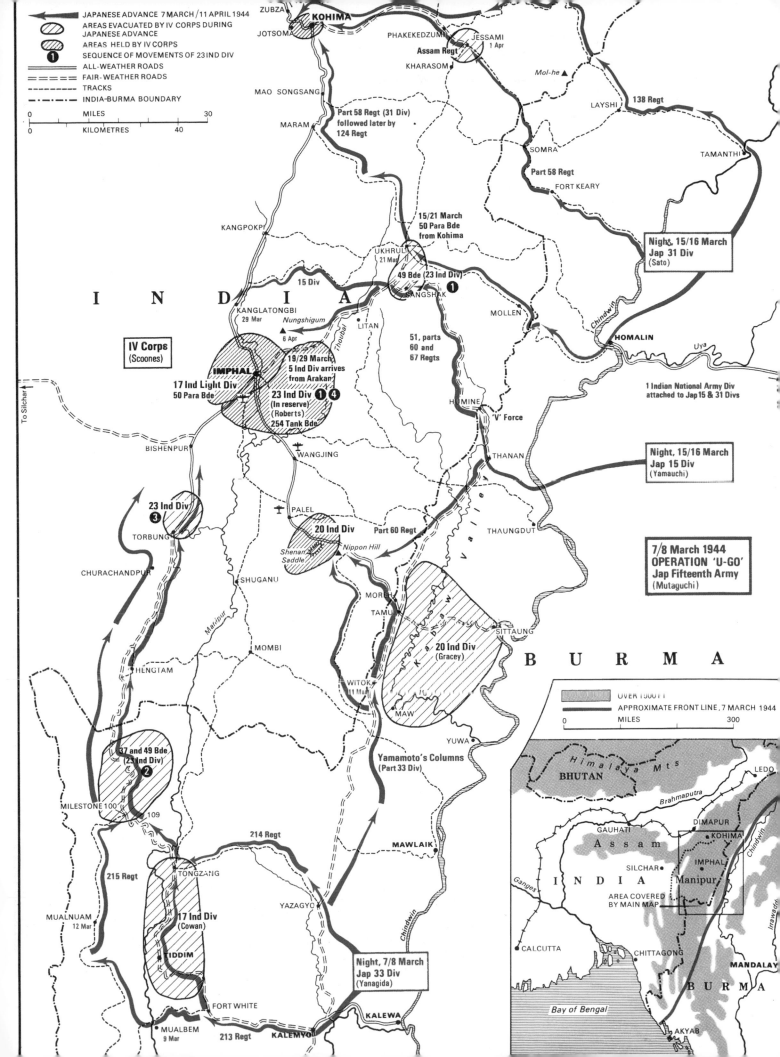

JAPANESE ADVANCE 7 MARCH/11 APRIL 1944
AREAS EVACUATED BY IV CORPS DURING JAPANESE ADVANCE
AREAS HELD BY IV CORPS
① SEQUENCE OF MOVEMENTS OF 23 IND DIV
ALL-WEATHER ROADS
FAIR-WEATHER ROADS
TRACKS
INDIA-BURMA BOUNDARY

| 0 | MILES | 30 |
| 0 | KILOMETRES | 40 |

ZUBZA
KOHIMA
PHAKEKEDZUMI
JESSAMI 1 Apr
Assam Regt
KHARASOM
Mol-he ▲
JOTSOMA
LAYSHI
138 Regt
MAO SONGSANG
MARAM
Part 58 Regt (31 Div) followed later by 124 Regt
SOMRA
TAMANTHI
Part 58 Regt
FORT KEARY

KANGPOKPI
15/21 March 50 Para Bde from Kohima
UKHRUL 21 Mar
49 Bde (23 Ind Div) ①
SANGSHAK
MOLLEN
Chindwin
HOMALIN

15 Div
KANGLATONGBI 29 Mar
Nungshigum 6 Apr ▲
LITAN
51, parts 60 and 67 Regts
HUMINE
Uya

I N D I A

IV Corps (Scoones)
IMPHAL
17 Ind Light Div
50 Para Bde
19/29 March 5 Ind Div arrives from Arakan
23 Ind Div ① ④ (In reserve) (Roberts) 254 Tank Bde
1 Indian National Army Div attached to Jap 15 & 31 Divs

Thoubal
'V' Force
THANAN
Night, 15/16 March Jap 15 Div (Yamauchi)

BISHENPUR
WANGJING

23 Ind Div ③
PALEL
20 Ind Div
Part 60 Regt
THAUNGDUT
7/8 March 1944 OPERATION 'U-GO' Jap Fifteenth Army (Mutaguchi)

TORBUNG
Shenam Saddle
Nippon Hill

CHURACHANDPUR
SHUGANU
MOREH
TAMU

Kabaw Valley

MOMBI
SITTAUNG
20 Ind Div (Gracey)

B U R M A

HENGTAM
Maripur
WITOK 11 Mar
MAW

37 and 49 Bde (23 Ind Div) ②
MILESTONE 100
109
YUWA
Yamamoto's Columns (Part 33 Div)

MUALNUAM 12 Mar
214 Regt
TONGZANG
YAZAGYO

215 Regt
17 Ind Div (Cowan)
TIDDIM
MAWLAIK

Chindwin

Night, 15/16 March Jap 31 Div (Sato)

FORT WHITE
MUALBEM 9 Mar
213 Regt
KALEMYO
KALEWA

Night, 7/8 March Jap 33 Div (Yanagida)

Inset map:

OVER 5000 FT
APPROXIMATE FRONT LINE, 7 MARCH 1944
| 0 | MILES | 300 |

Himalaya Mts
BHUTAN
Brahmaputra
LEDO
GAUHATI
DIMAPUR
Assam
KOHIMA
SILCHAR
IMPHAL
Manipur
I N D I A
Ganges
AREA COVERED BY MAIN MAP
CALCUTTA
CHITTAGONG
MANDALAY
Irrawaddy
Bay of Bengal
AKYAB
B U R M A

THE BATTLE AT KOHIMA AND IMPHAL

The investment of Kohima by the Japanese was completed on 7 April 1944 (**Map 1**), and there then followed twelve days of desperate struggle by the small garrison to hold off the constant Japanese attacks until help could arrive. The relief operation was entrusted to Stopford's XXXIII Corps, which pushed on its British 2 Division as soon as possible. On 14 April its leading brigade over-whelmed the Japanese road-block at Zubza and pushed on to relieve 161 Indian Brigade trapped in Jotsoma. The 2 Division's 5 Brigade then pushed on to relieve Kohima itself on 18 April.

After reinforcing the garrison, 5 Brigade pulled back to take part in a sweeping pincer movement intended to trap the Japanese, with 5 Brigade cutting down from the north and 4 Brigade up from the south. The counterattack was only partially successful, however, 5 Brigade linking up with the garrison on Firs Hill on

the 27th, but 4 Brigade being held on Mount Pulebadze and not managing to take GPT Ridge until 4 May.

On 4 May an attack by 6 and 33 Brigades to take the Japanese line between the District Commissioner's Bungalow and Jail Hill failed in the face of stubborn Japanese resistance, and the attack was called off on the 7th. It was renewed on 11 May and the hills were retaken on the 13th.

An attack on Hunters Hill and Gun Spur by 33 Brigade was repulsed between 15 and 31 May, as was an attack to clear Aradura Spur in the south between 25 and 28 May but a final attack by 7 Indian Division broke through the Japanese positions around the Naga Village on 1 June and allowed 5 Brigade to outflank the Aradura Spur on 3 June, this last making the final Japanese positions at Kohima untenable. The battle had been won. The 2 Division advanced south.

Meanwhile, to the south I V Corps

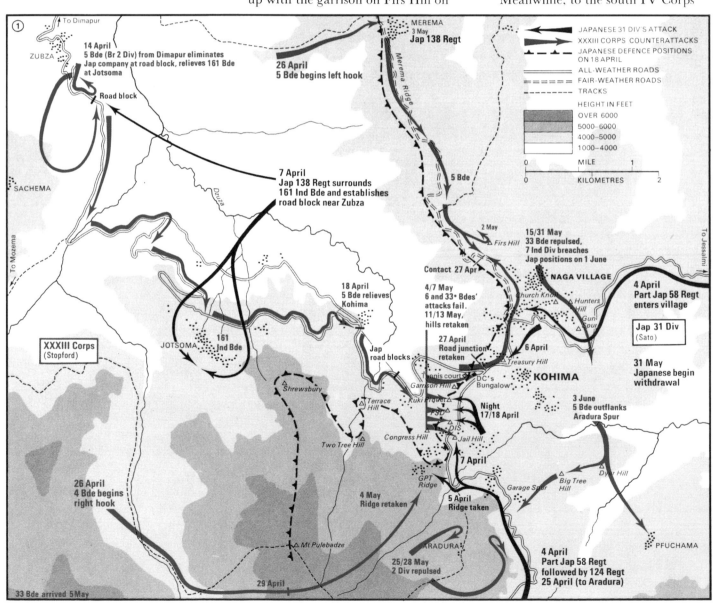

had been involved in a desperate struggle around Imphal (**Map 2**). The original defence perimeter had proved too large, and even the inner one was penetrated by the Japanese in attacks towards Ningthoukhong, Palel, Nungshigum, and Sengmai, attacks that were only held after some of the most vicious fighting seen in the theatre. Supply dropping and landing proved more difficult than had been imagined, and both sides found themselves quickly on the edge of starvation. Additional forces were flown in by Slim throughout the siege to replace these losses, until the British strength in Imphal was about 100,000 men.

Despite this, the Japanese continued to fight superlatively in the face of overwhelming odds to prevent the relief of Imphal by British 2 Division advancing from Kohima, and it was not until 22 June that IV and XXXIII Corps met at Milestone 107 on the road between the sites of the two sieges, the longer of which, that of Imphal, had lasted 88 days.

The remnants of the Japanese Fifteenth Army started to pull back to the River Chindwin, with British air and land forces hard on their heels. They did not entirely disintegrate in the face of this massive British counteroffensive, but nevertheless the campaign had cost them some 65,000 dead.

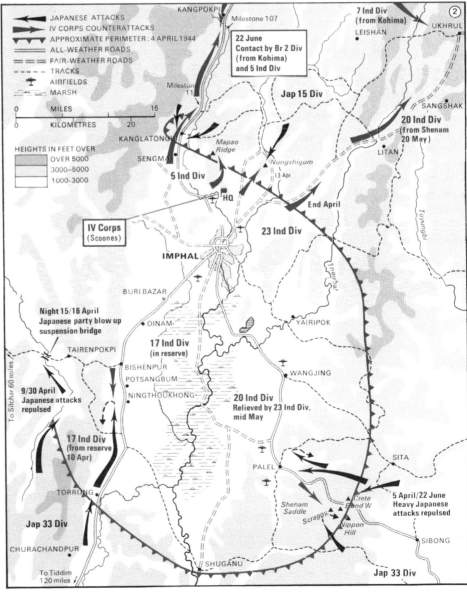

Above right: Mortars firing on Japanese positions near Imphal

THE ADVANCE TO MANDALAY AND MEIKTILA

After their defeats at Kohima and Imphal, the Japanese were pressed back steadily across the Kabaw Valley and to the Chindwin by the British Fourteenth Army (Lieutenant-General W. Slim), which now prepared to cross this major barrier at a number of points.

The disaster that had befallen the Japanese Fifteenth Army brought disgrace to Kawabe, who was replaced as commander of the Burma Area Army by General Hoyotaro Kimura, and to Mutaguchi, who was replaced as commander of the Fifteenth Army by Lieutenant-General Shihachi Katamura. Kimura spent the summer

months rebuilding his shattered forces, and planned to allow the Allies to push on into central Burma, where their overextended lines of communications, combined with the shortened Japanese lines, would allow his ten divisions to inflict a crushing reverse on Lieutenant-General O. Leese's Allied Land Forces South-East Asia, made up of Stilwell's Northern Combat Area Command, the British Fourteenth Army, and the XV Corps in the Arakan.

Operation Extended Capital, the crossing of the Chindwin and advance on Mandalay, started on 19 November with IV Corps at Sittaung and XXXIII Corps at Mawlaik and Kalewa (**Map 1**). The three bridgeheads were secure by 4 December. The British pushed on and met up with advance elements of Stilwell's command on 15 December at Banmauk, and by the end of the year the Allied forces were closing on the Irrawaddy line from Katha to Seikpyu.

Of all the Allied leaders in Burma, Slim was the only one to appreciate what Kimura was attempting to do, as well as his intention of destroying the Fourteenth Army as it crossed the Irrawaddy north of Mandalay. So leaving 19 Division to act as a decoy for IV Corps in this area, he had

secretly switched the corps to the south of XXXIII Corps, to cross the river at Pakokku and cut off the Fifteenth and Thirty-third Armies.

Slim was proved right when 19 Division was heavily counterattacked when it crossed the Irrawaddy at Thabeikkyin on 11 January. Further south, and closer to Mandalay, XXXIII Corps had also advertised its intentions so as to draw Japanese forces away from the area in which IV Corps was to make the major crossings – at Pakokku still further to the south. On 12 February, XXXIII Corps started its operations to cross the Irrawaddy at Ngazun, and immediately ran into heavy opposition, just as 19 Division had at Thabeikkyin in January. But when IV Corps started its crossing at Nyaungu just south of Pakokku on 13 February, only light opposition was encountered. Slim's analysis of the Japanese intentions, and his deception to exploit them, had proved accurate.

As planned, the main effort was now to be made by IV Corps, to cut the Japanese lines of communication from the south by a swift eastward advance. Thus the corps' 17 Indian Division rushed forward from the bridgehead to Meiktila (**Map 2**), which it took from astounded Japanese rear area

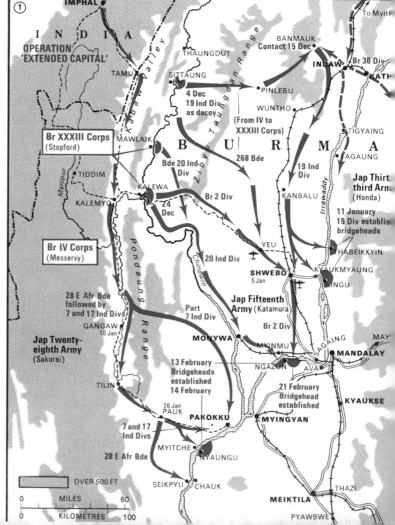

troops on 3 March. Meanwhile, the defence of IV Corps' bridgehead was entrusted to 4 Indian Division.

Meiktila, and the nerve centre of rail communications in the area, was clearly the key to the situation, to the almost complete exclusion of the larger city of Mandalay, and both sides acted promptly. The 17 Division dug itself in and Kimura virtually denuded the defences of Mandalay to provide a force sufficiently powerful to retake Meiktila. Confused fighting continued up to 15 March before the Japanese were able to invest 17 Division in Meiktila with parts of three divisions. Bitter fighting raged up to 29 March, when Kimura realized that his position was no longer tenable: with most of his troops involved around Meiktila and its vital communications to Rangoon, the British were advancing steadily on Mandalay against the weakened Japanese defence. So Kimura decided to pull back, which he did with considerable skill through the smaller rail junction at Thazi, to the east of Meiktila.

To the north, XXXIII Corps had kept the defence of Mandalay pinned down while 19 Division finally took the city in heavy house to house fighting on 20 March. Freed of the need to keep Mandalay's defence pinned, XXXIII Corps was then able to advance south to relieve the hard-pressed 17 Division in Meiktila.

Opposite left: Gurkha troops approach Mandalay

Below: Supplies being brought down the Chindwin

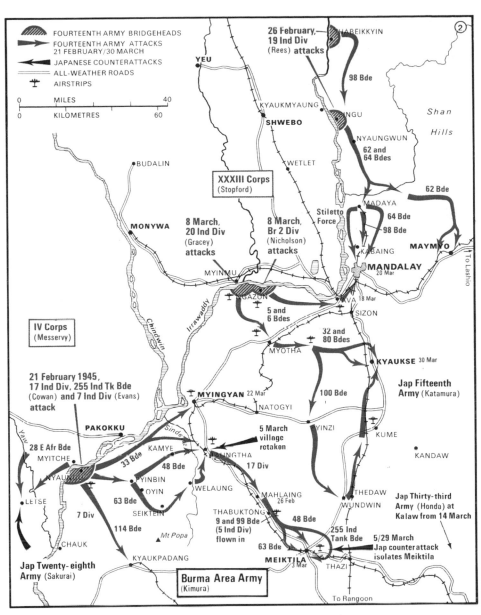

THE CAPTURE OF RANGOON

The monsoon season was now nearly upon Burma, and Slim ordered his forces into a rapid drive on Rangoon, so that he could make full use of his armour before the rains rendered it useless. The Japanese, almost completely exhausted, still offered some resistance, but their lines of communications were harassed by the Burma National Army under General Aung San, which had been ordered north to help Kimura's forces but had revolted.

The British, driving on from Meiktila, advanced along the lines of the Irrawaddy in the west and the Sittang in the east, with the eastern drive soon pulling ahead (**Map 1 opposite**). The monsoon broke on 1 May, and the next day 17 Indian Division entered Pegu. On the other side of the Pegu Yoma, 20 Indian Division took Prome on 3 May.

Both these drives were beaten to the capture of Rangoon by XV Corps from Akyab. Operation Dracula brought 26 Indian Division round from Arakan by sea and landed it south of Rangoon on 2 May. The Japanese realized that their position was untenable and evacuated the city, which was occupied by 26 Division on the 3rd. The 17 and 26 Indian Divisions met at Hlegu on 6 May. XV Corps seaborne operation which resulted in the capture of Rangoon was made possible by the third and last Arakan campaign, Operation Talon (**Map 2**). Kimura, who wished to fight the decisive battle for Burma around Mandalay and Meiktila, had stripped the defences of Arakan to the minimum, and there was little to hold XV Corps when it advanced on Akyab from 12 December 1944. Akyab itself was taken on 4 January 1945 and the whole coast secured in a series of amphibious landings at Myebon, Kangow, and Ramree island.

The war in southern Burma ended without further major battles, just a series of skirmishes between the Allied forces consolidating their positions in the main areas and the Japanese holding out between the west coast and the Irrawaddy, the Irrawaddy and Sittang, and between the Sittang and Thailand, all areas rendered virtually impenetrable by the monsoon.

Above right: Indian troops assault a village after the Rangoon landings

Below right: A 25-pounder being brought ashore during the landings

Opposite right: Indian troops advance under cover of smoke

OPERATION 'TALON': XV Corps (Christison) ②

Jap Twenty-eighth Army (Sakurai)

Jap 54 Div

82 W Afr Div 81 W Afr Div

MAUNGDAW

HTIZWE

74 Bde (25 Ind Div)

DONBAIK
23 Dec
Foul Point

MYOHAUNG

SEIKPYU

Irrawaddy

NGAPE

AKYAB 4 Jan

MYEBON

AN

0942, 21 Jan 1945
71 Bde (26 Ind Div)

KYAUKPYU

SANE 2 Feb

LETPAN

Ramree

Bay of Bengal

MAYIN

RAMREE 9 Feb

TAUNGUP

CHEDUBA

MILES 60
KILOMETRES 80

Op 'Dracula', 26 Ind Div for Rangoon landing on 2 May

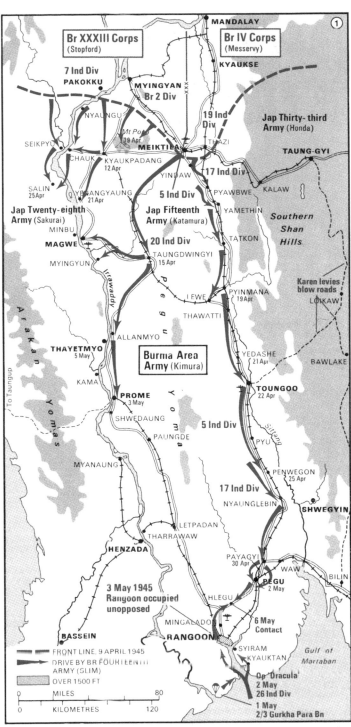

THE WAR IN NORTHERN BURMA

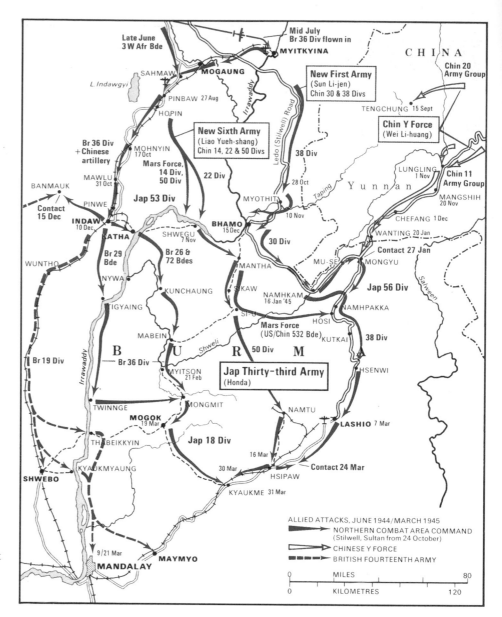

Stilwell's last advance in northern Burma started on 15 October 1944, and was a large scale pincer movement intended to trap Lieutenant-General Masaki Honda's Thirty-third Army between his own Northern Combat Area Command and the Chinese Y Force (General Wei Li-huang). Progress was slow but sure.

In China, however, matters were desperate, and when Stilwell recommended measures that Chiang Kai-shek ought to take, the latter demanded that Stilwell be replaced. Major-General A. Wedemeyer took over from him as chief-of-staff to Chiang and Lieutenant-General D. Sultan as head of the Northern Combat Area Command.

The British, American, and Chinese forces continued south, the Chinese 22 Division crossing the Irrawaddy at Shwegu on 7 November as the first part of the closing pincer movement. The movement was held up for a month, however, by the Japanese defence of Bhamo, which ended only on 15 December, when survivors of the garrison fought their way out to rejoin 56 Division south-east of Bhamo. At this point Chiang Kai-shek removed two divisions for service elsewhere in China, and Sultan had to alter Stilwell's plan from an envelopment to just opening the road from Bhamo via Namkham to the Burma Road.

The advance continued into the new year, and the two arms met at Mongyu on 27 January. The Japanese 56 Division managed to slip away, but the Burma Road had been reopened. The campaign in northern Burma ended after the Japanese had resisted the advancing Allies all the way to Lashio and Kyaukme. The British 36 Division reached Mandalay and returned to Fourteenth Army control on 21 March.

Right: General Stilwell watching his troops cross a river

THE WAR IN CHINA

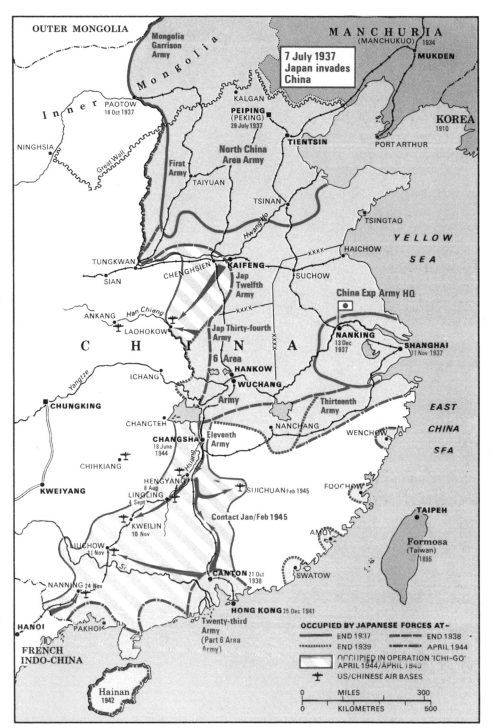

Japan's war against China had started in 1937, and initial successes had come thick and fast against a weak and poor China, already divided by the conflict between the Nationalists under Generalissimo Chiang Kai-shek and the Communists under Mao Tse-tung. Although a truce between the two Chinese parties was established, their rivalry was to dog the Chinese war effort throughout the Second World War. By 1939 Japan held most of China as far west as a line from French Indo-China in the south to the south-eastern border of Outer Mongolia in the north, and as these comprised the richest areas of China, Japan was content to hold here. America in particular was sympathetic to the Chinese cause, and enormous quantities of material were shipped to China, during the war via the Burma Road or 'Over the Hump' by aircraft. Perhaps as important, General Joseph Stilwell was loaned to Chiang as his chief-of-staff and military adviser in retraining the Chinese army.

1942 saw little action as the Japanese were too tied up with the opening and initial consolidation phases of their war against the Western Allies and the Chinese were too weak.

1943 was used by the Japanese for 'rice offensives', designed to give new formations battle experience against weak opposition and to seize the rice crop from previously unoccupied areas. The Chinese were at their lowest ebb and could offer no real resistance until the end of the year, when they managed to repulse, with American air support, one rice offensive in the Battle of Changteh. A dispute between Stilwell and Brigadier-General Claire Chennault about priority of supplies for the Chinese army or the Chinese air-force had been decided in the latter's favour, and the new US 14th Air Force as it became started to inflict severe damage on the Japanese all over China and as far away as Formosa. Increased hostility towards the

Communists also weakened Chiang's already overextended forces.

1944 was marked by a *de facto* truce with the Communists, which allowed greater activity against the Japanese. But the Japanese, disturbed by the success of the 14th Air Force operating from airfields at Linchow, Kwerlin, Lingling, Hengyang, and Chihkiong, launched Operation ICHI-GO in April to capture these and force China out of the war. The Chinese defence crumbled alarmingly, though there were local successes, but the offensive in northern Burma had to be called off and the loss of the 14th Air Force's airfields hindered the US advance in

the Pacific. The situation was finally stabilized on 10 December.

1945 saw further Japanese offensives to consolidate their previous year's gains, but the threatening situation in Manchuria and his own overextended deployment led General Okamura, commanding the China Expeditionary Army, to shift much of his strength north, which allowed the Chinese to cut off the corridor to Indo-China. The position remained approximately thus until the end of the war, when the civil war between the Nationalists and the Communists was soon resumed.

RUSSIA
FIGHTS
BACK

Hitler, when he launched Barbarossa, had miscalculated Russian military strength. Even so his initial onslaught had inflicted terrible casualties, and if he had not, like Napoleon before him, entered Moscow itself he had come perilously near it. When planning the campaign Hitler had, according to Colonel-General Halder, expressed the opinion that the seizure of Moscow 'was not so very important'. When late in the year the Germans did begin their onslaught against the Russian capital they did so without proper logistic preparation and were foiled not only by the weather but by the inadequacy of their own resources. Although the long Russian retreat was by no means the calculated withdrawal that Stalin would have had people believe, it did give time for the organization of new Russian armies. In December 1941 German intelligence still credited the enemy with 280 rifle or cavalry divisions and forty-four mechanized or armoured brigades. The remarkable resilience of the Russians was demonstrated by their great winter counteroffensive.

Even so they were disappointed by its results for they had hoped that this winter campaign would wipe out an exhausted enemy. But the Germans proved to have more staying power than they calculated. Stalin, it seems, held a meeting on 5 January, and without so much as asking for anyone else's opinion, announced that the time was opportune for a general counter-offensive. This led to a dissipation of effort. Nor were the various offensives, which involved six different Fronts, closely co-ordinated from the strategic point of view. Had the Russians concentrated on the destruction of Army Group Centre they might have achieved better results. It must be appreciated that the Russians, though better prepared administratively for winter warfare, also suffered from the weather. They too felt the cold; they too needed food and ammunition. The great Soviet counteroffensive eventually lost its momentum because the lines of communication were becoming too long as it progressed westwards. Moreover their state of training was still poor. Inexperienced commanders with untrained staffs tended to use their tanks in penny packets and to hound their infantry into action without properly co-ordinated artillery support. In truth the Red Army operated in a fashion very strange to the armies of the Western Allies, where it was not the thing for the higher commanders to become involved in the details of the tactical battle. This is well-illustrated by Colonel Albert Seaton in his account of the attack on 6 Rumanian Corps on the Stalingrad Front on 20 November 1942: 'The Red Army system of command and control was very different from that in use in western armies, and instead of commanding the attack by map, radio and liaison officers, all higher commanders, even the front commander himself, would establish battle command posts on prominent ground within sight of the enemy. This meant that in the sectors selected for the main attack within one or two thousand yards of the forward defended localities, regimental, divisional, army and front commanders would be watching the progress of the battle, each commander being accompanied by his personal staff, signallers, orderlies and clerks, and his artillery commander and the commanders of his main arms. The front commander would in addition have a telephonic or short wave radio telephonic rear link to Moscow and Stalin.' The Russian dictator was just as prone to interfere in operations and personnel selection as was the German.

By this stage the tide of war was turning against an over-extended Germany. The Allied victories at El Alamein, Stalingrad, and Tunis were landmarks on the road back to the *Reich*. Hitler's strategy was over-ambitious. He thrust to the Caucasus and the Volga simultaneously when his resources were scarcely adequate for even one of these objectives. Unable, as he was to tell Goebbels (8 May 1943), to overcome the problems of movement and supply he had left his unfortunate soldiers, as usual in Russia, to live from hand to mouth. Even had he allowed Paulus to try to break out of Stalingrad the move would probably have failed for lack of fuel. Göring's assurances that the place could be supplied by air were valueless. Nobody else on the staff of the Luftwaffe believed them.

Hitler did not have to cut the Volga at Stalingrad. By fighting the Russians in a built-up area he played into their hands, for the Soviet troops, outclassed in open warfare, were formidable in the ruins of a city. As Eremenko put it: 'the greatest error of the German High Command was to underestimate the power of the Soviet nation and its armed forces, at the same time overestimating its own ability.' When, as occasionally happened, the German generals were able to persuade Hitler to give them a free hand they were still capable of scoring a telling success. An example was von Manstein's daring counter-attack with Army Group South, which brought to an end the hitherto successful Soviet offensive in the winter 1942–3. Von Manstein and von Kluge, having prevailed upon Hitler to allow them to shorten the front and build up a reserve by withdrawing troops from the line, were able to counterattack with advantage in the Ukraine. With three experienced and fresh Panzer divisions (*Leibstandarte*, *Das Reich*, and *Totenkopf*) they were too much for tired opponents who had temporarily outrun their supports and supplies.

On 31 May 1943 there was a conference in Berlin. When it was over General Guderian seized Hitler's hand and asked to be allowed to speak to him. The Führer listened and Guderian urged him to abandon the plan for a summer offensive on the Russian Front on the grounds that 'the great commitment would certainly not bring us equivalent gains; our defensive preparations in the West were sure to suffer considerably. I ended', Guderian writes, 'with the question: "Why do you want to attack in the East

at all this year?" Here Keitel joined in, with the words: "We must attack for political reasons." I replied: "How many people do you think even know where Kursk is? It's a matter of profound indifference to the world whether we hold Kursk or not. I repeat my question: Why do we want to attack in the East at all this year?" Hitler's reply was: "You're quite right. Whenever I think of this attack my stomach turns over." Well it might.'

Kursk, the greatest armoured battle of all time, was a costly failure. The German offensive lost its momentum in the first 48 hours. The Anglo-American landings in Sicily gave Hitler the opportunity to break off an unprofitable operation in which he had never really believed. He was now in the situation, dreaded by German strategists, compelled to fight on land on two European fronts. 'The time was soon to come,' as Colonel Seaton points out, 'when a number of German formations were permanently lost to the war effort as they were shunted throughout Europe in an effort to plug gaps.' Soviet historians would have us believe that the Kursk battle compelled the Germans to withdraw divisions from the Mediterranean thus permitting the Allies to land in Sicily and leading to the defeat of Italy. It is evident, however, that in the long term the Italian campaign and that in Normandy eased the pressure on the Eastern Front whilst, in the short term, the Sicily landings provided the occasions for Hitler to break off the Kursk battle. What he did not appreciate, since he still underestimated them, was that the Russians were about to launch their own summer offensive. He had irretrievably lost the initiative on the Eastern Front. Even had Hitler wished to make peace, nobody was so stupid as to trust him to keep any terms he might make. And as for the Russians, who had suffered so much, they were determined to drive their tanks through the ruins of Berlin. Hitler himself recognized that the situation had changed. In his Directive No. 51 (3 November 1943) we read: 'The danger

in the East remains, but a greater danger now appears in the West; an Anglo-Saxon landing! In the East, the vast extent of the territory makes possible for us to lose ground, even on a large scale, without a fatal blow being dealt to the nervous system of Germany.' He now began to reinforce the defences in the West, especially the areas from which the V-1 and V-2 campaign against England was to be waged. Thus the Germans some 3,000,000 strong found themselves facing some 5,700,000 Russians, who greatly outnumbered them in tanks and guns, and who, thanks largely to the Americans, were well-supplied, and to whom the White half-track had given a new mobility. Hitler spoke of losing ground, but at a time when he should have withdrawn at least to the Bug, he still hoped to retake Kiev and to make an offensive in the Crimea.

In January 1944 at long last the Russians raised the thirty month siege of Leningrad (St Petersburg), then in February the Russians reached the northern frontier of Rumania. This was the occasion for Hitler to dismiss his greatest general, von Manstein — that master of manoeuvre. He now reverted wholeheartedly to his idea of an inflexible defence – 'All that counts now is to cling stubbornly to what we hold' . . . His choice to carry out this plan was the bold, inexhaustible Field-Marshal Walther Model, a determined fighting man, who did not belong to any high-born Prussian clan. Truly Hitler's tactical ideas were those of the Somme and Verdun. He can hardly be classed as a subtle tactician, and he was not the man to learn from his mistakes – if only because, like most dictators, he was not given to the admission that he ever made any. If 1944 became for the Russians 'The Year of the Ten Victories' it was largely thanks to Hitler, who as late as 2 April could announce 'The Russians have exhausted and divided their forces', could declare that it was imperative to hold firmly to the Crimea, and to hold or win back the line of the Dniester.

Hitler's judgment, never of the best, became decidedly warped after the attempt on his life on 20 July 1944. Guderian tells us that 'the deep distrust he already felt for mankind in general, and for General Staff Corps officers and generals in particular, now became profound hatred . . . in his case what had been hardness became cruelty, while a tendency to bluff became plain dishonesty. He often lied without hesitation, and assumed that others lied to him . . . It had already been difficult enough to deal with him; it now became a torture that grew steadily worse from month to month.' But he still had courtiers like Göring and Ribbentrop to bolster his self-esteem, and he still trusted *treuer* Heinrich Himmler, who had no kind of pretension to high military command, to command the Replacement Army. And as late as 20 April 1945 Field-Marshal Schörner, who after a meteoric rise, now commanded Army Group Centre, could visit him in the famous bunker in Berlin and restore him to good spirits and optimism. But by that time the Third Reich was dissolving in a crazy dream world.

Irrespective of all his strategic and tactical errors Hitler himself brought about the ultimate defeat of his Germany when by a gross political misjudgment he condemned her to wage the two-front war which every good German strategist from Frederick the Great onwards has always dreaded.

Opposite left: Civilians of Bryansk greet the Red Army

Opposite right: A Soviet assault begins

Above left: Troops crossing the Dniepr under fire

Above right: Soviet troops advancing in the Ukraine

THE RED ARMY ATTACKS IN THE SOUTH

Hitler's changes of mind in 1941 had robbed his forces both of the prize of Moscow and of any decisive gains in the south. As 1942 opened the German forces in the east were deployed from Finland to the Crimea in a series of huge defensive camps (nicknamed 'hedgehogs'), between which the tide of Russian counteroffensives ebbed and flowed. In the south the Germans held all the territory up to a line from Kharkov to Taganrog on the Sea of Azov, including all of the Crimea save Sevastopol and the Kerch peninsula (**Map 1**). In this area the major German hedgehogs were Kharkov, Artemovsk, and Taganrog.

In spite of their staggering losses in 1941, the Russian's were able to maintain a constant pressure on the Germans throughout the winter of 1941/42. Part of the reason for this was that the Russians, with the whole of their eastern empire at their back, were able almost immediately to make up their manpower losses, particularly in the infantry, with first rate, hardy troops. The importance of their losses in armour was to some extent mitigated by the frost, which for long periods immobilized German tanks and aircraft. Therefore the Russian winter counteroffensives, hastily planned and lacking in strong logistic support though they were, enjoyed considerable success. But the bulk of the German forces, esconced in their hedgehogs, were not effected.

One such counteroffensive, planned for Kostenko's South-West Front and Malinovsky's South Front to take place in January 1942, was to be launched across the River Donets between Kharkov and Artemovsk, wheeling south to trap the German forces in Artemovsk and Taganrog and freeing ports on the north coast of the Sea of Azov. A smaller force was to wheel north to attack the hedgehog of Kharkov.

Launched on 18 January, this attack did not meet its objectives (**Map 2**). The Russian Sixth, Fifty-seventh, and Ninth Armies of the South-West Front encountered sharp opposition from the German Sixth and Seventeenth Armies. By 31 January, although they had established a substantial salient in German-occupied territory, they were still far from their objectives. Elements of Fifty-seventh Army, thrusting south in accordance with the plan, were repulsed by the German Group 'Mackensen', hastily brought into action by the commander of Army Group South, Bock, to save the lateral railway communication from Pavlograd to Taganrog.

In March the spring thaws brought activity on both sides to a halt. Apart from the difficulties of movement, both sides were at the end of extended lines of supply, and short of all vital matériel. Not until May was either side ready for further action.

On 12 May Kostenko's South-West Front took the offensive again in an attempt to make good one of the objectives of his original plan by encircling Kharkov (**Map 3**). But by this time the Germans were able to move outside their hedgehogs, and their armies had been substantially reinforced. (A total of fifty-one new divisions from the satellite countries, Italy, Rumania, Hungary, and Slovakia, and one Spanish volunteer division had been added to the German armies in the east in April 1942). Also their tanks and aircraft were superior to anything the Russians could bring against them at the time. Kostenko's attacks were halted and turned back,

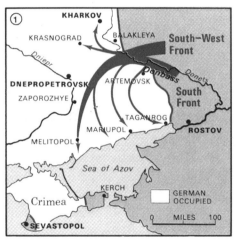

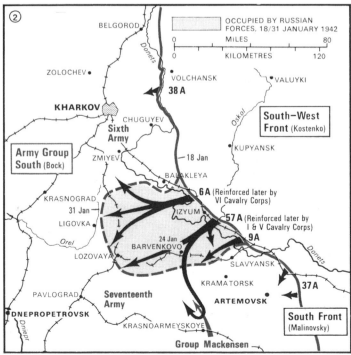

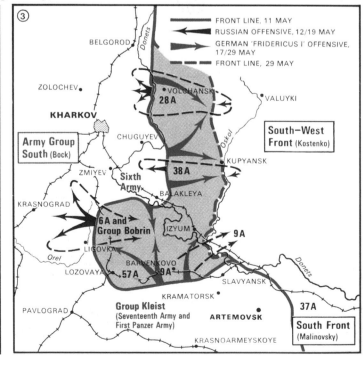

and the German Sixth Army and Group Kleist were able to eliminate the Russian salient and push back their line east of Kharkov. These operations, codenamed 'Fridericus I', were completed by the end of May.

Also in May Manstein's Eleventh Army cleared the Kerch Peninsula, inflicting 150,000 casualties on the Russians, and renewed attacks on Sevastopol, but it was not until 18 June that any significant progress was made (**Map 4**). In a series of concerted attacks the German LIV Corps from the north, the Rumanian Mountain Corps from the east, and the German XXX Corps from the south closed in on Sevastopol. They were helped by the largest artillery piece ever to grace a siege train. Eventually an amphibious assault by LIV Corps sealed the fate of the city and between 30 June and 2 July the remnants of the Russian garrison were evacuated by sea. They had lost a further 100,000 men.

Right: German troops surrender during the Russian spring attacks

Below right: Sailors loading a gun for shipment to besieged Sevastopol

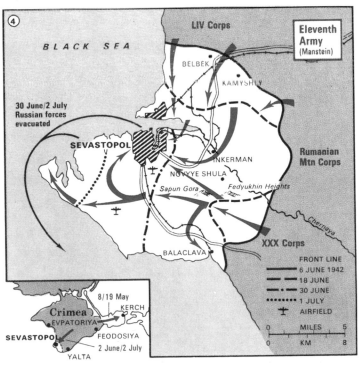

193

THE DRIVE TO THE VOLGA

The situation that faced Hitler in the spring of 1942 was very different to that which had faced him a year before. Then his armies had been everywhere victorious. Of his enemies only Britain remained in the field, and she with scant effect. But in 1942 his magnificent armies had lost their cutting edge. Huge numbers of them were committed deep in Russia with no prospect of release. The United States had entered the war, and the prospect of a war on two fronts, Germany's recurrent nightmare, was imminent. Above all, as his economic advisers never ceased to remind him, Germany's oil situation was critical,

and Hitler made the goal of his 1942 campaign the capture of the Caucasus oilfields. His initial aim was to occupy the oilfields in the northern part of the Caucasus, and to establish a defensive line along the River Don from Voronezh to Stalingrad (**Map 1**). To this end he planned first to burst through the Russian front between Kursk and Rostov. He reorganized Bock's Army Group South into Army Group A (Field-Marshal List), and Army Group B (initially under Bock; from 13 July under General Weichs). Army Group A was to thrust south into the Caucasus, capture the oilfields, and defeat the Russian forces facing it. Army Group B was to establish the protective front along the Don, but at this stage Hitler gave it a second objective – Stalingrad itself (**Map 2**). From being a covering operation the task of Army Group B became a major offensive while Army Group A was ordered to occupy all the oilfields to a line from Batumi to Baku. Even as a protective flank the role of Army Group B was radically unsound. A glance at the map will show that a concerted Russian thrust from the Stalingrad area towards Rostov, enjoying the protection of the 'elbow' of the Don on its right flank, could easily sever Army Group A from Army

Group B. Now Hitler planned to disperse the effort of his armies still further by giving them two major objectives to be taken simultaneously.

On 28 June the German summer offensive opened with a drive by the German Second Army and the Fourth Panzer Army against Voronezh. On 30 June the German Sixth Army (General Paulus) began its drive down the Donets Corridor (**Map 3**). It was not until 9 July that Army Group A broke into the Donets Basin and headed south to cross the Don between Rostov and Tsirilyansky. With Army Group A poised to cross the Don, and Army Group B racing for the Don elbow and Stalingrad, Hitler made the second of three moves that ruined the campaign, and sowed the seeds of his defeat. The first had been his change of plan on 13 July designating Stalingrad a major objective. Now, on 17 July, fearful that Army Group A would not be powerful enough to force the Don crossings, he diverted the Fourth Panzer Army from the eastward drive against Stalingrad to the southern drive against the Caucasus. In spite of this diversion, Army Group B was able to clear the Don elbow and arrive on the Volga north of Stalingrad by 23 August. But without Fourth

Panzer Army its progress was slow.

In spite of their decline in men, matériel, and morale during the long winter sieges, Hitler's armies carried out his extraordinary orders with remarkable success. By 29 July, Army Group A and Fourth Panzer Army had driven a deep wedge into the Caucasus, reaching to within 70 miles of the Caspian sea. The Russian Trans-Caucasus Front was threatened with separation and complete disruption.

At this point Hitler made the third of his mistakes. Enraged by the slow progress of Sixth Army, he ordered the Fourth Panzer Army to turn round yet again and rejoin Army Group B in its attacks toward Stalingrad. List and the German Chief-of-Staff, Halder, daring to protest at these moves, were relieved of their appointments. Army Group A, under the distant and erratic personal command of the Führer, was left holding a front of 500 miles in the Caucasus and at the same time trying to maintain an offensive to gain the original objective of the Batumi–Baku line. Not surprisingly, no significant progress was made.

Hitler's total failure to grasp even the most elementary military principles was not the only difficulty his armies had to contend with in 1942. The losses of Russian manpower of 1941 had been made good from the subject peoples of the Soviet empire in Asia. These were recruited mainly into the infantry and cavalry, and though, because of their illiteracy, tactical plans had to be simple, they were possessed of matchless endurance and tenacity. From a general's point of view they were ideal troops, needing minimal logistic backing. In the field of armour, too, the Russians had the edge over their opponents by the summer of 1942. The T34 tank, just coming into service, though simple to the point of crudity, was, in the crucial ratio of gun, armour, and speed, superior to anything the Germans could show against it. By mid-August any serious attempt to secure the oilfields was as good as over, and Hitler had diverted all his energies to the attack on Stalingrad.

Left: German artillery bombards a Russian position

Above right: German infantry advancing across the steppes

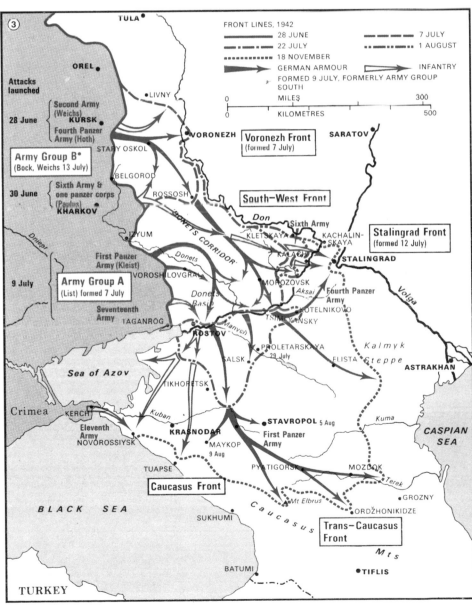

THE ASSAULT ON STALINGRAD

In 1942 Stalingrad was a city of 500,000 inhabitants straggling for 18 miles along the western bank of the Volga. Its industrial importance was considerable. It was a large inland port, and its factories produced over a quarter of the Russians' tractors and vehicles, as well as tanks, guns, and weapons. In the immediate vicinity of Stalingrad the Volga pursued a serpentine course through a number of different channels, posing a formidable bridging problem and making it virtually impossible for the Germans to invest the city from the east. An obvious solution to this problem was to establish a bridgehead north (upstream) of the city, stop all river traffic and prevent the reinforcement of the city. In spite of fact that they reached the Volga on 23 August (**Map 1**) the Germans failed to do this. Anyway their slow advance, caused by the removal of Fourth Panzer Army, had already allowed the Russians considerably to strengthen the defences of Stalingrad.

On 17 August, Paulus' Sixth Army struck across the Don, and the now-restored Fourth Panzer Army advanced from the south (**Map 1**). The Russian Fourth Tank, First Tank, and Fifty-first Armies fell back before them, and by the end of the month the Germans had squeezed the Russian defenders into a small perimeter some 30 miles by 18 miles. At this stage various alternatives were still open to the Germans: an upstream crossing, encirclement, siege – all could have been attempted. But they elected to carry the city by direct attack. The result was one of the most terrible battles of the war. Stalin's determination not to lose the city of his name, and Hitler's equal determination to take it, blinded both sides to other tactical and strategic considerations. Stalingrad became the Verdun of the Second World War.

By 12 September the Russian perimeter had been reduced to a total of 30 miles and the battle for the city proper began. Street by street, house by house, the Germans fought their way towards the Volga. The brunt of the fighting fell on the infantry, much of it at appallingly close quarters. By 13 October the river had been reached in the south, but in the north the factory area remained unconquered (**Map 2**). The attackers were exhausted, and Hitler ordered a change in tactics. Instead of a direct assault the city was to be reduced by artillery fire and bombardment, followed by a steady advance by the ground troops. This was next to nonsense. As the Allies were to find to their cost at Monte Cassino, heaps of rubble make better defensive positions even than standing buildings. All this order succeeded in doing was to make the task of the attacking troops still more difficult. By 18 November, although elements of Sixth Army had reached the river in the north, the Russian Sixty-second Army still held substantial areas on the west bank (**Map 2**).

By 18 November (the approximate date of the onset of the Russian winter freeze) Hitler had failed to carry either of the twin objectives of his 1942 summer campaign. He had succeeded in placing his armies in untenable positions with large gaps between them, tenuous supply lines and weakly defended, extended flanks direly vulnerable to Russian counterattack.

Above right: The first German troops arrive on the outskirts of Stalingrad

Right: A German anti-tank gun in action amid the ruins of Stalingrad

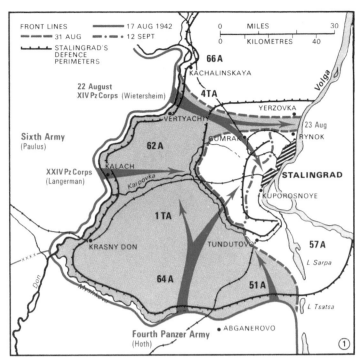

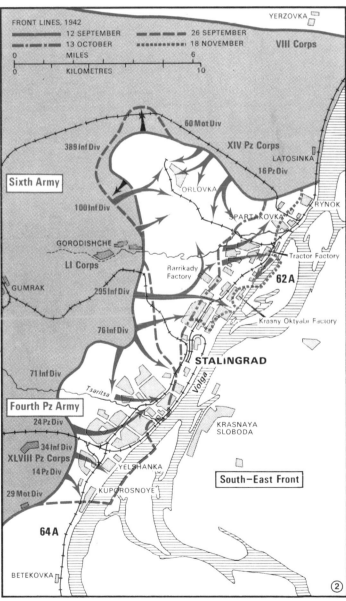

THE RUSSIAN COUNTER ATTACKS

On 19 November 1942 came the Russian counterattack that the extended German flank in south Russia had been inviting since July. Timed to coincide with the frosts and the Allied landings in North Africa, this offensive had been long in preparation. Both planning and execution were excellent, and demonstrated how far the Red Army had come in these respects since 1941.

From north of the Don the South-West Front (Vatutin) and the Don Front (Rokossovsky) were to drive south, pinching out the Don elbow, and trapping the German forces between the Don and the Volga (**Map 1**). A day later, 20 November the Stalingrad Front (Eremenko) was to attack westward to meet up with the northern attack and complete the encirclement of the Germans in Stalingrad. The two forces met on 23 November, and the German Army Group B under Weichs was only just able to reel back in time to save itself from total defeat. Sixth Army and part of Fourth Panzer Army, however, were completely trapped. On the same day (23 November) five encircled Rumanian divisions in the north surrendered.

Although the Russians had achieved encirclement, they were not yet sufficiently organized to prevent Paulus and the German Sixth Army from breaking out. This he was urged to do by Weichs, but the chain of command between Weichs and Paulus had been bypassed by Hitler, who assumed direct command of Sixth Army himself. On hearing of the Russian offensive, even Hitler was at first inclined to order Paulus to escape, but he was easily persuaded to order him to stay put when Göring undertook to supply Sixth Army by air to the tune of 500 tons of supplies per day. Like many of Göring's assurances this was wildly unrealistic, but it was enough for Hitler. Paulus was ordered to form 'Fortress Stalingrad', and plans to relieve him were put in train.

Manstein's Eleventh Army was moved from the Leningrad front, renamed Army Group Don and allotted the task of opening a corridor

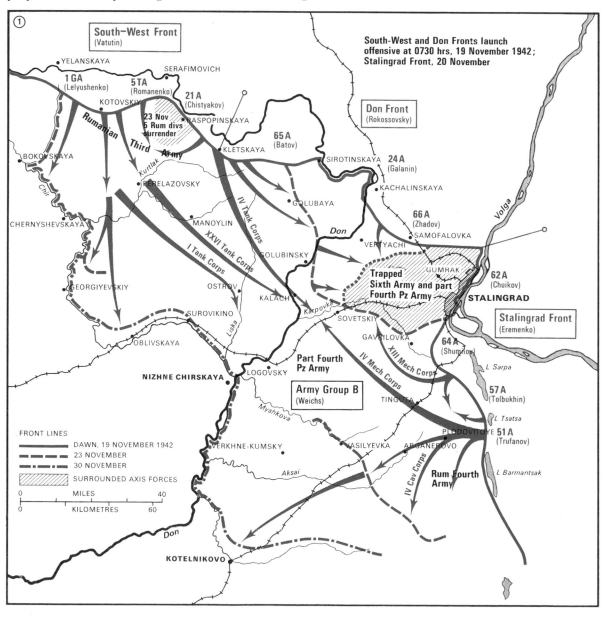

to Sixth Army, re-establishing its supply lines, and restoring the original front. Manstein organized his force in two groups, Group Hoth south of the Don (**Map 2**) and Operational Group Hollidt north of the river. His plan (largely dictated by Hitler) was to attack Yeremenko's Stalingrad Front, roll it back, and then, in concert with Paulus attacking from Stalingrad, fall on Rokossovsky's Don Front.

On 12 December Manstein launched his offensive. For two days progress was brisk, but Russian opposition was stiffened by reinforcements and Manstein's pace became slower. However by 23 December he had got within 30 miles of Stalingrad. His position here became so critical that he defied Hitler and sent Paulus a message ordering him to abandon what he could not carry and break out of Stalingrad to join forces with Group Hoth on the Myshkova. Paulus again refused to act on his own initiative, and declined to leave Stalingrad without direct authority from Hitler. This was the nearest that the attempt to relieve Paulus came to success.

Above left: A Stuka over Stalingrad

Left: German troops in a snow storm during the attempt to relieve Stalingrad

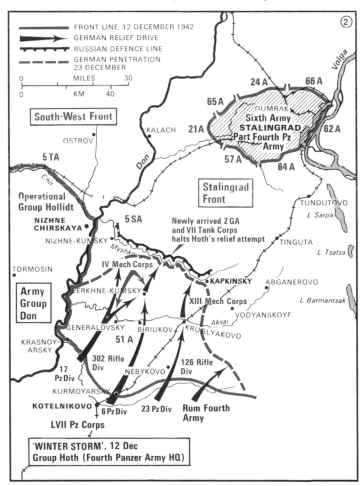

FRONT LINE, 12 DECEMBER 1942
GERMAN RELIEF DRIVE
RUSSIAN DEFENCE LINE
GERMAN PENETRATION 23 DECEMBER

MILES 0 — 30
KM 0 — 40

South-West Front

OSTROV
KALACH
5 TA
Chir
Don

24 A
66 A
65 A
21 A
GUMRAK
Sixth Army
STALINGRAD
Part Fourth Pz Army
62 A
57 A
64 A

Stalingrad Front

Operational Group Hollidt
NIZHNE CHIRSKAYA
5 SA
NIZHNE-KUMSKY
Myshkova

Newly arrived 2 GA and VII Tank Corps halts Hoth's relief attempt

TUNDUTOVO
L Sarpa
TINGUTA
L Tsatsa

TORMOSIN

Army Group Don

IV Mech Corps
VERKHNE-KUMSKY

KAPKINSKY
ABGANEROVO
L Barmantsak
XIII Mech Corps
VODYANSKOYF
Aksai
KRUGLYAKOVO

GENERALOVSKY
BIRIUKOV

KRASNOY-ARSKY

51 A
302 Rifle Div
NEBYKOVO
126 Rifle Div

17 Pz Div
KURMOYARSKY

KOTELNIKOVO
6 Pz Div
23 Pz Div
Rum Fourth Army

LVII Pz Corps

'WINTER STORM', 12 Dec
Group Hoth (Fourth Panzer Army HQ)

199

THE END AT STALINGRAD

Manstein's order to Paulus to break out and join him was prompted by the increasing insecurity of his own position. Operation Group Hollidt (see **Map 2** on previous page) found its front on the Chir threatened by Vatutin's South-West Front, and on 24 December, a day after Manstein's message to Paulus, the Russian South-West and Stalingrad Fronts erupted onto Manstein's tired forces (**Map 1**) leaving Rokossovsky's Don Front to invest Stalingrad. On Christmas Day Manstein was in full retreat, and by the end of the month had been driven back beyond all hope of relieving Stalingrad. It was all he could do, indeed, to try to keep open a narrow corridor east of Rostov to permit the withdrawal of Kleists' Army Group A, threatened with complete isolation in the Caucasus.

In Stalingrad itself Paulus' position was desperate. His force was dwindling rapidly through disease, battle casualties, but most of all through frostbite. His first estimated requirement of 700 tons of supplies per day was based on his then existing reserves. These reserves exhausted, his needs were at least double that. In spite of valiant efforts, the Luftwaffe was unable to make good Göring's vain-glorious boast. Between 23 November 1942, and the Russian capture of the airfields in early 1943, airlifted supplies into Stalingrad never averaged more than 70–80 tons per day.

At the moment of encirclement the German force in Stalingrad numbered some 200,000. The Russians were slow to realize the extent of their success – at first they thought they had trapped a pocket of a few divisions. On 8 January Rokossovsky called on Paulus to capitulate. This being refused, he launched an offensive against the German perimeter on 10 January (**Map 2**). Surrounded by seven Russian armies, Sixth Army's fate was a foregone conclusion, but Hitler would countenance no surrender. By 13 January the Russians had pinched out the western end of the German position, and by the 14th had captured the most important airfield, Pitomnik. By the 25th the remaining airfield had been lost, and Paulus' last contact with the outside world was gone. By 31 January there was nothing left for Paulus to defend. Continued fighting would merely involve the slaughter of his troops. The whole of Sixth Army except XI Corps laid down their arms, and XI Corps followed suit on 2 February.

It has been estimated that the matériel lost at Stalingrad represented six months of German production. Of the original 200,000 beleaguered Germans 100,000 had been killed and 34,000 evacuated by air. The remainder surrendered. In addition the Luftwaffe lost nearly 500 transport planes. Far more serious than these losses was the psychological effect of Stalingrad. The invincible Wehrmacht had suffered a resounding, shattering defeat. Coupled with the Allied successes in Africa this disaster preshadowed for both the Allies and the Axis the probable outcome of the war. The German generals, too, who had seen their armies and campaign wrecked by interference, suffered a sharp decline in confidence at a moment when their Russian counterparts were gaining both confidence and competence with every week that went by.

Opposite: A mortar crew supports advancing Russian infantry

Below left: Russian troops in the ruins of Stalingrad

Opposite below: Field Marshal von Paulus after the surrender at Stalingrad

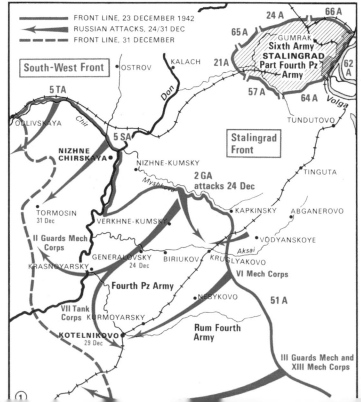

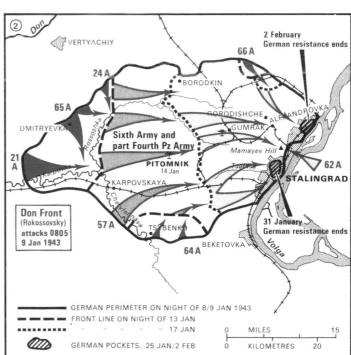

THE ADVANCE TO KHARKOV

The battles to encircle Stalingrad placed the Russian Stalingrad Front in a position to strike straight at Rostov and sever Kleists' Army Group A from the German forces to the north. Such an event would be catastrophic for Kleist, and a simultaneous offensive by the Russian Trans-Caucasus Front would seal his fate. Already, by the end of December 1942, the Stalingrad Front was within 70 miles of Rostov, and when the Northern Group of the Trans-Caucasus Front attacked from the River Terek (**Map 1**) on 1 January 1943, Kleist's position was so perilous that

he had no alternative but to fall back as fast as possible. Manstein, in charge of Army Group Don (later Army Group South), fought desperately to keep open the Rostov corridor for Kleist's escape. Only the First Panzer Army escaped through this corridor. By 14 February Rostov had fallen to the Russians, and the remainder of Kleist's Army Group A had been compelled to take refuge in the Taman peninsula. Here simultaneous attacks by the Black Sea Group and Northern Group of the Trans-Caucasus Front drove Kleist back into a still smaller bridgehead around Novorossiysk.

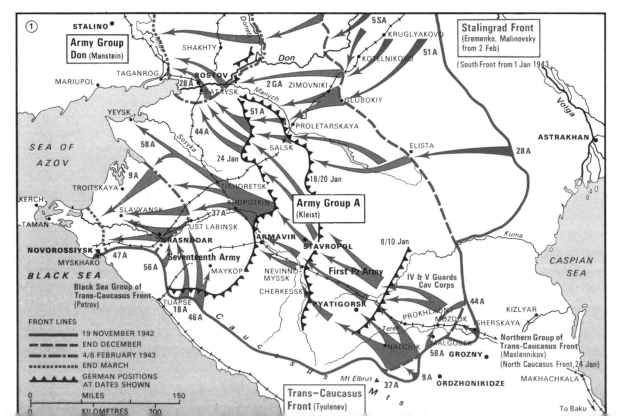

Here for the time being, in strong positions, he was able to hold out.

North of the Don the last and greatest act of the 1942/43 winter campaign was enacted. On 12 January, on a front stretching from Orel to Rostov (**Map 2**) four Russian Fronts, the Bryansk Front, Voronezh Front, South-West Front, and South Front (a regrouping of Stalingrad Front), broke out and fell upon Army Group Don in the south and Army Group B under Weichs. Their objective was Kharkov. On the right flank of the Russian offensive their armour literally flooded westward, surrounding elements of the German Second Army, and forcing the rest of it to fall back well beyond Kursk. In the centre Kharkov fell early in February to troops of the Russian Fortieth Army and Third Tank Army. In the south, the Russian left, the Germans fared somewhat better. By brilliant handling of his reserves Manstein was able to halt the Russian offensives and, then, in the face of numerical odds of seven to one, to counterattack the vulnerable Russian salients, recapture Kharkov, and establish a slightly more favourable line along the Donets before the spring thaw brought movement to an end at the end of March. Near miraculous though Manstein's achievement was, the Russian winter offensive had struck a decisive blow at German power. Their losses had been crippling. Accurate figures do not exist but estimates put the German dead during the winter battles of 1942/43 at over 1,000,000. The Russians claimed the destruction or capture of 5,000 aircraft, 9,000 tanks, 20,000 guns, and thousands of trucks and other vehicles. Russian losses, even more difficult to establish, were probably just as great, but they at least had the satisfaction of having recaptured all the territory lost in 1942, and of the knowledge that their strength was now many times greater than the Germans, and growing.

Opposite above: Soviet troops storm a water obstacle

Above right: A Soviet anti-tank gun supports advancing infantry

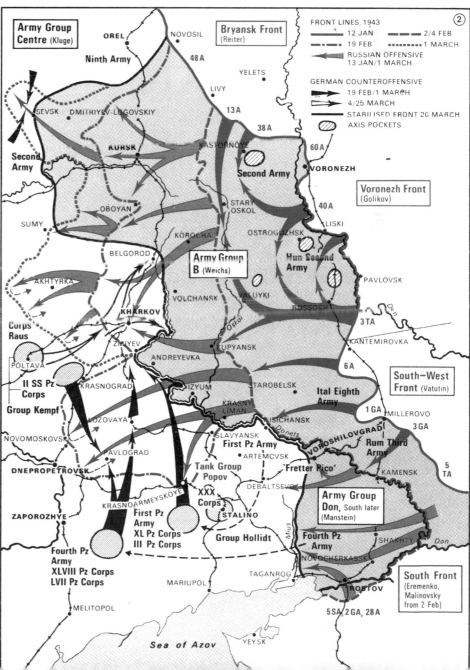

THE BATTLE OF KURSK

The success of the Russian offensive in the first months of 1943, and the German counterattacks in the south left a huge salient around Kursk, a bulge that the Germans were determined to pinch out (**Map 1**). The period March to June 1943 was one of relative inactivity on the Eastern Front. Both sides had lost heavily during the winter, and both needed a long period of recuperation. Yet, to the Germans, such a period was not without peril. With American and British aid now flowing freely, Russian recuperative power was greater than German, and any prolonged pause favoured their chances.

Operation Citadel, the plan to eliminate the Kursk salient, was scheduled for the beginning of July. Two German armies, Ninth and Fourth Panzer, enormously strong in armour were to attack north and south of the salient respectively. The Russian's were well aware of the weakness of the salient, and had been at pains to strengthen it. Two Fronts, Central and Voronezh, occupied the salient, and eight concentric lines of defence had been built. They constituted the most formidable defences the Germans had ever prepared to assault. The result, now called the Battle of Kursk, was the biggest tank battle ever fought, involving over two million men, 6,000 tanks, and 4,000 aircraft. Although best known as a tank battle, Kursk was also an important air battle, and the Luftwaffe's loss of supremacy in the air is as important and interesting as the Wehrmacht's

loss of supremacy in armour.

From the start Operation Citadel was doomed. Not only were the Germans attacking forces numerically inferior to their own, but the Russians were well aware of their intentions, both in broad outline and in detail – the reward of good Intelligence and of the work of the 'Lucy' spy ring operating from Switzerland.

On 5 July the German offensive opened, slightly behind schedule as a result of a preventive Russian bombardment that had hit the German forward areas as they were forming up. In the north Ninth Army

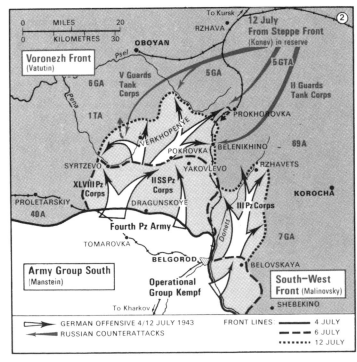

gained a mere six miles at the cost of 25,000 killed, and 200 tanks and 200 aircraft lost (**Map 3**). By the 10th the whole of the German strike force in the north had been committed with no further gains.

In the south Manstein's forces enjoyed greater success. A wedge 25 miles deep was driven into the Russian defences, but again at high cost – 10,000 men and 350 tanks lost (**Map 2**). Reinforcements from the Russian Steppe Front, stationed in reserve, halted Manstein's attacks.

Between 12 and 15 July the Russian forces took to the offensive (**Map 3**), and by the 20th all Russian formations were advancing and the Germans were in full retreat. By the 23rd the Germans were back beyond their start lines, and Citadel had been destroyed without coming even distantly within sight of success. But the Russians were not going to stop there. In the north, Army Group Centre was compelled to abandon Orel, and was forced back to the Hagen Line. In the south the Voronezh and Steppe Fronts converged on Kharkov and, by 22 August, the Germans began to withdraw from the town, finally abandoning it to the Russians on 23 August. Manstein, keeping his forces intact as skillfully as ever, defied Hitler's order to stand fast, and fell back towards the Dniepr.

Opposite: A Soviet anti-tank gun is moved into position

Below: Russian tanks during the Kursk counterattacks

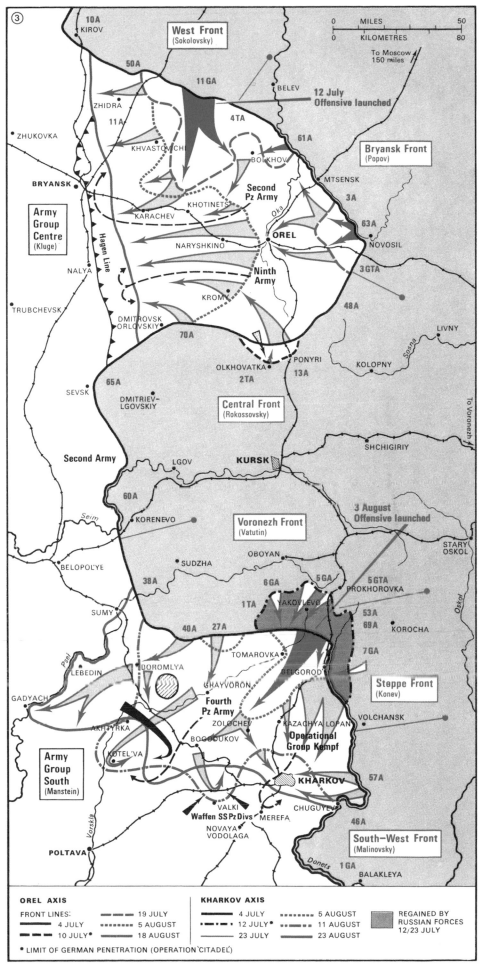

THE DNIEPR AND SMOLENSK BATTLES

Kursk marked the end of German mass efforts in the east. Hitler, alarmed by the Allied landings in Sicily, had transferred many of his best divisions to the west. His generals in the east, now hopelessly outnumbered by the great masses of Russian armour, hung on grimly and with great skill, keeping their forces intact, and giving ground grudgingly and always at a cost.

From July to December 1943, the Russians launched a series of blows along the whole length of the Eastern Front from Smolensk to Rostov. By 23 August their line lay from the Donets in the south, through Kharkov,

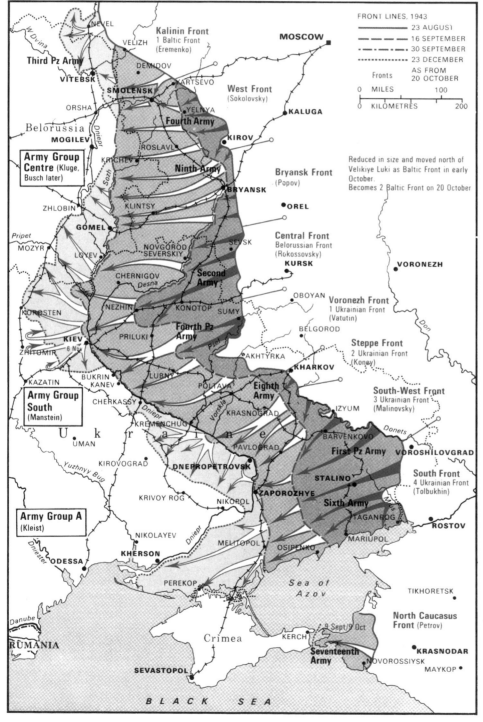

FRONT LINES, 1943

———————— 23 AUGUST
– – – – – 16 SEPTEMBER
–·–·–·– 30 SEPTEMBER
············· 23 DECEMBER
AS FROM 20 OCTOBER

Fronts

0   MILES   100
0   KILOMETRES   200

Reduced in size and moved north of Velikiye Luki as Baltic Front in early October.
Becomes 2 Baltic Front on 20 October

to the Dvina north of Smolensk
(see map). Three German Army
Groups were faced by eight Russian
Fronts. By September 16 the Russians
were threatening Smolensk in the
north and Kiev in the centre. In the
south the Donets was crossed and the
Dniepr bend was being approached.
By the end of September the Russians
were on the Dniepr along most of its
length, and Smolensk had fallen. Also
during September the German Army
Group A was rescued in the nick of
time from its Caucasus bridgehead to
operate on the right of Manstein's
Army Group South. By the end of the
year the Russians had crossed the
Dniepr in great force around Kiev
(which fell on 6 November) and in
Manstein's sector in the south.
Manstein's insistence that the German
Seventeenth Army be evacuated
from the Crimea was overruled by
Hitler in another of his 'No Retreat'
orders. By the end of the year it was
cut off in the Crimean peninsula.

The Russian forces had pressed
these offensives against very skilled
and determined opposition, and in
spite of their enormous territorial
gains they had lost heavily in
men and matériel.

Left: Russian infantry in action on the banks
of the Dniepr

Below left: The first Russian troops crossing
the Dniepr on a makeshift bridge

THE RELIEF OF LENINGRAD

In 1941 the advancing German forces bypassed Leningrad and advanced on the left bank of the Neva to Lake Ladoga. This manoeuvre trapped the Russian forces in Leningrad (and other Russian forces around Oranienbaum cutting them off from the rest of Russia (see The Attack on Leningrad). For 900 days Leningrad remained isolated, without supplies of food, fuel or arms. By the end of the siege its citizens were dying of hunger, cold, and disease at the rate of 20,000 a day. In addition to their other sufferings, the inhabitants had to endure constant German bombardment. But a combination of patriotism, fear of German occupation, and severe Soviet discipline kept the Leningraders active throughout the siege. Production never entirely ceased in the factories; vigilante organizations were always at hand, however hungry and enfeebled, to put out fires, clear up rubble, construct defences.

There is some evidence that Stalin allowed the siege to go on longer than he needed for political reasons connected with his dislike of the Leningraders independent spirit, and a feud between him and the Leningrad party leader, Zhdanov. Nonetheless some relief operations were attempted. In August 1942 the Leningrad Front and the Volkhov Front (**Map 1**) planned to raise the siege by severing

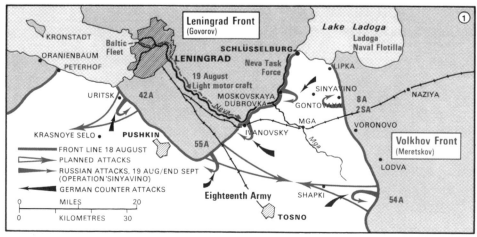

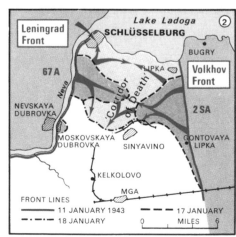

the German-held corridor between Tosno and Lake Ladoga, and with a thrust north of Pushkin to link up with the Oranienbaum forces. The attempt lasted from 19 August to the end of September, but was checked at all points by the German Eighteenth Army.

It was not until January 1943 that the Leningraders received their first gleam of hope. On 11 January another concerted effort by the Leningrad Front and Volkhov Front succeeded in securing a narrow corridor south of Lake Ladoga. Through this a thin trickle of supplies was able to reach Leningrad (**Map 2**), and with this Leningrad had to be content for the remainder of 1943.

Real release for the Leningraders did not come until January 1944. Between 14 January and 19 January three Russian Fronts, Leningrad Front, Volkhov Front, and 2 Baltic Front launched attacks against the German Army Group North. By 27 January the Moscow–Leningrad railway was cleared (**Map 3**). Novgorod fell to the Russian Fifty-ninth Army on 19 January, and the threat of encirclement compelled the withdrawal of the whole of Army Group North out of the area east of Lake Chudskoye. By 1 March the Russians had reached the River Narva in the north, Pskov in the centre, and Pustoshka in the south.

Opposite above: Nevsky Prospekt during the siege of Leningrad

Above: A Russian patrol sets out during fighting south of Lake Ilmen

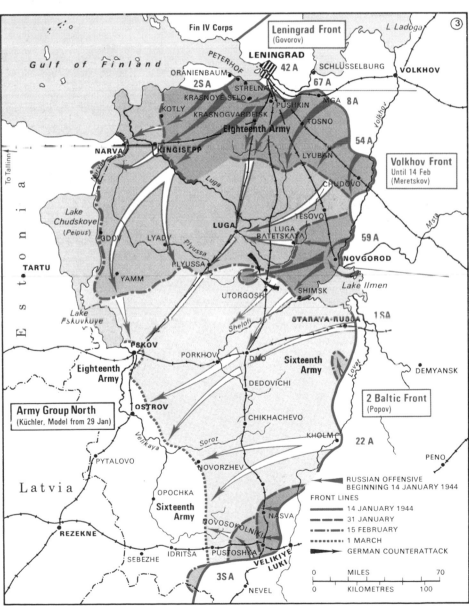

THE BATTLES IN THE UKRAINE

While Leningrad was being relieved in the north, the German forces in south Russia were given no rest. On 24 December 1943, and 5 January 1944, the 1 and 2 Ukrainian Fronts erupted from their bridgeheads over the Dniepr, falling upon Manstein and Kleist's Army Groups and trapping the German First Panzer Army. Instant counterattacks by Manstein bogged down in blizzards and appalling weather. The Russian advance continued towards the Rivers Bug and Dniestr in spite of desperate counterattacks by Manstein (see map).

Meanwhile the trapped First Panzer Army conducted a brilliant behind-lines rearguard action. An improvised airlift kept the army supplied, and eventually it fought its way out almost completely intact south of Tarnopol. To the south Army Group A had also taken a considerable beating. Attacked by 2 and 4 Ukrainian Fronts, Kleist fell back to Odessa, leaving behind surrounded elements of Sixth and Eighth Armies. On 10 April he was compelled to abandon Odessa, and by mid-April the Russian front had been extended from Odessa in the south nearly to Brest Litovsk in the north.

With the Russians poised on the borders of Poland and in the foothills of the Carpathians the German situation in the east was desperate. The abandoned Seventeenth Army was cleared out of the Crimea by troops of the 4 Ukrainian Front during April (see inset) and Sevastopol finally fell on 12 May.

Hitler, infuriated by these losses, relieved Manstein and Kleist of their commands. Model replaced Manstein in command of Army Group North Ukraine, and Schörner replaced Kleist in charge of Army Group South Ukraine.

In summary it must be stressed that the tenacity of the German generals in south Russia in the face of the Russian onslaught was nothing short of miraculous. Manstein, in particular, since being called in to relieve Stalingrad, had fought continuously, untiringly, and at great cost to the Russians.

Below: German sentries on the alert as a flare goes up

Opposite below: During the spring offensive, Russian infantry attack with tank support

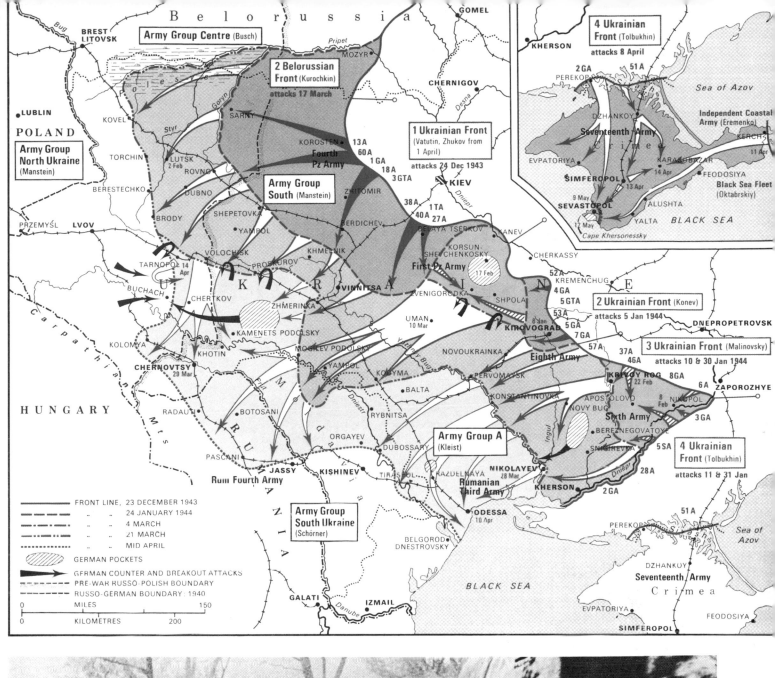

THE THRUST INTO POLAND

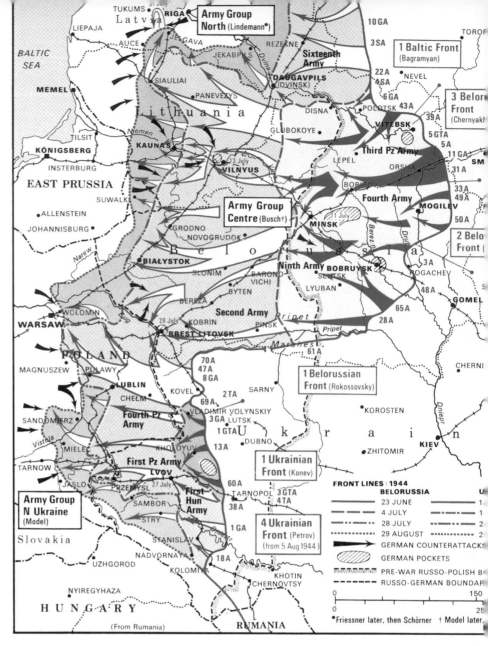

Following the appalling reverses of the winter of 1943/44 the only course open to the Germans in the east was to fall back to a shorter front and reorganize on strong defensive positions sited in depth. If the pause during the spring thaws of 1944 had been occupied in doing this, there might have been some hope of blunting the Russian offensives of the summer of 1944. But Hitler's obsession with holding territory at all costs left his forces dangerously overextended, holding a vast 1,400-mile front with scant reserves.

The Russian blow fell at the end of June. On the 23rd three Russian Fronts, 1, 2, and 3 Belorussian, under the overall command of Marshal Zhukov (now deputy supreme commander) struck at General Busch's Army Group Centre. A simultaneous outburst of partisan activity in Busch's rear came close to destroying his communications, and when Zhukov's forces (supported by a density of almost 400 guns *per mile* of front) assaulted on a 350-mile front (see map) he was unable to co-ordinate the movements of his formations. Russian air superiority was complete, many Luftwaffe units having already been taken west. Busch's army group was torn apart. By 4 July Minsk had fallen, and to the north 1 Baltic Front was driving for Riga. By the end of July, Vilnyus and Brest Litovsk were in Russian hands. Twenty-five out of Busch's thirty-three divisions had been trapped, and the Russians claimed 158,000 captured, almost 400,000 dead, 2,000 tanks, 10,000 guns, and 57,000 motor vehicles captured or destroyed. Hitler instantly replaced Busch with Model. By the end of August Zhukov's offensive had reached the gates of Warsaw in the south, and Riga in the north. The Russians stood on the frontiers of East Prussia. The German Army Group North was threatened with being trapped with its back to the Baltic, and Model, now commanding what was left of Army Group Centre, only just succeeded in stopping the Russians in front of Warsaw. (In this he was assisted by the Russians themselves who paused before Warsaw to resupply and to allow the German SS to crush the non-communist Warsaw insurrection.)

To the south of Warsaw the Russian 1 and 4 Ukrainian Fronts had surged through Lvov, isolating elements of the Army Group North Ukraine, and by the end of August had reached and crossed the Vistula.

In two months the Russian armies had advanced 450 miles, and had outstripped their own supply capabilities. Operations on this front came, temporarily, to a halt.

Opposite above: Soviet infantry disembark from tanks in preparation for an attack

Opposite below: Members of the Polish Home Army whose rising in Warsaw was crushed

CLEARING THE BALTIC STATES

The defeat of Finland was undertaken in June 1944 by the Russian Karelian Front under Meretskov. There is some irony in reflecting that the last time the Russians had conquered Finland it had been as the ally of Nazi Germany. From the south, operating on both sides of Lake Ladoga, units of the Karelian Front attacked the strong Finnish fortifications, between Lake Ladoga and the sea and on the east of the lake, between 8 June and 11 July. West of the lake (**Map 1**) they enjoyed success. The formidable Mannerheim Line was breached, and on 20 June Viipuri was captured. East of the lake, although the Russian attacks were repulsed at the Finnish U Line, the Murmansk railway had been cleared, and the Finns had been pushed back from their positions between Lake Ladoga and Lake Onega.

Below right: Civilians take cover during fighting in Karelia

In the north, the Russian Fourteenth Army pushed the German Twentieth Mountain Army off its positions on the Litsa, and by executing amphibious landings on its flanks, forced it back into Norway by the end of October (**Map 2**). In the same sector the Russian Nineteenth Army pushed units of the Twentieth Mountain Army back to Salla, clearing the last German/Finnish troops from Russian soil.

Having withdrawn from Leningrad in January 1944, the German Army Group North was, by July, situated in the Baltic states with its back to the sea. It was placed in extreme jeopardy by Zhukov's successful offensive against Army Group Centre, which threatened to destroy its corridor of escape to Germany, and bottle it up in the Baltic states. Guderian (by July 1944 Chief of the German General Staff) tried to persuade Hitler of its peril, but Hitler clung to his 'No

Retreat' principle until it was too late. At the same time that the Russian 3 Belorussian Front seized Vilnyus, the 1 Baltic Front drove for Memel and Riga, separating Army Group North from Army Group Centre, cutting off its retreat, and forcing it back until by the end of September it was locked up in the Kurland Peninsula. Here the bulk of it remained blockaded until the end of the war, although some units were taken off by the German navy. Meanwhile 2 and 3 Baltic Fronts and the Leningrad Front had overrun Estonia and Latvia, capturing Riga on 15 October (**Map 3**).

Left: German paratroops prepare for action on the borders of East Prussia

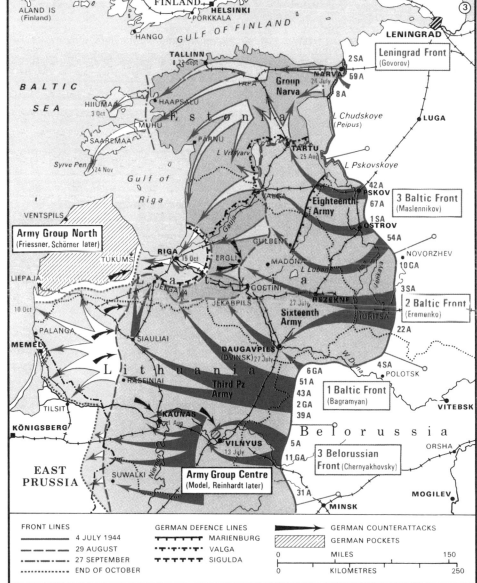

215

CLEARING THE BALKANS

Zhukov's June/July attacks in Belorussia pushed out a large salient that left the German Army Group South Ukraine on the southern or 'under' side of it. If driven further south this Army Group might well lose contact with the other German Eastern Front groups, and if this were done swiftly enough the pursuing Russian forces might well cut off the German armies in Greece and the Balkans from their homeland (see map).

In this, due to the speed of their own advance, and Hitler's now predictable delay in ordering a withdrawal, the Russians very nearly succeeded. On 20 August 1944, the 2 and 3 Ukrainian Fronts under Malinovsky and Tolbukhin attacked Friessner's Army Group South Ukraine, trapping the German Sixth Army and the Rumanian Third Army (see map). They drove south, reaching the Danube by 29 August. On 30 August the bulk of the Russian forces turned west and then north, overrunning Rumania by 24 September. A smaller group of 3 Ukrainian Front headed south over the Danube into Bulgaria, forcing the withdrawal of elements of Weichs' Army Group F.

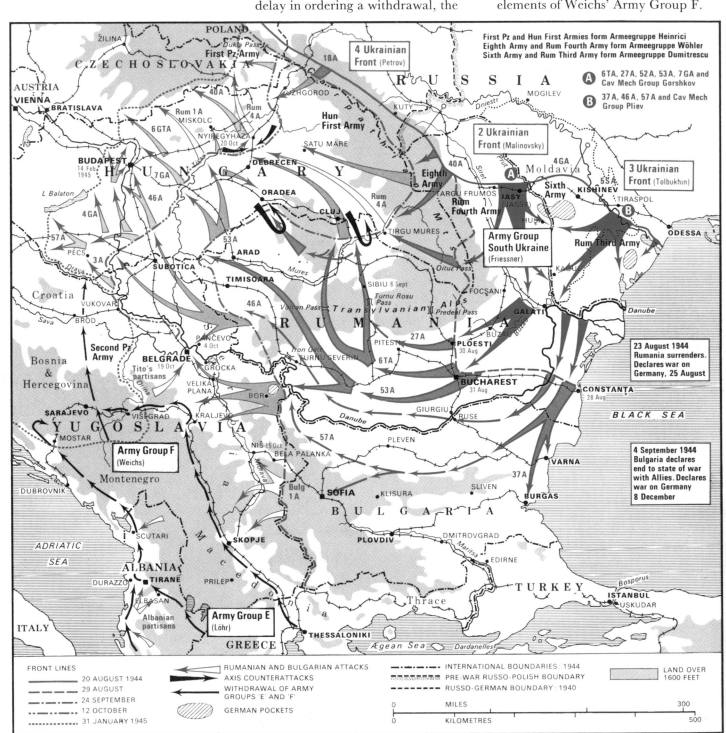

First Pz and Hun First Armies form Armeegruppe Heinrici
Eighth Army and Rum Fourth Army form Armeegruppe Wöhler
Sixth Army and Rum Third Army form Armeegruppe Dumitrescu

A 6TA, 27A, 52A, 53A, 7GA and Cav Mech Group Gorshkov

B 37A, 46A, 57A and Cav Mech Group Pliev

23 August 1944
Rumania surrenders. Declares war on Germany, 25 August

4 September 1944
Bulgaria declares end to state of war with Allies. Declares war on Germany 8 December

FRONT LINES
20 AUGUST 1944
29 AUGUST
24 SEPTEMBER
12 OCTOBER
31 JANUARY 1945

RUMANIAN AND BULGARIAN ATTACKS
AXIS COUNTERATTACKS
WITHDRAWAL OF ARMY GROUPS 'E' AND 'F'
GERMAN POCKETS

INTERNATIONAL BOUNDARIES: 1944
PRE-WAR RUSSO-POLISH BOUNDARY
RUSSO-GERMAN BOUNDARY: 1940

LAND OVER 1600 FEET

0   MILES   300
0   KILOMETRES   500

By early October Rumania and Bulgaria were in Russian hands, and the German Army Groups E and F were within an ace of being trapped in southern Yugoslavia and Greece. In the nick of time they retreated north and west, and took up a position on the right of Friessner's retreating Army Group South Ukraine. During October the two Russian Fronts, supported by the 4 Ukrainian Front on the right, overran the larger part of Hungary. And during November, December, and January the remainder of Hungary, up to Lake Balaton and the Czechoslovak border, fell. Budapest, encircled on 24 December, held out until 14 February 1945.

The Russian advance through Rumania, Bulgaria, and Hungary was made much easier by the activities of Tito's Yugoslav partisans, and by the defection of Rumania and Bulgaria to the Allied cause.

Right: Russian troops enter Bucharest

Below: Soviet artillery in the Carpathians

217

THE DRIVE TO THE ODER

Their advances of 1944 had brought the Russians to the borders of East Prussia, and by January 1945 they were ready to invade the German Fatherland for the first time since 1914. On 12 January Rokossovsky's 2 Belorussian Front, fielding nine armies (**Map 1**), fell upon the German Second Army along the Narew north of Warsaw. The Russian Forty-seventh Army encircled Warsaw, which fell on 17 January. The remainder of Rokossovsky's forces drove north-west along the right bank of the Vistula towards Danzig, isolating Reinhardt's Army Group Centre. To the north of Rokossovsky the Russian 3 Belorussian Front and the 1 Baltic Front also closed in on Army Group Centre forcing it back until, by 8 February, the Germans occupied a few isolated pockets along the Bay of Danzig. More than 500,000 German troops were cut off, but during April and March these pockets were successfully evacuated by the German navy. On 9 May the remaining German beachheads surrendered.

The operations of the German Baltic Fleet, which had included the evacuation of part of Army Group North from the Kurland Peninsula, succeeded in rescuing an estimated million and a half fugitives, many wounded, and four army divisions. The cost, due to lack of air cover, was virtually the whole strength of the fleet. Only the cruisers *Prinz Eugen* and *Nürnberg* were still afloat at the end of April.

At the same time as Rokossovsky's attack north of the Vistula (**Map 1**), the Russian 1 Belorussian Front (Zhukov) and the 1 Ukrainian Front (Konev) launched an assault on a wide front from Warsaw to Jasło in the south. In one of the most massive, costly, and fastest advances of the war Zhukov's forces had reached the Oder by 31 January. Pockets of German resistance were bypassed and mopped up at leisure. Russian armies of over 1,500,000 men, supported by 28,000

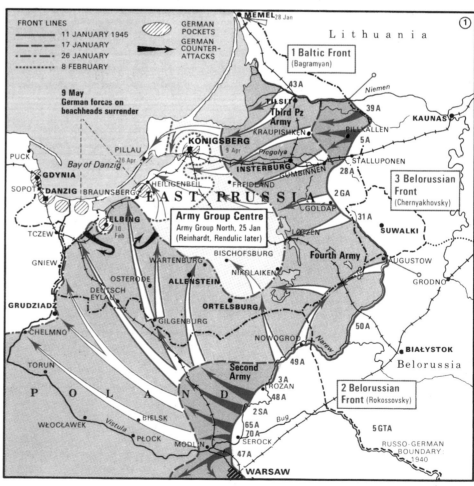

guns, 3,300 tanks, and 10,000 aircraft, faced German forces of 596,000 men, 8,230 guns, 700 tanks, and 1,300 aircraft. Against odds like these the Germans could not contend. Army Groups Vistula and A were torn apart (**Map 2**). Torun, Poznan, and Breslau were surrounded and held out for some time, but the remainder of the German armies were swept back. By 24 February Pomerania in the north, and Silesia in the south, had fallen, so that the Russian forces presented a solid front along the Oder less than 40 miles from Berlin.

Opposite: Russian artillery bombard German positions before an assault

Right: German anti-tank guns going to the front

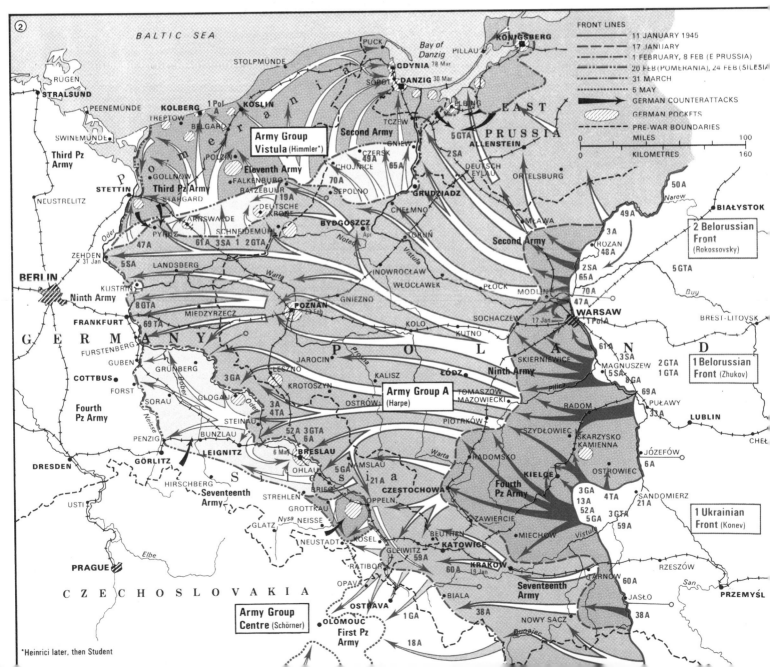

THE INVASIONS OF AUSTRIA AND HUNGARY

After the fall of Budapest on 14 February 1945 the Russian 2 and 3 Ukrainian Fronts stood poised to overrun the rest of Hungary and strike at Vienna. However, on 6 March 1945, Hitler, in a desperate attempt to save the Balaton oil fields, launched a counterattack north and south of Lake Balaton. North of the Lake the Sixth SS Panzer Army was to break out and strike north and south to Budapest and Baja, establishing a line along the Danube. South of the lake, Second Panzer Army was also to strike towards the Danube – due east. In hideously muddy conditions this counterattack, codenamed *Frühlingserwachen*, was ground to a halt by weather, lack of fuel, and stiff opposition. On 16 March the Russians resumed their advance against Army Group South. By 4 April they were within five miles of Vienna, which finally fell on 14 April.

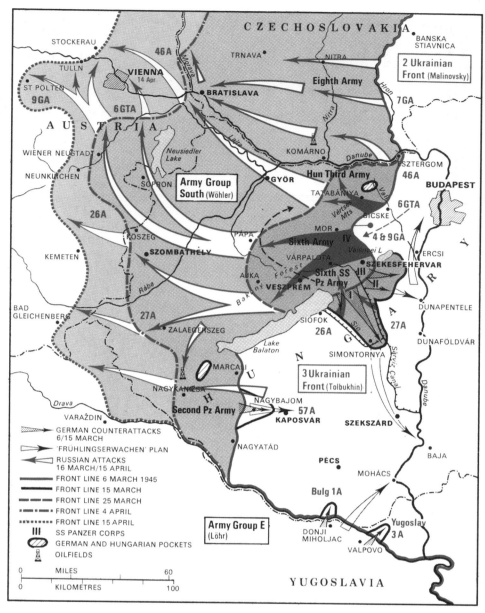

Right: German troops move forward during the abortive 'Frühlingserwachen' offensive

220

THE DRIVE INTO CZECHO-SLOVAKIA

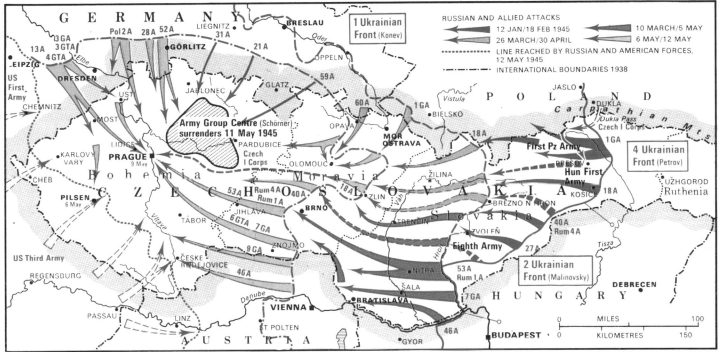

After the fall of Berlin (next page) only one sizeable German force was left in Europe – Schörner's Army Group Centre now in Czechoslovakia. In spite of madcap Nazi plans to form a 'national redoubt' on the German/Czechoslovak border based on this force, Schörner's position was without hope. On three sides, north, east, and south the Russians surrounded him. From the west Patton's US Third Army was approaching. But his armies, numbering nearly 1,000,000 men, held the Reich's last important industrial area.

The Russian 2 and 4 Ukrainian Fronts had already by 6 March overrun much of Slovakia (see map). By 6 May they were well into Moravia, having occupied more than a half of Czechoslovakia. At the same time Czech partisans in Prague and elsewhere rose against the Germans, capturing much of Prague and further disrupting the German forces, especially their communications.

On 8 May an all-enveloping Russian offensive began. From the north troops of Konev's 1 Ukrainian Front bore down on Prague, while 2, 3, and 4 Ukrainian Fronts struck from the south and east. Prague was liberated on 9 May, and contact with the US Third Army made on 12 May along a line from Karlovy Vary to Linz. On 11 May, completely surrounded, Schörner surrendered. After nearly six years, the war in Europe was over.

Above: A Russian tank knocked out during the Czech campaign

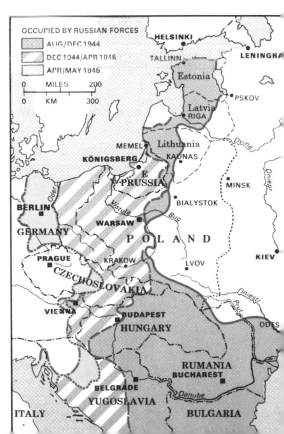

THE BATTLE OF BERLIN

easy one. Simultaneously, in the north, Rokossovsky's 2 Belorussian Front was to occupy all of northern Prussia up the Elbe.

Employing an unprecedented artillery concentration of one gun per 13 feet of front, Zhukov and Konev opened their bombardment of the German forces on 16 April. It was the prelude to one of the most ferocious slogging matches of the war, the Germans, having few illusions as to what a Russian breakthrough would mean, fighting desperately. In two days, 18 April, only small bridgeheads 3–7 miles deep had been established (see main map). But by 20 April the German resistance on the Oder had been smashed, and the Russian advance to encircle and capture Berlin could continue. By 25 April Konev and Zhukov's armies had met on the west of Berlin. On the same day Russian and US forces made contact on the Elbe at Torgau. Apart from the garrison of Berlin itself, all that remained of the Wehrmacht in Germany itself was a few isolated remnants of Army Groups Centre and Vistula, all trying desperately to surrender to the Western Allies rather than the Russians.

At the moment of encirclement Berlin contained 2,000,000 civilian

inhabitants and about 30,000 garrison troops. Since January the city had been preparing for a siege, but its defences were rudimentary – certainly no match for the enormous Russian forces encircling them. Even so the Russian attack on the city of Berlin was no walk-over. Every street – every house – was bitterly contested.

On 26 April Zhukov's armies from the north, and Konev's from the south drove in on the Berlin defences. Two days of fighting brought Zhukov's armies to the River Spree in the Moabit area (see map below). From the south Konev's forces had advanced almost to the Tiergarten. Both threatened to cut the city in half – east from west. Between them lay the Reichstag and Hitler's command bunker in the garden of the Chancellery. The distance between the two Russian forces was less than a mile, and some idea of the savagery of the Berlin fighting is given by the fact that it was not until 2 May that they met across the Charlottenberg Chaussee. In the meantime the Reichstag had fallen on 30 April, and Hitler had killed himself, naming as his successor Admiral Dönitz.

Once safely ensconced on the Oder the Russians were able to prepare for the Red Army's greatest exploit – the capture of Berlin. Zhukov's 1 Belorussian Front, and Konev's 1 Ukrainian Front were given the task of taking Berlin and driving beyond to establish the Russian armies on the Elbe. In spite of the losses they had taken, the Germans were still able to deploy 1,000,000 men in the defence of Berlin, situated in strong defensive positions on the west bank of the Oder. Although between them Konev and Zhukov could command nearly 2,500,000 men, their task was not going to be an

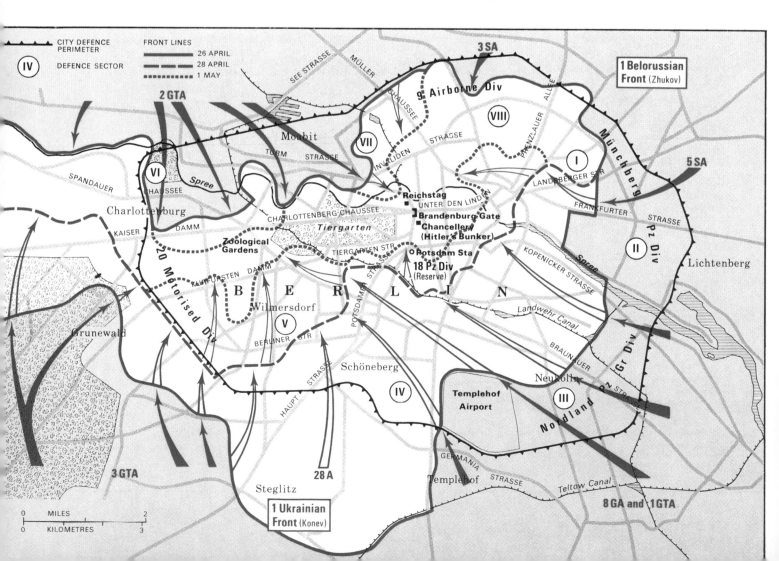

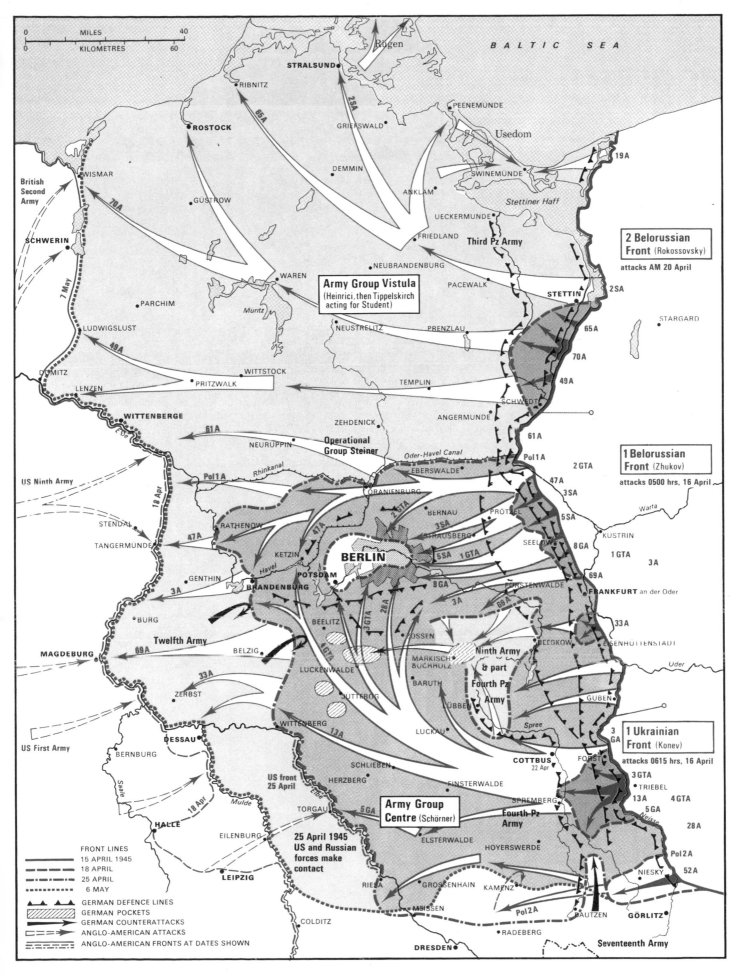

BALTIC SEA

Rügen

STRALSUND

• RIBNITZ

• ROSTOCK

2SA

GRIEFSWALD

DEMMIN

PEENEMUNDE

Usedom

19A

WISMAR

85A

SWINEMUNDE

ANKLAM

Stettiner Haff

British Second Army

GÜSTROW

WAREN

UECKERMUNDE

FRIEDLAND

Third Pz Army

2 Belorussian Front (Rokossovsky)

attacks AM 20 April

70A

SCHWERIN

NEUBRANDENBURG

PACEWALK

STETTIN

2SA

STARGARD

7 May

PARCHIM

Muritz

Army Group Vistula
(Heinrici, then Tippelskirch acting for Student)

PRENZLAU

65A

49A

LUDWIGSLUST

49A

NEUSTRELITZ

70A

DOMITZ

WITTSTOCK

TEMPLIN

49A

LENZEN

PRITZWALK

SCHWEDT

WITTENBERGE

ZEHDENICK

ANGERMUNDE

61A

61A

NEURUPPIN

Operational Group Steiner

Oder-Havel Canal

Pol1A

1 Belorussian Front (Zhukov)

US Ninth Army

Rhinkanal

EBERSWALDE

2 GTA

Pol 1 A

attacks 0500 hrs, 16 April

18 Apr

Pol 1 A

ORANIENBURG

47A

3SA

Warta

STENDAL

47A

RATHENOW

BERNAU

PRÖTZEL

5SA

KUSTRIN

TANGERMUNDE

KETZIN

2 GTA

3SA

STRAUSBERG

SEELOW

8 GA

1 GTA

3A

BERLIN

47A

Havel

POTSDAM

5SA

1 GTA

69A

GENTHIN

BRANDENBURG

8 GA

FÜRSTENWALDE

FRANKFURT an der Oder

3A

3A

69A

BURG

Twelfth Army

3 GTA

2 BA

BEELITZ

33A

EISENHÜTTENSTADT

MAGDEBURG

69A

BELZIG

ZOSSEN

Ninth Army

BEESKOW

Oder

LUCKENWALDE

MARKISCH BUCHHOLZ

& part Fourth Pz Army

33A

ZERBST

33A

JÜTERBOG

BARUTH

GUBEN

US First Army

BERNBURG

Saale

WITTENBERG

LÜBBEN

Spree

3 GA

DESSAU

13A

LUCKAU

1 Ukrainian Front (Konev)

SCHLIEBEN

FINSTERWALDE

COTTBUS
22 Apr

FORST

attacks 0615 hrs, 16 April

3GTA

HERZBERG

SPREMBERG

TRIEBEL

US front 25 April

Army Group Centre (Schörner)

Fourth Pz Army

13A

4 GTA

Mulde

TORGAU

5 GA

5 GA

28A

HALLE

EILENBURG

25 April 1945 US and Russian forces make contact

ELSTERWALDE

HOYERSWERDE

Neisse

LEIPZIG

RIESA

GROSSENHAIN

KAMENZ

Pol 2 A

NIESKY

52 A

MEISSEN

Pol 2 A

BAUTZEN

GÖRLITZ

COLDITZ

RADEBERG

DRESDEN

Seventeenth Army

0 MILES 40
0 KILOMETRES 60

FRONT LINES
———— 15 APRIL 1945
— — — 18 APRIL
—·—·— 25 APRIL
······· 6 MAY

▲▲▲ GERMAN DEFENCE LINES
▨ GERMAN POCKETS
GERMAN COUNTERATTACKS
⇨ ANGLO-AMERICAN ATTACKS
ANGLO-AMERICAN FRONTS AT DATES SHOWN

223

THE WAR IN NORTH-WEST EUROPE

Opposite: US troops go ashore
on D-Day

On 6 June nine Allied divisions invaded Normandy over the open beaches between the Cherbourg Peninsula and the mouth of the River Orne at Ouistreham. Ten weeks later when the Allies broke out from Normandy they had destroyed the German Seventh Army, some 500,000 strong. Yet on the first day of the invasion the Allies landed a force which was scarcely the equivalent of ten divisions: six infantry divisions; three airborne divisions; two Commando brigades; and one Ranger battalion. In all 5,300 ships and craft were to put ashore 150,000 men and 1,500 tanks during the first forty-eight hours of the Second Front. There were 12,000 aircraft in support.

On sea and in the air the German defenders were completely outclassed, but Field-Marshal von Rundstedt, the Commander-in-Chief, West, had sixty divisions, including eleven armoured divisions, with which to defend Holland, Belgium, and France. Of these, six, including one Panzer division, were in or near the area of the beachhead. With so many troops at his disposal it was well within the bounds of possibility the Germans would either crush the invaders on the beaches, or with a swift concentration of a mass of armour break into the beachhead before the Allies could get set and consolidate. In order to prevent these unpleasant possibilities the Allies devised the most elaborate and successful deception plan which military history records.

The objects of this plan were to persuade Hitler and his entourage that the Normandy assault was just a cunning diversion, and that the main invasion must be expected elsewhere, probably in the Pas de Calais. The idea was to prevent the Germans reinforcing Seventh Army from the nineteen divisions of Fifteenth Army, which included some of their best formations. Had this happened in the early days of the invasion when bad weather delayed the build-up, smashed

one of the artificial (Mulberry) harbours and hampered air support, it is by no means certain that Montgomery could have continued to hold the original bridgehead. The British had been remarkably successful in rounding up German agents working in England. This greatly facilitated the Allied deception team's task of selling fake intelligence to the enemy. By 31 May 1944 German intelligence credited the Allies with the equivalent of eighty-seven combat divisions, including eight airborne, in Britain. In fact there were less than fifty-two, and only thirty-seven were available for operations on the continent. Some of these would not be going to France until seven months after D-Day. It is no exaggeration to say that the German Fifteenth Army was kept idle for seven crucial weeks by a Phantom Army, the US First Army Group (FUSAG), under General George S. Patton, Jr., which was waiting with its twenty-five large formations, and perhaps five airborne divisions, to embark in South-East England and pounce on the Pas de Calais. Since Hitler himself expected an attack in that area it is little wonder that the Germans bought the Allied deception plan. Another Phantom Army, the 'Fourth' under Lieutenant-General Sir A. F. A. N. Thorne (Commander-in-Chief, Northern Command) was 'assembled' in Scotland with the object of discouraging any movement of German troops from Norway to France. Hitler, convinced of the importance of Norway, was receptive to the suggestion that it was imperilled.

Montgomery's campaign in Normandy went more or less according to plan. There were times when he was criticized, quite unfairly, because it was going more slowly than some hoped. He can, of course, be criticized upon points of detail. It may be, for example, that the employment of an airborne division in Operation Goodwood (the attack on Caen) might have made all the difference at a moment when

victory was almost within his grasp, but for all his tactical soundness, Montgomery was an unimaginative general.

As the end of the battle of Normandy came in sight a serious inter-Allied controversy blew up: the Broad Front/Narrow Front question.

There was a brief moment round about 4 September when, at least in Rundstedt's view the Allies might have broken through the shattered German front. If he was correct Montgomery's idea of thrusting with a solid mass of some forty divisions towards Antwerp, Brussels, Aachen, and Cologne, may have been right. But the Americans were now the senior partners in the alliance and Bradley has told us what was in their minds: 'The first or predominantly American plan called for emphasis on a thrust to the Reich straight through the middle of France to the Saar and beyond the Saar to the Rhine in the vicinity of Frankfurt . . . Both the First and Third American Armies . . . would be required for this major effort.'

In the event the Allies approached the German frontier on a broad front, and Eisenhower ended up in a situation not unlike that of Joffre in 1914. Had his whole army been of one nation it would have been a grave error. As things were it was perhaps inevitable. The American nation would never have stood for the British and the Canadians reaping all the glory.

Montgomery was still determined – although the Russians were still the other side of the Vistula – to gain a foothold beyond the Rhine before winter. Hence his somewhat belated and ambitious Operation Market Garden (the airborne landing at Arnhem). At a time when the Allies were still being supplied over the open beaches of Normandy he would probably have done better to concentrate upon clearing the seaward approaches of the port of Antwerp.

The dramatic German offensive in the Ardennes, which took the

Americans by surprise, showed Eisenhower in a good light. He had but a small reserve but this he deployed to advantage. The Allied air forces, thinking the German army no longer capable of a counteroffensive had failed to detect its concentration. The defence of Bastogne was a splendid demonstration of what the American soldier can do when he means business. In the event the offensive only succeeded in destroying Hitler's last effective reserves. When the time came for the Allies to cross the formidable obstacle of the Lower Rhine the Germans found themselves left with too few troops to defend it. There were three more rivers to cross before Hamburg should fall, but the war was as good as won.

Touring his victorious troops soon after the surrender Montgomery told them that the Western Allies had won for four main reasons. Firstly, the Germans' mistakes; second, Allied domination of the air; third, Anglo-American co-operation; fourth, the fighting qualities of the British, Canadian, and American soldiers. As so often he had got to the heart of the matter.

For most of the German mistakes Hitler himself must bear the blame, for it was no longer the great General Staff that controlled operations but the Führer himself. The flair for military affairs which he occasionally showed in the earlier part of the war, had long since abandoned him. He had spent his last reserves in the Ardennes offensive. He had clung to the Reichswald too long. Like so many bad generals he wished to hold everything, and ended up by being weak everywhere. He believed only such Intelligence as fitted in with his own prejudices and mistrusted the majority of his best qualified commanders.

Allied air supremacy was a pearl of great price, even though the Allied air marshals may be said to have got out of political control, and might have given direct support to the other services in a more generous – not to say more

accurate – fashion. It is not easy, on moral grounds, to justify their policy of area bombing. Herman Göring, who consistently exaggerated the strength and capabilities of the Luftwaffe, must take some of the credit for the fact that the Allied airmen got the upper hand.

For Anglo-American co-operation Eisenhower must take much of the credit. His strategic errors, due in part to lack of proper political direction, are obvious enough. Nevertheless he could get on with Churchill and Alanbrooke and Montgomery and won the liking and trust of the British as well as the American soldier. His own generals, Bradley and Patton were men who needed a firm superior. Patton, despite his arrogant temper, was a thruster with real talent. Bradley, though an effective writer, was what Napoleon would have called *bon général ordinaire*, or as Montgomery once rather maliciously is said to have described another – British – colleague, 'a good, plain cook'.

Most of the Allied generals have either found biographers or have given us their own recollections. An exception is one of the best of them: General Sir Miles Dempsey. As Major L. F. Ellis says: 'He was always in firm control of all that was done by Second Army. Much of his day was usually spent in visits to formations chiefly involved, to confer with commanders on their problems and progress and to give them clear and concise verbal orders. The directives he received left him little scope for any conspicuous initiative but his understanding of Montgomery's purpose, his own knowledge of the troops he commanded and his quiet and steady personality continued to give both his superior and his subordinates confidence in his judgement and in his leadership.' Given the character of Montgomery and the nature of Second Army he was the ideal man for his job.

The fighting qualities of the British, Canadian, and American soldiers is a subject of great interest, but it is a vast one for in the nature of things the various

formations varied in quality and experience. The great majority of those who went to France in 1944 had never been in action before, but they were on the whole pretty well trained. It is no exaggeration to say that early disasters at Dunkirk and elsewhere had led the Allies to overhaul their tactics, a process in which the Commandos, paratroops, and Rangers led the way, if only by arousing in the ordinary infantry divisions a spirit of emulation. One of the chief lessons of modern warfare is that however much air or gunfire support may be available, the infantryman and the tank crew must sooner or later come to close quarters with the enemy and fight it out. A very experienced soldier and historian, Major-General H. Essame, writes: 'There is some truth in the statement that he who has not fought the Germans does not know what war is.' They remained formidable to the end when 'they were outfought on the Western front by troops, . . . as well-trained, as well-led and as tough as themselves'.

Opposite left: Shipping massed off the coast of Normandy

Opposite right: Troops coming ashore on one of the Mulberry artificial harbours

Above right: The crowds waiting for General de Gaulle's entry into Paris

Above left: US engineers blow up German fortifications during the attack on Cherbourg

PREPARATION FOR D-DAY

As agreed at the Trident Conference in Washington in 1943, the Western Allies laid plans for an invasion of Europe in 1944. Ignoring the fact that they already held a foothold in Europe, Italy, the American and British planners yielded to political pressures and selected France as the target of a cross-channel assault. The Normandy beaches between Cherbourg and Le Havre were chosen as the targets of this attack for a number of reasons. First, the area was in easy reach of the fighter bases of southern England. Secondly, the beaches and the countryside inland were favourable. Thirdly, the water distance for the force, and its subsequent supplies, to cross was the shortest available if the Pas de Calais were ruled out. Fourthly, the Germans were expecting the blow to fall across the Pas de Calais, and the Normandy beaches were correspondingly less heavily defended.

By 1944 an enormous Allied army had been built up in Britain –

Americans, British, Canadian, and French – and with supporting naval and air units it totalled nearly 3,000,000 men (**Map 1**). The assault forces, in essence the US First Army and the British Second Army, were to sail from their embarkation ports, assemble offshore, and make a landing on a front of four corps. Essential to the plan was the airborne operation by the US 82 and 101 Airborne Divisions and the British 8 Airborne Division. These were to be dropped right and left of the target beaches respectively and act as flank guards to the landings.

The whole operation was covered by the most elaborate programme of deception of the whole war. Every effort was made to persuade the Germans that the Pas de Calais was the real target. For every sortie flown west of Le Havre, two were flown north of it; for every ton of tombs dropped west of Le Havre, two were dropped to its north. In Kent, a likely stepping off point for a Pas de Calais crossing, dummy headquarters and railway sidings were built.

By the beginning of June, 1944, every precaution that could be taken to safeguard 'Overlord' had been taken. But one important and imponderable factor remained – the weather.

Across the channel the Allies were faced by Field-Marshal Gerd von Rundstedt, and more immediately by Army Group B (Rommel) and Seventh Army (Dollmann). Between them they could field thirty infantry divisions and six armoured divisions (**Map 2**). Many of the infantry divisions were 'coastal' or training divisions and of inferior quality. Moreover Rundstedt's Western

Command spread from the Arctic circle in Norway to the Mediterranean in France, and his relationship with his subordinates was complicated by Hitler's habit of bypassing him and issuing orders direct to his Army Group commanders. In fact, the Germans had no effective chain of command in the west, and this was to tell heavily against them when the moment arrived. The situation was further complicated by the fact that the Third Air Fleet, although stationed in France, came under Göring's command. It was virtually a paper organization anyway, having only ninety bombers and seventy fighters fit for action.

Perhaps the greatest weakness of the German position in the north of France lay in the topography itself The whole of Normandy is almost enclosed by the rivers Loire and Seine. To destroy the crossings on these rivers would virtually isolate all the forces in Normandy, and leave them only the small gap between Paris and Orleans through which to escape.

Below: A German sentry stands outside a coastal gun emplacement in France

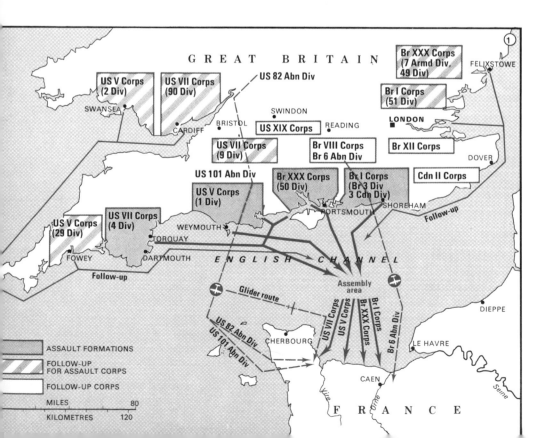

Above: Spitfires flying on a mission prior to the D-Day landings

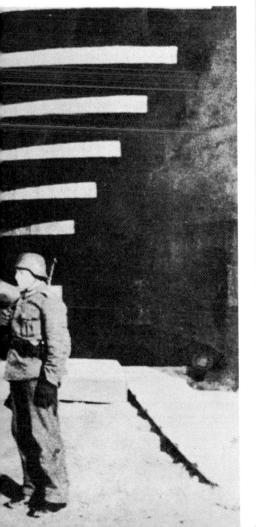

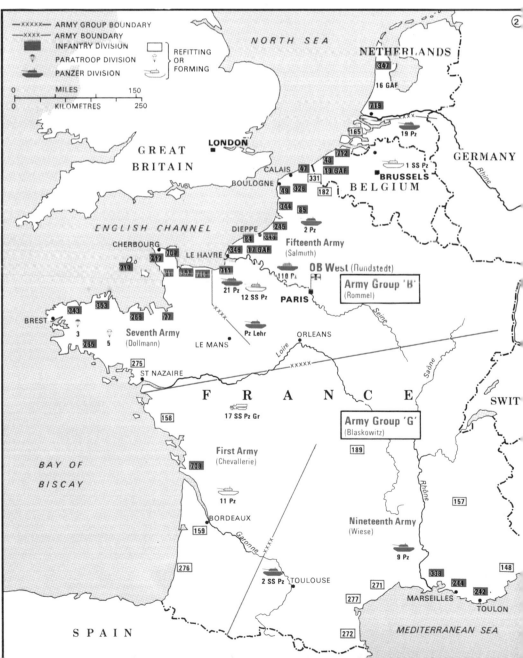

②

ARMY GROUP BOUNDARY
ARMY BOUNDARY
INFANTRY DIVISION
PARATROOP DIVISION
PANZER DIVISION
REFITTING OR FORMING

0 — MILES — 150
0 — KILOMETRES — 250

NORTH SEA

NETHERLANDS
347
16 GAF
719
165
712
48
19 GAF
1 SS Pz
19 Pz

GREAT BRITAIN

LONDON

CALAIS 47
BOULOGNE 331
BRUSSELS
BELGIUM
49 326
182
344 85
2 Pz

ENGLISH CHANNEL

DIEPPE 245
84 346
CHERBOURG 346 17 GAF
247 709 LE HAVRE
210 711
441 243 716 116 Pz OB West (Rundstedt)
21 Pz 12 SS Pz PARIS
Fifteenth Army (Salmuth)
Army Group 'B' (Rommel)

343 353
BREST 266 77
3 Pz Lehr
265 5 Seventh Army (Dollmann) LE MANS ORLEANS
Loire
Seine
xxxxx
Saône

F R A N C E

275
ST NAZAIRE

158
17 SS Pz Gr

Army Group 'G' (Blaskowitz)

First Army (Chevallerie)
189
708

BAY OF BISCAY

11 Pz

157

BORDEAUX
159
Nineteenth Army (Wiese)
Rhône
9 Pz
438 148
2 SS Pz TOULOUSE 271 244 242
276 277 MARSEILLES
TOULON

SPAIN

SWIT

MEDITERRANEAN SEA

272

D-DAY

June 1944 opened with cold weather and high winds, a serious matter to the Allied planners. There were only a few days in each month on which the optimum conditions of moon and tide for the landings occurred, and the first week of June formed such a period. Command of the Overlord operation had been assumed by General Eisenhower earlier in the year, and the landing forces themselves were commanded by General Montgomery. The naval forces were commanded by Admiral Ramsay, and the air forces by Air Marshal Leigh Mallory.

Taking advantage of a break in the weather the landings went ahead on 6 June. Some 4,000 ships carried 176,000 troops and their material; 600 warships escorted the force; and 2,500 bombers and 7,000 fighter-bombers 'softened-up' the beaches and combed the skies. At 0200 hours the American and British airborne forces were dropped or landed on their targets. Tactical surprise was complete, and both airborne forces were able to consolidate a position. At 0314 hours the aircraft bombardment of the beaches began, augmented at 0550 hours by the guns of the 600 escorting warships. At 0630 hours the first waves went ashore (see map). In the west the US First Army tackled Utah beach

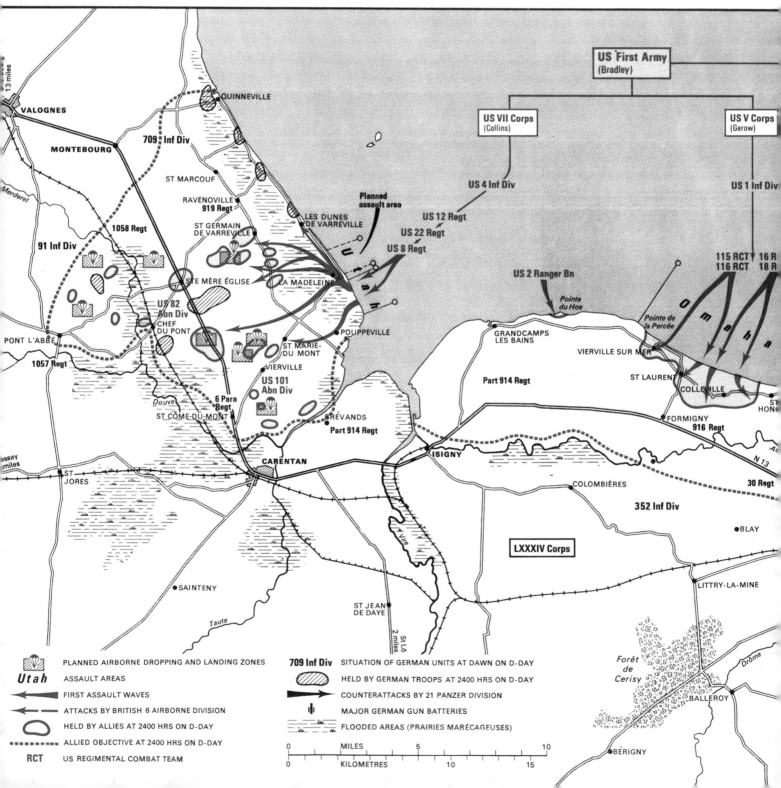

⛨	PLANNED AIRBORNE DROPPING AND LANDING ZONES	
Utah	ASSAULT AREAS	
←	FIRST ASSAULT WAVES	
←	ATTACKS BY BRITISH 6 AIRBORNE DIVISION	
◯	HELD BY ALLIES AT 2400 HRS ON D-DAY	
▪▪▪▪	ALLIED OBJECTIVE AT 2400 HRS ON D-DAY	
RCT	US REGIMENTAL COMBAT TEAM	

709 Inf Div	SITUATION OF GERMAN UNITS AT DAWN ON D-DAY	
▨	HELD BY GERMAN TROOPS AT 2400 HRS ON D-DAY	
►	COUNTERATTACKS BY 21 PANZER DIVISION	
╫	MAJOR GERMAN GUN BATTERIES	
≋	FLOODED AREAS (PRAIRIES MARÉCAGEUSES)	

MILES 0 — 5 — 10

KILOMETRES 0 — 5 — 10 — 15

(US VII Corps) and Omaha beach (US V Corps): in the east the British Second Army attacked Gold beach (British XXX Corps) and Juno and Sword beaches (British I Corps). On Sword, Juno, and Gold the British and Canadian divisions, using specialized armour to overcome specific obstacles, met stiff resistance in some places, but in most were able to press on towards Caen. The Bayeaux via Creuilly road was captured, and a counterattack by 21 Panzer Division was repelled.

In the west Utah beach was quickly overrun, contact was made with the airborne forces and a depth of six miles was reached. Only on Omaha beach did things go seriously wrong. The regimental combat teams of the US V Corps, deprived of full amphibious tank support by the rough seas, remained pinned down on the beach by the fire of the German 352 Division. Not until nightfall were they able to fight their way forward to the coast road.

By 2400 hours on D-Day the Allies had not attained their predetermined objectives, but, with the exception of Omaha, all the landings had secured comfortable beachheads, and, with the artificial harbours in position the flow of supplies and reinforcements could easily be maintained.

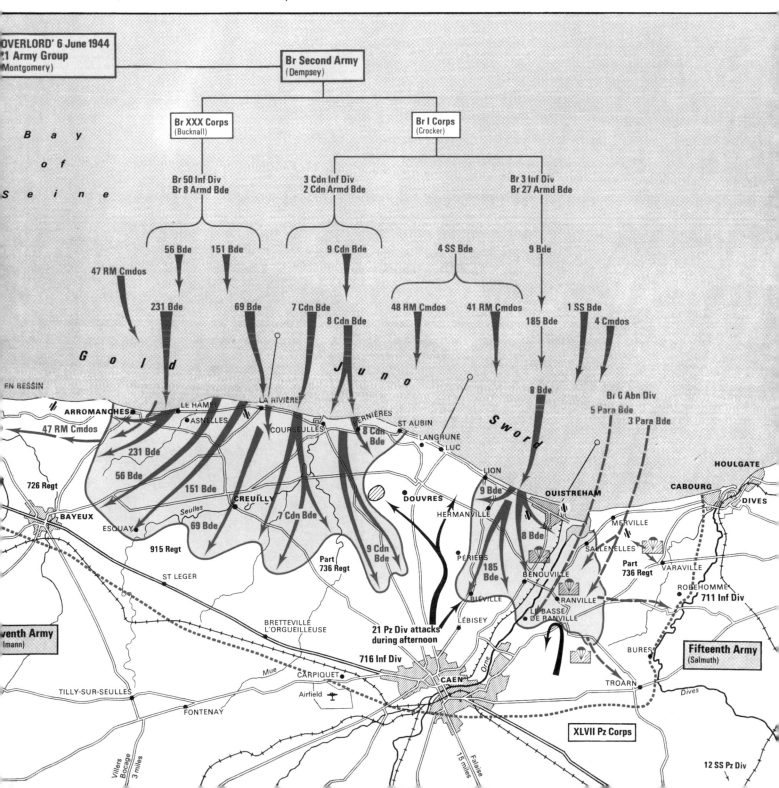

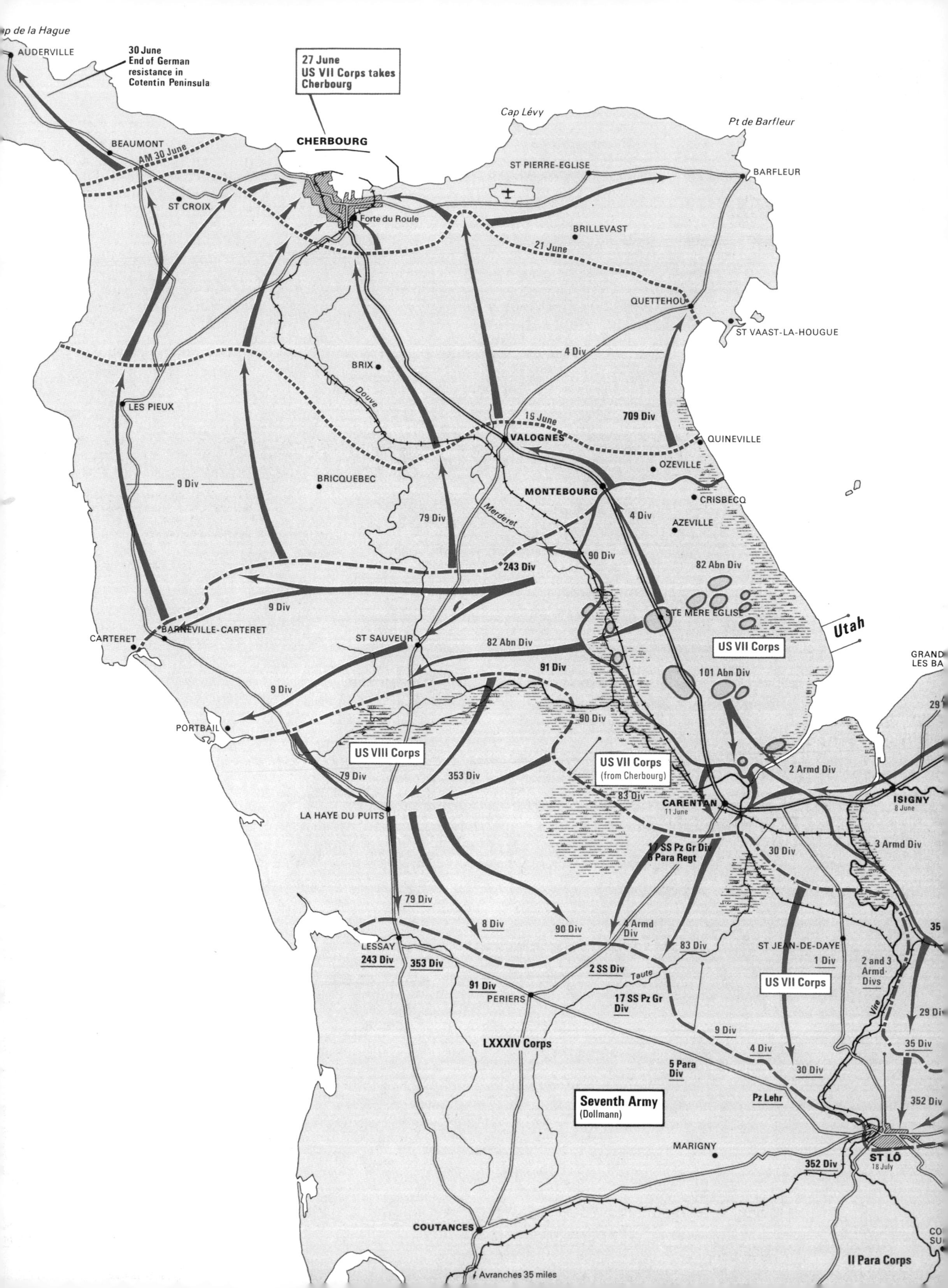

Cap de la Hague

AUDERVILLE

30 June
End of German
resistance in
Cotentin Peninsula

27 June
US VII Corps takes
Cherbourg

Cap Lévy

Pt de Barfleur

BEAUMONT
AM 30 June

CHERBOURG

ST PIERRE-EGLISE

BARFLEUR

ST CROIX

Forte du Roule

BRILLEVAST

21 June

QUETTEHOU

ST VAAST-LA-HOUGUE

LES PIEUX

Douve

BRIX

15 June

709 Div

QUINEVILLE

VALOGNES

OZEVILLE

9 Div

BRICQUEBEC

MONTEBOURG

CRISBECQ

4 Div

AZEVILLE

79 Div

Merderet

9 Div

243 Div

90 Div

82 Abn Div

CARTERET

BARNEVILLE-CARTERET

9 Div

ST SAUVEUR

STE MERE EGLISE

Utah

82 Abn Div

US VII Corps

GRAND
LES BA

9 Div

91 Div

101 Abn Div

PORTBAIL

90 Div

29

US VIII Corps

79 Div

353 Div

US VII Corps
(from Cherbourg)

2 Armd Div

LA HAYE DU PUITS

83 Div

CARENTAN
11 June

ISIGNY
8 June

17 SS Pz Gr Div
6 Para Regt

30 Div

3 Armd Div

79 Div

8 Div

90 Div

4 Armd
Div

83 Div

ST JEAN-DE-DAYE

1 Div

2 and 3
Armd
Divs

35

LESSAY

243 Div   **353 Div**

2 SS Div

Taute

US VII Corps

Vire

29 Div

91 Div

17 SS Pz Gr
Div

9 Div

35 Div

PERIERS

LXXXIV Corps

5 Para
Div

4 Div

30 Div

352 Div

Seventh Army
(Dollmann)

Pz Lehr

MARIGNY

352 Div

ST LÔ
18 July

COUTANCES

CO
SU

Avranches 35 miles

II Para Corps

THE BATTLE OF THE BUILD-UP

Rundstedt and Rommel were hampered by three important factors in any attempt to 'kill' the Allied invasion on the beaches. Firstly the Allies held total command of the air. Secondly since the beginning of 1944 the Allied bomber offensive had been geared to destroying communications, particularly rail communications, in the north of France. In this it had been successful, and this, combined with the efforts of the Maquis, made movement for the German forces very difficult. Thirdly Hitler himself still insisted that the real invasion would fall across the Pas de Calais, and he interfered with and hindered Rommel's attempts to mobilize reserves.

Nonetheless the Allies' breakout from their beachheads was a painful process. In the west the first task of Bradley's US First Army was to sever the Contentin peninsula, and then to capture Cherbourg, the Allies' first hope of a proper harbour (see map). By 17 June the US 9 Division had reached Carteret and Portbail, and by 21 June Cherbourg was besieged by 9 Division, 79 Division, and 4 Division of VII Corps. After a brief but bitter siege Cherbourg fell on 27 June, but so thoroughly had the Germans wrecked the harbour that it was unusable until August. Turning south VII Corps, joined by VIII Corps, struck at Dollmann's Seventh Army and, by 24 July, had captured St Lô. The Contentin peninsula was occupied.

From Omaha beach the US XIX and V Corps had broken out southwards on 10 June, and by 17 June had reached Caumont on the Caen-St Lô road. On 19/22 June the Channel was swept by gales which destroyed the artificial Mulberry harbour on Omaha beach and badly damaged that on Gold. This inevitably set back Allied plans by reducing the flow of reinforcements and supplies. (The storm destroyed nearly five times as many landing craft as German fire had done on D-Day.)

Throughout June the British Second Army made slow progress towards Caen. It was, admittedly, part of the Allied plan that the advance on Caen should draw off most of the German opposition, leaving the Allied right free to wheel round south and east, but opposition was fiercer than expected.

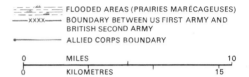

HELD BY ALLIES AT 2400 HRS ON D-DAY	FLOODED AREAS (PRAIRIES MARÉCAGEUSES)
FRONT LINE ON MORNING, 10 JUNE	BOUNDARY BETWEEN US FIRST ARMY AND BRITISH SECOND ARMY
FRONT LINE MIDNIGHT 17 JUNE	ALLIED CORPS BOUNDARY
FRONT LINE MIDNIGHT 30 JUNE	
FRONT LINE MIDNIGHT 24 JULY	
2 Div 326 Div SITUATION OF ALLIED AND GERMAN FRONT LINE DIVISIONS AT MIDNIGHT 24 JULY	MILES 0 10
GERMAN COUNTERATTACKS	KILOMETRES 0 15

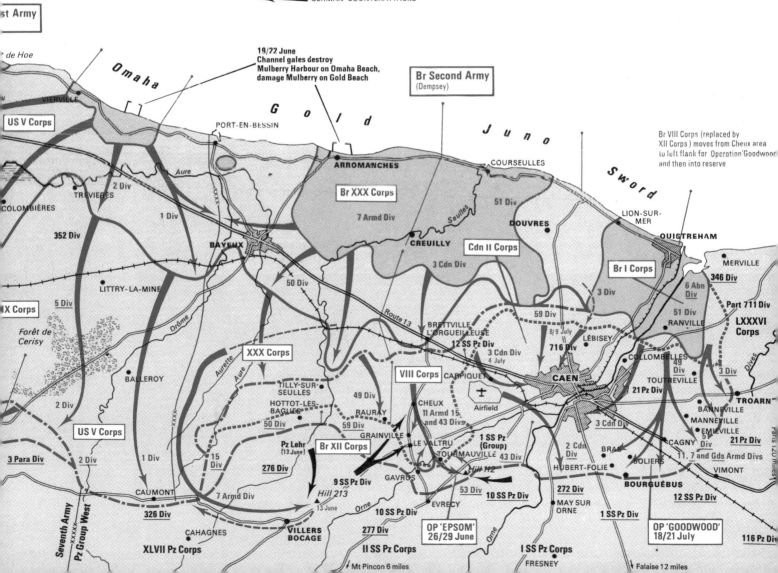

THE BATTLE FOR NORMANDY

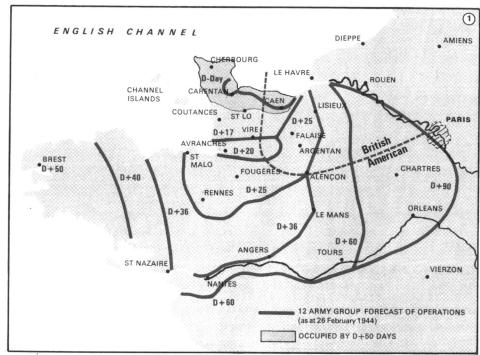

The close-set hedges of the Normandy bocage favoured the defence, and of this the Germans were quick to take advantage. After heavy bombing that hindered rather than helped the attackers, Allied troops reached the outskirts of Caen on 13 July.

Reinforcements had now reached Rommel from the south of France, and this enabled him to regroup his armour for a decisive blow at the Allied armies. It was essential for Montgomery to prevent this, and accordingly he mounted two operations, Epsom and Goodwood, as a preventive strike against Rommel's forces (see previous pages). The first was a costly failure,

but Operation Goodwood (**Map 3**) was pushed forward against strong opposition and had the effect of pinning down German units around Caen.

On the left of the Allied front the Canadian II Corps fought its way into Caen street by street, and by 18 July was occupying most of the town.

During the next two days the remainder of the town fell. The British I Corps, bypassing Caen in a great sweep as part of Operation Goodwood, was brought to a halt by the guns of the 1 and 12 SS Panzer Divisions. By the 20th Caen had fallen, and the Allied front extended some miles beyond the town.

On 26 February 1944, Twelfth

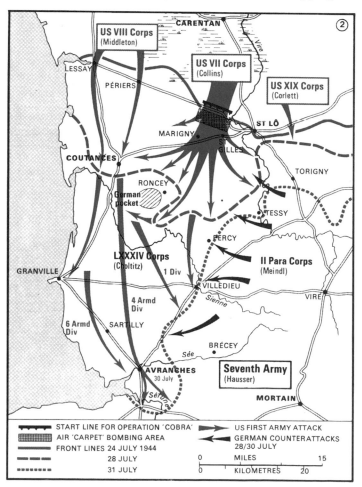

Army Group forecast the progress to be expected as the result of landings on the Normandy beaches (**Map 1**). They expected to reach Brest by D+50, and Paris by D+90. Actual progress was rather more modest. By D+50 (27 July) only the Contentin peninsula and the Normandy coast were in Allied hands.

By the end of July the Allied strength ashore was nearly 1,000,000 men, 150,000 vehicles, and a million tons of supplies. They had lost about 122,000 men, as against German losses of 114,000 plus about 41,000 prisoners.

The British and Canadian attacks on and around Caen had drawn away so many of the German forces on the Allied right that, by the end of July, Bradley's US First Army was in a position to break out through the German defences west of St Lô. On 25 July, after a prolonged air bombardment of a new kind called 'carpet' bombing, the US VII, VIII, and XIX Corps attacked (**Map 2**). The VII Corps poured through the gap caused by the bombing and in spite of strong opposition had reached Avranches by 30 July. German counterattacks, ordered by Hitler personally, failed to check this move.

Above: Canadian troops near Caen
Below: The ruins of Caen after its occupation

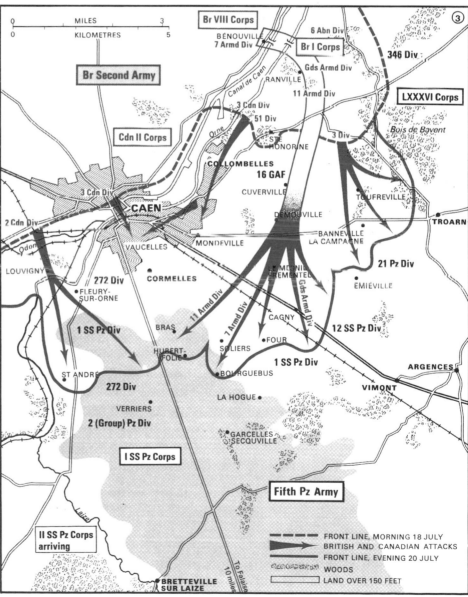

THE ANVIL LANDINGS

In yielding to Stalin's demand for a second front the Allies allowed themselves to lose sight of the fact that they already had a second front in Italy. From the first a strong school of thought among the Allied planners favoured the reinforcing of the Italian campaign with all the troops and supplies earmarked for a second front. There can be no doubt that with the extra strength in men, guns, aircraft, and landing craft, the war in Italy would have been transformed. An advance on Vienna and beyond would have been quite possible, and the German forces in the west could have been left to wither on the vine without incurring the cost of attacking them. This was very much a British idea, born of memories of the 'might have been' of Gallipoli, and it cannot be denied that behind it was a desire not only to defeat Germany, but to prevent the Russian armies establishing themselves too far to the west. This political motive was certainly present, but militarily the plan made sense. A move northward from the Po would have imperilled all the German forces in the Balkans, and if executed swiftly, might even have cut them off. The German forces in Italy itself could have been surrounded and destroyed by twin enveloping amphibious movements 'up the leg' of Italy. Germany, finding herself attacked through Austria, would have been compelled to transfer the bulk of her strength from the west to oppose such a move.

The American planners were deeply suspicious of this idea. They saw it as an attempt by the imperialist powers to involve American lives in political schemes of doubtful military value. In this they were backed by President Roosevelt who was anxious to go out of his way to please Stalin. Stalin, not unnaturally, wanted the Anglo-American effort made as far to the west as possible. To the Italian venture, therefore, the Americans opposed an exploitation of Overlord supported by an invasion of southern France, Anvil

(**Map 1**). Except that logistically Overlord was comparatively easy to support from England, this scheme had little to recommend it. The greatest possible distance was interposed between the invaders and their final objective; the enemy was attacked at a point where he was comparatively strong; and the troops earmarked for Anvil were virtually wasted – a sufficiently threatening advance across the north of France would have compelled the withdrawal of any forces in the south without the necessity of a supporting operation.

Nonetheless the Anvil plan was adopted. How far political or military considerations shaped this decision is not known, but with the abandonment of the plan for a campaign over the Alps towards Vienna and the Danube, a great opportunity was lost.

At 0800 hours on 15 August 1944, the US Seventh Army under Lieutenant-General Patch made landings in the South of France between Toulon and Cannes (**Map 2**). These landings were supported by airborne forces. The landings' object was to free Marseilles for supply purposes and to secure Eisenhower's southern flank. Opposition was light (only 183 men were killed in the landings) and, by last light on the 15th, 94,000 men and 11,000 vehicles were ashore. Immediately the French II Corps (General De Lattre Tassigny) was passed through Patch's forces and took up the advance.

While De Lattre's forces and the US 3 and 45 Divisions made west for Toulon, a task force under Butler headed north to Gap and then west to Montelimar, closing the trap on the German Nineteenth Army (Wiese). Much of Wiese's army managed to escape but Butler's artillery and Allied aircraft took a terrible toll. 15,000 German prisoners were taken and some 4,000 vehicles. At the same time De Lattre had captured Toulon and Marseilles taking 47,717 prisoners.

After these successes Patch's task

was simple. On 29 August he started out on the trek north up the Rhône valley. Contact with Patton's Third Army was made on 12 September. Patch's Seventh Army and the newly-formed French First Army became the US 6 Army Group under Lieutenant-General Devers.

Above: Landing craft set out for the shore as the invasion of southern France begins

Opposite: Allied paratroops dropping as part of the Anvil assault

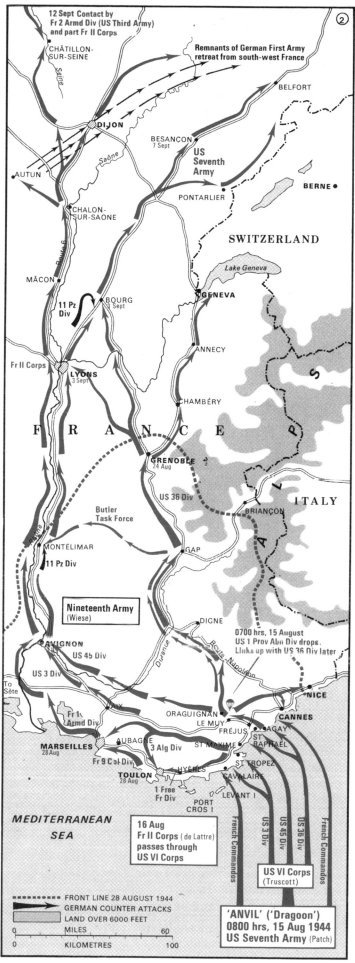

12 Sept Contact by
Fr 2 Armd Div (US Third Army)
and part Fr II Corps

CHÂTILLON-
SUR-SEINE

Remnants of German First Army
retreat from south-west France

BELFORT

DIJON

BESANÇON
7 Sept

US
Seventh
Army

BERNE

AUTUN

Saône

PONTARLIER

CHALON-
SUR-SAONE

SWITZERLAND

MÂCON

Lake Geneva

BOURG
3 Sept

GENEVA

11 Pz
Div

ANNECY

Fr II Corps

LYONS
3 Sept

CHAMBÉRY

F R A N C E

GRENOBLE
24 Aug

US 36 Div

ITALY

A L P S

BRIANÇON

Butler
Task Force

MONTÉLIMAR

GAP

11 Pz Div

Nineteenth Army
(Wiese)

DIGNE

0700 hrs, 15 August
US 1 Prov Abn Div drops.
Links up with US 36 Div later

Route Napoléon

AVIGNON

US 45 Div

Durance

US 3 Div

NICE

To
Sète

AIX

Fr 1
Armd Div

ORAGUIGNAN

LE MUY

CANNES

FRÉJUS

AGAY

MARSEILLES
28 Aug

AUBAGNE

3 Alg Div

ST MAXIME

ST
RAPHAEL

Fr 9 Col Div

HYÈRES

ST TROPEZ

TOULON
28 Aug

CAVALAIRE

1 Free
Fr Div

LEVANT I

PORT
CROS I

MEDITERRANEAN
SEA

16 Aug
Fr II Corps (de Lattre)
passes through
US VI Corps

French Commandos

US 3 Div

US 45 Div

US 36 Div

French Commandos

US VI Corps
(Truscott)

•••••••• FRONT LINE 28 AUGUST 1944
━━━▶ GERMAN COUNTER ATTACKS
▨ LAND OVER 6000 FEET

MILES   60
0
KILOMETRES   100
0

'ANVIL' ('Dragoon')
0800 hrs, 15 Aug 1944
US Seventh Army (Patch)

THE BREAKOUT

After Bradley's advance on Avranches the Allied forces were reorganized. The US 12 Army Group was formed under Bradley comprising the US First Army (Hodges) and as from 1 August the US Third Army (Patton). The British forces became the British 21 Army Group under Montgomery, comprising the British Second Army (Dempsey) and the Canadian First Army (Crerar). Montgomery remained in overall command of Eisenhower's land forces until September.

On 1 August, Patton's Third Army poured through the Avranches gap. His armour overran Brittany (see inset) and swept south towards the Loire (**Map 1**). His infantry made for Le Mans. At the same time the US First, the British Second, and the Canadian First armies attacked south and east driving the German opposition before them. By 16 August the British and American forces in the north, and Patton's forces from the south had squeezed the German forces into a salient between Falaise and Argentan (**Map 2**). Through this gap the disorganized German Seventh and Fifth Panzer armies were escaping. Hitler's insistence on last-minute counterattacks had left these troops in a vulnerable position, and only some dilatoriness by the Allies allowed them to escape. As it was, by the time the pocket was closed by Canadian II Corps and US V Corps, some 50,000 Germans were captured and some 10,000 lay dead.

Kluge, who had replaced Rommel in July after Rommel had been wounded by Allied aircraft, was now in full retreat, with four Allied armies on his tail, making for the safety of the Seine crossings. Patton's armour reached the Seine at Fontainebleau on the same day that the Falaise gap was closed, and the US XV Corps established a bridgehead downstream of Paris. On the 25th the city was liberated. Kluge's reward for salvaging a remarkable proportion of Army Group B was to be replaced by Model.

The Allied breakout from Normandy was a remarkable military operation. It decisively defeated the German forces in Western Europe and should have opened the door for a pursuit to Berlin.

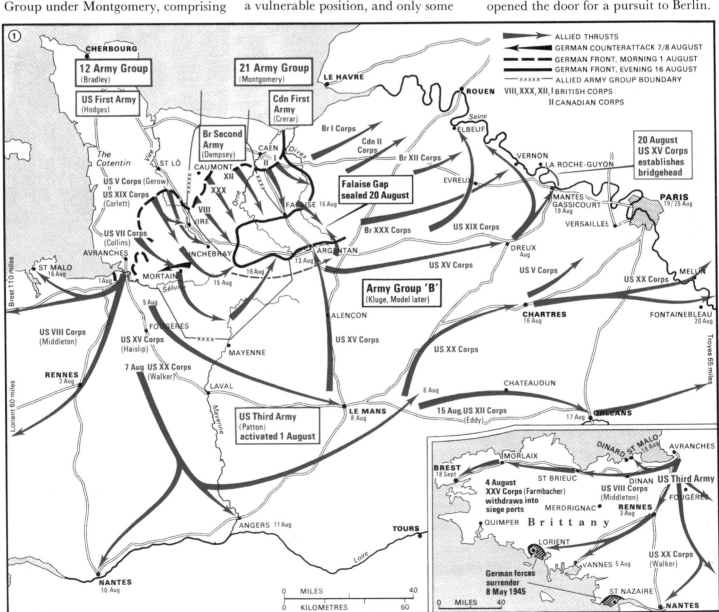

Above: American forces are greeted as they drive through a Normandy village

Below: Canadian artillery moves up to the front as the drive on Paris begins

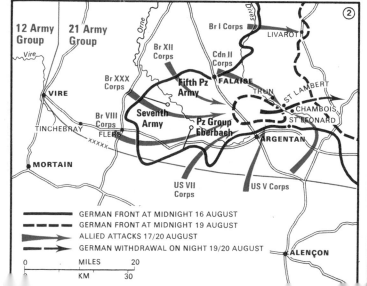

GERMAN FRONT AT MIDNIGHT 16 AUGUST
GERMAN FRONT AT MIDNIGHT 19 AUGUST
ALLIED ATTACKS 17/20 AUGUST
GERMAN WITHDRAWAL ON NIGHT 19/20 AUGUST

THE DRIVE TO THE RHINE

Standing on the Seine, the German forces defeated and disordered, the problem that faced the Allies in late August 1944 was one of pursuit. Again the Allied commanders found themselves split, but this time it was not a simple split along lines of nationality. A straight pursuit by all four Allied armies was impossible. The supply demands would be far too great, and already the petrol situation was critical. But a strong thrust by a part of the Allied armies, through Belgium, encircling the Ruhr and on to Berlin might yield enormous benefits. Both Montgomery and Bradley favoured this plan, although neither was prepared to be subordinate to the other. Eisenhower, on the other hand, favoured a slow advance in line by all his forces. To a certain extent he was motivated by the need to keep the peace between his extremely fractious subordinates, but he also had military reasons for disliking the 'single strong thrust' plan. The German forces opposing him, although defeated, were still partially intact. Their chain of command remained, and their standards of morale and leadership were high. They were far from out of the game. Eisenhower feared that a deep thrust into Germany would expose flanks very vulnerable to attack by forces of this kind. A pencil-like thrust, as he described it, would stand too great a risk of being bitten off.

The maps (**1 and 2**) show the alternatives. It is easy with hindsight to accuse Eisenhower of being over-cautious. The Allied command of the air, and their enormous predominance on the ground, almost certainly outweighed the risks of the narrow front plan – a plan which held out the prospect of ending the war in 1944 with the Red Army still east of the Oder.

Broad front or narrow front, the Allies' most pressing need in August 1944 was a port. The 300-mile logistical haul from Normandy was stretched almost to breaking point. Over the Seine the Allies advanced rapidly (**Map 3**). By 4 September Brussels and Antwerp had fallen, and by the 15th the whole of Belgium and Luxembourg had been cleared. However this lightning advance by British Second Army was performed at the cost of the US First and Third Armies who found themselves short of petrol.

On 3 September Eisenhower assumed direct command of ground operations. Hitler recalled Rundstedt to command in the west two days later.

Although the Germans had been cleared from Antwerp they still commanded the Scheldt estuary. Also some time had to be devoted to clearing the Channel ports and eliminating the missile sites in the Pas de Calais area. These tasks were both discharged by the Canadian First Army by the end of September.

In spite of these checks, by 15 September the Allies stood on the borders of Germany. Since their landings in June they had put more than 2,000,000 men on French soil, and they had lost some 40,000 dead. German losses had been catastrophic – 500,000 from the field forces, and a further 200,000 from the coastal fortresses.

Left: Allied units arrive in Eindhoven

Opposite: US engineers bridging the Seine

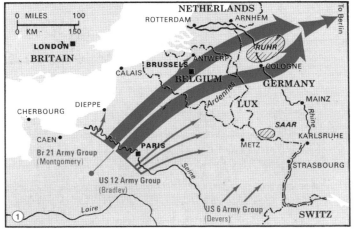

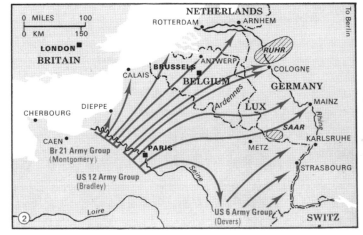

240

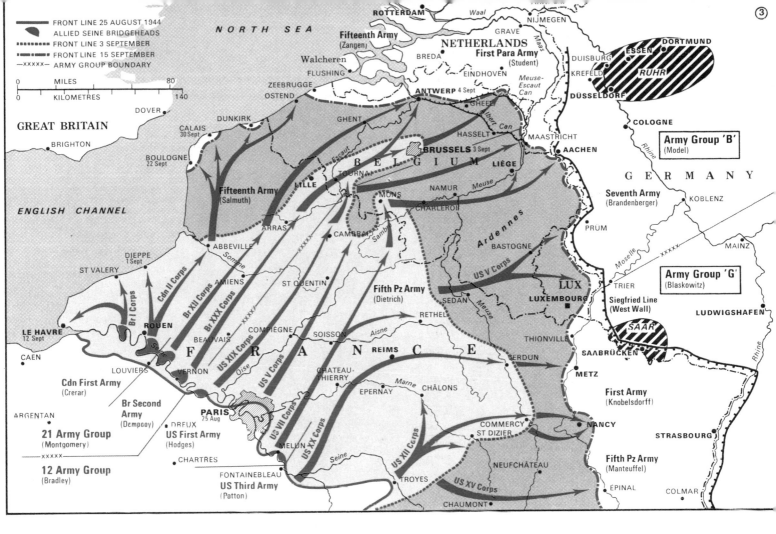

FRONT LINE 25 AUGUST 1944
ALLIED SEINE BRIDGEHEADS
FRONT LINE 3 SEPTEMBER
FRONT LINE 15 SEPTEMBER
××××× ARMY GROUP BOUNDARY

MILES 80
KILOMETRES 140

NORTH SEA

GREAT BRITAIN

ENGLISH CHANNEL

ROTTERDAM
Waal
NIJMEGEN
Grave
Maas

Fifteenth Army
(Zangen)
BREDA
EINDHOVEN
NETHERLANDS
First Para Army
(Student)

DUISBURG
KREFELD
DORTMUND
ESSEN
RUHR
DÜSSELDORF

Walcheren
FLUSHING
Meuse-
Escaut
Can
ANTWERP 4 Sept
Gheel
Albert
Can

COLOGNE

ZEEBRUGGE
OSTEND
DUNKIRK
GHENT
HASSELT
MAASTRICHT
AACHEN

Army Group 'B'
(Model)

DOVER
CALAIS
30 Sept
BOULOGNE
22 Sept
LILLE
TOURNAI
BRUSSELS 3 Sept
LIÈGE

GERMANY

BRIGHTON
Br I Corps
Cdn II Corps
ARRAS
Escaut
BELGIUM
NAMUR
Meuse
CHARLEROI

Seventh Army
(Brandenberger)
KOBLENZ

ABBEVILLE
Somme
AMIENS
ST QUENTIN
CAMBRAI
Sambre
MONS

Ardennes
BASTOGNE
US V Corps

PRUM

DIEPPE
1 Sept
ST VALERY
Br XII Corps
Br XXX Corps
BEAUVAIS
COMPIEGNE
SOISSON
Aisne
Fifth Pz Army
(Dietrich)
SEDAN
Meuse

LUX
LUXEMBOURG
TRIER

Moselle
MAINZ

LE HAVRE
12 Sept
ROUEN
US XIX Corps
VERNON
Oise
REIMS
F R A N C E
RETHEL

Siegfried Line
(West Wall)

Army Group 'G'
(Blaskowitz)

LUDWIGSHAFEN

CAEN
LOUVIERS
Seine
US V Corps
CHATEAU-
THIERRY
EPERNAY
Marne
CHÂLONS
THIONVILLE
VERDUN
METZ

SAAR
SAARBRÜCKEN

Cdn First Army
(Crerar)

PARIS
25 Aug
US VII Corps

COMMERCY
ST DIZIER
NANCY

First Army
(Knobelsdorff)

STRASBOURG

ARGENTAN
Br Second
Army
(Dempsey)
DREUX
US First Army
(Hodges)
MELUN
US XX Corps
Seine

NEUFCHÂTEAU

Fifth Pz Army
(Manteuffel)

21 Army Group
(Montgomery)
CHARTRES
FONTAINEBLEAU
US Third Army
(Patton)
TROYES
US XII Corps
US XV Corps

EPINAL
COLMAR

12 Army Group
(Bradley)
CHAUMONT

Rhine

THE ARNHEM OPERATION

After the liberation of Belgium, the 21 Army Group was faced by the complex of rivers and estuaries where the Rhine and the Meuse empty into the North Sea. To secure a continuous northward advance, Montgomery planned to drop three airborne divisions to capture the bridges at Veghel, Grave, Nijmegen, and Arnhem, creating an airborne corridor for Second Army, led by XXX Corps, to advance along. Planned for 17 September, the operation consisted of a landing by the US 101 Airborne Division at Veghel (**Map 1**), a landing by the US 82 Airborne Division at Grave, and a landing by the British 1

Airborne Division supported later by the Polish parachute brigade at Arnhem. The intention was to co-ordinate the advance of XXX Corps with these drops to achieve maximum surprise and dislocation.

The landings of 101 and 82 Divisions were successful and XXX Corps linked up with the airborne forces on schedule on the 18th. On the 20th the Nijmegen bridge fell to a combined attack by XXX Corps and 82 Division, but they could get no farther. The British 1 Airborne Division had encountered powerful opposition. Only one battalion got through to the bridge, and was instantly cut off. The remainder of the force was surrounded, but held out until the 26th. 2,200 survivors managed to escape, but 7,000 were left behind to be killed, wounded, or captured.

Many factors contributed to the British disaster at Arnhem. The major one was the readiness and flexibility of the German defence, but it must also be mentioned that the British airborne forces' doctrine of landing some distance from the objective was a risky one that threw away the surprise and shock that are the essence of airborne operations.

Before Antwerp could be of use to the Allies, the German forces in the Scheldt estuary had to be cleared (**Map 2**).

The Canadian First and British Second armies undertook this, and by 8 November the area was clear. Minor line mending took place around Venlo on the German border, and by the US First Army around Aachen. Bradley's 12 Army Group was enlarged by the arrival of the US Ninth Army (Simpson), and, to the south, Devers' 6 Army Group pushed through the Vosges mountains to the German border. By 15 December the Allies were poised for their next obvious objective – the crossing of the Rhine.

But German resistance west of the Rhine could be expected to be strong. Rundstedt's command, OB West, comprised Army Group H (Student), Army Group B (Model), Army Group G (Balck), and Army Group Oberrhein (Himmler). The broad front policy had given the Germans a breathing space, and they had used it to reorganize their defences.

Below: Allied paratroops dropping on Arnhem

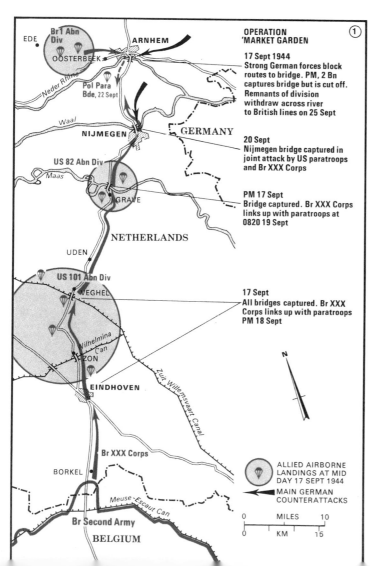

OPERATION 'MARKET GARDEN'

17 Sept 1944
Strong German forces block routes to bridge. PM, 2 Bn captures bridge but is cut off. Remnants of division withdraw across river to British lines on 25 Sept

20 Sept
Nijmegen bridge captured in joint attack by US paratroops and Br XXX Corps

PM 17 Sept
Bridge captured. Br XXX Corps links up with paratroops at 0820 19 Sept

17 Sept
All bridges captured. Br XXX Corps links up with paratroops PM 18 Sept

ALLIED AIRBORNE LANDINGS AT MID DAY 17 SEPT 1944

MAIN GERMAN COUNTERATTACKS

Above: German troops counterattack the British landings

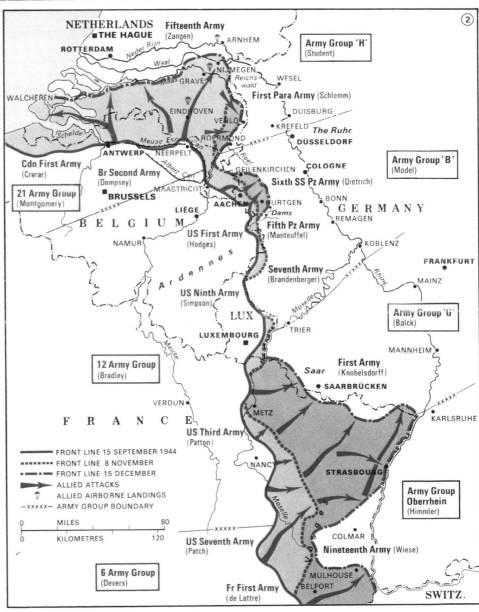

②

NETHERLANDS **Fifteenth Army** (Zangen)

THE HAGUE

ROTTERDAM

Neder Rijn

ARNHEM

Waal

Army Group 'H' (Student)

NIJMEGEN

Maas GRAVE

Reichs-wald

WESEL

WALCHEREN

Schelde

EINDHOVEN

VENLO

First Para Army (Schlemm)

DUISBURG

KREFELD

The Ruhr

DÜSSELDORF

Meuse Escaut Can

ROERMOND

ANTWERP

NEERPELT

Albert Can

Roer

GEILENKIRCHEN

COLOGNE

Army Group 'B' (Model)

BONN

REMAGEN

Cdn First Army (Crerar)

Br Second Army (Dempsey)

MAASTRICHT

AACHEN

HÜRTGEN

Dams

Sixth SS Pz Army (Dietrich)

21 Army Group (Montgomery)

BRUSSELS

LIÈGE

BELGIUM

GERMANY

NAMUR

US First Army (Hodges)

Fifth Pz Army (Manteuffel)

KOBLENZ

Ardennes

Seventh Army (Brandenberger)

Rhine

FRANKFURT

MAINZ

US Ninth Army (Simpson)

Moselle

LUX

LUXEMBOURG

TRIER

Army Group 'G' (Balck)

MANNHEIM

Meuse

12 Army Group (Bradley)

Saar

First Army (Knobelsdorff)

SAARBRÜCKEN

VERDUN

METZ

FRANCE

KARLSRUHE

US Third Army (Patton)

NANCY

STRASBOURG

Army Group Oberrhein (Himmler)

Moselle

FRONT LINE 15 SEPTEMBER 1944
FRONT LINE 8 NOVEMBER
FRONT LINE 15 DECEMBER
ALLIED ATTACKS
ALLIED AIRBORNE LANDINGS
ARMY GROUP BOUNDARY

0 MILES 80

0 KILOMETRES 120

US Seventh Army (Patch)

COLMAR

Nineteenth Army (Wiese)

MULHOUSE

6 Army Group (Devers)

Fr First Army (de Lattre)

BELFORT

SWITZ.

THE BATTLE OF THE ARDENNES

Poised for their attack toward the Rhine the Allies had entirely dismissed the possibility of a German offensive against them. Hitler, on the other hand, had determined to attack the Allies before they reached Germany. His plan (**Map 1**) was to break through the Allied front in the Ardennes, split the Americans from the British, and capture Antwerp, disrupting Allied supplies and destroying their armies piecemeal.

For this offensive Hitler had scraped together what was in effect his last remaining strategic reserve – twenty-four divisions, ten of them armoured deployed in the Sixth SS Panzer, Fifth Panzer, and Seventh Armies.

The offensive was daring and imaginative and came very close to success. One vital factor that the Germans lacked was air cover, and they were lucky that their offensive was covered by low cloud and heavy snowfall. On 16 December, eight Panzer divisions fell upon the US VIII Corps (**Map 2**). Tactical and strategic surprise was complete, and confusion was made worse confounded by the presence of English-speaking German soldiers in Allied uniforms behind the US lines. So great was the German success that Eisenhower was compelled to commit his reserves, the airborne

divisions still resting after Market Garden. One of these, the US 101 Airborne Division, arrived in Bastogne just in time to be trapped by 15 Panzer Grenadier Division. By 20 December, Bastogne was encircled and the German forces stood ready to make for the Meuse.

But by 20 December the Allies were beginning to recover from their surprise. Eisenhower transferred command of all troops north of the 'bulge' to Montgomery, leaving only Patton's army under Bradley to the south. Despite the desperate defence of St Vith by the US 7 Armoured Division it fell on the 22nd, but the delay had been fatal to German plans. The 24th saw the high water mark of the German offensive. With empty fuel tanks and against stiffening opposition, the Ardennes offensive ground to a halt.

The Allies now proceeded to squeeze out the bulge. From the north Hodges' US First Army, and from the south Patton's Third Army closed in on the German salient (**Map 3**). The battle for Bastogne saw the last major effort by the Luftwaffe, with some 800 planes attacking airfields in France, Belgium, and Holland. It had no effect on the air offensive being conducted over the Ardennes in support of the

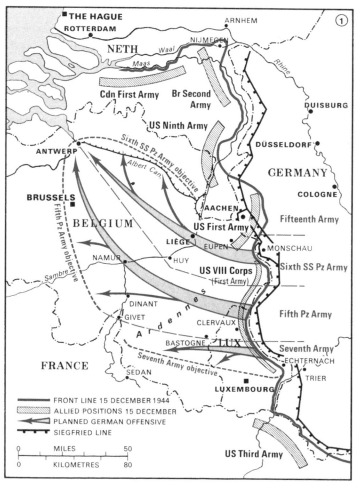

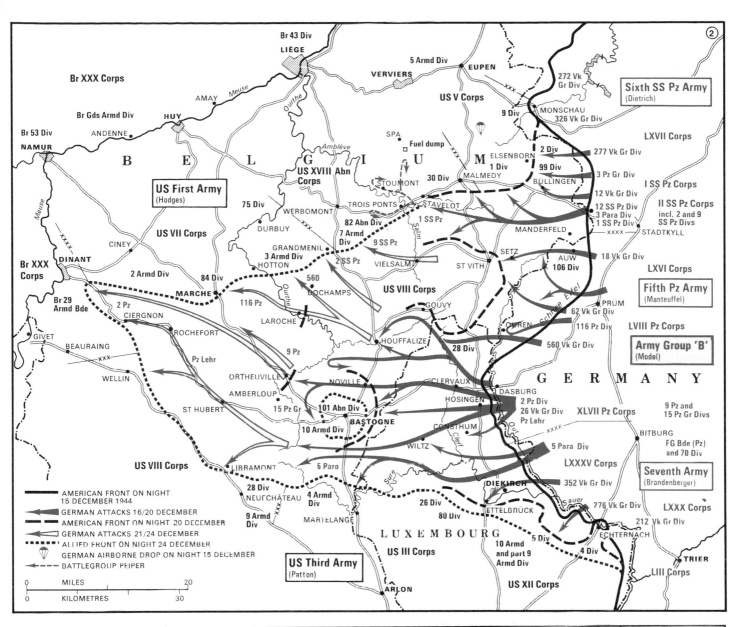

Br 43 Div
LIÈGE
Br XXX Corps
5 Armd Div
VERVIERS   EUPEN
272 Vk Gr Div
US V Corps
Sixth SS Pz Army
(Dietrich)
AMAY
Meuse
9 Div
MONSCHAU
326 Vk Gr Div
LXVII Corps
Br Gds Armd Div
HUY
ANDENNE
SPA
Fuel dump
ELSENBORN
2 Div
277 Vk Gr Div
Br 53 Div
Amblève
1 Div
99 Div
3 Pz Gr Div
NAMUR
BELGIUM
MALMEDY
BÜLLINGEN
I SS Pz Corps
US First Army
(Hodges)
US XVIII Abn
Corps
30 Div
12 Vk Gr Div
12 SS Pz Div
II SS Pz Corps
incl. 2 and 9
SS Pz Divs
Meuse
STOUMONT
1 SS Pz
3 Para Div
1 SS Pz Div
US VII Corps
75 Div
WERBOMONT
TROIS PONTS
STAVELOT
MANDERFELD
xxxx   STADTKYLL
DINANT
DURBUY
82 Abn Div
7 Armd
Div
9 SS Pz
SETZ
ST VITH
AUW
106 Div
18 Vk Gr Div
LXVI Corps
CINEY
GRANDMENIL
3 Armd Div
VIELSALM
Fifth Pz Army
(Manteuffel)
Br XXX
Corps
2 Armd Div
84 Div
HOTTON
2 SS Pz
560
US VIII Corps
PRÜM
62 Vk Gr Div
MARCHE
BOCHAMPS
GOUVY
DUREN
116 Pz Div
LVIII Pz Corps
Br 29
Armd Bde
116 Pz
Ourthe
LAROCHE
HOUFFALIZE
560 Vk Gr Div
Army Group 'B'
(Model)
2 Pz
CIERGNON
ROCHEFORT
9 Pz
28 Div
GERMANY
GIVET
BEAURAING
Pz Lehr
ORTHEUVILLE
NOVILLE
CLERVAUX
DASBURG
2 Pz
26 Vk Gr Div
Pz Lehr
9 Pz and
15 Pz Gr Divs
WELLIN
AMBERLOUP
HOSINGEN
XLVII Pz Corps
15 Pz Gr
101 Abn Div
BITBURG
ST HUBERT
BASTOGNE
CONSTHUM
FG Bde (Pz)
and 70 Div
10 Armd Div
WILTZ
5 Para Div
Seventh Army
(Brandenberger)
US VIII Corps
LIBRAMONT
6 Para
LXXXV Corps
28 Div
NEUFCHÂTEAU
4 Armd
Div
DIEKIRCH
352 Vk Gr Div
LXXX Corps
9 Armd
Div
MARTELANGE
26 Div
80 Div
ETTELBRÜCK
276 Vk Gr Div
212 Vk Gr Div
ECHTERNACH
AMERICAN FRONT ON NIGHT
15 DECEMBER 1944
GERMAN ATTACKS 16/20 DECEMBER
AMERICAN FRONT ON NIGHT 20 DECEMBER
GERMAN ATTACKS 21/24 DECEMBER
ALLIED FRONT ON NIGHT 24 DECEMBER
GERMAN AIRBORNE DROP ON NIGHT 15 DECEMBER
BATTLEGROUP PEIPER
LUXEMBOURG
US Third Army
(Patton)
US III Corps
10 Armd
and part 9
Armd Div
5 Div
4 Div
TRIER
LIII Corps
MILES   20
KILOMETRES   30
ARLON
US XII Corps

ground forces. By 7 February the salient had been eliminated. Hitler's gamble had failed, due to the German's inability to overrun the Allied fuel dumps and thus replenish their tanks. The result was a delay of six weeks in the Allies' operations, and the loss of the only German forces that might have checked the coming Russian spring offensive.

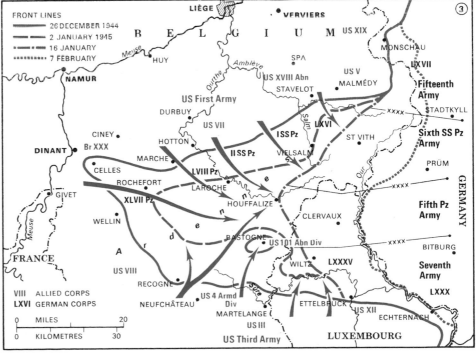

FRONT LINES
26 DECEMBER 1944
2 JANUARY 1945
16 JANUARY
7 FEBRUARY
LIÈGE
VERVIERS
BELGIUM
US XIX
MONSCHAU
LXVII
HUY
Amblève
SPA
US V
Fifteenth
Army
NAMUR
US XVIII Abn
STAVELOT
MALMÉDY
STADTKYLL
Meuse
Ourthe
Salm
LXVI
Sixth SS Pz
Army
DINANT
DURBUY
US VII
I SS Pz
ST VITH
PRÜM
CINEY
HOTTON
II SS Pz
VIELSALM
MARCHE
LVIII Pz
Fifth Pz
Army
CELLES
ROCHEFORT
LAROCHE
GERMANY
WELLIN
XLVII Pz
HOUFFALIZE
CLERVAUX
BITBURG
FRANCE
BASTOGNE
US 101 Abn Div
US VIII
WILTZ
LXXXV
Seventh
Army
Sure
RECOGNE
NEUFCHÂTEAU
US 4 Armd
Div
ETTELBRÜCK
LXXX
MARTELANGE
US XII
ECHTERNACH
VIII   ALLIED CORPS
LXVI   GERMAN CORPS
US III
US Third Army
LUXEMBOURG
MILES   20
KILOMETRES   30

Left: German troops pass a disabled US half-track

245

CROSSING THE RHINE

Above: US artillery shelling German positions across the Rhine

The tactical importance of the Rhine in 1945 was great enough, but this was enhanced by its symbolic importance. To both the Allies and the Germans it was the 'frontier' behind which lay the German heartland. The Allies could therefore expect the Germans to defend the Rhine, the most formidable water obstacle in Western Europe, with the utmost tenacity.

In early 1945 the flanks of the Allied armies had reached the Rhine in the north (Nijmegen) and in the south (Strasbourg). In the centre, however, the Ardennes offensive and the Siegfried Line had held back the Allied advance, and it was not until March that the Allies reached the Rhine along its whole length.

As the Allies approached the Rhine the hope grew that it might be possible to 'jump' a bridge intact but, even if this were to happen, there was no assurance that it would be in a vital or even useful quarter. All units, therefore, had to face the possibility of an opposed crossing of this wide, fast-flowing river. In the north, where Montgomery's 21 Army Group faced the widest stretch of the river, the defence could be expected to be at its hottest to deny the Allies access to the Ruhr and to the north German plain. In the south, however, where Devers' US 6 Army Group approached the Rhine between Strasbourg and Mannheim, the river, although narrower, was tricky and fast flowing. Also the Germans were able to control its flow by regulating dams on the east bank feeder rivers.

Then, on 7 March, the hoped-for happened. Speeding towards the Rhine, men of Hodge's US First Army captured intact the bridge at Remagen. Showing great flexibility and speed the Americans instantly exploited this opportunity, and by the evening of the 7th a substantial bridgehead had been established.

Useful though this was, however, it was not a decisive gain. The Remagen bridgehead could not be exploited alone. More substantial crossings were needed both up and down stream.

It was not until 22 March that a further crossing was made. On that day the US Third Army pushed its 5 Division across at Nierstein. On the following day after massive preparation British 51 (Highland) Division and Canadian 3 Division crossed near Rees and Emmerich. On the same day the US 9 Division crossed near Rheinberg.

These crossings were followed on 24/25 March by US 87 Division's successful storming of the river at St Goar. On the same day US 4 Armoured Division reached Darmstadt, and British and US airborne forces landed east of the Rhine and joined up with the advancing ground forces. On 26 March the US Seventh Army crossed near Worms and linked up with Patton's Third Army on the east bank. Finally on 27 March 80 Division of Third Army forced a crossing near Mainz and captured Wiesbaden.

The Allies had now cleared the Rhine from Nijmegen to Mannheim. From 31 March onwards the French First Army began to force crossings south of Mannheim, and by the first week in April the Germans had lost all their footholds on the east bank of the Rhine.

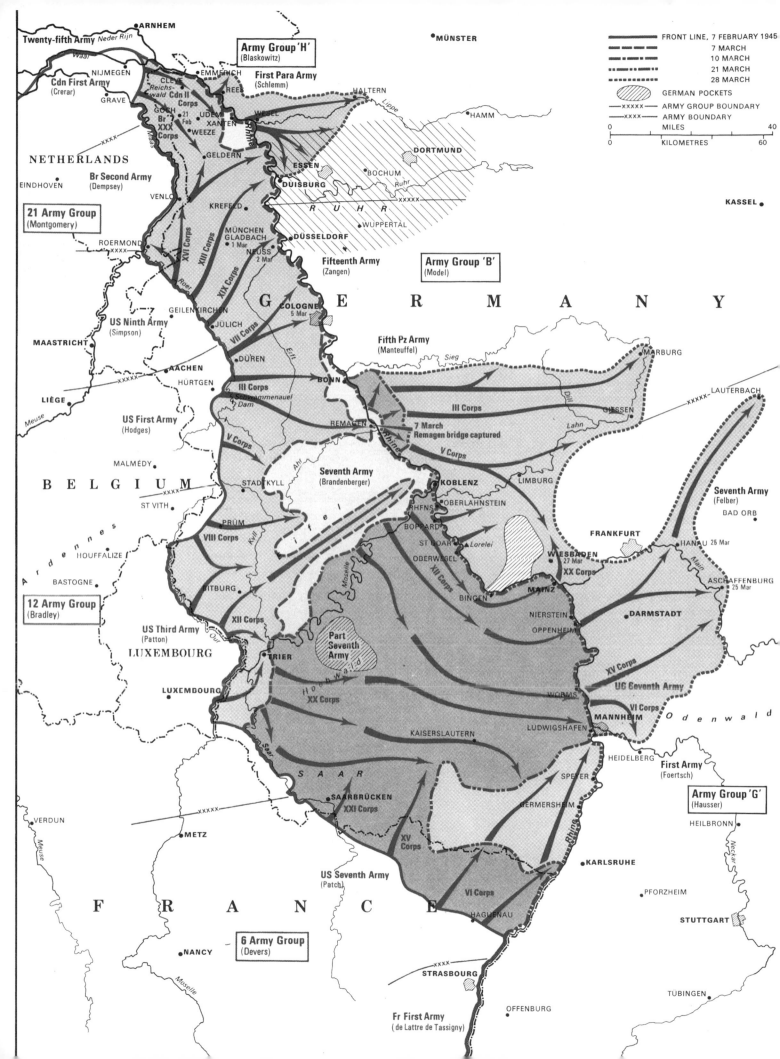

THE DRIVE INTO GERMANY

The Allied advance from the Rhine to link up with the Russian forces on the Elbe was marked in a few places by bitter opposition, but for the most part fighting was sporadic and isolated (map on right). Where a German officer of particularly determined character commanded seasoned troops, a well organized and spirited defence could be expected. Most German units, however, leaderless, lacking air cover, often short of rations and ammunition, were only too thankful that they were facing the Americans and British and not the Russians, and they surrendered in increasing numbers. Town after town greeted the Allies with white flags. Communication and command in the German armies had broken down, and no airy talk by Hitler of a 'national redoubt' in the mountains could disguise this fact.

There is no doubt that during April the Allies could have reached both Berlin and Prague before the Russians, but, in keeping with undertakings made to the Russians, Eisenhower announced that the Allied advance would halt on the Elbe. Also, as the advance through Germany uncovered Belsen, Buchenwald, and other camps, the British and American attitudes to the Germans hardened.

By 7 May the 21st Army Group had cleared Holland and north Germany up to the Elbe and the Danish border; the 12th Army Group had cleared central Germany south of the Ruhr; and the 6th Army Group had driven through Bavaria and penetrated Austria. Small German pockets were left in the Ruhr itself, the Hartz Mountains, and on the north coast.

On 4 May General Montgomery accepted unconditional surrender of Admiral Dönitz's plenipotentiaries at Lüneberg Heath. On 7 May 1945 the war in Europe formally came to an end. There now remained the problems of what to do with Germany and what to do with the many thousands of Nazis, great and small. It was decided to divide Germany, and Berlin which fell deep within the Soviet area, into four zones each under one of the four major allies (**Maps 1 and 2**).

Below: US troops march through a devastated German town

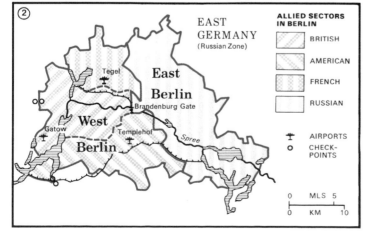

DENMARK

BALTIC SEA

NORTH SEA

FLENSBURG

RÜGEN

KIEL
Kiel Canal

ROSTOCK

7 May
LÜBECK
WISMAR
SCHWERIN

STETTIN

WILHELMSHAVEN
EMDEN
BREMERHAVEN

HAMBURG
3 May

NEUSTRELITZ
STARGARD

GRONINGEN
OLDENBURG

18 Apr
BREMEN
26 Apr

Lüneberg

DANNENBERG
DÖMITZ
WITTENBERG

Oder
KÜSTRIN

AMSTERDAM

Army Group 'H'
(Blaskowitz)

OSNABRÜCK

Teptoburger Wald
MINDEN

Weser

4 Apr

Belsen □
Heath
ÜLZEN

TANGERMÜNDE

BERLIN

POTSDAM
FRANKFURT

NETHERLANDS
Twenty-fifth Army

ARNHEM

MÜNSTER
First Para Army

HAMELN
HANNOVER
10 Apr

US Ninth Army

BRUNSWICK

MAGDEBURG

Twelfth Army

ROSSLAU
COTTBUS

Cdn First Army
(Crerar)

WESEL

HAMM
LIPPSTADT
PADERBORN

Leine

Eleventh Army
Harz Mts
BLANKENBURG
Brocken Pk

BARBY
DESSAU
24 Apr

Br Second Army
(Dempsey)
US Ninth Army
(Simpson)

ESSEN
DORTMUND
BOCHUM
WUPPERTAL

Ruhr
Sauerland

GÖTTINGEN

US First Army

HALLE
Saale

LEIPZIG

Neisse

21 Army Group
(Montgomery)

DUISBURG
DÜSSELDORF

Fifteenth Army

KASSEL

4 Apr

NORDHAUSEN

MERSEBURG
WEISSENFELS

GÖRLITZ

COLOGNE

Fifth Pz Army

Army Group 'B'
(Model)

MARBURG

GOTHA
ERFURT
OHRDRUF

WEIMAR
JENA

ZEITZ

COLDITZ

DRESDEN

LIÈGE

BONN

Sieg
REMAGEN
Rhine

GIESSEN
Dill

FULDA 2 Apr
BAD ORB

Buchenwald □

Mulde

CHEMNITZ

USTÍ

BELGIUM

KOBLENZ
Lahn

US First Army
(Hodges)

Seventh Army

Thüringian Forest

US Third Army

Seventh Army

Erzgebirge

KARLOVY VARY

12 Army Group
(Bradley)

WIESBADEN

FRANKFURT
Main
HANAU

HAMMELBURG
SCHWEINFURT

HOF

PRAGUE

LUX
UXEMBOURG

Moselle
TRIER

MAINZ
OPPENHEIM

US Third Army
(Patton)
ASCHAFFEN-
BURG

Spessart Mts

WÜRZBURG

BAMBERG

BAYREUTH

CZECHOSLOVAKIA

PLSEN

THIONVILLE

WORMS

Odenwald

KITZINGEN 5 Apr

4 Apr

NÜREMBERG
20 Apr

Bohemian Forest

US Seventh Army
(Patch)

MANNHEIM

Army Group 'G'
(Hausser)

FÜRTH

ANSBACH

18 Apr

7 May

CESKE
BUDEJOVICE

SAARBRÜCKEN

First Army
HEILBRONN

Neckar

REGENSBURG 26 Apr

Vltava

6 Army Group
(Devers)

KARLSRUHE
4 Apr
PFORZHEIM

Löwenstein Hills

US Seventh
Army

Franconian Jura

NANCY

Fr First Army
(de Lattre de Tassigny)

8 Apr
STUTTGART

INGOLSTADT

Danube

LANDAU
PASSAU

ESSLINGEN
KIRCHHEIM

DONAUWÖRTH

Isar
LANDSHUT
30 Apr

LINZ
5 May

STRASBOURG

TÜBINGEN

DILLINGEN

First Army

Inn

BRAUNAU

FRANCE

Nineteenth
Army

Swabian Highlands

ULM 23 Apr

AUGSBURG

Dachau □

LANDSBERG

US Third Army

COLMAR

Schwarzwald

SIGMARINGEN

EHINGEN

MUNICH

ROSENHEIM

SALZBURG
4 May

BERCHTESGADEN
4 May

FREIBURG

Fr First Army
Lake Constance

MEMMINGEN

US Seventh Army

Enns

BASLE

OBERAMMERGAU
FÜSSEN

GARMISCH-
PARTENKIRCHEN

KUFSTEIN

KITZBÜHEL

SWITZERLAND

Oberjoch Pass
BREGENZ
Fern Pass

INNSBRUCK

A U S T R I A

TAMSWEG

Aarlberg Pass

T y r o l

LANDECK

A

Brenner Pass

4 May

KLAGENFURT

Resia Pass

BOLZANO

US Fifth Army

ITALY

YUGOSLAVIA

▨	OCCUPIED BY ALLIED FORCES, 28 MARCH 1945
⇢	BRITISH ATTACKS
→	US ATTACKS
→	FRENCH ATTACKS
▨	GERMAN POCKETS
▨	OCCUPIED BY RUSSIAN FORCES, 16 APRIL
□	CONCENTRATION CAMPS

0   MILES   120

0   KILOMETRES   200

THE NAVAL WAR

On land or in the air the Germans were formidable opponents. This was abundantly clear after the Polish campaign of 1939. Only at sea did the French and British allies enjoy the advantage. In the First World War unrestricted submarine warfare had wrought terrible havoc amongst the Allied merchant shipping in the Atlantic. In the Second the Germans lost no time in embarking upon a similar policy, indeed every U-boat fit for sea had been sent out before war was declared. But though they did a good deal of damage, and by March 1940 had sunk 222 ships totalling 764,766 tons, the Germans did not in fact have very many submarines when the war began, and during the first few months they lost eighteen, about one-third of their total. During that time only eleven new ones were commissioned. Later in the war Hitler gave a higher priority to their construction, and at one time or another they had 1,162 U-boats in service. Of these 785 were destroyed, 500 of them by British ships or aircraft.

The Germans were perhaps fortunate in that their High Seas Fleet had been scuttled in Scapa Flow at the end of the First World War. In consequence all their ships were of modern design, whereas the British, with their magnificent personnel, were handicapped by a lot of old iron. Of Britain's fifteen capital ships thirteen had been built before 1918. The ten *Queen Elizabeth* and R class battleships had all been designed before 1914. Not only were many of the British warships obsolescent they were by no means as numerous as could have been desired. The Norwegian campaign of 1940 highlighted this weakness, the legacy of a series of parsimonious governments. There was soon a serious shortage of destroyers.

A very serious weakness in the Royal Navy was the lack of aircraft-carriers and of modern aircraft. Off Norway, Crete, and Malaya the Royal Navy was to pay heavily for its neglect of the air

arm. Naval officers were slow to realize that war is waged in three dimensions.

During the campaign in Norway the German surface fleet suffered very serious losses, so much so that it may be doubted whether Operation Sealion, the invasion of Britain was ever really a practical possibility. But with the fall of France the powerful and efficient French navy was lost to the Allies, and the entry of Italy into the war added to the Admiralty's problems. It was fortunate indeed that there were admirals of the calibre of Sir Andrew Cunningham, Sir Bertram Ramsey, and Sir James Somerville to weather the storms of those fateful days.

The British had expected the war to develop on much the same lines as that of 1914–18. An expeditionary force would be built up in France and the tasks of the Royal Navy, besides destroying the German fleet if it would come out and fight, would be to escort convoys of soldiers crossing the channel or supplies crossing the Atlantic. With the fall of France all this was changed. The Blue Water school had to face the fact that raids, landings and invasions were now inevitable. The idea was not popular in the Royal Navy. All the same British history was studded with combined operations – Gibraltar, Quebec, Aboukir Bay, the Dardanelles to name but a few. Amphibious warfare calls for special equipment and special techniques. At the outbreak of war the Royal Navy did have two landing craft, each capable of lifting a platoon. These were both lost in Norway, and it was not until late in 1940 that assault landing craft, carried by converted cross-channel steamers, came into service in any numbers.

Amphibious warfare makes special demands on planners and staff officers alike, for it has its own peculiar problems: where and when to land; naval gunfire support; the organization of ship to shore movement and so on. Techniques which had been mastered in the 18th century had been forgotten by the time of Gallipoli. The lessons of

Suvla, Zeebrugge, and Ostend were by no means fresh in the memories of the senior officers of 1940. The achievement of Combined Operations Headquarters was not only in the sphere of planning but of training. To those who appreciate the complete neglect of preparation for amphibious warfare it is remarkable indeed that the defeats of 1940 should have been followed so soon by the landings in North Africa, Sicily, Italy, and Normandy.

As the war developed and one operation followed another the eyes of the public were constantly being focused on new problems, new crises. Dunkirk, the Battle of Britain, the various raids and landings: so far as the Admiralty was concerned there was always one deadly battle going on whose loss must mean defeat: the Battle of the Atlantic. In this long drawn out struggle each side in turn strove to work out new tactics. In 1939 Grand-Admiral Dönitz had published a book in which he forecast the tactics of the 'wolf-pack': German submarines would operate by night on the surface, in much the same fashion as torpedo-boats. The Admiralty does not appear to have given this book the attention it deserved. At first the British, instead of using the maximum number of vessels as escorts, spent a great deal of energy in hunting for U-boats in the open ocean. Few of the escorts had radar, and few had the speed to catch a submarine on the surface. Asdic which had now been introduced was designed to detect submerged submarines.

By mid 1941 escorts were becoming stronger and this compelled the U-boats

Above left: The British destroyer H M S *Eskimo* during a raid on the Norwegian coast

Above right: A U-boat in stormy seas

Opposite left: H M S *Furious* at speed in the Mediterranean

Opposite right: Sailors examine the hulk of the *Tirpitz* after she had been sunk by British bombers

to attack in force. In June 1941 ten U-boats attacked south of Iceland. The Admiralty riposted by sending the escorts of two others to the relief of convoy HX 133. A protracted battle followed in which the Germans lost two submarines and the Allies five merchantmen. This action led to the evolution of 'support groups' a distinct tactical advance.

The invasion of Russia by drawing off German bombers to the eastern front led to a drop in the sinkings for July and August. American co-operation – even before Pearl Harbor – the build-up of Coastal Command, and the departure of U-boats to the Mediterranean, all conspired to reduce losses during the last quarter of 1941.

Another significant tactical advance was the introduction in December of the escort carrier, helping to close the 'air gap' in the Central Atlantic, which was out of range of land-based air cover.

The invasion of Russia had brought some easing of the pressure in the Battle of the Atlantic. The entry of Japan into the war was a grave setback. The Americans were now compelled to send numbers of their best warships to the Pacific. During the first four months of 1942 American losses on the east coast of the USA were very heavy, and included many tankers, in the period before they adopted the convoy system. 1942 was the worst year of the battle. U-boats accounted for 1,160 of the 1,664 Allied ships sunk – a total of 7,790,697 tons. But by the autumn the Allies navies had once more gained the upper hand, driving the U-boats southward to the Caribbean and the Gulf of Mexico and extending the 'Interlocking Convoy System'. British and Canadian escorts, now numbering some 450, were still too few for their tasks at a time when Dönitz had some 400 U-boats at his command. Despite the demands of Bomber Command, Coastal Command was gradually being given the long-range aircraft it needed to make its rôle decisive.

The climax of the Battle of the

Atlantic came in May 1943 when sinkings fell to fifty and cost the Germans, in all theatres, forty-one U-boats. Dönitz was compelled to withdraw his submarines from the North Atlantic. But the Germans were still producing forty U-boats a month including new types with a higher underwater speed. The introduction of the 'schnorkel' breathing-tube allowed them to recharge their batteries whilst submerged, thus helping to prevent their detection by radar.

June 1943 was a bad month for the Germans who lost seventeen U-boats without a single attack being made upon a North Atlantic convoy. Dönitz continued to probe far afield, and by using U-tankers or 'milch-cows' to support his submarines managed to cause casualties in the Indian Ocean and off the Brazilian coast.

Heavy German casualties between June and August, seventy-four U-boats sunk, were largely inflicted by Allied aircraft. In return the Germans managed to sink fifty-eight ships. Only in the Indian Ocean were they still scoring without unacceptable losses to themselves. There the demands of the Sicily and Italy landings had deprived the Eastern Fleet of sufficient escorts. In the autumn Dönitz tried to regain control in the North Atlantic, but despite some German success the Allies now had his measure.

Captain E. J. Walker (2 Escort Group) had devised tactics which are described by Captain S. W. Roskill, the Official Historian of the Royal Navy: 'His method was to station a "directing ship" astern of the enemy to hold Asdic contact, while two others, not using their asdics crept up on either side, to release a barrage of depth charges by signal from the directing ship at the critical moment. The U-boat thus never knew when the depth charges were released, and could not take avoiding action while they were descending.'

In October 1943 the Allies made an agreement with Portugal by which they

were enabled to set up naval and air bases in the Azores. At a time when long-range aircraft were proving their value as escorts this helped to tighten their grip on the battle. Already losses had fallen to a most gratifying extent. In September and October of 2,468 merchant ships crossing the Atlantic only nine were lost. In early 1944 matters improved still further: between January and March 3,360 ships crossed for the loss of three, whilst their escorts disposed of twenty-nine submarines.

Later in the year a kind of stalemate developed, for whilst the U-boats were not scoring heavily, and no longer operated on the surface in 'wolf-packs', their numbers were still rising, and continued to do so until in March 1945 they had 463. The Allied escorts found it extremely difficult to find the schnorkelling submarines. One (U-1199) remained submerged for fifty days!

By the end of the war Bomber Command had dropped such numbers of mines in the Western Baltic that the Germans were doing their training in Oslo Fjörd. When at last the Germans surrendered they still had 377 submarines: 221 were scuttled by their crews. In all the German U-boats had sunk 2,828 Allied or neutral ships of 14,687,231 tons. The British merchant navy, which in 1939 had comprised 9,488 vessels, totalling 21,215,261 tons, sustained losses amounting to 11,500,000 tons. During the war the Royal Navy lost 51,578 men, and the merchant navy 30,248. Of these the great majority lost their lives through U-boat action. The Germans for their part lost practically all their merchant navy to the Royal Navy and the RAF. Nor did many of their surface ships survive. The cruisers *Prinz Eugen* and *Nürnberg* were still fit for sea. *Hipper* and *Seydlitz* were scuttled. Bombing had accounted for *Emden, Köln, Lützow* and *Scheer*. The damaged *Leipzig* fell into the hands of the Royal Navy whilst the Russians captured the wrecked *Gneisenau* at Stettin, and the incomplete *Graf Zeppelin* at Gdynia.

THE BATTLE OF THE RIVER PLATE

Admiral Erich Raeder, commander-in-chief of the German navy, had decided to send the first of his commerce raiders, the pocket battleships *Deutschland* and *Admiral Graf Spee*, together with their supply ships *Westerwald* and *Altmark*, to their operational areas before the beginning of hostilities. *Graf Spee* sailed from Wilhelmshaven on 21 August 1939 and reached her waiting area in mid-Atlantic undetected, there to await the order to commence her mission. Though this was ostensibly commerce raiding, it was in fact more than this. Commerce raiding was only the secondary mission, the first being to post a threat to Allied sea communications, and thus dislocate Allied naval efforts against Germany by causing hunting groups to be set up at all points where the two raiders might strike. In this respect the Germans were remarkably successful.

Deutschland's commerce raiding activities were neither successful nor extended – she returned to port on 15 November 1939 having sunk only two ships of 7,000 tons – but *Graf Spee* had greater success (**Map 1**). Operating south of the equator, she was sent into action on 23 September, and opened her account by sinking the *Clement* off Pernambuco. The Allies were confused as to how many German raiders there were and set up five hunting groups in the South Atlantic on 5 October, the day that *Graf Spee* captured the *Newton Beech* north of Saint Helena. *Ashlea* and *Huntsman* followed in quick succession on 7 and 10 October, and then the *Trevanion* on 22 October. After this *Graf Spee* headed round the Cape of Good Hope to the Indian Ocean, where she sank the *Africa Shell* and stopped the *Mapia* on 15 and 16 November respectively, before heading back into the Atlantic once again. Here she sank the *Doric Star* on 2 December and the *Tairoa* on 3 December, before heading to the rich hunting grounds off the River Plate. *En route* she met and sank the

Streonshalh on 7 December. It was *Graf Spee*'s last success, bringing her tally to nine ships of 50,000 tons.

Commanding Force G, based on Port Stanley in the Falkland Islands, was Commodore H. Harwood with the heavy cruisers *Cumberland* and *Exeter* and the light cruisers *Ajax* and *Achilles*. At the time of the Battle of the River Plate, *Cumberland* was detached from the rest of the force, however. For some time Harwood had thought that Langsdorff, captain of the *Graf Spee*, would be attracted to the Plate, and so concentrated his three cruisers 150 miles off the mouth of the great river.

On 13 December Harwood's assessment was proved right for the pocket battleship was sighted. Though outgunned, Harwood had decided to attack immediately (**Map 2**). *Ajax* and *Achilles* were to go in from the west, and *Exeter* from the south, thus forcing Langsdorff either to concentrate his fire on one ship or group – leaving the other free to close right in – or divide the fire of his main battery, giving both the British subdivisions a better chance of closing and inflicting mortal damage. Langsdorff first chose the second, but soon directed the fire of his main battery on to *Exeter* alone. The German fire was formidably accurate, and the British cruiser was soon no

more than a battered wreck. *Exeter* was ordered to break off and make for the Falklands.

Graf Spee could now turn her attentions to the light cruisers, which continued the action alone, harrying the pocket battleship as she made for Montevideo. Langsdorff had decided to seek a temporary respite in this neutral port to have his casualties tended for and to make repairs before breaking out to Germany. *Graf Spee* reached Montevideo at midnight on 13/14 December, and there followed a spate of legal wrangles between the two belligerent powers and Uruguay about the terms of *Graf Spee*'s stay in port. British ruses finally persuaded Langsdorff that a far superior British force was now waiting for him outside territorial waters, and he decided not to throw away the lives of his crew in a futile battle. In fact only the two light cruisers were patrolling to seaward. Be that as it may, Langsdorff took *Graf Spee* out into Montevideo Roads on 17 December and there scuttled her. The crew were interned, and three days later Langsdorff shot himself.

Above: The German pocket battleship, *Admiral Graf Spee*

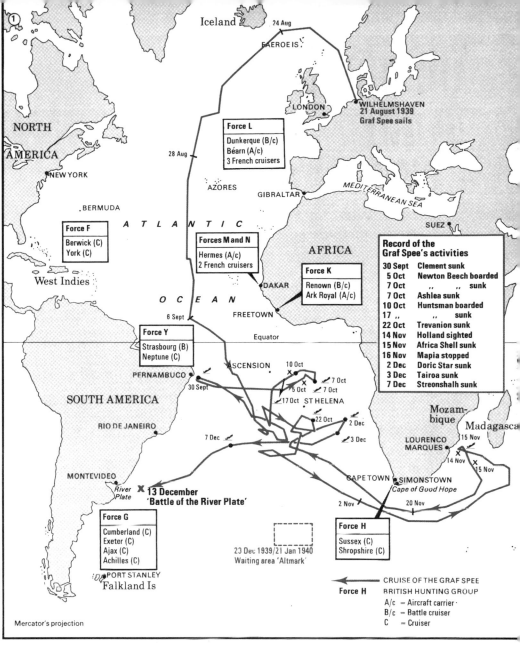

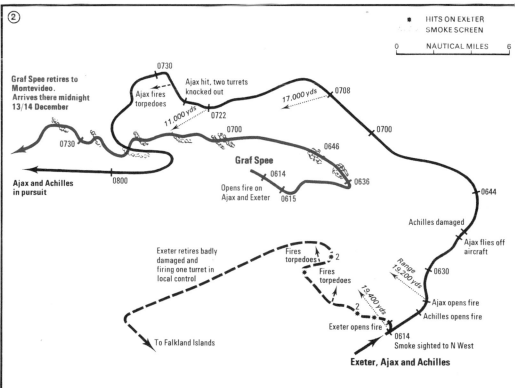

THE RAIDERS

Early in the war with the voyages of the *Graf Spee* and the *Deutschland*, the German navy found out how much the conventional naval dispositions of their enemies were dislocated by the threat of surface raiders. This left considerable scope, if the dislocation could be increased by the use of disguised merchant raiders, for Germany's small but efficient regular forces to chip away at the Allies' naval superiority. Beside contributing towards this end, the merchant raiders would be able to take a worthwhile toll of Allied merchant shipping.

Work was put in hand soon after the beginning of the war to convert several merchantmen to the new role. Clearly armament was of prime importance, and all the raiders were fitted with between six and eight 5·9-inch guns, giving a firepower equal to most Allied light cruisers. Other armament consisted of cannon, torpedoes, mines, and spotter aircraft. Range was also of vital significance, and all the raiders were capable of staying at sea for about a year, receiving fresh supplies of food, ammunition, and fuel from supply ships that waited for them in designated areas. Finally, to avoid arousing suspicion, all the raiders were made to look inconspicuous as possible, and were fitted with equipment to enable their crews to alter salient features of their vessels so that the raiders might assume different identities at will.

Seven merchant raiders were sent on cruises varying in duration from four to eighteen months (**Map 1**):

Atlantis (known to the Germans as 'Ship 16' and the British as 'Raider C') sailed on 31 March 1940 and before being sunk by the British cruiser *Devonshire* on 22 November 1941, captured or sank twenty-two ships of 145,697 tons.

Orion (Ship 36, Raider A) sailed on 6 April 1940 and sank nine ships of 57,744 tons before returning to base on 21 August 1941.

Widder (Ship 21, Raider D) sailed on 6 May 1940 and sank or captured ten vessels of 58,645 tons before returning home on 31 October 1940.

Thor (Ship 10, Raider E) sailed on 6 June 1940 and before arriving home led an eventful career, which included engagements with the British armed merchant cruisers *Alcantara* and *Carnarvon Castle*, the sinking of a third, *Voltaire*, and the dispatch of eleven ships of 83,000 tons.

Pinguin (Ship 33, Raider F) sailed on 22 June 1940 and before being sunk by the British cruiser *Cornwall* on 8 May 1941 disposed of twenty-eight ships (including eleven whalers) of 136,551 tons.

Komet (Ship 45, Raider B) sailed from Germany on 9 July 1940 and sailed round the north of Russia to the Pacific with the aid of Russian icebreakers. Before returning to base she sank six ships of 42,959 tons.

Kormoran (Ship 41, Raider G) sailed on 3 December 1940 and sank or captured eleven ships of 68,274 tons before being sunk by the Australian cruiser *Sydney* on 19 November 1941.

All in all the German disguised merchant raiders proved remarkably efficient and economical weapons, dislocating Allied shipping seriously and inflicting considerable casualties.

German warships sent on raider missions were not as successful,

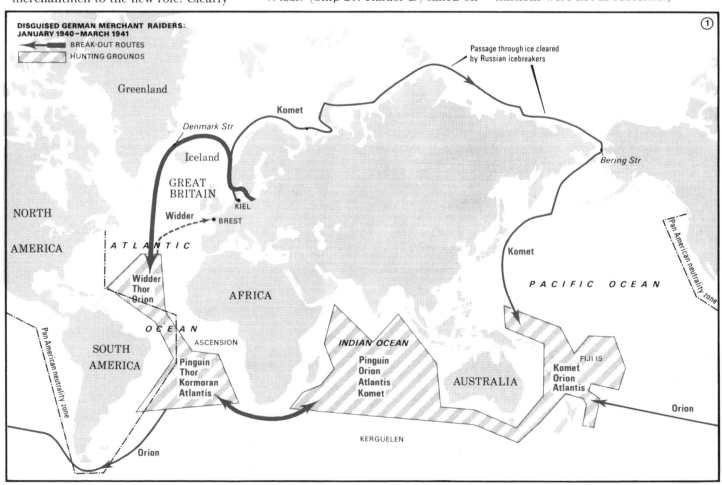

DISGUISED GERMAN MERCHANT RAIDERS: JANUARY 1940–MARCH 1941

BREAK-OUT ROUTES
HUNTING GROUNDS

Passage through ice cleared by Russian icebreakers

Greenland

Komet

Denmark Str

Iceland

GREAT BRITAIN

KIEL

Widder

BREST

NORTH AMERICA

ATLANTIC

Widder
Thor
Orion

OCEAN

AFRICA

ASCENSION

SOUTH AMERICA

Pinguin
Thor
Kormoran
Atlantis

Pan American neutrality zone

Orion

KERGUELEN

INDIAN OCEAN

Pinguin
Orion
Atlantis
Komet

AUSTRALIA

Bering Str

Pan American neutrality zone

PACIFIC OCEAN

Komet

Komet
Orion
Atlantis

FIJI IS

Orion

however. Their range was limited, and they therefore had to act in the main shipping lanes, where the chances of meeting serious opposition in the form of Allied major units was much greater. As a further complication, Hitler ordered that they were to take no risks at all in the event of meeting such Allied opposition.

One really successful cruise was by the pocket battleship *Admiral Scheer* (**Map 2**). She sailed on 23 October 1940 and sank sixteen ships of 99,059 tons before returning home on 1 April 1941. She also sank the British armed merchant cruiser *Jervis Bay* on 5 November 1940.

The two battle-cruisers *Scharnhorst* and *Gneisenau* sailed from Germany on a raiding cruise on 21 January 1941, and in the course of the next two months, before returning to Brest on 22 March 1941, they cost the Allies twenty-two ships of 115,622 tons.

Other German surface raiders were the cruiser *Admiral Hipper*, which made two forays (30 November 1940 to 27 December 1940 and 1 February 1941 to 13 February 1941), in which she sank nine ships of 40,078 tons, and finally the battleship *Bismarck* and cruiser *Prinz Eugen* whose voyage is described later.

Below: The end of an Allied merchantman caught by a raider

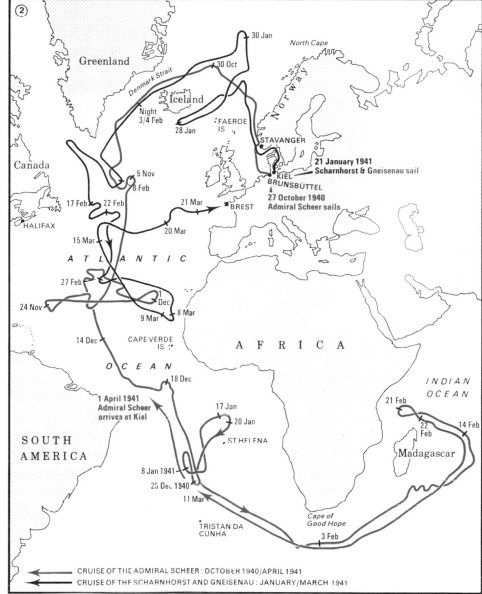

② CRUISE OF THE ADMIRAL SCHEER : OCTOBER 1940/APRIL 1941
CRUISE OF THE SCHARNHORST AND GNEISENAU : JANUARY/MARCH 1941

21 January 1941
Scharnhorst & Gneisenau sail

27 October 1940
Admiral Scheer sails

1 April 1941
Admiral Scheer arrives at Kiel

THE NAVAL WAR IN THE MEDI-TERRANEAN

The naval situation in the Mediterranean was a difficult one for the Royal Navy: the Italian navy was modern in equipment and enjoyed a position from which it could bring superior forces to bear on either of the two major British forces in the Mediterranean, Force H at Gibraltar and the Mediterranean Fleet at Alexandria, a split which was inevitable but nonetheless very dangerous for the Royal Navy. In the centre, where it would have to take the full brunt of the Italian naval and air attack, was Malta, on which it was thought advisable to base only light and submarine naval forces. Commanding the Mediterranean Fleet, Admiral Sir Andrew Cunningham used his limited forces with great verve and aggression, constantly seeking for ways in which to whittle down the Italians' great superiority.

On 9 July 1940, while cruising off the coast of Calabria, Cunningham's three battleships, one aircraft-carrier,

five light cruisers, and several destroyers encountered an Italian force of two battleships, six heavy, and twelve light cruisers, and their destroyer escort. In the following action, one Italian battleship and a cruiser were severely damaged, with little or no loss to Cunningham's forces.

On 19 July the Australian light cruiser *Sydney* and four destroyers met two Italian light cruisers off Crete, and sank one of them.

The scales were not significantly altered, for all this, but Cunningham finally found a way of attacking the Italian fleet in harbour, with little danger to his own command. It was planned to launch twenty-one Fairey Swordfish torpedo-bombers to deliver a night attack on the Italian fleet in Taranto on the night of 11 November (**Map 1**). The strike was extremely successful, sinking the new battleship *Littorio* and two older but modernized battleships, very severely damaging two cruisers and two fleet auxiliaries. All

but two of the Swordfish returned to the carrier *Illustrious*. Cunningham's position was now far happier.

Above: Italian battleships firing on the British fleet

Below: A British cruiser lays a smoke screen during an engagement with the Italian fleet

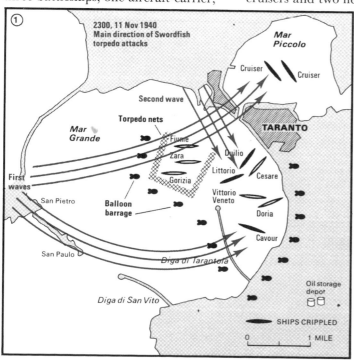

Map 1 — 2300, 11 Nov 1940. Main direction of Swordfish torpedo attacks. Labels: Mar Piccolo, Cruiser, Cruiser, Second wave, Torpedo nets, Mar Grande, Fiume, TARANTO, Zara, Duilio, Gorizia, Littorio, Cesare, First waves, San Pietro, Balloon barrage, Vittorio Veneto, Doria, Cavour, San Paulo, Diga di Tarantola, Oil storage depot, Diga di San Vito, SHIPS CRIPPLED, 0 — 1 MILE

A further heavy blow was inflicted on the Italian navy at the Battle of Cape Matapan on 28 March 1941 (**Map 2**). It was clear that an Axis invasion of the Balkans was imminent, and to bolster the Greeks, it was decided to ship in a contingent of British troops. These movements could not be concealed from the Axis, and the Germans urged the Italians to strike at the convoys carrying the troops with all the power they could muster. Cunningham realized that an Italian threat might emerge, and planned accordingly. Vice-Admiral H.D. Pridham-Wippell and his four cruisers were ordered to patrol to the south of Gávdhos, while the destroyer force in Piraeus was ordered to be ready to move south if needed. Naval and airforce strike aircraft were readied, and submarines were ordered to watch for an Italian force heading eastward.

On the evening of the 27th, RAF reports indicated a force of three Italian cruisers heading east, and Cunningham decided to put to sea from Alexandria with three battleships, one aircraft-carrier, and their destroyer escorts, at the same time summoning Pridham-Wippell to a rendezvous south of Crete. Air searches the next morning proved somewhat confusing, and it was uncertain how many battleships the Italians were using. In fact the force heading east was the battleship *Vittorio Veneto*, while the battleships reported south of Crete, heading south west, were a group of three heavy and two light cruisers. Air strikes on *Vittorio Veneto* were launched, but only one torpedo hit was scored, at 1510. All the Italian forces were now heading for home at top speed. But at 1930 a torpedo hit on *Pola* stopped the Italian cruiser, and the heavy cruisers *Zara* and *Fiume* were sent back to help. Admiral Angelo Iachino, commanding the Italian force, thought that the British were still far to the east, whereas in fact they were not far behind, now

closing on the three Italian heavy cruisers very swiftly. The battleship *Valiant* spotted the two returning Italian cruisers on radar, and Cunningham's battleships blasted them from the water at a range of 3,000 yards. The *Pola* was found and sunk later.

By now it was too late to catch *Vittorio Veneto*, and though a search was made for her, Cunningham soon realized the futility of this and ordered his scattered forces to rendezvous south-west of Cape Matapan before withdrawing.

Above: Italian cruisers under fire during the action off Cape Matapan

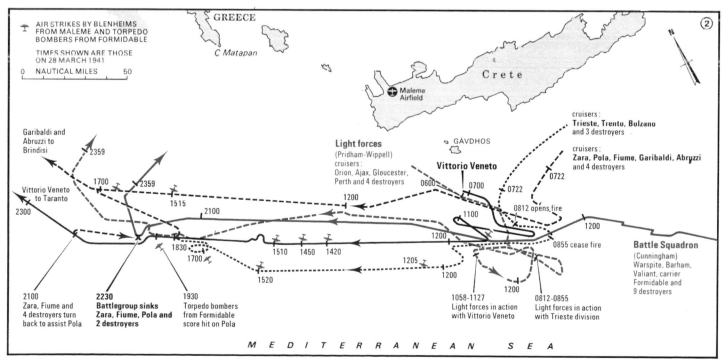

AIR STRIKES BY BLENHEIMS FROM MALEME AND TORPEDO BOMBERS FROM FORMIDABLE

TIMES SHOWN ARE THOSE ON 28 MARCH 1941

0   NAUTICAL MILES   50

GREECE

C Matapan

Crete

Maleme Airfield

GÁVDHOS

Light forces
(Pridham-Wippell)
cruisers:
Orion, Ajax, Gloucester,
Perth and 4 destroyers

Vittorio Veneto

cruisers:
Trieste, Trento, Bolzano
and 3 destroyers

cruisers:
Zara, Pola, Fiume, Garibaldi, Abruzzi
and 4 destroyers

Garibaldi and
Abruzzi to
Brindisi

2359

1700

2359

Vittorio Veneto
to Taranto

2300

1515

2100

1200

0600

0700

0722

0722

1100

0812 opens fire

1200

1830

1200

1200

0855 cease fire

1510 1450 1420

1205

1700

1520

1200

1200

Battle Squadron
(Cunningham)
Warspite, Barham,
Valiant, carrier
Formidable and
9 destroyers

2100
Zara, Fiume and
4 destroyers turn
back to assist Pola

2230
Battlegroup sinks
Zara, Fiume, Pola and
2 destroyers

1930
Torpedo bombers
from Formidable
score hit on Pola

1058-1127
Light forces in action
with Vittorio Veneto

0812-0855
Light forces in action
with Trieste division

M E D I T E R R A N E A N   S E A

HUNTING THE BISMARCK

In the spring of 1941, two of Germany's newest surface units finished their trials and were judged ready for action. These were the superb battleship *Bismarck*, armed with 15-inch guns and protected by massive armour plate and first class internal compartmentalization, and the heavy cruiser *Prinz Eugen*, sister ship of the *Admiral Hipper*. Admiral Raeder decided that they could cut their operational teeth on a raiding sortie into the Atlantic.

On 18 May the two warships sailed from Gdynia for Bergen, where on the 21st they were spotted by RAF reconnaissance aircraft. Clearly the only reason for their presence in Norwegian waters could be a foray into the Atlantic, and all elements of the Royal Navy in the Atlantic and around Britain were warned to hold themselves ready for the inevitable battle.

On the same day that they were discovered, the two raiders, under the command of Vice-Admiral Günther Lütjens, put to sea in foggy weather and headed north to enter the Atlantic via the Denmark Strait. Although the British soon found out that the two German ships had sailed, it was not until late on 23 May that the cruisers *Suffolk* and *Norfolk*, patrolling in the Denmark Strait, spotted them and radioed a report. Vice-Admiral L. Holland, commanding the Battle-Cruiser Squadron (*Hood* and the new battleship *Prince of Wales*, which had not even been completed), altered course to intercept the German raiders.

The two forces met early the next morning, but as *Hood* closed on *Bismarck*, a shell from the latter plunged through the weak deck armour of the British battle-cruiser into one of the aft magazines. *Hood* blew up, and only three of her 1,500 man crew survived. *Bismarck* then turned her attention to *Prince of Wales*, scoring several hits on her and forcing her to break off the action, though not before one of the British ship's 14-inch shells had hit *Bismarck*, causing a tell-tale streak of fuel to leak from a ruptured tank.

Prince of Wales and the two cruisers continued to shadow the German squadron until the Home Fleet could close on it, but as *Bismarck* turned to head for Brest, *Prince Eugen* broke away south and finally returned safely to Brest on 1 June. Though contact with *Bismarck* was lost, a Catalina of the RAF spotted her in the morning of the 26th.

Force H, which was moving up north-east from Gibraltar, contained the carrier *Ark Royal*, and a torpedo strike by her Swordfish further damaged *Bismarck*, jamming her rudder and thereby sealing her fate. The next morning, the battleships *Rodney* and *King George V* arrived on the scene and started pouring heavy calibre shells on to the hapless *Bismarck*. The German battleship was soon a blazing wreck, but it was not until the cruiser *Dorsetshire* closed in and torpedoed her that she sank, taking with her all but 110 of her 2,300 man crew.

Opposite above: The *Bismarck* sets out from Bergen on her last voyage

Opposite below: *Bismarck* in action against HMS *Hood*. A photograph taken from the *Prinz Eugen*

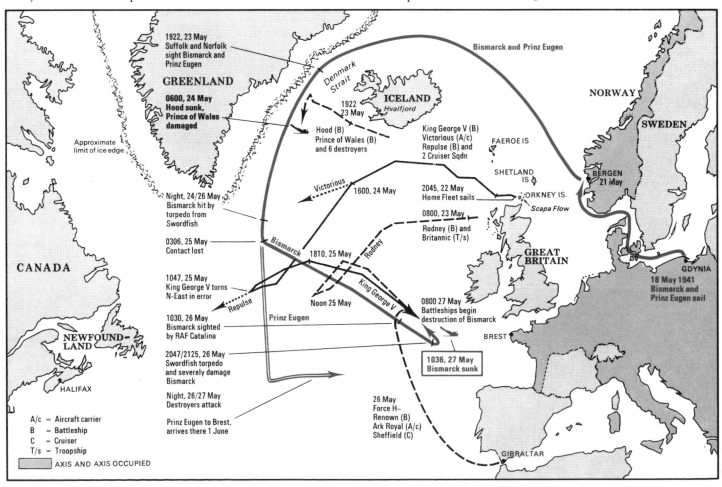

THE CHANNEL DASH

German naval sorties into the Atlantic in 1941 had left three vital ships all but stranded in Brest: the battle-cruisers *Scharnhorst* and *Gneisenau* and the heavy cruiser *Prinz Eugen*. Hitler, obsessed by the idea that Norway was the 'zone of destiny' and that its invasion by the British was imminent, demanded against Raeder's better judgement that the squadron in Brest be brought home to Germany, and recommended that a quick dash up the Channel was the best way to achieve this. Since surprise was all important, the squadron would leave Brest at night, even though this meant that it would pass through the Straits of Dover in daylight.

German preparations, organized by Vice-Admiral Ciliax, were excellent: passages were swept through minefields and then marked so that the squadron could travel at top speed, and a permanent aerial umbrella was arranged with General Adolf Galland of the Luftwaffe. The British were aware that preparations for some venture were under way as the clearing of channels in the minefields had been observed, and therefore the ineptitude of their reaction when the day came is all the more to be condemned. Three air patrols by Coastal Command Hudsons fitted with air-to-surface radar were instituted to cover the night hours.

The German squadron's departure was delayed for more than three hours on 11 February, and it was not until 2245 hours that they sailed. The Hudson patrolling off Brest spotted nothing on its radar. In the second Hudson, north of Ushant, there was a radar failure. The German squadron did not get within range of the third Hudson's radar. And so, despite considerable German aerial activity being spotted by British surface radar, it was not until three Spitfires returned from patrol and their pilots were debriefed at 1130 hours on 12 February that any definite Intelligence of the

breakout was received. Time was now of the essence, and it was decided to send all available aircraft into the attack as soon as they were ready. The Royal Navy 825 Squadron attacked at 1245 and all its aircraft were lost (its commander, Lieutenant-Commander E. Esmonde, was awarded a posthumous VC). Motor torpedo boat attacks also proved futile, as did all subsequent aircraft and destroyer attacks.

Although *Scharnhorst* hit a mine at 1431, she was soon making 25 knots again. The same happened to *Gneisenau* at 1955, but she too was only slightly damaged. However, when *Scharnhorst* hit a second mine at 2134 the damage was serious and she had to be left behind by the other two ships. However, she was able to limp on, and all three German ships reached port on the morning of 13 February.

Below: The German squadron in line ahead during the Channel Dash

Opposite: The German ships as they passed through the Straits of Dover

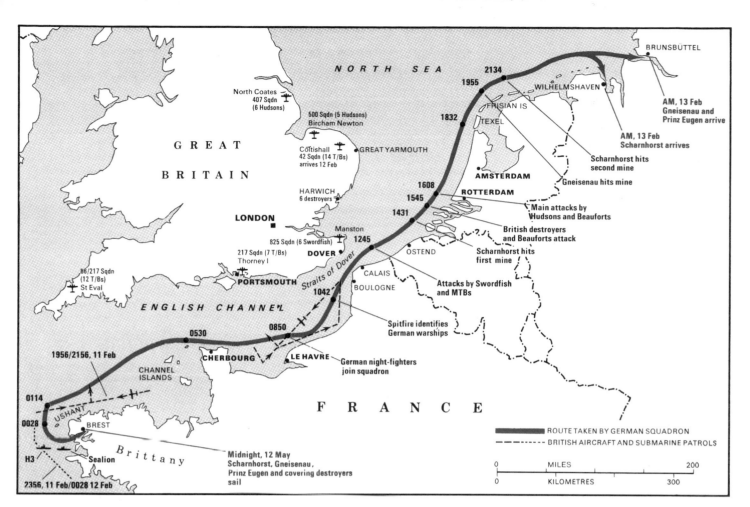

THE MALTA CONVOYS

Malta's position in the middle of 1942 was desperate – astride the Axis supply lines to North Africa, she was under continual air attack by the German and Italian airforces and supply convoys were suffering such heavy losses that they had had to be suspended. Although the success of missions ferrying aircraft in to the island's defences meant that Malta could continue her unequal struggle with the bombers of the Luftwaffe and Regia Aeronautica, it was abundantly clear that food and fuel for military and civilians alike had to be got in or the island would fall. It was decided that another attempt to pass a convoy through to Malta from the west should be made early in August. The importance of what was at stake can be gauged by the naval forces massed to protect this one convoy of fourteen merchantmen: two battleships, three aircraft-carriers, seven cruisers, thirty-two destroyers, and eight submarines, not counting lesser craft. At the same time, the aircraft-carrier *Furious* was to ferry more fighters in for the RAF squadrons on the island. The convoy left the Clyde on 3 August, escorted by Vice-Admiral E.N.Syfret's warships. Operation Pedestal was under way.

The convoy passed through the Strait of Gibraltar in fog early on the morning of the 10th. The same day a dummy convoy left Port Said, apparently for Malta, as a diversion, and then turned back the next day. As the Mediterranean fleet's other contribution to the operation, a cruiser force bombarded Rhodes on the 13th. But by the afternoon of the 10th the Axis had got wind of the main operation, and from the next morning onwards the convoy was constantly shadowed by reconnaissance aircraft.

During the afternoon of the 11th, *Furious* flew off her aircraft to Malta and turned back that same evening. But the Axis also made its first move, when a U-boat sank the aircraft-carrier *Eagle* at 1323. During the evening, a

first air attack was made, but no hits were scored on the convoy.

In the second Axis raid on the convoy on the 12th, the freighter *Deucalion* was damaged and had to leave the convoy, being sunk later that evening. In the afternoon the convoy passed through the main concentration of Axis submarines, one of which, the Italian *Cobalto*, was rammed and sunk by the destroyer *Ithuriel*. No Allied ships were lost. But in the evening the destroyer *Foresight* was badly damaged and had to be sunk, and the carrier *Indomitable* suffered three heavy bomb hits, which put her flight deck out of operation. Soon after this Syfret, as planned, turned back with the main covering forces, leaving Rear-Admiral H.M.Burrough to escort the convoy the rest of the way with his four cruisers. Two of these were hit by torpedoes at about 2000. *Nigeria* turned back to Gibraltar, but *Cairo* had to be sunk. The American tanker *Ohio* was hit at the same time but stayed with the convoy. Just at dusk, the convoy once again came under bombing attack, which cost it the merchantmen *Empire Hope* and *Clan Ferguson* sunk, while the *Brisbane Star* was hit but managed to reach Malta. The next casualty was the cruiser *Kenya*, torpedoed by the Italian submarine *Alagi*, but she managed to stay with the convoy.

At 0120 on the morning of the 13th the cruiser *Manchester* was hit by a torpedo, and was later scuttled. At the same time five merchantmen (*Santa Eliza*, *Wairangi*, *Almeria*, *Lykes*, and *Glenorchy*) were lost, the result of the convoy having become stretched out by the attacks of the previous afternoon and evening. Soon after dawn the air attacks were renewed, resulting in the loss of the *Wairanama* and further damage to the *Ohio*, which was disabled in a later attack, during the course of which the *Rochester Castle* and *Dorset* were also hit. Soon afterwards, light forces from Malta met the main body of the convoy, which now consisted

only of *Port Chalmers*, *Melbourne Star*, and *Rochester Castle*. Behind them *Dorset*, *Ohio*, and *Brisbane Star* struggled to make port, though the first two were again damaged by bombs, *Dorset* sinking. The gallant *Ohio* and her precious fuel cargo were finally towed into Valletta on the 15th. Her master was awarded the George Cross.

And so ended Operation Pedestal. Five of the fourteen merchantmen got through and enabled Malta to hold on and even strike back, but nine others had been sunk, together with one aircraft-carrier, two cruisers, and a destroyer, with a further carrier and two cruisers severely damaged.

Above: British aircraft-carriers forming part of the escort of a Malta convoy

Opposite: The destroyer HMS *Malcolm* passes through a convoy

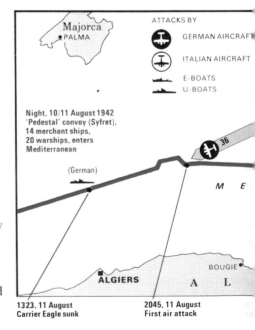

Majorca
• PALMA

ATTACKS BY

GERMAN AIRCRAFT

ITALIAN AIRCRAFT

E-BOATS

U-BOATS

Night, 10/11 August 1942
'Pedestal' convoy (Syfret),
14 merchant ships,
20 warships, enters
Mediterranean

(German)

M E

36

BOUGIE

ALGIERS

A L

1323, 11 August
Carrier Eagle sunk

2045, 11 August
First air attack

0   NAUTICAL MILES   120

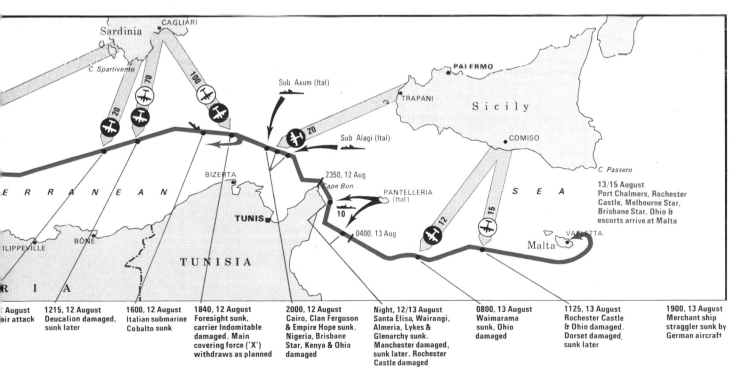

THE ARCTIC CONVOYS

In conditions far different to the Mediterranean convoys, the Arctic convoys also provided tales of great heroism under savage attack and appalling weather as Allied seamen struggled to push supplies through to Russia. The convoys were begun in August 1941 shortly after Germany invaded Russia and continued until September 1943 (**Map 1**). During the summer, when the edge of the pack ice retreats northward, convoys could stand off further from the German-occupied coastline of Norway and that of her ally Finland, with all their air bases, but then the length of the day made them relatively

easy prey for the U-boats. During the winter the ice edge moved south again, driving the convoys in closer to the air bases, but shorter days meant that the threat of U-boats was lessened. Allied air bases, being on the outside of the great curve described by Scandinavia, could not cover the convoys the whole way, there being a considerable gap between Jan Mayen Island to north of Murmansk.

In these waters, however, there occurred one of the war's most tragic episodes, the loss of Convoy PQ–17, which sailed for Russia on 27 June 1942 with thirty-six merchant ships. Because of the threat posed by German heavy units based in northern Norway, the convoy was given a heavy escort. Close cover was provided by four cruisers and three destroyers, as far as Bear Island. Distant cover was provided by two battleships, one carrier, two cruisers, and fourteen destroyers. Close escort was provided by three minesweepers and four trawlers, which sailed with the convoy. The long-range escort, of six destroyers, four corvettes, and two submarines, joined the convoy on 30 June.

The next day the convoy was spotted by U-boats and aircraft, but U-boat attacks were all driven off. The next afternoon PQ–17 passed the homeward

bound QP–13. An air attack was beaten off that evening, by which time the close cover was 40 miles to the north of the convoy. Then in fog the convoy lost its shadowing aircraft as it turned east to pass just north of Bear Island. Meanwhile, back in Britain, air reconnaissance had revealed that the German heavy surface ships had left their southern bases.

Early on the 4th a German aircraft spotted the convoy through the fog and torpedoed a merchantman. An air attack at 0830 cost the convoy two ships, but a third managed to keep up, though damaged. Meanwhile, *Tirpitz*, *Scheer*, and *Hipper* had reached Altenfjord, but Hitler's standing orders forbade their dispatch towards the convoy. The First Sea Lord, Sir Dudley Pound, who was controlling the operation from London, thought it inevitable that the German surface vessels would move out to intercept the convoy, and as the distant cover had been withdrawn according to plan, the convoy and the close cover would be destroyed. He thus ordered the distant cover to return. However, as they were still some 800 miles from Archangel, their destination, Pound thought that the individual ships of the convoy might be able to evade the German raiders if they scattered, and he

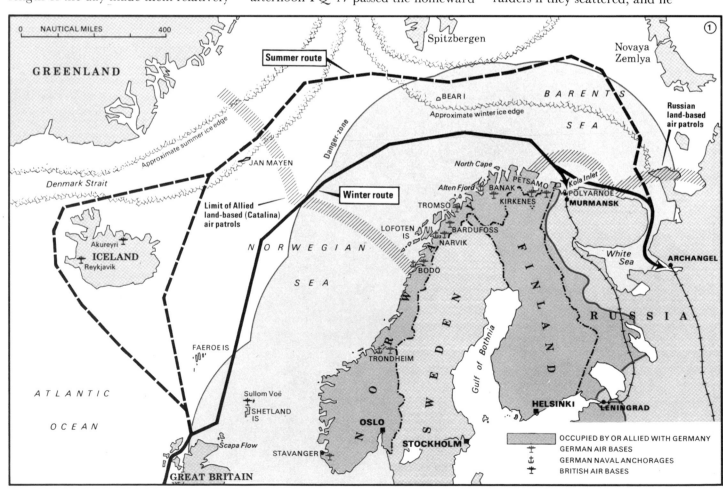

ordered them to do this at 0936 hours on 4 July. The long-range escort, except for the submarines, left the convoy to rendezvous with the close cover. The commander of the long-range escort, Commander J.E.Broome, wished to rejoin the convoy, but the commander of the close escort, Rear-Admiral L.H.K.Hamilton, under the impression that he was moving back to join up with the Home Fleet, as a result of poorly worded messages from the Admiralty, would not let him do so. The convoy was now scattered and defenceless.

The reason for the 'scatter' order, the presence and imminent threat of three major German ships, in fact materialized on the morning of the 5th: the three ships sailed from Altenfjord, but on receipt of the news that U-boats and aircraft were dealing satisfactorily with the scattered remnants of the convoy they turned back.

The four days from 5 to 8 July were terrible ones for the convoy, with most of its ships sunk. One of many notable feats was that of the armed trawler *Ayrshire*. She led three merchantmen up into the ice, where they painted their upper works white and waited for the crisis to pass before making for Archangel. Only eleven of the original

thirty-six merchantmen made Russia. Among the cargo lost were 3,350 vehicles, 430 tanks, 210 aircraft, and 99,316 tons of other cargo.

Right: A near miss on an Allied destroyer

Below: A convoy enters Archangel harbour

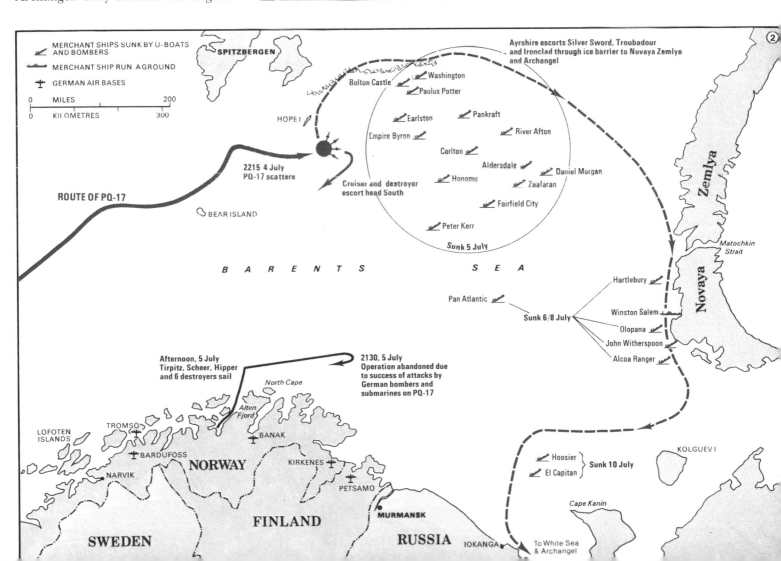

BATTLES OF THE BARENTS SEA

After the disaster of PQ–17 and the savaging that the next Arctic convoy, PQ–18, received, there was an interval before Russian convoys were resumed, with a different code (JW) and different tactics, whereby instead of one large convoy there would be two smaller ones (A and B), much easier to handle and defend. The new system got off to a flying start when the first such convoy, JW–51A, got through without loss. As soon as it arrived off Murmansk, its escort of the two cruisers *Sheffield* and *Jamaica*, under Rear-Admiral R.L. Burnett, turned back to meet the second instalment of the convoy, JW–51B, which was at present escorted by six destroyers under Captain R. Sherbrooke.

A U-boat, however, spotted JW–51B and radioed a sighting report. Raeder saw this as a golden opportunity to test *Lützow*, with a view to sending her on a raid into the Atlantic if she was successful. The German plan was simple and could have been effective

but for the crippling tactical restrictions imposed on all surface ship actions by Hitler. The force was to consist of the heavy cruiser *Hipper*, the pocket battleship *Lützow*, and six destroyers, commanded by Vice-Admiral Oscar Kummetz. *Hipper* would take on the escort, while *Lützow*, commanded by Captain Stänge, destroyed the convoy. Though Kummetz was ignorant of the presence in the area of Burnett's cruisers and a covering force of one battleship, one cruiser, and three destroyers commanded by Vice-Admiral Sir Bruce Fraser, the plan started auspiciously enough. The German squadron sailed 30 December 1942 and approached the convoy the following morning. Seeing the convoy to the south of himself, Kummetz turned towards it, but was spotted by the destroyer escort, one of which started to lay a smoke screen between the Germans and the convoy while the others made dummy attacks on *Hipper*. The latter turned away but then decided to try another attack. Sherbrooke had meanwhile sent two of his destroyers back towards the convoy to deal with the German destroyers, which were closing in, and thus found himself in dire straits as *Hipper* returned to the fray, severely damaging *Onslow*. Kummetz once again withdrew. Burnett, meanwhile, had seen the gun flashes to the south and was closing as fast as he could. But the other half of the German pincer, *Lützow*, now appeared from the south, with no British destroyers between herself and the convoy. However, she too turned away, uncertain whether she was about to meet friend or foe.

Above: The *Scharnhorst* in Norwegian waters

Opposite right: HMS *Sheffield* seen from *Duke of York* during the hunt for the *Scharnhorst*

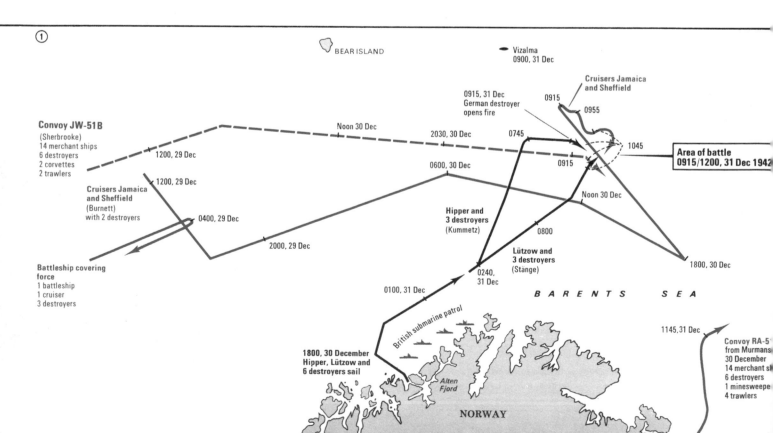

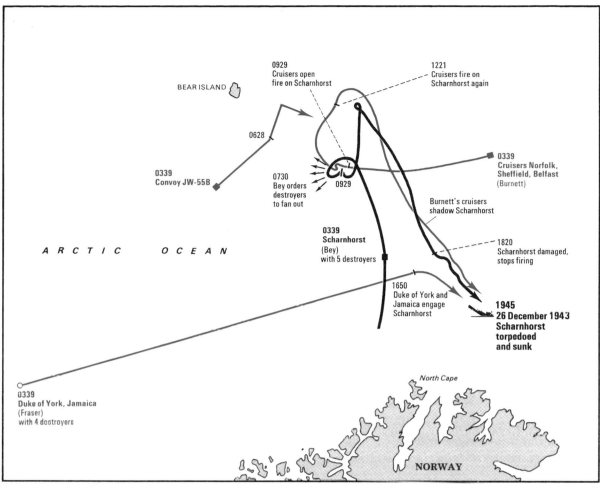

0929
Cruisers open
fire on Scharnhorst

1221
Cruisers fire on
Scharnhorst again

BEAR ISLAND

0628

0339
Convoy JW-55B

0730
Bey orders
destroyers
to fan out

0929

0339
Cruisers Norfolk,
Sheffield, Belfast
(Burnett)

Burnett's cruisers
shadow Scharnhorst

1820
Scharnhorst damaged,
stops firing

A R C T I C   O C E A N

0339
Scharnhorst
(Bey)
with 5 destroyers

1650
Duke of York and
Jamaica engage
Scharnhorst

1945
26 December 1943
Scharnhorst
torpedoed
and sunk

North Cape

0339
Duke of York, Jamaica
(Fraser)
with 4 destroyers

NORWAY

Hipper now returned, sinking the destroyer *Achates* before flinching away from the threat of torpedo attack, only to find herself caught between Burnett's cruisers and the destroyers. Three hits were soon scored on *Hipper* before two German destroyers were met. One of these was sunk. To the south again, Stänge at last opened fire on the convoy, but was then foiled by a smoke screen laid by the destroyers. Kummetz then broke off the action and ordered his ships to retire to the south.

The Germans had had all the advantages: superior firepower, surprise, and all the tactical advantages. But yet they had thrown them all away by poor co-ordination and lack of initiative, especially by the destroyer captains. Hitler, quite rightly, was incensed and ordered the major units of the surface fleet to be scrapped. Raeder managed to dissuade him, but felt obliged to resign. He was succeeded as commander-in-chief of the German navy by Admiral Karl Dönitz.

Almost exactly a year later, the German navy suffered another major reverse in the north. The battle-cruiser *Scharnhorst* sailed from Altenfjord on 25 December 1943 to intercept Convoy JW–55B, which was escorted by fourteen destroyers, and covered by

Admiral Burnett's cruisers *Belfast*, *Sheffield*, and *Norfolk*, which had the double task of protecting the westbound RA–55A and the eastbound JW–55B. Distant cover was provided by Sir Bruce Fraser with the battleship *Duke of York*, the cruiser *Jamaica*, and four destroyers. Rear-Admiral Erich Bey took *Scharnhorst* and her five escorting destroyers due north. At about 0730 on the 26th Bey ordered his destroyers to fan out and search to the south-west, and then lost touch with them. *Scharnhorst* was on her own from now on.

At 0840 *Belfast* picked up *Scharnhorst* on her radar and then illuminated her with starshell at 0924. Burnett's squadron opened fire at 0929, but *Scharnhorst* hauled round to the south and withdrew from the cruisers before trying to work her way round to the north-east. This move was spotted by *Belfast*'s radar, but the German ship was considerably faster in the prevailing seas, and Burnett decided to keep himself between the convoy and where he expected the German ship to reappear.

Burnett's move was proved right shortly after noon when *Belfast* once again picked up *Scharnhorst* by radar. A short action ensued in which both sides received damage. *Scharnhorst* then broke away to the south – exactly

where Fraser's force was waiting for her. *Duke of York*'s radar picked up the German ship at 1617. *Belfast* illuminated her with starshell at 1650 and *Duke of York* and *Jamaica* immediately opened fire. Try as she might, *Scharnhorst* could not escape the sandwich she was in between Fraser and Burnett. *Duke of York*'s 14-inch shells, plunging down steeply at long range, tore through the German ship's deck armour. She was soon reduced to a wreck and sank at 1945. The surface threat to the Arctic convoys was over.

THE EARLY COMMANDO RAIDS

With the realization in the middle of 1940 that the fall of France almost certainly precluded the use of major military forces on the European continent for some time to come, it was decided to raise a force of men who, with special training and equipment, would make small forays against German-controlled installations on the continent. These would have the dual purposes of keeping up British morale by showing that some military effort was being made, and of keeping German forces that might have been used profitably elsewhere tied up guarding installations that might be raided (**Map 1**).

The first target for the Commandos, as they became known was the fish oil factories of the Lofoten Islands (**Map 2**). Some 500 commandos from Nos 3 and 4 Commandos sailed from Scapa Flow in two converted cross-Channel steamers under the command of Brigadier J.C. Haydon on 1 March 1941, escorted by five destroyers under Captain C. Caslon. On 4 March the attack went in, meeting no opposition until it had landed. All the fish oil installations were destroyed, 200 German prisoners were taken, 300 Norwegian volunteers were picked up, and the navy sank the fish factory ship *Hamburg* and numerous small cargo ships.

The next raid was carried out by a predominantly Canadian force. This was the destruction of the coal installations on Spitzbergen (**Map 1**). The force, under the command of Rear-Admiral P. Vian sailed for the island on 19 August. All went smoothly. Stocks of coal were burnt, the installations destroyed, three colliers captured and sent to Britain, and the Norwegian inhabitants of the island evacuated. Vian sailed for home on 3 September, *en route* encountering the German training ship *Bremse*, which he sank.

The next raid was planned as a bigger affair. The major landings were to be made on Vaagsö Island, with subsidiary landings on Maaloy Island (**Map 3**). The main force sailed from Scapa Flow on 21 December 1941 under Rear-Admiral L.H.K. Hamilton, escorted by a cruiser and eight destroyers. One of the two troop transports broke down, so the main operation was confined to small landings and the capture of two

small coasters. All the forces were back in Scapa by 1 January 1942. The secondary landings had greater success, however. Coastal batteries were silenced by bombing and gunfire, and the landing parties destroyed all the German installations on the island, while the navy disposed of some 16,000 tons of shipping. All the Vaagsö forces returned to Scapa by 28 December.

On 27 February 1942, an important raid was made on a German radar station at Bruneval on the northern coast of France (**Map 4**). Parachutists were dropped just inland from the site, captured the station, took parts for examination by British scientists, destroyed the rest of the station, and were then evacuated by the Navy. British casualties were three killed and seven wounded.

An altogether more ambitious Commando operation was launched in May 1942. Japanese operations in the Indian Ocean had led to fears that

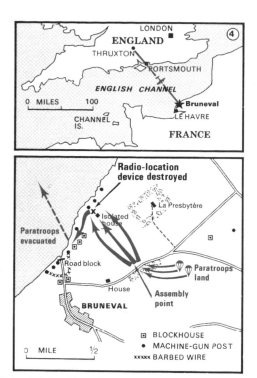

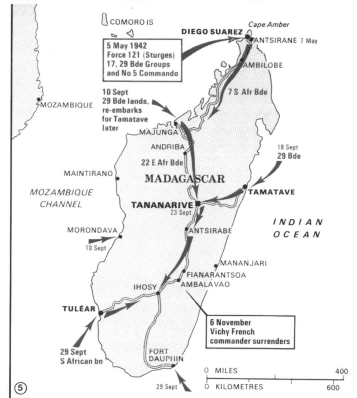

Madagascar, part of the Vichy French
Empire, might be captured and used as
a base for attacks on Allied sea routes
from Suez to the Far East and
Australia. Between 5 and 7 May a
force under the command of Rear-
Admiral E.N.Syfret attacked and took
the port of Diego Suarez in the extreme
north of the island (**Map 5**). But on the
29th a Japanese aircraft was spotted
over the harbour and the next day the
battleship *Ramillies* was damaged in
Diego Suarez by a midget submarine,
this leading to the notion that the
Japanese had a secret base on the
island. In fact both craft had been
launched from a submarine. It was,
however, decided to overrun the rest
of the island.

This proved a difficult undertaking.
The conquest did not get under way
until September, and it was not until
6 November that the Vichy French
governor capitulated to the troops
under Lieutenant-General Sir William
Platt. The island was handed over to the
Free French early the following
January.

Above: British commandos attacking under
cover of a smoke screen during the
Vaagsö operation

Right: Commandos withdrawing from Maaloy

271

THE RAID ON ST NAZAIRE

The threat that the new German battleship *Tirpitz* might, like her sister ship *Bismarck*, break out into the Atlantic was a constant worry for the Admiralty at the beginning of 1942. But there was only one place in which so large a vessel could be dry-docked in France, and if this dock should be destroyed, the Admiralty thought that there was a good chance that *Tirpitz* might not attempt the breakout. The dock in question was the Normandie dock in St Nazaire, and a bold scheme to destroy it was set in motion.

The plan was for an old destroyer, one of the fifty 'four-stackers' provided by the Americans, to be lightened so that she could steam straight up the Loire regardless of sand banks and ram the outer lock gate. Later, explosive charges in her bows would go off, destroying the outer gate entirely. The escort force of one motor gun boat as headquarters ship, sixteen motor launches, and one motor torpedo boat. Troops were to be landed from the expendable destroyer, *Campbeltown*, and from the motor launches to carry out other demolition work before being evacuated.

The force left Falmouth on 26 March 1942. By 0130 on the 28th the force had got within two miles of its objective without being spotted, but then it was illuminated by German searchlights. The defence was confused by fake identification signals, and several minutes passed before the Germans opened fire. At 0134 *Campbeltown* rammed the lock gate and stuck fast, while the commandos she was carrying stormed ashore. The smaller craft had a more difficult time of it, however. The Germans were now fully alert, and of the landings planned (the right hand column at the Old Entrance and the left on the Old Mole), only three craft succeeded, including MGB 314, the headquarters craft. The evacuation was a confused affair, and many commandos were left behind.

Campbeltown blew up just before mid-day as a large party of German officers was inspecting her, and completely destroyed the lock gate. The primary task of the operation had been achieved. Fourteen small craft were lost, and total losses were 144 dead and missing. Five Victoria Crosses were awarded.

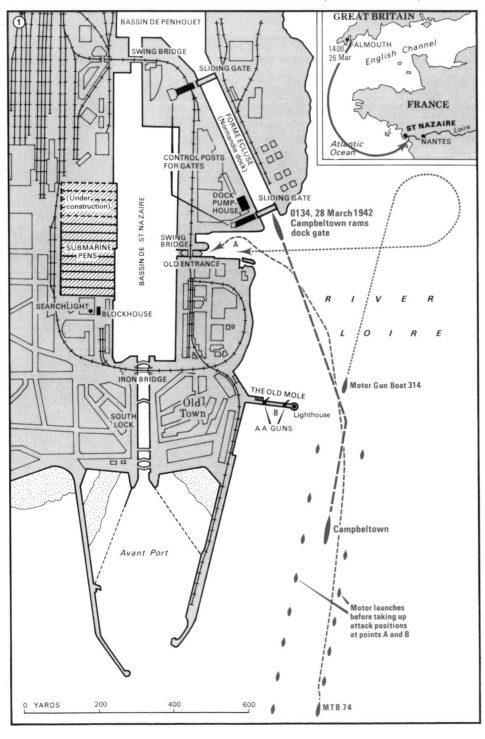

① BASSIN DE PENHOUET
SWING BRIDGE
SLIDING GATE
FORME ECLUSE (Normandie dock)
CONTROL POSTS FOR GATES
(Under construction)
DOCK PUMP-HOUSE
SLIDING GATE
BASSIN DE ST NAZAIRE
0134, 28 March 1942 Campbeltown rams dock gate
SWING BRIDGE
OLD ENTRANCE
SUBMARINE PENS
SEARCHLIGHT
BLOCKHOUSE
IRON BRIDGE
THE OLD MOLE
Old Town
SOUTH LOCK
A A GUNS
Lighthouse
Avant Port
RIVER LOIRE
Motor Gun Boat 314
Campbeltown
Motor launches before taking up attack positions at points A and B
MTB 74

GREAT BRITAIN
1400 26 Mar FALMOUTH
English Channel
FRANCE
ST NAZAIRE
Loire
Atlantic Ocean
NANTES

0 YARDS 200 400 600

THE DIEPPE OPERATION

The large-scale landing at Dieppe on 19 August 1942 was an altogether different matter. It was felt that with large numbers of troops ready for action in the British Isles, a reconnaissance in force might be made on to the continent of Europe. The raid would provide battle experience for the troops and provide much useful information on German defensive methods. This latter would prove very useful in planning the D-Day landings.

The site selected was Dieppe, as it was typical of German defended localities the destruction of whose port and defence installations would be worthwhile, but was still within the range of fighters operating from England. The troops chosen for the raid were from 2 Canadian Division, commanded by Major-General J.H.Roberts, with commandos providing the two flank forces that were to land on either side of the town and silence the coastal batteries which would otherwise seriously jeopardize the whole operation. The total land forces amounted to slightly over 6,000 men, carried in nine landing ships escorted by eight destroyers.

The outer flank attacks were to silence the heavy batteries at Vasterival and Berneval, the inner ones those at Pourville and Puys, all at dawn. The main assault was to follow 30 minutes later. All German forces in the area were to be destroyed by the combined land forces before the town was evacuated.

Indications that the raid was going to fail started with the first landings: the eastern outer flank could not silence the guns that were its objective. The eastern inner flank assault was late, surprise was not obtained, and the force was pinned down as soon as it landed. Greater success was obtained on the other flank, however. There the commandos silenced their objective and then withdrew successfully. The inner flank made some progress inland but was then halted by German reinforcements. As the advance by the main assault from the town failed to materialize, the inner flank force had to pull back.

The main landings proved an almost total failure. The landing craft were met by a withering hail of fire, which pinned them down on the beach, and the tanks that did manage to scale the sea wall and reach the promenade were halted there by German obstacles. From that moment onwards the enterprise was doomed. The Canadians fought with enormous courage, but were in a hopeless position. The evacuation started at 1100 hours, and by 1300 what remained of the force started to sail back to England.

The raid had proved an appalling blunder, whose sole mitigating factor had been the lessons learnt. In particular that any attempt to capture a port by direct assault would certainly fail, and that any landings on the continent of Europe must be made over the open beaches. Canadian casualties were 3,363 out of 4,961, the commandos lost 247 out of 1,057. The Navy lost a destroyer and thirty-three landing craft, together with 550 men, and the RAF lost 106 aircraft and 190 men. German casualties were only about 600.

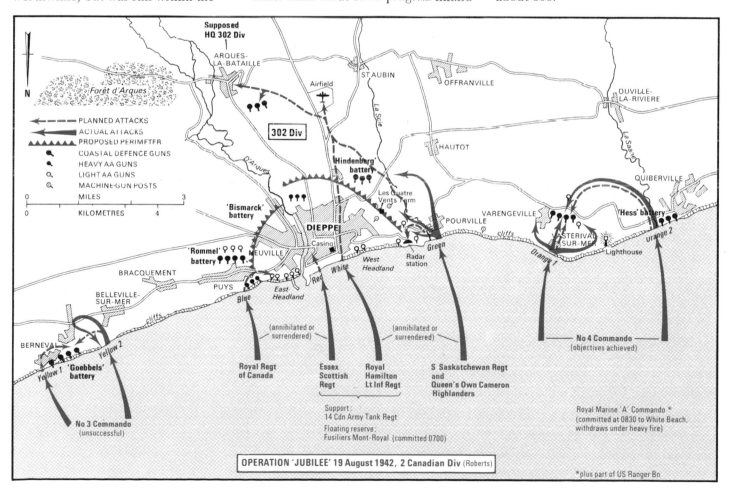

THE WAR IN THE AIR

If a single bomb drops on Berlin
you can call me Meyer!
Hermann Göring

On 11 June 1917 a formation of fourteen Gothas dropped 118 high explosive bombs on London, killed and wounded 588 people, scored a direct hit on Liverpool Street Station, and convinced General Smuts, the *eminence grise* of the British Government in two world wars, that the air arm 'can be used as an independent means of war operations'. This view was shared by the Italian Brigadier-General Giulio Douhet whose *The Command of the Air* (1921) had a wide influence among the airmen of all the great powers, as well as upon influential authors such as H. G. Wells. It was Douhet's thesis that once the airforce has won command in the skies control of land and sea must follow as the night the day. In Britain men like Trenchard and Harris subscribed whole-heartedly to this view. In Germany it had the support of Göring, and in America of Mitchell. Above all it was a view widely accepted by press and public in all the countries that were to be involved in the Second World War. The techniques that were to permit the North Vietnamese to survive the recent attentions of the US Air Force were as yet unimagined.

During the Second World War both sides made effective use of the air arm, yet on the whole desire seems to have outrun performance. The Germans were, at least at first, too much inclined to regard the Luftwaffe as a form of close support artillery. The Allies whose Bomber Command was a weapon of relatively slow growth, expected from it a weapon of precision which could destroy selected targets in the German economy. Instead of a rapier they found they had armed themselves with a bludgeon.

At the Washington Conference on the Limitation of Armaments (1922) it was agreed that 'Aerial bombardment for the purpose of terrorizing the civilian population, or destroying or damaging private property not of a military character, or of injuring non-combatants is prohibited' (Article 22, Part II). From the very first day of the Second World War this article was a dead letter for bombing, aimed at getting the enemy population on to the roads so as to obstruct troop movements, was a deliberate part of the German *Blitzkrieg*. The Luftwaffe and notably the Stuka dive-bomber played a vital part in the conquest of Poland, the Low Countries, and France. When the Battle of Britain began German air power was at its height: Field-Marshals Kesselring and Sperrle could dispose of 2,830 aircraft and neither they nor their followers foresaw much difficulty in their two-fold task of denying the English Channel to

Allied shipping and of destroying the Royal Air Force. The latter with fifty-five fighter squadrons, a strength of 600 or 700 planes seemed to everyone but themselves to be hopelessly outmatched. The disparity in numbers was offset to some extent by the development of radar, which helped the defenders to differentiate between genuine and feint attacks and to deploy accordingly.

Meeting a resistance at once more efficient, determined, and flexible than they had expected, the Germans allowed themselves to be deflected from the objectives they had set themselves, and embarked on the series of operations known to history as the London blitz. In its first three months they killed 12,696 Londoners, but on 12 October Hitler found himself compelled to cancel Operation Sealion, the plan to invade England.

Slowly the initiative began to pass to the Allies. As early as 1940 the British, who then had only a very small bomber force, made concentrated attacks on Mannheim, Bremen, Wilhelmshaven, Kiel, and other targets. In March 1941 they devoted much attention to the *Scharnhorst* and *Gneisenau* at Brest. It was a relief to the RAF when the two battle-cruisers escaped up the Channel, and they were able to turn their attentions to German targets once more.

When after two and a half years of war Sir Arthur Harris took over Bomber Command he found that his total force was only 378 serviceable aircraft. It would be another year before the Americans could develop their potential strength to the full. At this time the RAF was receiving about 200 new bombers each month, and could not, therefore, afford heavy casualties. Successful attacks on Lübeck and Rostock raised the morale of Bomber Command. By May 1942 when the first of the 'thousand bomber raids' was mounted, bomb damage in Germany already equalled that inflicted on England. It was now that the real Bomber Offensive began. It had the effect of compelling the Germans to redeploy much of the Luftwaffe to defend their industry. When the German army invaded Russia in 1941 50 per cent of their aircraft were there in support. By the end of 1943 only 20 per cent were available for army co-operation.

In August 1942 the British improved the accuracy of their concentrated bombing by the introduction of the Pathfinder Force. By December Harris had at his disposal an average front-line strength of about 340 aircraft, including some 260 heavy bombers. The Lancaster bomber,

with four engines and capable of taking the 22,000-lb. 'Grand Slam' bombs, was now in service.

The Casablanca Conference of January 1943 outlined the strategy for the Combined Bomber Offensive: 'The progressive destruction and dislocation of the German military, industrial, and economic system, and the undermining of the morale of the German people to a point where their capacity for armed resistance is fatally weakened.' What this meant is explained by 'Bomber' Harris himself who wrote: 'After the extent of devastation in a number of towns had been compared with the loss of output in these towns over a period of months, a definite correlation was found between acreage of concentrated devastation and loss of man hours; . . .'

On the night 5/6 March the Battle of the Ruhr began when 442 aircraft made a severe and successful attack on Essen. On the night 16/17 May No. 617 Squadron breached the Möhne and Eder Dams releasing some 330,000,000 tons of water and flooding parts of Kassel.

At the end of July 7,196 tons of bombs were dropped on Hamburg, causing 80,000 casualties, destroying 6,200 acres of the built-up area and knocking out the city economically. The great shipbuilding yards, which had produced so many U-boats were severely damaged. A million of the inhabitants fled, and in the words of Colonel Adolf Galland: 'A wave of terror radiated from the suffering city and spread throughout Germany.' Everywhere people were saying 'What happened to Hamburg yesterday can happen to us tomorrow'. The famous fighter ace adds that 'in the wide circle of the political and military command could be heard the words: "The war is lost." ' But though Speer, the minister for war production, thought that six more such attacks could bring Germany to her knees, it somehow did not come to pass: at least not yet.

Meanwhile at Peenemünde the Germans were working on the second of Hitler's famous secret weapons – the V-2 – an 80-ton rocket with with a warhead containing ten tons of explosives. Its development was seriously delayed by an attack by 600 aircraft (17/18 August) which killed many of the staff and caused heavy damage.

The American 8th Air Force now made its debut in Europe. It believed in daylight precision bombing by Boeing B-17 'Flying Fortresses', which might or might not have fighter escort. Casualties were heavy from the first but the raid on the great German ball-bearing factory at Schweinfurt (14 October) was a disaster. Once past Aachen the Fortresses were beyond the range of fighter cover, and though they did much damage, sixty were shot down and 138 damaged out of 291 aircraft taking part. The Americans now realized that they must have a long-range fighter and with truly amazing drive had the P.51 Mustang in service only two months later. The Mustang, turned down by the USAAF in 1940, was given a Rolls Royce engine and was superior to the German fighters not only in speed, manoeuvrability, and range, but in numbers. By the end of the war 14,000 had been produced.

The Battle of Berlin, sixteen attacks on the German capital, made up Bomber Command's offensive in the bitter winter of 1943–1944. Perhaps 14,000 people were killed and 3,000,000 made homeless: 5,000 acres of the city were devastated. Gradually the German night fighters got the upper hand and the battle cost the RAF 300 aircraft.

Strange though it seems the Luftwaffe was still growing in strength and from February to April 1944 the Allies gave first priority to bombing the German aircraft industry. By dispersing their plant the Germans managed to save about 80 per cent of their production.

From April to September 1944 support of Operation Overlord, the Second Front, had priority, and the consequent lull in strategic bombing gave German industry six months in which to make up for the heavy damage during the previous year.

In the summer of 1944 thirty-seven Allied divisions drove sixty German divisions out of France, destroying their Seventh Army, 500,000 strong. The disparity on the ground was offset by almost complete superiority at sea and in the air.

The pre-D-Day bombing of the French railway system, and the destruction of bridges over the Rivers Seine and Loire made the movement of German reinforcements to the bridgehead area both slow and hazardous. Command of the air made it possible to secure the flanks of the lodgement area by dropping three airborne divisions.

In June 1944 the Allies were able to turn their attention to a massive attack on German oil production. This was remarkably effective. The production of aviation gasoline was reduced from 170,000 tons a month in June 1944 to 52,000 tons in March 1945. Training became impossible and numbers of aircraft were actually grounded for lack of fuel. The army suffered as badly as the Luftwaffe.

The Bomber Offensive's last great spectacular raid was also its most

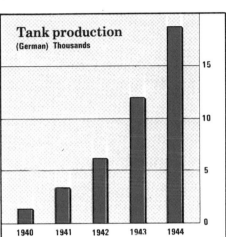

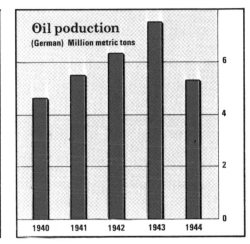

controversial: Operation Thunderclap. On the night of 13/14 April 1945 800 bombers attacked Dresden, by far the biggest German city which was still undamaged. Its pre-war population was 630,000 and there were some 200,000 refugees. The casualties were somewhere between 250,000 and 400,000. Dresden, besides its industrial importance, was the centre of communications for the southern sector of the Eastern Front. It is easy to condemn such destruction but it must be remembered that the unconditional surrender of Germany still lay some three months in the future.

The Bomber Offensive, whilst undoubtedly effective was extremely costly. Bomber Command is thought to have lost 7,122 aircraft, with 55,573 aircrew and 1,570 ground staff killed, 22,000 wounded and 11,000 captured. The USAAF lost 23,000 aircraft and suffered 120,000 battle casualties.

The USAAF also mounted another major air offensive, this time in the Pacific against Japan. The main problem here was the great distances from US held territory to the target area. On 18 April 1942 Major Doolittle had led a raid on Tokyo in which his bombers were launched from the aircraft carrier *Wasp* off the coast of Japan and then flew on to land in China. Although this

raid caused little material damage it had a profound effect on Japanese civilian morale. It was not until 1944 when the Mariana islands had been taken that the Americans had bases from which their Superfortress bombers could strike at Japan directly. The early high-level, unescorted attacks suffered terrible losses, but once tactics had been changed to lower-level attacks with incendiaries, and fighter escorts could be provided from Okinawa, the US 20th Air Force was able to devastate the industrial towns of Japan, and have a truly major effect upon Japan's ability to rearm and support her forces.

Above: Four diagrams showing the relative ineffectiveness of the Allied campaign. Only on oil did the bombing have a significant effect in decreasing German production

THE BOMBER OFFENSIVE ON GERMANY

The first major Allied air raid of the war took place in the spring of 1940, but it was not until late 1943 and the widespread entry into action of American 8th Air Force units that the grand strategic bombing offensive can really be considered to have got into its stride. It was only in the spring of 1944 that the increasing range of escort fighters allowed deep penetration raids over the whole of Germany.

At first results matched the weakness of the effort made by the Allies. But with increasing experience, the introduction of new aircraft and electronic aids, and the growth of the number of aircraft available, that the success rate improved. RAF Bomber Command, using the greater number of aircraft, concerned itself mostly with area bombing of Germany's urban areas by night; the US 8th Air Force, however, concentrated on precision bombing of specific military targets by day. Initial heavy losses slowed down the American effort, but the arrival of long-range fighter escorts (see map) enabled heavy raids to be conducted deep into Germany. The effect of most of the early raids is still a moot point, but with the major effort being made on transport systems and oil production towards the end of the war, the Allies at last found and destroyed targets that considerably shortened the war. The following are some of the raids that marked turning points in the bombing offensive.

The first truly strategic air raid took place on 15/16 May 1940, when ninety-nine RAF aircraft bombed the Ruhr, losing one of their number. Damage caused was very slight.

The night of 16/17 December 1940 witnessed the RAF's first night area raid, when 134 aircraft bombed Mannheim. Three aircraft were lost, and again damage was slight, as the bombing was extremely inaccurate.

Lübeck was visited on 28/29 March 1942 by 234 British bombers, of which twelve were lost. The raid was the first to see the widespread use of incendiary bombs, and though extensive material damage was caused, war production was back to normal after only one week.

The city of Cologne was the next target to witness a milestone in bombing history: on the last night of May 1942 it received the first '1,000-bomber raid'. The very bottom of Bomber Command's barrel was scraped to gather the necessary aircraft, and 1,046 were despatched. Of these, forty were lost and 116 damaged. Half the target area was destroyed, under 500 Germans were killed, but 40,000 were made homeless. Reconstruction work was remarkably swift.

The American 8th Air Force entered the lists on 17 August 1942, when twelve Flying Fortresses attacked the marshalling yards near Rouen. Damage was slight, but the Americans lost no aircraft and as a result committed themselves firmly to this pattern of day precision bombing.

The 8th Air Force despatched 291 bombers to attack the Schweinfurt ball-bearing factory on 14 October 1943. Damage to the factory held up production for a short time, but American losses were crippling: sixty destroyed and 138 damaged. This destroyed the theory that the bomber 'boxes' could fight their way through unescorted, and the American effort was held up until adequate escort fighters were available.

Berlin was raided by 444 RAF bombers on the night of 18/19 November, and serious damage was caused, with RAF losses only nine. This was the first of sixteen major raids on the German capital, which almost completely destroyed it.

With the arrival of escort fighters the 8th Air Force could resume its efforts, and on 8 March 1944 590 bombers attacked the Erkner ball-bearing factory in Berlin. Damage held up production considerably, and the Americans lost thirty-seven aircraft.

On 30/31 March 1944 Bomber Command attacked Nuremberg with 795 aircraft, and suffered the heaviest defeat in its history. Damage caused was not very extensive, but ninety-five bombers were lost and seventy-one damaged. After this, the British abandoned area raids on distant objectives.

Bomber Command did not restrict itself entirely to area bombing, as the raid on the Dortmund–Ems Canal on the night of 23/24 September 1944 proves. 141 aircraft took part, and 14 were lost, but eleven 12,000-lb. 'Tallboy' bombs were used, and a six-mile stretch of the canal emptied of water.

The most controversial raid of the European war took place on 13/14 February 1944, when 805 Bomber Command aircraft destroyed some 1,600 acres of Dresden, together with an unknown number of civilians (estimates vary between 35,000 to 135,000). British losses were eight aircraft. The city, which was of no conceivable military value, was attacked by 400 8th Air Force aircraft the next day.

KEY BOMBING TARGETS

Industrial

1 Le Mans (aircraft)
2 Paris
3 Rouen
4 Siracourt (V-bombs)
5 Lottinghem
6 Mimovecques (V-bombs)
7 Watten
8 Wizernes (V-bombs)
9 Lille
10 Brussels (aircraft)
11 Rotterdam
12 Amsterdam (aircraft)
13 Le Havre
14 Boulogne
15 Dunkirk
16 Metz
17 Emden (U-boats)
18 Wilhelmshaven (U-boats)
19 Vegesack (U-boats)
20 Bremen (aircraft)
21 Hamburg
22 Flensburg (U-boats)
23 Kiel (U-boats)
24 Lübeck
25 Hannover
26 Brunswick
27 Magdeburg
28 Oschersleben (aircraft)
29 Dessau (aircraft)
30 Essen
31 Dortmund

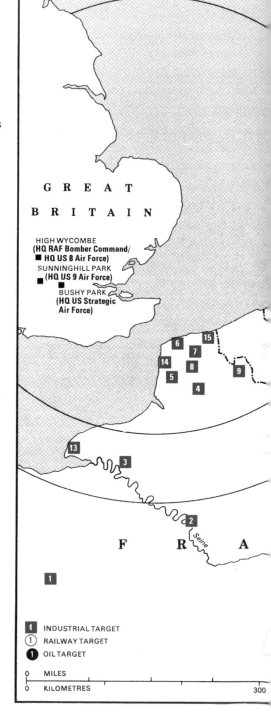

GREAT BRITAIN

HIGH WYCOMBE
(HQ RAF Bomber Command/
■ HQ US 8 Air Force)
SUNNINGHILL PARK
■ (HQ US 9 Air Force)
BUSHY PARK
■ (HQ US Strategic Air Force)

FRA

Seine

▣ INDUSTRIAL TARGET
◎ RAILWAY TARGET
● OIL TARGET

0 MILES
0 KILOMETRES

300

32 Duisburg
33 Düsseldorf
34 Cologne
35 Bonn
36 Möhne Dam
37 Wuppertal
38 Eder Dam
39 Sorpe Dam
40 Kassel (aircraft)
41 Leipzig
42 Dresden
43 Liegnitz
44 Berlin
45 Rostock
46 Peenemünde
   (V-bombs)
47 Stettin
48 Erfurt
49 Gotha (aircraft)

50 Schweinfurt
   (ball-bearings)
51 Fürth
52 Nuremberg
53 Regensburg
   (aircraft)
54 Augsburg (aircraft)
55 Munich
56 Ulm
57 Stuttgart
58 Ludwigshafen
59 Saarbrücken
60 Bochum
61 Karlsruhe
62 Friedrichshafen
63 Chemnitz
64 Prague
65 Wiener Neustadt
   (aircraft)

Railways
1 Frankfurt
2 Hanau
3 Aschaffenburg
4 Koblenz
5 Oberlahnstein
6 Giessen
7 Siegen
8 Schwerte
9 Soest
10 Hamm
11 Löhne
12 Osnabrück
13 Rheine
14 Bielefeld
15 Altenbecken
   Neuenbecken
16 Seelze
17 Lehrte
18 Hameln

19 Paderborn
20 Bebra
21 Stendal
22 Halle
23 Gera
24 Breslau
25 Minden
26 Mulhouse
27 Freiburg
28 Offenburg
29 Rastatt . .
30 Karlsruhe
31 Heilbronn
32 Treuchtlingen
33 Pasing
34 Munich
35 Rosenheim
36 Salzburg
37 Strasshof
38 Würzburg

39 Mannerheim
40 Darmstadt
41 Mainz
42 Bingen
43 Vienna
44 Munster

Oil
1 Wesseling
2 Reisholz
3 Dülmen
4 Gelsenkirchen
5 Salzbergen
6 Nienburg
7 Farge
8 Heide
9 Hitzacker
10 Dollbergen
11 Derben
12 Pölitz

13 Salzgitter
14 Lützkendorf
15 Leuna
16 Ruhland
17 Böhlen
18 Rositz
19 Mölbis
20 Zeitz
21 Brüx
22 Neuburg
23 Freiham
24 Linz
25 Moosbierbaum
26 Korneuburg
27 Floridsdorf
28 Schwechat
29 Lobau
30 Ploesti

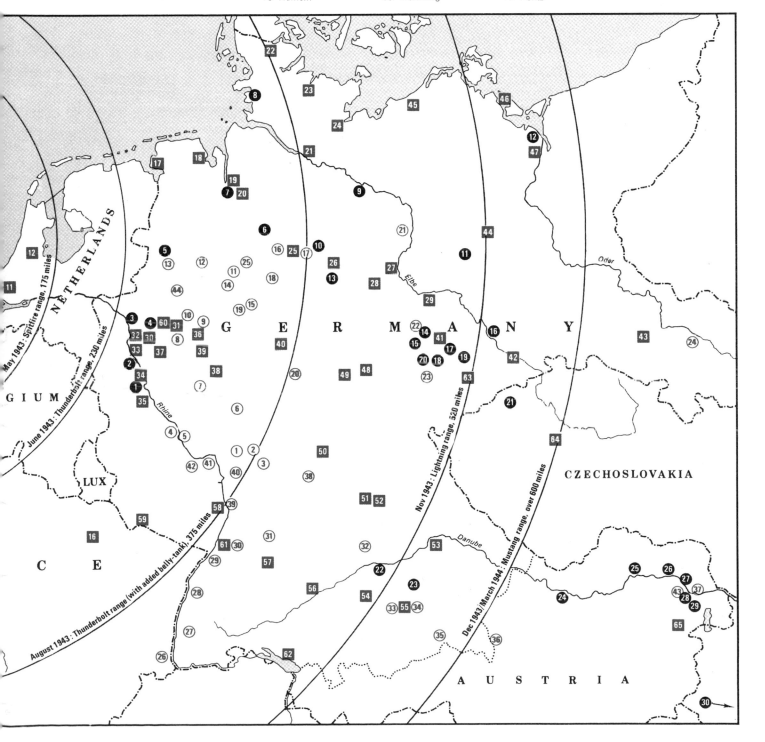

279

THE BOMBER OFFENSIVE ON JAPAN

As the Japanese homeland could only be attacked at long range, for lack of bases close to the islands of the Japanese archipelago, a special aircraft was needed, and this was found in the Boeing B-29 Superfortress, operating for the most part from huge airfields constructed in the Marianas islands. Initially, the success rate was not good, as the Japanese defences proved to be more efficient than anticipated, and bombing accuracy severely troubled by the high winds at the bombing altitude of 30,000 feet, the effect of ice on instruments and performance, and fog at ground level. Losses were running at the unacceptably high rate of 6 per cent. The 20th Air Force's new commander, General Curtis Le May, set about overcoming these difficulties. The answer involved a complete reappraisal of American bombing tactics: instead of high altitude raids with high explosive, the new tactics called for low level raids with incendiaries.

Success was immediate. The first raid, on Tokyo, was carried out by 334 B-29's, dropping some 1,667 tons of incendiaries from 7,000 feet. Fifteen square miles of the city were destroyed. The next four raids proved the success of the new tactics. Operating at the new altitude, the B-29's could carry about three times the bomb load they had at 30,000 feet, but raided at night to avoid the worst efforts of the Japanese anti-aircraft fire. In all, 9,365 tons of incendiaries were dropped, gutting 32 square miles of urban areas. Losses were reduced dramatically: of the 1,595 sorties despatched, only twenty-two aircraft were lost, a loss rate of only 1·4 per cent. With the arrival of the first escort fighters operating from Iwo Jima on 7 April, American losses fell still further, and with the constantly growing number of B-29's available, Japanese industry suffered mortal blows in the period of total American air superiority between May and August 1945.

The Japanese continued to resist, however, and it was not until the awesome import of the two Atom bomb raids had been digested that the Japanese sued for peace.

Below: USAAF Superfortresses releasing incendiary bombs over Yokohama

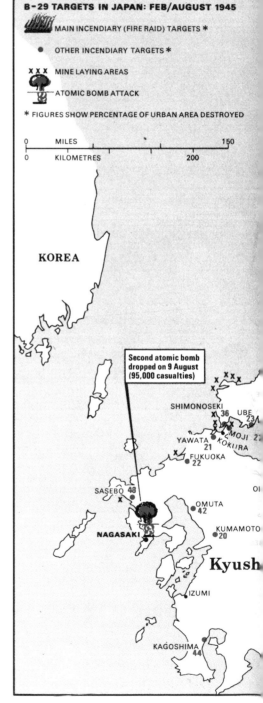

B-29 TARGETS IN JAPAN: FEB/AUGUST 1945

MAIN INCENDIARY (FIRE RAID) TARGETS *

OTHER INCENDIARY TARGETS *

XXX MINE LAYING AREAS

ATOMIC BOMB ATTACK

* FIGURES SHOW PERCENTAGE OF URBAN AREA DESTROYED

MILES 0 — 150
KILOMETRES 0 — 200

KOREA

Second atomic bomb dropped on 9 August (95,000 casualties)

SHIMONOSEKI
UBE 23
MOJI 27
YAWATA 21 KOKURA
FUKUOKA 22
SASEBO 48
OMUTA 42
KUMAMOTO 20
NAGASAKI
Kyush
IZUMI
KAGOSHIMA 44

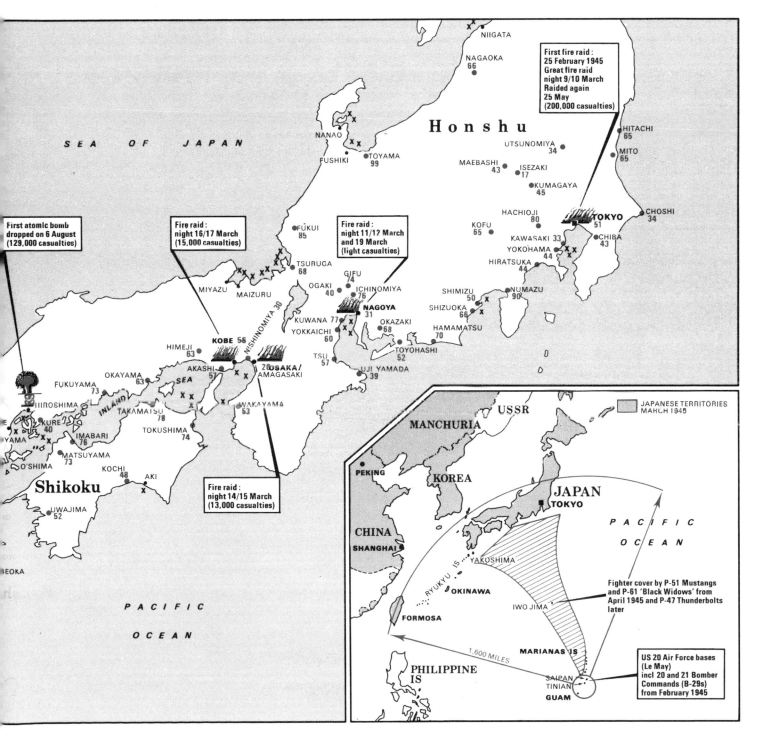

SEA OF JAPAN

Honshu

NIIGATA

NAGAOKA
66

First fire raid :
25 February 1945
Great fire raid
night 9/10 March
Raided again
25 May
(200,000 casualties)

HITACHI
65

NANAO

TOYAMA
99

FUSHIKI

UTSUNOMIYA
34

MITO
65

MAEBASHI
43

ISEZAKI
17

KUMAGAYA
45

HACHIOJI
80

TOKYO
51

CHOSHI
34

KOFU
65

CHIBA
43

FÚKUI
85

Fire raid :
night 11/12 March
and 19 March
(light casualties)

KAWASAKI 33
YOKOHAMA
44

HIRATSUKA
44

Fire raid :
night 16/17 March
(15,000 casualties)

First atomic bomb
dropped on 6 August
(129,000 casualties)

TSURUGA
68

GIFU
74

OGAKI
40

ICHINOMIYA
76

SHIMIZU
50

NUMAZU
90

MIYAZU

MAIZURU

NISHINOMIYA 30

NAGOYA
31

SHIZUOKA
66

HAMAMATSU
70

KUWANA 77

OKAZAKI
68

YOKKAICHI
60

TSU
57

TOYOHASHI
52

HIMEJI
63

KOBE 56

OSAKA/
AMAGASAKI

UJI YAMADA
39

AKASHI
57

SEA

OKAYAMA
63

INLAND

WAKAYAMA
53

FUKUYAMA
73

HIROSHIMA

TAKAMATSU
78

KURE
40

IMABARI
76

TOKUSHIMA
74

MATSUYAMA
73

KOCHI
48

AKI

Shikoku

O'SHIMA

Fire raid :
night 14/15 March
(13,000 casualties)

UWAJIMA
52

BEOKA

PACIFIC

OCEAN

JAPANESE TERRITORIES
MARCH 1945

USSR

MANCHURIA

KOREA

JAPAN

TOKYO

PEKING

PACIFIC

OCEAN

CHINA

SHANGHAI

RYUKYU IS

YAKOSHIMA

OKINAWA

IWO JIMA

Fighter cover by P-51 Mustangs
and P-61 'Black Widows' from
April 1945 and P-47 Thunderbolts
later

FORMOSA

1,600 MILES

MARIANAS IS

PHILIPPINE
IS

SAIPAN
TINIAN

GUAM

US 20 Air Force bases
(Le May)
incl 20 and 21 Bomber
Commands (B-29s)
from February 1945

(Map references are shown by 'M' following page number. Forces are arranged by nationality (e.g. BRITISH FORCES) and then by theatres of war (e.g. in Europe) and size of unit.)

Aachen, 241M, 242, 243M, 247M, 277
Abe, Vice-Admiral, 144
Abyssinia, 52M1, 53M2,3; and see Ethiopian campaign
Achates, British destroyer, 268–9
Achilles, British cruiser, 254, 255M
Acroma, 60, 61M1,2
Adem, El, 54, 54M, 61M2
Aden, 52, 53M3
Addis Ababa, 52, 52M, 53M3
Admiral Graf Spee, German battleship, 254, 255M, 256
Admiral Hipper, German cruiser, 20M, 253, 257, 260, 266, 267M, 268–9, 268M
Admiral Scheer, German battleship, 253, 257, 257M, 266, 267M
Admiralty Islands, 150M1, 151, 151M4
Agedabia, 54, 54M, 59M4, 60, 60M, 72, 72M
Agheila, El, 48, 50, 51M2, 54, 54M, 58, 59M4, 60, 60M, 72, 72M
Ajax, British cruiser, 254, 255M
Akagi, Japanese carrier, 134, 138, 138M2
Akyab, 172, 173M, 174, 174M, 185
Alam Halfa Ridge, battle of, 49, 66, 67M
Alam el Onsol, 64, 65M
Alamein, El, 48, 63, 63M2, 73M; first battle of, 64, 65M; second battle of, 49, 68–9, 68M, 69M, 190
Alanbrooke, Viscount see Brooke, Sir Alan
Albania, 36–8, 39M, 41M, 42, 43M, 216M
Albert Canal, 12, 23M, 24M, 241M, 243M, 244M
Albert Line, 128, 128M
Alexander, Gen., later Field Marshal, Sir Harold: and N. Africa, 49, 64, 75, 78, 79; and Burma, 97, 112; and Italian campaign, 117, 123, 124, 129
Aleutian Islands, 98–9M, 134, 138, 138M1, 139
Alexandria, 32, 36, 48, 63M2, 73M, 258, 259
Algeria, 48, 70, 70M, 71M, 74M, 75M
Algiers, 70, 70M
Aliakmon Line, 42, 43M
Alor Star, 102, 102M
Alten Fjord, 266, 267, 267M, 268M, 269
Altmark, German supply ship, 20M, 254
Amba Alagi, 52, 53M3
Amboina, 110, 110M

Ambrosio, General Vittorio, 116–17
Andalsnes, 20, 20M
Anderson, Lieut.-Gen. Kenneth, 74
Antelat, 60, 60M, 72M
Antwerp, 226; falls to Allies, 240, 241M, 242, 243M, 244, 244M
Anzio, 120M; Allied landings at, 124, 125, 126, 126M1,2
Aradura Spur, Kohima, 180, 180M
Arakan Battles, 172, 174, 174M, 184
Archangel, 266, 266M
Arctic Ocean: convoys in, 266–9, 266M–9M; Commando raids in, 270, 270M1,2
Ardennes, 12, 22, 22M, 23M; Panzer crossing of, 24, 24M, 25M, 243M; battle of, 227, 244–5, 245M, 246
Argenta Gap, 130, 131M1
Argentan, 238, 238M, 239M, 241M
Ark Royal, British carrier, 255M, 260, 260M
Arnhem, 241M; Operation, 242, 242M, 247M
Arnim, General von, 74
Arno Line, 128, 128M
Arras, 12, 24, 24M, 25M3
Artemovsk, 192, 192M1,2,3
Asmara, 52, 53M3
Assam, 178, 179M (inset)
Astoria, US cruiser, 134, 142, 142M1
Athens, 36, 43M
Atlantic, Battle of, 253
Atlantis, German raider, 256, 256M
Auchinleck, Gen. Claude, 48, 49, 58, 63, 64, 66
Aung San, General, 184

AUSTRALIAN FORCES
in Mediterranean, 258
in North Africa, see under British forces in North Africa
in Pacific War:
Army: 7 and 9 Divisions, in New Guinea, 146–7, 146M, 147M; 17 Brigade, in New Guinea, 147, 147M
Navy: and German raiders, 256; Task Force 44: in Coral Sea, 136, 137M
in Malaya, 96, 102, 102M

Austria: annexed to Reich, 14, 15M; Russian invasion of, 220, 220M, 221M; at end of war, 248M
Avranches, 234M, 238, 238M
Azores, 255M; Allied bases in, 253
Azov, Sea of, 192, 192M1

Bab el Qattara, 64, 65M, 66, 67M
Badoglio, Marshal Pietro, 37, 117
Baja, 220, 220M
Baku, 194, 194M1,2, 195

Balaton, Lake, 216M, 217, 220, 220M; oilfields of, 220
Balck, General, 242
Bali, Japanese invasion of, 110, 110M
Balikpapan, 110, 110M
Balkans: campaign in, 36–45, 82, 259; partisans in, 117; Russian invasion of, 216–21, 216M–21M
Baltic Sea, 16, 208, 212, 212M, 213M, 215M; Western, bombing of, 253
Baltic states, clearing of, 214–15, 215M
Banmauk, 182, 182M
Bardia, 54M, 56M; capture of, 50, 51M2, 56M, 57, 57M, 58M, 59M, 73M
Barents Sea, battles of, 268–9, 268M, 269M
Bari, 120M
Bastogne, US defence of, 226, 244, 245M
Bataan Peninsula, 106, 108, 109M, 162M, 163
Batumi, 194, 194M1,2, 195, 195M
Bayeux, 231, 231M
Bear Island, 266, 266M, 267M, 268M, 269M
Beaverbrook, Lord, 83
Beja, 70, 70M
Belfast, British cruiser, 269, 269M
Belgium: defences of, 12, 23M; invasion of, 24, 24M, 25M; Allies enter, 226, 229M; liberation of, 240, 240M, 241M, 242, 243M, 244M, 245M
Belgian army: in 1940, 23M; and fall of France, 24M, 25M3, 26M
Belgrade, 40, 41M, 216M
Belorussia, 87M, 215M, 216
Ben Gama, 54, 54M
Benghazi, 36, 54, 54M, 55, 59M4, 60, 60M, 72M
Berbera, 52, 53M2,3
Berdyansk, 90, 90M
Berezina, river, 86, 87M
Bergen, 20, 20M, 260, 260M
Berlin: Battle of, 277, 278; Russian advance to, 219, 219M; fall of, 221, 222, 222M, 223M; Allied advance to, 240, 249M; division of, 248, 248M
Berneval, 273, 273M
Betio, 152M2, 152–3, 153M3
Bey, Adm. Erich, 269
Bhamo, 186, 186M
Bialystock, 84–5, 85M, 86, 87M
Bilin river, 112, 113M
Binalonan, 106, 107M
Bir el Gubi, 58, 58M, 59M1,2, 62M2,3
Bir Hacheim, 51M2; battle of, 48, 49, 60–1, 60M, 61M2,3
Bismarck, German battleship, 257, 260, 260M
Bizerta, 70M, 71M, 78, 79M, 118M
Black Sea, 202, 202M
Blamey, Sir Thomas, 147
Blücher, German cruiser, 20, 20M
Bock, Field Marshal von, 12, 83, 84, 192, 194
Bodö, 20, 20M
Bohemia, 221M
Bologna, 128M, 129, 129M3, 130, 131M1,2
Bône, 70, 70M, 74, 74M
Borneo, 128M, 129; Japanese attack on, 110, 110M, 159, 159M
Bou Arada, 70, 71M
Bougainville, 98M, 142, 150–1, 151M1
Bougie, 70, 70M
Boulogne, fall of, 24, 25M, 229M, 241M
Bradley, General Omar, 227; and invasion of Normandy, 226, 233, 235, 238; and Allied drive through Europe, 240, 242, 244
Brazil, 253
Bremen, bombing of, 276, 279M
Breslau, surrender of, 219, 219M, 221M

Brest: German naval base, 256M, 257, 257M, 260, 260M, 262, 263; bombing of, 276; and Allied invasion of Normandy, 229M, 234–5
Brest-Litovsk, 16, 16M, 17M3,4, 210, 211M
Brindisi, 37, 41M, 117, 120M
Britain: pre-war relations with Germany, 14; and battle of Low Countries, 24; and fall of France, 26; and Operation Sealion, 28, 28M; and see Operation Sealion; Battle of, 30, 31M, 276; and destruction of French fleet, 32; defence of Greece, 36–7, 38; and Yugoslav coup, 37; and German dash to Channel, 262, 263M; and Pearl Harbor, 96; and North African campaign, 49; aid to Russia, 82; and Burma campaign, 172; and invasion of Normandy, 226, 228, 228M, 229M; and choice of Second Front, 236, 236M; V-2 campaign against, 191; and see British forces

BRITISH FORCES
in Arctic:
Merchant Navy: and German raiders, 256–7; and Arctic convoys, 266–9, 266M, 267M; losses of, 253
Royal Navy: and Arctic convoys, 266–9, 267–9M; and Commando raids, 270, 270M1,2
Commandos: 3 & 4, assault on Lofoten Islands, 270, 270M2
Convoys: HX133, 255; JW51A, 268; JW51B, 268, 268M; JW55B, 269, 269M; PQ17, loss of, 266–7, 267M, 268; QP13, 266; RA55A, 269
in Atlantic: and Battle of River Plate, 254–5, 255M; and Battle of Atlantic, 252–3; and destruction of French fleet, 30, 32, 32M; and sinking of Bismarck, 260, 260M
Royal Air Force, and sinking of Bismarck, 260, 260M
Royal Navy, and sinking of Bismarck, 260, 260M
Force H, 32, 260, 260M; Swordfish aircraft, 260
in Balkans:
Army, 36; defence of Greece, 37, 38, 42, 43M; on Crete, 44, 44M
Brigades: 5 New Zealand, 44, 44M
'W' Force in Greece, 43M
Royal Air Force, 36, 37, 39M, 44
Royal Navy, 36, 37, 252
in Burma:
Army: Burma Army and fall of Burma, 112, 113M; Fourteenth Army in Burma Campaign, 97, 172–86, 174M–86M
Corps: IV, 178, 179M, 181–3, 181M–4M; XV, 174, 174M, 175M, 182, 184, 184M, 185M; XXXIII, 178, 180–3, 181M–3M, 185M; Burma Corps, and loss of Burma, 97
Divisions: (2), 180–1, 180M, 181M, 183M, 185M; (36), 186, 186M; 5 Indian, 174, 175M, 181M, 185M; 7 Indian, 174, 175M, 180, 180M, 183M, 185M; 12 Indian, 181M; 14 Indian, 147, 147M; 17 Indian, 112, 181M, 182–4, 183M–5M; 19 Indian, 182–3, 182M, 183M, 185M; 20 Indian, 179M, 181M, 183M, 184, 185M; 23 Indian, 179M,

181M; 26 Indian, 184, 185M
Brigades: (4, 5 and 6), 180, 180M; (16) 177, 177M; (33), 180, 180M; 3 Commando, 184; 77 Indian, 176–7, 176M, 177M; 161 Indian, 180, 180M
Chindits, 172, 176–7, 176M, 177M
Ghurkas, 176
Royal Air Force, 173
in Europe: strength of, 12, 13, 276; and German invasion, 12–31; and Allied invasion of Europe, 238–49
Army: 21 Army Group (British Second Army and Canadian First Army): and breakout from Normandy, 238, 238M, 239M; and drive to Germany, 240–2, 240M–5M; invasion of Germany, 226, 227, 246, 247M; victory of 248, 249M
Corps: XXX, 242, 242M, 245M
Divisions: Airborne, 242, 242M, 246, 247M; 1 Canadian, 26; 51 Highland, 26, 246, 247M
British Expeditionary Force, 12, 23M, 24, 24M, 25M, 26, 26M
Commandos: 270, 271M4, 273, 273M
Merchant Navy, and Battle of Britain, 30
Royal Air Force: strength of, 276; and Dunkirk, 26; and Dieppe operation, 273; raids on Germany, 276–8; and Allied invasion of France, 277
Bomber Command, 253, 276–8, 279M
Coastal Command, 253, 262, 263M
Fighter Command, 30, 31M, 276
Pathfinder Force, 276
Royal Navy: defence of Norway, 20, 20M, 252; and Dunkirk, 26, 26M2; and German Channel dash, 262, 263M; raid on St Nazaire, 272, 272M; and Dieppe operation, 273, 273M
and see British forces in Italian Campaign, British forces in Normandy
in Far East: and loss of Malaya and Singapore, 96–7, 97, 102, 102M, 103M; and fall of Hong Kong, 104, 104M
Army: Divisions: 8 Australian, 102, 102M; 11 Indian, 102, 102M
Royal Air Force, attacks on Malayan bases, 102
Royal Navy, weakness of in Malay, 252
and see British forces in Burma
in Italy:
Eighth Army in Italian campaign, 119–30, 119M–31M
Corps: V, 122M, 128–9, 129M, 131M; X, 121, 121M, 122M, 124, 124M, 125M, 131M1; XIII, 119M, 122M, 125M, 131M; XXX, 119M, New Zealand, 124, 124M
Divisions: 1 Airborne, 120M; 8 Indian, 130, 131M
in Mediterranean:
Merchant Navy, and Malta Convoys, 264, 264M
Royal Air Force, 259, 259M, 264
Royal Navy, 258–9
Force H (Gibraltar), 258, 260
and see British forces in Balkans, above

in Normandy:
Second Army: strength of, 226, 227, 228, 228M; and invasion of Normandy, 230–5, 230M–5M; and breakout from Normandy, 238, 238M; *and see* British forces in Europe, *above*
Corps: I, 228M, 231, 231M; and Operation Goodwood, 234, 235M; X X X, 228M, 231, 231M, 238M, 239M
Divisions: Airborne, 226, 228, 228M, 230; 8 Airborne, 228, 228M
Commandos, 226, 227, 231M
Paratroops, 227
in North Africa:
Eighth Army: strength of, 48, 68; and German offensive, 50–61, 51M–61M; and fall of Tobruk, 62, 62M; and first Battle of Alamein, 63, 63M2,3, 64, 65M; and Battle of Alam Halfa, 66, 67M; and second Battle of Alamein, 48, 49, 68–9, 68M, 69M; advance and victory in Tunisia, 72, 72M–3M, 76–7, 76M, 77M
Western Desert Force, 50, 51M
Corps: X, 63, 63M1,2; at El Alamein, 68–9, 68M, 69M; in Tunisia, 73M, 76, 76M2, 77M; X I I I, 58, 58M, 59M1, 60, 61M2,3; and first Battle of Alamein, 63, 64, 65M; at Alam Halfa, 67M; and second Battle of Alamein, 69, 69M; X X X, 58, 58M, 59M3,4, 61M2; and first Battle of Alamein, 63, 63M1, 64, 65M; 67M; and second Battle of Alamein, 68–9, 68M, 69M; in Tunisia, 72M–3M, 76, 76M2
New Zealand, 76, 76M1, 77M
Divisions: (50), 61M2,3, 69M, 76, 76M2; (51(H)), 69M, 72M, 76M2, 79M2; 11 and 12 African, in Ethiopia, 53M3
1 Armoured: and German offensive, 61M2,3, 63, 63M1,2, 65M; and Battle of Alamein, 68M, 69, 69M; in Tunisia, 76, 76M2, 77M, 79M
2 Armoured, 54–5
6 Armoured, 78–9, 79M
7 Armoured: and German offensive, 50, 51M1, 57, 58M, 61M2,3, 65M; defends Alam Halfa, 66, 67M; and Battle of Alamein, 69M; and Tunisia, 72M, 76M1,2, 78, 79M
10 Armoured, 67M, 68M, 69, 69M
6 Australian, 50
7 Australian, 55
9 Australian, 54, 55, 64, 65M, 68M, 69, 69M
4 Indian, 50, 51M1, 53M3, 57, 57M, 58, 58M, 69M2,3, 69, 69M, and Allied victory, 76, 76M2, 78, 79M
5 Indian, 53M3, 63M, 65M, 67M
New Zealand: and German offensive, 50, 51M, 58, 58M, 59M2, 63, 63M; and first Battle of Alamein, 64, 65M; and Battle of Alam Halfa, 66, 67M; and second Battle of Alamein, 69, 69M; advance to Tunisia and victory, 72, 72M, 76, 76M, 77M, 79M
1 South African, 53M3, 58M, 59M2, 61M2,3; at battles of Alamein, 65M, 67M, 68M, 69, 69M
2 South African: at Tobruk,

61M2,3, 62, 62M
Brigades: (150), 60, 61, 61M2
4 Armoured, 57, 57M, 58, 58M, 59M1, 60, 61M2,3, 63M1,2, 64, 65M
7 Armoured, 56, 56M, 57, 57M, 58, 58M, 59M2
8 Armoured, 67M, 76, 76M
22 Armoured, 58, 58M, 59M2, 61M2,3, 65M, 66, 67M
22 Guards, 56M, 57, 58, 58M
201 Guards, 76, 76M1
3 Indian, 54, 55
4 Indian Motor, 60, 61M2
131 Lorried Infantry, 76, 76M1
7 Motor, 60, 61M2,3, 63M2, 65M, 67M
5 South African, 58
Battalions: 2 Parachute, 70, 71M
Regiments: 7 Tank, 50, 51M1
Eastern Task Force, 70, 70M
Selby Force, takes Sidi Barrani, 60
in Pacific: strength of, 99; and sinking of Force Z, 105, 105M
in Palestine and Transjordan:
Army: 32, 32M3
Divisions: 7 Australian, 32; Free French, 32
Brigades: 4 Indian, 32

British Somaliland, 52, 53M2,3
Brittany, Allies overrun, 238, 238M
Brooke, General Sir Alan (Viscount Alanbrooke), 36, 37, 227
Broome, Commander J. E., 267
Bruneval, 270, 271M4
Brunsbuttel, 257M, 263M
Brussels, 24, 24M, 25M; falls to Allies, 240, 241M, 243M
Bryansk, 90, 91M, 92M, 93
Bucharest, 216M
Buckner, General, 166
Budapest: falls to Russians, 216M, 217, 220, 220M 221M
Buerat, 72, 72M
Bug, river, 210, 211M
Bulgaria: joins Axis, 36–7; German army in, 40, 41M; Russian conquest of, 216, 216M, 221M; joins Allies, 217
Buna, 116, 146M
Buq Buq, 50, 51M1, 54M, 55
Burma, 97, 98M, 99; Japanese invasion of, 112, 113M; campaign in, 172–87, 173–86M
Burma National Army, 184
Burma road, 99, 172, 186, 186M, 187
Burnett, Rear Adm. R. L., 268–9
Burrough, Rear-Adm. H. M., 264
Busch, General, 212
Buthidaung, 174, 174M, 175M
Butler, General, 236
Bzura, battle of the, 16, 17M3

Caen, 228M, 231, 231M, 233, 233M; Allies enter, 234–5, 235M, 238M
Cairo, British cruiser, 264, 265M
Calabria, 120M, 121, 258
Calais, 22, 22M, 24, 25M, 26, 26M, 229M, 241M
Calcutta, 174, 179M (inset)
Callaghan, Rear-Admiral, 144
Cambeltown, British destroyer, 272, 272M

CANADIAN FORCES
in Arctic: Commando raids on Spitzbergen, 270, 270M1
in Battle of the Atlantic (navy), 235
in Europe:
First Army: and breakout from Normandy, 238, 238M; clears Channel Ports, 240, 241M; clears

Scheldt estuary, 242, 243M; and invasion of Germany, 226, 227, 246, 247M, 248M
Divisions: (2), and Dieppe operation, 273, 273M; (3), crossed Rhine, 246, 247M
and see Canadian forces in Italy, Canadian forces in Normandy
in Italy:
Army: I Corps, 125M, 129, 129M
in Normandy:
First Army: and invasion of Normandy, 228, 228M, 231, 231M, 234, 238, 239M
Corps: (II), and invasion of Normandy, 228M; and fall of Caen, 234, 235, 235M; closes Falaise Gap, 238, 239M

Canéa, 44, 44M
Cannes, 236, 237M
Cap Bon, 78, 79M
Cape Esperance, battle of, 140, 142–3, 143M3
Capuzzo, Fort, 54M, 56, 56M, 57, 57M, 58, 58M, 59M2,3
Caribbean Sea, 253
Carpathian Mountains, 191, 210, 211M
Casablanca, 32, 70, 70M
Casablanca Conference (1943), 276
Caslon, Captain C., 270
Cassino, 122M, 123; battles of, 124–7, 124M–6M
Castellano, Gen. Giuseppe, 116, 117
Catania, 116, 119, 119M
Caucasus, oilfields of, 83, 194, 194, 194M1,2; German thrust to, 190, 194–5, 194M1,2, 195M, 200, 202, 202M, 207
'Cauldron', the, 61, 61M2,3
Caumont, 233, 233M
Cavallero, Marshal Ugo, 120
Cavalry Point, 108, 109M
Celebes, 98M; Japanese attack, 110, 110M
Channel, English, 28, 28M, 30, 31M, 276; German dash through, 262, 263M, 276
Channel Ports, clearing of, 240, 241M
Chang Kai-shek, Generalissimo, 172, 186, 187
Changteh, 187M; Battle of, 187
Chennault, Brig.-Gen. Claire, 187
Cherbourg, 226, 228, 228M, 229M; US capture of, 232M, 233, 233M
Chukhiang, 187, 187M
China: civil war in, 187; war with Japan, 96, 98M, 99, 187, 187M; and Burma campaign, 112, 113M, 172, 179, 186, 186M; US forces in, 135, 187

CHINESE FORCES
in Burma, 112, 113M, 176–7, 177M, 186, 186M
in Sino-Japanese war, US aid to, 187

Chindwin, river, 172, 173M, 179M, 181, 181M, 182, 182M, 183M
Chir, river, 198M, 199M, 200, 200M
Choiseul Island, 150–1, 151M
Choltitz, Gen. von, 191
Christison, Gen., 174, 184
Chudskoye, Lake, 209, 209M
Churchill, Winston S.: and France, 12, 26; and defence of Balkans, 36, 37; and invasion of Russia, 82; and Malaya, 106; and N. Africa, 49, 58, 64; and Burma, 172; and Anglo-American co-operation, 227
Ciano, Count, 96
Ciliax, Vice-Adm., 262
Clark, Gen. Mark., 121, 124, 127, 129, 130

Clark Field, Luzon, 106, 107M, 160, 162, 162M
Cologne, bombing of, 241M, 243M, 244M, 278, 279M
Commacchio, Lake, 130, 131M
Commandos, 270–1, 270M, 271M; *and see* Dieppe, Normandy, St Nazaire
Constantine, 74, 74M
Coral Sea, 98M; Battle of, 134, 136–7, 137M
Coriano Ridge, 129, 129M2
Corinth, 42, 43M
Corregidor, 96, 97, 107M, 108, 108M, 109M, 134; US capture, 162M, 163
Cotentin Peninsula, 232M, 233, 235, 238M
Cox's Bazaar, 174, 174M
Crace, Rear-Adm., 136
Crerar, General, 238
Crete, 36, 37, 43M; and Battle of Cape Matapan, 258, 259M; fall of, 32, 44, 44M, 252
Crimea, 87M, 93M, 191; German forces in, 83, 192, 192M1, 206, 207, 210, 211M
Cruewell, General, 58, 60
Crutchley, Rear-Adm., 142
Cumberland, British cruiser, 254, 255M
Cunningham, Gen. Sir Alan, 48, 52, 58
Cunningham, Adm. Sir Andrew, 36, 252, 258, 259
Cyrenaica, 48, 51M, 54M, 56M, 57M, 58M, 60, 72–3M
Cyzechoslovakia: and Sudetenland, 14, 15M; and Russian advance, 216, 217, 219M, 220M; Russian offensive in, 221, 221M; partisans in, 221; at end of war, 248M

Dakar, 32, 32M1
Damascus, Allies take, 32, 32M3
Danzig: 218, 218M, 219M; Bay of, 218, 218M, 219M; Corridor, 14, 15M
Darmstadt, 246, 247M
Daugavpils, 86, 87M
Davao, 98M, 110, 110M, 163M
D-Day, 228, 228M–31M
De Gaulle, Gen. Charles, 26, 32
De Lattre Tassigny, Gen., 236
Deir el Shein, 64, 65M
Dempsey, Gen. Sir Miles, 227, 238
Demyansk, 92M, 93
Denmark, invasion of, 20, 20M
Denmark Strait, 256M, 257M, 260, 260M, 266M
Depienne, 70, 71M
Derna, 50, 51M2, 54M, 55, 59M4, 60M, 72M
Dessie, 52, 53M3
Deutschland, German battleship, 254, 256
Deveraux, Major James, 96
Devers, General, 242, 246
Devonshire, British cruiser, 256
Diego-Suarez, 271, 271M5
Dieppe: Allied landing at, 229M, 241M, 273, 273M
Dinant, 24, 24M, 25M
Djebel Bou Aoukaz, 78, 79M
Djebel Merda, 76, 77M
Djedeida, 70, 71M
Dniepr, river, 86, 87M, 90, 90M, 93M; in Russian offensive, 205, 206M, 207, 207M, 210, 211M
Dniester, river, 191, 210, 211M
Dollman, Gen., 228, 233
Don, river, 194, 194M1,2, 195M, 198, 198M
Donets, river, 90, 90M, 93M, 195M; basin, 83, 194, 195M; and Russian offensive, 192, 192M2,3, 206–7, 206M, 207M
Donetz Corridor, 194, 195M
Donbaik, 174, 174M
Dönitz, Grand-Adm. Karl, 252, 253, 269; Hitler's successor, 222; surrenders, 248

Doolittle, Major James, 277
Doorman, Rear-Adm. Karel, 110
Dorsetshire, British cruiser, 260, 260M
Dortmund-Ems Canal, 278
Dover, 263M; Strait of, 262, 263M
Dresden, 219, 221M, 223M; bombing of, 277, 278, 279M
Dubrovnik, 40, 41M
Duke of York, British battleship, 269, 269M
Dunkerque, French battlecruiser, 32, 255M
Dunkirk: evacuation of, 12, 24, 24M, 26, 26M, 227, 241M
Dusseldorf, 241M, 243M, 244M, 247M, 249M

DUTCH FORCES
in Far East, Army, 99
in Pacific, Navy, 98M, 110

Dutch East Indies, 98M, 99; fall of, 110, 110M
Japanese withdrawals from, 135
Dvina, river, 86, 87M, 206, 207M
Dyle, river, 12, 23M

East Prussia, 14, 16M, 17M, 84, 84M, 87M; Russians approach, 212, 212M, 213M, 215M; Russians invade, 218M, 219M, 221M; at end of war, 248M
Eastern Solomons, Battle of, 140, 142, 142M2
Eastern Dorsale, Tunisia, 74, 75M
Eben Emael, 12; capture of, 24, 24M, 25M
Eder Dam, 276, 277
Eden, Anthony, 36, 37
Egypt, 32, 44, 50, 52M1, 54M, 56M–9M, 63, 63M2, 72, 73M
Eichelberger, Gen., 163
Eindhoven, 241M, 242M, 243M
Eisenhower, Gen. Dwight D., 49, 226, 227, 230, 237, 240, 244
Elbe, river, 222, 223M
Ellice Islands, 98M, 152
Emmerich, 246, 247M
Empress Augusta Bay, 151, 151M3
Enfidaville, 78, 79M
England: blitz on, 30, 31M, 276; plan to invade, *see* Operation Sealion; V-1 and V-2 campaign on, 191; *and see* Britain
Eniwetok Atoll, 98M, 153, 153M5, 154
Enterprise, US carrier, 138–9, 138M2, 142, 142M2, 143, 143M4, 144
Epirus, the, 36, 37, 38, 39M
Er Regima, 60, 60M
Eremenko, Gen., 190, 198
Eritrea, 52, 52M3
Esmonde, Lieut.-Comm., 262
Essaine, Maj.-Gen. H., 227
Essen, bombing of, 276, 279M
Estonia, 213M, 215, 215M, 221M
Ethiopian campaign, 52, 52M1, 53M2,3
Etna, Mount, 116, 119M, 120M
Europe, Allied invasion of, 226–48, 228M–49M; at end of war, 248M; *and see* individual countries
Exeter, British cruiser, 254, 255M

Falaise, 238, 238M, 239M
Falkland Islands, 254, 255M
Fériana, 74, 75M
Ferrara, 130, 131M1
Fiji Islands, 98M, 134, 152
Finland: Russian invasion of, 18, 18M, 19M, 82, 84M, 87M, 88, 89M; and German invasion of Russia, 88, 88M; Arctic convoys and, 226, 226M, 267M; German forces in (1942), 192; Russian defeat of, 214, 214M, 215M2

First World War, 12, 13, 48, 226, 252

Fiume, Italian cruiser, 258M, 259, 259M

Fitch, Rear-Adm., 137

Fletcher, Rear-Adm., 134, 136–7, 139, 140, 142

Florence, 128M, 129M3

Flores Sea, 110, 110M

Foggia, 117, 120M

Fontainebleau, 238, 238M, 241M

Foresight, British destroyer, 264, 265M

Formosa, 98M, 135, 149; in Sino–Japanese war, 187, 187M; Plan, 149, 158; Japanese bases on, 162, 164

France: pre-war relations with Germany, 14; defences of, 12, 23M; and Japanese occupation of Indo-China, 96, 99; and battle of Low Countries, 24; fall of, 24, 26, 26M, 27M, 32, 252; blitz on, 276; Commando raids on, 270, 271M4, 273, 273M; railways bombed, 277; and invasion of Europe, 226, 241M, *and see* Normandy; southern, US invasion of, 236, 236M, 237M, 277; *and see* Free French forces, French forces

Frankfurt, 226, 243M, 247M, 249M

Fraser, Vice-Adm. Sir Bruce, 268

FREE FRENCH FORCES
Army: foundation of, 26
in French West Africa (Force M), 32
in Italy: French Expeditionary Corps, 122M, 124, 124M, 125M
in Madagascar, 271
in North Africa, 61M2,3, 69M, 70, 72M
in Palestine and Transjordan: Free French Division, 32

FRENCH FORCES
Army: strength of, 12, 22, 23M; defence of Norway, 20, 20M; and fall of France, 24, 24M, 25M3; and Allied invasion of Europe, 228, 236, 237M, 246, 247M
First Army: and fall of France, 24, 24M, 25M3, 26M; joins US 6th Army Group, 236; crosses Rhine, 246, 247M
II Corps: and US landings, 236, 237M

French Overseas Empire, 32, 32M; *and see* Indo-China, French; North Africa; Somaliland, French; Tunisia; West Africa, French

Freyberg, Maj.-Gen. Bernard, 44

Friessner, General, 216–17

Fuka, 72, 73M

Fuller, Maj.-Gen. J. F. C., 96, 117

Furious, British carrier, 264

Gabes, 76, 77M

Gabr Saleh, 58, 58M, 59M2,3

Gafsa, 74, 75M, 76

Galatas, 44, 44M

Galland, Gen. Adolf, 262, 276

Gamelin, Gen. Maurice, 12, 22

Garigliano, river, 120M, 121, 122M, 123, 124, 124M, 125M

Gavdhos, 259, 259M

Gavutu, 140, 140M

Gazala, 58, 59M4, 60–1, 60M, 61M2, 72M

Gela, Gulf of, 119, 119M

Gemmano, 129, 129M2

Geneva, 26, 27M, 237M

Gensoul, Admiral, 82

GERMAN FORCES
in Arctic:
Luftwaffe, and Arctic convoys, 266, 267M

Navy, and Arctic convoys, 266–7, 267M, 268, 269M
in Atlantic:
Navy: in battle of Atlantic, 252–3; raiders, 256–7, 256M, 257M, 260; and sinking of *Bismarck*, 260, 260M
U-boats, 252–3
in Balkans, 36–44, 41M–3M, 259
Army:
Twelfth Army: invasion of Yugoslavia, 40, 41M; invasion of Greece, 43M
Corps: XXX, 42, 43M; XLI Motorised, 40, 41M; XL Panzer, 42, 43M
Divisions: Panzer, in Yugoslavia, 40, 41M; 2 Panzer, invades Greece, 42, 43M
First Panzergroup, invades Yugoslavia, 40, 41M
Luftwaffe: 36, 37, 40, 44M
X Air Corps, attacks in Mediterranean, 37
Fliegerkorps XI, attack on Crete, 44, 44M
in Europe: strength of, 12–13, 14, 16, 22, 23M; and invasion of Europe, 12–29, 23M–7M; and Allied invasion of Europe, 236–46, 237M–47M; surrender of, 248, 249M
Army
Western Command (OB West), 228, 229M, 242, 243M
Army Groups: (A) 22, 23M, 24M, 26M, 27M, 28M; (B), 23M, 24M, 26M, 27M, 28M; and Allied invasion, 241M, 242, 243M, 245M, 247M, 249M; (C), 23M, 24M, 27M; (G), 241M, 242, 243M, 247M, 249M; (H), 242, 243M, 247M, 249M
Oberrhein, 242, 243M
Armies: First, and Allied invasion, 241M, 243M, 247M, 249M
Seventh: and Allied invasion, 241M, 243M, 247M, 249M; and Ardennes offensive, 244, 244M, 245M
Twelfth: in Low Countries, 24M
Fifteenth: and Allied invasion, 241M, 243M, 244M, 247M, 249M
Nineteenth: and Allied invasion, 236, 237M, 247M, 249M
Fifth Panzer: and Allied invasion, 241M, 243M, 247M, 249M; and Ardennes offensive, 244, 244M, 245M
Sixth SS Panzer, 243M, 244, 244M, 245M
Corps, Panzer, 17M, 22, 23M, 24, 24M, 25M, 26, 26M, 27M
Divisions: 15 Panzer, 244, 245M
Luftwaffe: and invasion of Europe, 16, 26, 28, 30; and Battle of Britain, 30, 31M, 276; and Channel dash, 262; and bombing of Germany, 277, 278, 279M; last major effort of, 244; and Allied air victory, 226
Third Air Fleet, 228
Navy: strength of, 16, 252; and invasion of Norway, 20M; and Operation Sealion, 28; bombed at Brest, 276; and Channel dash, 262, 263M; and raid on St Nazaire, 272, 272M; and Dieppe operation, 273, 273M; losses of, 252
in Russia: strength of, 82–3, 84; and invasion of Russia, 48, 49, 82–8, 84M–8M; and

siege of Leningrad, 89, 89M, 208; and battle for Moscow, 90–3, 90M–3M; and Russian offensive, 190–220, 192M–220M; and battle of Stalingrad, 190, 196–200, 197–201M; and battle for Kursk, 116, 190, 191, 204–5, 204M, 205M; and Russian advance, 212–21, 212M–21M; and fall of Berlin, 222, 222M, 223M
Army:
OKH (Oberkommando des Heeres), 84, 86
Army Groups: (A), and Caucasus, 194–5, 194M2, 195M, 200, 202, 202M, 206M, 207; and battles in Ukraine, 210, 211M; destruction of, 219, 219M
(B): and Stalingrad, 194, 194M2, 195, 195M, 198, 198M; and Kharkov, 203, 203M
Centre: and invasion of Russia, 84, 84M, 85M, 86, 87M, 88, 91M, 92, 92M, 93M; and Operation Citadel, 204M, 205, 205M, 206M, 211M; Zhukov attacks, 212, 212M, 215, 215M; retreat, 218, 218M, 219M; defeat, 221, 221M, 222, 223M
Don (later Army Group South), 198–9, 199M, 202, 202M, 203, 203M
(E), in Balkans, 216M, 217
(F), in Balkans, 216M, 217
Kleist, 192–3, 192M3
Mackensen, 192, 192M2
North, 84M, 85M; at Leningrad, 84, 86, 87M, 88, 88M, 89, 89M; and battle for Moscow, 90, 91M, 93, 93M; and relief of Leningrad, 209, 209M; and Russian advance, 212, 212M, 215, 215M
North Ukraine, 210, 211M, 212, 212M
South, 84M, 85, 85M, 90M; in Ukraine, 83, 90, 91M, 93M; and Russian offensive, 192, 192M2,3, 194, 204M, 205, 205M, 206, 207, 210, 211M, 220, 220M
South Ukraine, 210, 211M, 216–17, 216M
Vistula: destruction of, 219, 219M, 222, 223M
Armies: Second, and invasion of Russia, 86, 87M, 194; at Kharkov, 203, 203M; and Russian advance, 218, 218M, 219M
Sixth: and Russian offensive, 192–4, 192M2,3, 195M; and Battle of Stalingrad, 196–200, 197M–200M; in Ukraine, 210, 211M, 216, 216M
Eighth, 210, 211M, 221M
Ninth: and Battle of Kursk, 204–5M, 204M1,2, 205M, 219M, 223M
Eleventh, 193, 193M, 198
Seventeenth: and invasion of Russia, 86, 87M; and Russian offensive, 192, 192M2,3; in Crimea, 206M, 207, 210, 211M
Twenty-ninth, 92M, 93
First Panzer, retreat from Russians, 202, 202M, 210, 211M, 219M, 221M
Second Panzer: and battle for Moscow, 90, 91M, 92M; and Lake Balaton, 220, 220M
Fourth Panzer: and invasion of Russia, 86, 87M; and battle for Moscow, 91M, 92M, 93; and Caucasus, 194–6, 195M; and Battle of Stalingrad, 196–200, 197M 201M; and Battle of Kursk, 204, 204M1,2,

205M; and German defeat, 219M, 223M
Sixth SS Panzer, 220, 220M
Twentieth Mountain, 215, 215M
Rumanian Third, in Ukraine, 216, 216M
Rumanian Fourth, at Stalingrad, 198M, 199M, 200M, 211M
Corps: (II), 93; XI, at Stalingrad, 200; XXX and LIV, and Sevastopol, 193, 193M; 6 Rumanian, at Stalingrad, 190; Rumanian Mountain, and Sevastopol, 193, 193M
Divisions: Panzer, and invasion of Russia, 83, 84–5, 85M; Panzer and counterattack in Ukraine, 190; Rumanian, surrender at Stalingrad, 198, 198M
Panzergroups: (I) invasion of Russia, 86, 87M; takes Rostov, 90, 90M
(II), invasion of Russia, 86, 87M
(III), invasion of Russia, 86, 87; assault on Moscow, 90, 91M
(IV), takes Daugavpils, 86, 87M; and assault on Moscow, 90, 91M
Luftwaffe: and invasion of Russia, 82–3, 276; and Battle of Stalingrad, 190, 198, 200; and Battle of Kursk, 204; removal of units, 212
Navy: Baltic Fleet evacuates troops, 218
in Italy:
Army: and Allied invasion of Italy, 116–29, 120M–7M; surrender of, 130, 131M1,2
Army Groups: (B), 117; (C) (South-West), 127M, 130
Armies: Tenth, 120M, 121M, 122M, 123, 125M, 126, 127, 127M, 128M, 129M2, 130, 131M1,2
Fourteenth, 126–7, 126M2, 127M, 128M, 130, 131M12
in Mediterranean:
Luftwaffe, attacks on Malta, 264
Navy: U-boats, 264
in Normandy:
Army: strength of, 226, 227, 228, 229M; and Allied invasion, 230–9, 230M–8M
Army Group B, 228, 229M, 238, 238M
Armies: Seventh: and Allied invasion, 226, 228, 229M, 231M; and loss of St. Lô, 233, 234M, 235; escape of 238, 239M; destruction of, 277
Fifteenth: and Allied invasion, 226, 229M, 231M
Fifth Panzer: and battle for Normandy, 234–5, 235M, 238, 239M
Divisions: (352), 230M, 231; 21 Panzer, 231, 231M, 235M; 1 SS Panzer, 234, 235M; 12 SS Panzer, 231M, 234, 235M
in North Africa:
Army: strength of, 48–9, 68; offensives in Western Desert, 54–63, 54M–63M; and first Battle of Alamein, 64, 65M; and Battle of Alam Halfa, 66, 67M; and second Battle of Alamein, 68, 68M, 69M; and Allied and German landings, 70, 70M, 71M; retreat and defeat of, 72–9, 74M–9M
Africa Korps, 48, 58; *and see* DAK task force, *below*
DAK task force (Afrika Korps) (15 and 21 Panzer Divisions): and drive to Gazala, 60–1, 60M, 61M2,3; takes Tobruk, 62,

62M; and first Battle of Alamein, 63–4, 63M2, 65M; and Battle of Alam Halfa, 66, 67M; and Battle of Alamein, 69; in Tunisia, 75, 75M, 76, 76M1,2, 77M, 79M
Divisions: (164) in Tunisia, 76
5 Light, 54, 54M, 55, 55M, 57, 57M
90 Light, 58M, 59M; advance of, 60, 60M, 61M2,3, 63, 63M1,2; first Battle of Alamein, 64, 65M; and Battle of Alam Halfa, 67M; and second Battle of Alamein, 68M, 69, 69M; in Tunisia, 76M1,2, 77M, 79M2
8 Panzer: and Halfaya Pass, 56
10 Panzer: in Tunisia, 74–6, 75M, 76M1
15 Panzer, 57, 58, 58M, 59M2,3; *and see* DAK task force, *above*
21 Panzer, 58, 59M2,3; *and see* DAK task force, *above*
Regiments: 8 Panzer, attacks Halfaya, 56M, 57, 57M
Force Cruewell, 60, 61M

Germany: Hitler's plans for, 82; rise of, 12–14, 15M; invasion of Europe, 16–20, 17M–20M, and fall of France, 23M, 24, 26, 32; and Balkan campaign, 37, 38, 39, 40, 42, 44; and Tripartite Pact, 37; invasion of Russia, 36, 37, 48, 49, 82–3, 118; and US entry into war, 96; and Operation Sealion, 28, *and see* Operation Sealion; and North Africa, 49; and Italian campaign, 116–17; raids on England, 191; Allied bombing of, 276–8, 277M; tide of war turns against, 190, 200; and Stalingrad, 200; Russian invasion of, 218–19, 218M, 219M, 221M; and Allied invasion of Europe, 226, 227, 240–6, 240M–7M; capture of Berlin, 222, 222M, 223M; surrender of, 191, 222, 227, 248, 249M; division of, 248, 248M; *and see* German forces

Gibraltar, 32, 32M, 70M, 255M; British navy at, 258, 260, 260M; Strait of, 264

Gilbert Islands, 98M, 152, 152M1, 153

Gin Drinkers Line, 104, 104M

Gneisenau, German battle-cruiser, 20M, 253, 257, 257M, 262, 263M, 276

Goebbels, Dr Paul Joseph, 190

Gold Beach, Normandy, 231, 231M

Gomel, 86, 87M

Gona, 146, 146M

Gondar, 52, 53M3

Good Hope, Cape of, 254, 255M, 257M

Gorodischche, 86, 87M

Göring, Hermann, 227, 228, 276; and Stalingrad, 190, 198

Gorrahei, 52, 53M

Gothic Line, 128–9, 128M, 129M2,3

Goto, Rear-Adm., 136, 142

Gott, Brigadier, 56

Goubellat, 78, 79M

Grave, 241M, 242, 242M, 243M

Graziani, Marshal Rodolfo, 50

Greece, fall of, 32, 36–7, 38, 39M, 42, 43M, 48, 49; British naval support of, 259, 259M; German army in, 216M, 217

GREEK FORCES
Army: in Balkan campaign, 36–7, 38, 39M, 42, 43M, 44; in Crete, 44

Greenland, 257M, 260M, 266M

Griswold, Maj.-Gen. (later Gen.), 150, 162, 163
Guadalcanal, 98M, 135, 137M; battle for, 135, 140–1, 140M, 142, 142M; actions of, 144–5, 145M; in battle for Solomons, 151M1
Guam, 98M, 138M1, 154, 155M, 157M2,3
Guderian, Gen. Heinz, 24, 37; and Russia, 82, 83, 86, 90, 190, 191, 215
Gun Spur, Kohima, 180, 180M
Gustav Line, 121–7, 120M–7M
Guzzoni, Gen. Alfredo, 119
Gydnia, 253, 260, 260M

Hagen Line, 205, 205M
Halder, Gen. Franz, 82, 190, 195
Hale, Maj.-Gen., 152
Halfaya Pass, 55–8, 54M–9M, 72, 73M
Hall, General, 163
Halfid Ridge, 57, 57M
Halsey, Vice-Adm. Thomas, 152, 159, 160–1, 162
Hamma, El, plain of, 76, 77M
Hammamet, 79, 79M1
Hamman Lif, 79, 79M1
Hamburg, 227, 277, 279M
Hamilton, Rear-Adm. L. H. K., 267, 270
Hara, Admiral, 142
Harar, 52, 53M2,3
Harriman, Avrell, 83
Harris, Sir Arthur, 276–7
Harwood, Commodore H., 254
Hashimoto, Admiral, 144
Hawaii, 98M, 136, 138M, 152; and see Pearl Harbor
Haydon, Brigadier J. C., 270
Helena, US cruiser, 142, 143M3, 145M1
Henderson Field, Guadalcanal, 140–1, 140M, 143, 144, 151M1
Hengyang, 187, 187M
Heraklion, 44, 44M
Hering, Maj.-Gen., 146
Hermes, British carrier, 32, 255M
Herr, General, 130
Hester, Maj.-Gen., 150
Hiei, Japanese battleship, 144, 145M1
Himmler, Heinrich, 191, 242
Hiroshima, 168, 169M
Hiryu, Japanese carrier, 138, 138M2, 139
Hitler, Adolf: and Treaty of Versailles, 14; reoccupies Rhineland, 14, 15M; conquest of Poland, 14, 16; and Operation Sealion, 30, 276; and U-boats, 252; and naval raiders, 257; and Balkan campaign, 37; and Channel Dash, 262; and Arctic convoys, 266, 268, 269; and N. Africa, 49, 68; and invasion of Russia, 82, 83, 84, 86, 90, 116, 190–1, 192, 194–5; and Italian campaign, 116–17, 120; and Stalingrad, 196, 198–9, 200; 'No retreat' principle, 205, 207, 212, 215; and Russian offensive, 206, 210, 216, 220; and invasion of Normandy, 226, 233, 235, 238; and invasion of Europe, 227, 228, 240; and Ardennes offensive, 244–5; suicide of, 222
Hlegu, 184, 185M
Hodges, General, 158, 166, 238, 244, 246
Holland see Netherlands
Holland, Vice-Adm. L., 260
Hollandia operation, 147
Homs, 72, 72M
Honda, Lieut.-Gen. Masaki, 186
Hong Kong, 98M; fall of, 104, 104M
Honshu, 98M, 168
Hood, British cruiser, 32, 260, 260M
Hornet, US carrier, 138–9, 138M2, 143, 143M4
Horrocks, Lieut.-Gen. Sir Brian, 76, 78

Hosogaya, Admiral, 136
Hoth, General, 90
Houston, US cruiser, 110
Huon Peninsula, 147, 147M
Hub, Col.-Gen., 116, 119
Hukawng Valley, 176, 177M
Hungary, 116; falls to Russians, 216M, 217, 220, 220M, 221M
Hunter, Col. C. N., 177
Hunters Hill, Kohima, 180, 180M
Hutton, General T. J., 112
Iachino, Adm. Angelo, 259
Iceland, 253, 255M, 256M, 257M, 260M
Ichiki, Colonel, 140
Iida, General, 174
Illustrious, British carrier, 258
Imphal, 173, 173M, 178, 179M; battle at, 181, 181M, 182M
Indawgyi, Lake, 177, 177M
India, 98M, 113M; and Burma campaign, 173M, 174, 174M; Japanese invasion of, 178, 179M, 180–1, 180M, 181M

INDIAN FORCES
in Burma, see under British forces
in Malaya, 102, 102M
in North Africa, see under British forces

Indian Ocean: U-boats in, 253; Graf Spee in, 254, 255M; German raiders in, 256M, 257M; Japanese operations in, 270; Commando raids in, 270–1, 271M5
Indo-China, French: and Sino-Japanese War, 187, 187M; Japanese occupation of, 96, 98M, 99, 102, 105M, 110, 110M
Indomitable, British carrier, 264, 265M
Ino, Gen. Matsuichi, 135
Inouye, Adm. Shigeyoshi, 136
Ironbottom Sound, 140, 140M, 145, 145M3
Irrawaddy, river, 173, 173M, 176, 176M, 177M, 179M, 182, 182M, 183M, 184, 184M, 186, 186M

ITALIAN FORCES
in Balkans and Mediterranean:
Army: and invasion of Greece, 36, 38, 39M, 42, 43M; in Yugoslavia, 40, 41M
Navy: in Balkan Campaign, 36, 258–9, and battle off Calabria, 258; and Battle of Cape Matapan, 259, 259M; attacked off Taranto, 258, 258M
Regia Aeronautica: attacks on Malta, 264
in Italian campaign, 116 117, 119, 130, 131M2
Sixth Army, 119
Ligurian (Fascist) Army, 130, 131M2
in North Africa:
Army: strength of, 48–9, 50, 52, 68; defeat in Ethiopia, 52, 53M2,3; in Western Desert, 58–64, 58M–65M; at Alamein, 68, 68M, 69M; in Tunisia, 76M1,2, 77M, 78–9, 79M2
Corps: X, 60M, 61M3, 63M1,2, 65M
XX, 60, 60M, 61M2, 63M2,3, 65M, 76M2
XXI, 58M, 59M, 60M, 63M1,2, 76M2
Divisions: Ariete, 54M; and Axis advance, 58, 58M, 59M2, 61M3, 62M, 63M; and first battle of Alamein, 64, 65M; and Alam Halfa, 67M; and second battle of Alamein, 69M
Blackshirt, 50

Italy: and Tripartite Pact, 37; declares war, 26, 252;

invades France, 26, 27M; and Balkan campaign, 36–7; and US entry into war, 96; and N. Africa, 48–9, 50, 52; coup against Mussolini, 117; armistice with Allies, 117, 120–1; campaign in, 116–31, 118M–31M, 191; and Allied choice of Second Front, 236, 236M; and see Italian forces
Ithuriel, British destroyer, 264
Iwo Jima, 98M, 164, 164M, 280

Jamaica, British cruiser, 268, 268M, 269, 269M
Jan Mayen Island, 266M
Japan: war with China, 96, 98M, 99, 187, 187M; and Tripartite Pact, 37; occupation of Indo-China, 96, 98M, 99; and Pearl Harbor, 96, 98M, 99, 100; entry into war, 253; offensive in Far East and Pacific, 96–113; bombing of, 136, 277, 280, 281M; and Pacific War, 134–5, 149, 159: and Okinawa, 135; and Russian war, 116; atomic bombs on, 168, 169M, 280, 281M; and see Japanese forces

JAPANESE FORCES
in Burma:
Army: and invasion of Burma, 112, 113M; and campaign in Burma, 172, 174–86, 174M–86M
Armies: Burma Area, 178, 179M, 182, 183M, 185M
Fifteenth, 174, 174M, 176–7, 177M; and Kohima and Imphal, 170–9, 178M, 179M, 182; and British advance, 182–3, 182M, 183M, 185M
Twenty-third, 182, 182M, 183M, 186, 186M
Divisions: (15) and Imphal, 178, 179M, 181M; (18), US advance against, 177; (31) at Kohima, 178, 179M, 180M, (33) and Imphal, 178, 179M, 181M; (53), in N. Burma, 177, 186M; (55), and Arakan battles, 174, 175M; (56), in N. Burma, 186, 186M
in Far East:
Army: strength of, 96, 98M, 99; in Sino-Japanese war, 187, 187M; occupies Indo-China, 96, 98M, 99, 102, 105M, 110, 110M; invades Malaya, 102, 102M–3M, 105; takes Hong Kong, 104, 104M
Armies: China Expeditionary, 187, 187M
Fifteenth, 102, 112, 113M
Twenty-fifth, 102, 102M
Divisions: (5 and 18), and invasion of Malaya, 102, 102M; Imperial Guards, 102, 103M
Takumi Force, 102, 102M
and see Japanese forces in Burma, Japanese forces in Pacific
in Indian Ocean: Commando raids on, 270–1, 271M5
in Pacific: offensive of, 96–110, 98M–110M; in Pacific War, 134–66, 137M–66M
Air Force: strength of, 96; and Pearl Harbor, 100, 100M; sinking of Force Z, 105, 105M; and Philippines, 106, 108, 108M; losses at Saipan, 154; losses in Philippine Sea, 156; sink Princeton, 160; losses at Okinawa, 135, 166
Kamikaze missions, 161, 162, 166, 166M
Tokyo Night Express, 140, 142, 145
Armies:
Fourteenth: in Philippines,

106, 107M; and Luzon, 162–3, 162M; Shobo Group of, 162M, 163
Seventeenth: and Guadalcanal, 140–1; in battle for Solomons, 151M1
Eighteenth: in Papua, 146, 146M; in battle for Solomons, 151M
Thirty-first: and loss of Saipan, 154, 154M
Thirty-second: and Okinawa, 166, 166M
Thirty-fifth: defence of Philippines, 158, 158M, 163M
Central, Eastern and Western Forces, take Dutch East Indies, 110, 110M
Divisions: (2), and Guadalcanal, 140; (16) and Leyte Gulf, 158; (17), elimination of, 151M3
Navy: strength of, 96, 99; and Pearl Harbor, 98M, 100, 100M; in Pacific War, 134, 136, 137M, 140–5, 145M; loss of Marshalls, 152–3, 153M3; loss of Saipan, 154
Fleets: First Mobile, and Battle of Philippine Sea, 156, 156M, 157M2,3; Second, 138–9; Combined, and Battle of Leyte Gulf, 159, 159M
Forces: 'A', in Battle of Leyte Gulf, 159–60, 159M, 161M; 'C', in Battle of Leyte Gulf, 159, 159M
First Carrier, and Battle of Midway, 138, 138M1,2
Midway occupation, 138–9, 138M1
Northern (Carrier 'Decoy' Force), and Battle of Leyte Gulf, 159, 159M, 161, 161M
Pearl Harbor Strike, 98M, 100, 100M
Second Striking, 159, 159M
Southern and Battle of Philippine Sea, 156, 156M, 157M2,3
Task Force MO, 136
Second Destroyer Flotilla, 145, 145M3

Jaslo, 218, 219M, 221M
Java, 98M; Japanese attacks on, 110, 110M
Java Sea, Battle of, 110, 110M
Jean Bart, French battleship, 32
Jigjiga, 52, 53M3
Jimma, 52, 53M3
Jitra, 102, 102M
Joffre, Gen. Joseph, 12, 226
Jolo, 106, 110M
Jomard Passage, 136, 137M
Jotsoma, 180, 180M
Juba, river, 52, 52M3
Juno beach, Normandy, 231, 231M

Kalamata, 42, 43M
Kalewa, 179M, 182, 182M
Kalinin, 90, 91M, 92, 92M
Kaluga, 90, 91M
Kampar, 102, 102M
Kangow, 184, 184M
Karelia, 88, 88M, 89M
Karelian Isthmus, 18, 19M, 214M
Karlovy Vary, 221, 221M
Karpino, 89, 89M
Kashira, 90, 91M
Kassala, 52, 52M3
Kassel, 276, 279M
Kasserine, Battle of, 74–6, 74M, 75M
Katamura, Lieut.-Gen. Shihachi, 182
Katha, 177M, 182, 182M
Kawabe, Lieut.-Gen. Shozo, 178, 182
Kawaguchi, General, 140
Kazatin, 86, 87M
Kema, 110, 110M
Keitel, Field-Marshal, 190
Kendari, 110, 110M

Kenya, 52, 53M3
Kenya, British cruiser, 264, 265M
Kerch peninsula, 192, 192M1, 193, 193M
Keren, fortress of, 52, 53M3
Khartoum, 52, 53M3
Kesselring, Field-Marshal: and airpower, 276; and Italian campaign, 120, 121, 123, 124, 130
Kharkov, 83; German occupation of, 90, 90M, 93M, 192–3, 192M1,2,3; Russian advance to, 203, 203M, 205, 205M, 206, 206M, 207, 207M
Khota Baru, 102, 102M
Kiel, bombing of, 276
Kiev, 84, 84M1, 86, 87M, 90, 93M; Germans take, 83, 191; Russians take, 206M, 207, 207M
Kimura, Gen. Hoyotaro, 182–3, 184
King, Adm. Ernest J., 135
King George V, British battleship, 260, 260M
Kinkaid, Rear-Adm. Thomas, 144
Kirishima, Japanese battleship, 144, 145M1,2
Kismayu, 52, 53M
Kleist, Gen. Paul von, 24, 40, 90; in Russia, 200, 202, 210; dismissed, 210
Klopper, General, 62
Kluge, Field Marshal, 190, 238
Kohima, 173, 173M, 178, 179M; battle at, 180, 180M
Kokoda Trail, N. Guinea, 146, 146M
Köln, German cruiser, 253
Kolombangara, 150, 150M2, 151M1
Komet, German raider, 256, 256M
Kondo, Admiral, 138, 144
Konev, Marshal, 221, 222
Konigsberg, 218M, 219M, 221M
Kopels, Lieut.-Gen., 83
Koritza, 37, 38, 39M
Kormoran, German raider, 256, 256M
Korosten, 86, 87M
Kostenko, General, 192
Kra Peninsula, 102, 102M, 110M
Kremenchug, 86, 87M
Kristiansand, 20, 20M
Krueger, General, 158, 162, 163
Kuala Lumpur, 102, 102M, 110M
Kuantan, 105, 105M
Kula Gulf, Battle of, 150M2
Kummetz, Adm. Oscar, 268–9
Kuribayashi, Maj.-Gen., 164
Kurita, Adm. Takeo, 159, 160–1
Kurland Peninsula, 215, 215M, 218
Kursk, 190, 194, 194M1,2, 195M, 203, 203M; Battle of, 116, 190–1, 204–5, 204M, 205M
Kurzea, General, 16
Kwajalein Atoll, 98M, 153, 153M4
Kweilin, 187, 187M
Kyaukme, 186, 186M
Kyushu, 98M, 168

La Spezia, 129, 129M3
Ladoga, Lake, 88, 88M, 89, 89M, 208, 208M1,2, 209, 209M, 214, 214M
Lae, 147, 147M
Lanciano, 122M, 123
Lashio, 172, 173M, 186, 186M
Latvia, 212M, 213M; Russians overrun, 215, 215M, 221M
Le Havre, 228, 228M, 229M, 238M, 241M
Le Kef, 74M, 75, 75M
Le Mans, 238, 238M
Le May, Gen. Curtis, 280
Lebanon, 32, 32M
Lednevo, 89, 89M
Ledo, 173M, 177, 177M; Ledo road, 172, 176
Lee, Admiral Willis, 144
Leeb, General von, 84

Leese, Lieut.-Gen. Sir Oliver, 128–9, 182
Legaspi, 106, 107M
Leghorn, 128M, 129, 129M3
Leigh-Mallory, Air Marshal Sir T. L., 230
Leipzig, 221M, 223M
Leipzig, German cruiser, 253
Lemelsen, General, 130
Leningrad, 84, 84M; Germans attack, 86–9, 87M–9M; siege of, 89, 92, 93M, 208; relief of, 191, 208–9, 208M, 213M, 214M
Lentaigne, Maj.-Gen. W., 177
Lexington, US carrier, 100, 134, 136, 137M, 138
Leyte, 158, 158M, 159M, 162, 163, 163M
Leyte Gulf, battle of, 158–61, 158M–61M
Libya, 44, 50–62, 51M–62M, 72, 72M–3M
Liddell-Hart, Capt. Sir Basil, 135
Liège, 12, 23M, 25M
Lingayen Bay, 106, 107M
Lingayen Gulf, 162, 162M
Lingling, 187, 187M
Linz, 221, 221M
Liri, river, 122M, 123
List, Field-Marshal, 37, 194, 195
Lithuania, 212M, 213M, 215M, 221M
Litorio, Italian battleship, 258, 258M
Litsa, 215, 215M2
Liuchow, 187, 187M
Lodz, 16, 16M, 17M
Lofoten Islands, 270, 270M1,2
Loire, river, 228, 229M, 236M, 238, 238M; bridges of bombed, 277
Lokhvitsa, 86, 87M
Lombok Straits, 110, 110M
London: Free French in, 26; blitz on, 30, 31M, 276
'Longstop', 78, 79M
Loroag, 106, 107M
Los Negros, 150M1, 151, 151M4
Louisiade Archipelago, 136
Low Countries, 22, 23M; battle of, 24, 24M, 25M; blitz on, 276; *and see* Belgium, Netherlands
Lübeck, 276, 278, 279M
Lucas, Maj.-Gen. John, 126–7
Luga, river, 86, 87M
Lütjens, Vice-Adm. Günther, 260
Lützow, German battleship, 20, 20M, 268, 268M
Luxembourg: 24M; Allied invasion of, 240, 241M, 243M, 244M, 245M, 246M, 247M
Luzon, 98M, 106, 107M, 110M, 135, 156M, 158, 159M, 160; US assault on, 162–3, 162M
Lvov, 212, 212M, 213M
Lyons, 237M

MacArthur, Gen. Douglas, 96, 97; in Pacific War, 106, 108, 135, 147, 149, 152, 158, 168
McCreery, Lieut.-Gen. Richard, 129, 130
Macedonia, 36, 38, 39M, 42, 43M
Mackensen, Gen. Hans Georg von, 126
Madagascar, 270–1, 271M5
Maginot Line, 12, 15M, 22, 22M, 23M, 24M, 25M, 27M
Mainz, 241M, 243M, 246, 247M
Maitland, Gen. Sir Henry, 32
Makin Atoll, 98M, 152, 152M1
Malaya, Japanese invasion of, 96, 97, 98M, 99, 102M, 103M, 105, 105M, 110M; British naval weakness in, 252
Malème, 44, 44M
Malinovsky, Maj.-Gen., 192, 216
Malinta Tunnel, 108, 109M
Malta, 60, 258; convoys to, 264, 264M–5M
Manado, 110, 110M
Manchester, British cruiser, 264, 265M
Manchuria, 98M, 99, 187, 187M

Mandalay, 173M; British capture of, 182, 182M, 183M, 184, 186M
Mandalay–Myitkyina Railway, 172, 183M, 186M
Manila, 98M, 106, 107M, 110M, 159M; US assault on, 162M, 163
Manila Bay, 162M, 163
Manipur, 179, 179M (inset)
Mannerheim, Marshal, 88
Mannerheim Line, 18, 18M, 214
Mannheim: bombing of, 276, 278, 279M; 243M, 246, 247M
Manstein, Gen. Eric von, 22; and Russian offensive, 190, 193, 200, 203, 205, 207, 210; and Stalingrad, 198–9, 200, 210; dismissed, 191, 210
Manstein Plan, 22M
Mao Tse-tung, 187
Mareth Line, 72, 72M, 74, 74M, 76–7, 76M1,2, 77M
Mariana Islands, 98M1, 138M1, 156M; US conquest of, 154, 154M, 155M, 156; airbases on, 277, 280, 281M
Marseilles, 236, 236M, 237M
Marshall, Gen. George C., 172
Marshall Islands, 98M, 152M1, 152–3
Maruyama, General, 140–1, 143
Massawa, 52, 53M3
Matapan, Cape, Battle of, 259, 259M
Mateur, 78, 79M
Matmata Hills, 76, 77M
Maungdaw, 174, 174M, 175M, 184M
Mawlaik, 178M, 182, 182M
Mechili, 54, 54M, 55, 59M4, 60M
Medenine, 72, 72M, 76, 76M1, 77M
Mediterranean Sea: control of, 52, 52M1, 60; the war in, 36, 37, 253, 258–9, 258M, 259M, 264, 265M
Medjerda Valley, 78, 79M1
Medjez el Bab, 70, 71M, 78, 79M
Medvezhegorsk, 88, 88M
Mehdia, 70, 70M
Meiktila, 182–3, 182M, 183M, 184, 185
Meindl, General, 44
Melbourne Star, British merchantman, 264, 265M
Mersa Brega, 54, 54M, 59M4, 60M, 72, 72M
Mersa Matruh, 63, 63M1,2, 72, 73M
Messe, Marshal, 78
Messina, US occupation of, 110, 119M, 120M
Metaxas Line, 36, 42, 43M
Metsova, 36, 38, 39M
Meuse, river, 12, 23M, 24, 24M, 25M
Mexico, Gulf of, 253
Midway, US carrier, 134
Midway Island, 99M, 136, 138M1; Battle of, 134–5, 138M, 138–9, 140
Mikawa, Admiral, 142, 144
Mindanao, 98M, 106, 110M, 156M, 159M, 163M
Mindoro, 159M, 162, 162M, 163M
Minsk, 84, 85M, 86, 87M; falls to Russians, 212, 212M, 213M
Mitchell, General, 276
Miteirya Ridge, 68, 68M, 69M
Mitscher, Admiral Marc, 153, 154, 156, 160
Mius, river, 90, 90M
Model, Field Marshal Walther, 191, 210, 212, 238, 242
Mogadishu, 52, 53M3
Mogaung, 177, 177M, 186M
Möhne Dam, bombing of, 276
Monastir, 40, 41M; Gap, 42, 43M
Mongyu, 172, 186, 186M
Montelimar, 236, 237M
Montevideo, 254, 255M
Montgomery, Gen: later Field Marshal Sir Bernard Law: in N. Africa, 49, 64, 66, 68–9, 72, 76–7; and Italian campaign, 116, 119, 121, 123; and

invasion of Normandy, 226, 230, 234; in Europe, 238, 240, 242, 244; and Allied victory, 227, 248
Morava, river, 221, 221M
Moravia, 221, 221M
Moscow, 82, 83, 84, 84M, 86, 87M; battle for, 83, 90–3, 91M, 92M, 190, 206M, 207M
Moscow Conference, 83
Moscow–Leningrad railway, 209, 209M
Moskva, river, 90, 91M, 92M
Moulmein, 112, 113M
Mountbatten, Lord Louis, 172–3
Mozhaysk, 90, 91M
Msus, 54, 54M, 59M4, 60, 60M, 72M
Muar, river, 102, 102M
Munda, 150, 150M2, 151M1
Munich: bombing of, 276, 278, 279M; 243M, 246, 247M
Murmansk, 266, 266M, 267M, 268, 270M; railway, 88, 88M, 214, 214M
Musashi, Japanese battleship, 160
Mussolini, Benito: declares war, 26; and invasion of Greece, 36–7, 38; and Ethiopian campaign, 52; and invasion of Italy, 116–17; overthrow of, 117, 120
Mutaguchi, Lieut.-Gen. Renya, 174, 178, 182
Myebon, 184, 184M
Myitkyina, 173M, 176–7, 177M, 186M
Myshkova, river, 199, 199M

Nadzab, 147, 147M
Nagara, Japanese flagship, 134
Nagasaki, 98M; bombing of, 168, 169
Nagumo, Vice-Adm. Chuichi, 100, 134, 138–9, 142, 143, 154
Namkhan, 186, 186M
Namsos, 20, 20M
Namur, 24, 24M, 25M
Naples, 120, 120M, 121M, 122M
Narva, river, 209, 209M
Narvik, 20, 20M
Nasugbu, 162M, 163
Nazis, 14; and surrender of Germany, 248
Neame, Gen. Philip, VC, 54
Netherlands (Holland): defences of, 12, 23M; invasion of, 24, 24M; and Japanese occupation of Indo-China, 96; and Allied invasion of Europe, 226, 229M, 240M, 241M, 242M, 243M; *and see* Dutch forces
Neustadt, 219M
New Britain, 98M, 150M1, 151
New Caledonia, 98M, 134
New Georgia, 98M, 150, 150M2, 151M1
New Guinea, 98M, 134, 136, 137M, 146M, 146–7, 147M, 150, 150M, 151
New Hebrides, 98M, 152
New Ireland, 150M1, 151
New Zealand, 98M, 135, 141

NEW ZEALAND FORCES
and battle for the Solomons, 150–1
and see under British Forces

Ngazun, 182, 182M, 183M
Nibeiwa, 50, 51M1
Niemen, river, 82, 87M
Nierstein, 246, 247M
Nigeria, British cruiser, 264, 265M
Nijmegen, 241M, 242, 242M, 243M, 246
Nimitz, Adm. Chester W., 134, 135, 136, 139, 149, 152, 154, 158, 168
Ningthoukhong, 181, 181M
Nis, 40, 41M
Nishimura, Vice-Adm. Shoji, 159, 160, 161
Norfolk, British cruiser, 260, 269, 269M
Normandy: Allied invasion of, 49, 117, 127, 191, 228–33, 228M–32M; battle for, 226, 234–5, 234M–6M; breakout from, 238, 238M, 239M

North Africa, French: Allied landings in, 70, 70M, 71M; *and see* Tunisia
North Africa: bombing of ports, 116; supplies to, 264, 264M–5M; campaign in, 48–79, 198; Allied victory in, 12, 118
Norway, 88, 88M, 260M; German invasion of, 20, 20M; British naval weakness in, 252; importance of to Hitler, 262; Arctic convoys and, 266, 266M, 267M, 268M, 269M; Commando raids on, 270, 270M1,2; German troops in, 226, 253; German army retreats to, 215, 215M
Novaya Zemlya, 266M, 267M
Novgorod, 86, 87M, 93M; Russians take, 209, 209M
Novorossiysk, 202, 202M
Novi Borissov, 83, 87M
Nuremberg: bombing of, 278, 279M; Tribunal, 248
Nürnberg, German cruiser, 218, 253

Oahu, 98M, 100, 100M, 138M1
O'Connor, Maj.-Gen. Richard, 48, 49, 50, 54, 62
Oder, river, Russian advance to, 219, 219M, 222
Odessa, 87M, 93M, 207M, 210, 211M
Odeynoye Pole, 88, 88M
Okamura, General, 187
Okinawa, 156; battle of, 135, 166, 166M
Olendorf, Admiral J. B., 158, 160–1, 162
Olympia Pass, 43, 43M
Omaha beach, Normandy, 230M, 231, 233, 233M
Onega, Lake, 214, 214M
Operations:
Achse (Axis), 117
Anvil, 236, 236M, 237M
Barbarossa, 37, 82–4, 84M, 88, 190; *and see* Russia, invasion of
Citadel, 116, 204–5
Crusader, 58, 58M
Dragoon, 117
Epsom, 234
I C H I-G O, 187, 187M
Market Garden, 226, 242, 242M
Overlord, 228, 230–1, 230M–1M, 236, 236M; air support for, 277; *and see* Europe, Allied invasion of
Pedestal, 264, 264M–5M
Sealion, 28, 28M, 30, 252, 276
Thunderclap, 145, 277
Torch, 49, 70, 70M, 72
U-GO, 178, 179M
Oran, 32, 32M1, 70, 70M
Orel, 90, 91M, 203, 203M, 204M, 205M, 206M
Orienbaum, 208, 208M1, 209, 209M
Orion, German raider, 256, 256M
Ormoc, 158, 158M
Orne, river, 226
Ortona, 122M, 123
Ostrov, 86, 87M
Oudna, 70, 70M
Ouistreham, 226, 231M
Owen Stanley Range, 146, 146M
Ozawa, Vice-Adm. Jisaburo, 156, 159, 161

Pacific Ocean: German raiders in, 256, 256M; Japanese offensive in, 96, 99–110, 98M–110M, 253; Allied Command in (ABDA), 110; war in, 134–68, 137M–68M, 277
Pakokku, 182, 182M, 185M
Palel, 181, 181M
Palembang, 110, 110M
Palestine, 50
Pantelleria, bombing of, 116, 118–19, 118M
Panzers, *see under* German forces

Papagos, Gen. Alexander, 36
Papua, 98M, 134, 137M, 146, 146M, 147M, 150M1, 151, 151M (inset)
Paris: falls to Germans, 26, 27M; and Normandy landings, 228, 229M, 235, 236M; liberation of, 238, 238M, 241
Parry Island, 135, 135M5
Pas de Calais, 226, 228, 233, 240, 241
Patch, Lieut.-Gen., 236
Patani, 102, 102M
Patton, Gen. George S., 119, 221; and invasion of Europe, 226, 227, 236, 238, 244, 246
Paul, Prince of Yugoslavia, 37
Paulus, General, 190, 194, 196; in Stalingrad, 198–9, 200
Pavlograd–Taganrog railway, 192, 192M2,3
Pavlov, General G. D., 83
Pearl Harbor: Japanese attack on, 96, 99M, 99, 100, 100M, 106; US base at, 138, 138M1
Pegu, 184, 185M
Peleliu, 135
Peloponnese, 42, 43M
Percival, Lieut.-Gen. A. E., 96, 97, 102
Pernambuco, 254, 255M
Perth, HMAS, 110
Pervomaysk, 86, 87M
Pétain, Marshal Philippe, 26, 96
'Peter's Corner', 78, 79M
Petrozavodsk, 88, 88M
Philippines, 98M, 110M; Japanese invasion of, 96, 99, 106, 106M, 135; Philippine plan, 149, 158; US assault on, 158–63, 158M–63M
Philippine Sea, battle of, 154, 156, 156M, 157M
Pinguin, German raider, 256, 256M
Piraeus, 43M; British fleet at, 259
Pitomnik airfield, 200, 201M
Platanias, 44, 44M
Platt, Lieut.-Gen. Sir William, 52, 271
Po, river, 130, 131M2
Pola, Italian cruiser, 259, 259M
Poland: invasion of, 14, 16, 16M, 17M, 252, 276; Russians invade, 210–12, 212M, 213M, 218M, 219M, 221M; at end of war, 248

POLISH FORCES
Air force, 16
Army: and German invasion, 12, 16, 16M; and defence of Norway, 20, 20M; in Italian campaign, II Corps, 124, 125M, 129M2, 131M1; parachute brigade, at Arnhem, 242, 242M

Pomerania, fall of, 219, 219M
Porac Line, 106, 107M
Port Moresby, 98M, 134–7, 137M, 146–7, 146M, 147M, 150M1
Port Said, 73M, 264
Port Stanley, 254, 255M
Portbail, 233, 233M
Portsmouth, 263M
Portugal, 36, 253
Pound, Adm. Sir Dudley, 266–7
Pourville, 273, 273M
Poznan, 219, 219M
Prague, 219M, 221, 221M
Pridham–Wippell, Vice-Adm. H. D., 259
Prince of Wales, British battleship, 105
Prinz Eugen, German cruiser, 218, 253, 257, 260, 260M, 262, 263M
Pripet, river, 84–5, 84M, 85M, 87M
Prussia, East *see* East Prussia
Prome, 112, 113M, 184, 185M
Pskov, 209, 209M
Pulau Ubin, 102, 103M
Pulebadze, Mount, 180, 180M

Pustoshka, 209, 209M
Puys, 273, 273M

Qattara Depression, 66, 67M

Rabaul, 98M, 136, 137M, 146, 146M, 149, 150M1, 152
Raeder, Adm. Erich, 254, 260, 262, 268; resigns, 269
Rafina, 42, 43M
Ramsay, Adm. Sir Bertram, 230, 252
Ramillies, British battleship, 271
Ramree Island, 184, 184M
Rangoon, 98M, 112, 113M, 173M, 183; British capture, 184, 185M
Rapido, river, 122M, 123, 124, 124M, 125M, 126
Rathedaung, 174, 174M
Rees, 246, 247M
Reggio di Calabria, 120–1, 120M
Remagen, 243M, 246, 247M
Rendova Island, 150, 150M2, 151M1
Repulse, British battle-cruiser, 105
Resolution, British battleship, 32
Retimo, 44, 44M
Reynaud, Paul, 26
Rheinberg, 246, 247M
Rhine, river: Allied drive to, 226, 240, 241M, 242, 242M, 243M; Allied crossing of, 227, 246, 247M
Rhineland, Hitler reoccupies, 14, 15M
Rhodes, bombing of, 264
Rhône, river, US drive up, 236, 236M, 237M
Ribbentrop, Joachim von, 96
Richelieu, French battleship, 32
Riga, 212, 212M, 213M; fall of, 215, 215M
Rimini, 128M, 129, 129M3
Rintelen, General von, 116
Ritchie, General N., 63
River Plate, battle of, 254, 255M
Roberts, Maj.-Gen. J. H., 273
Rodney, British battleship, 260, 260M
Rokossovsky, General, 198, 200, 218, 222
Rome: bombing of, 116–17, 117, 120M, 126, 126M; capture of, 127, 127M, 128
Rommel, Field Marshal Erwin: in North Africa, 48–9, 54–77 *passim*; and Italian campaign, 117; and invasion of Normandy, 228, 233, 234; replaced, 238
Roosevelt, President Franklin D., 96, 117, 149
Roskill, Captain S. W., 253
Rostock, Allied bombing of, 276
Rostov, 90, 90M, 194, 194M1,2, 195M; Russians take, 202, 202M, 203, 203M, 206, 206M, 207M
Rotterdam, 24M; blitz on, 24
Rouen: bombing of, 238, 241M, 278, 279M
Ruhr, Battle of, 276, 278, 279M; and Allied invasion of Europe, 240, 240M, 241M, 243M, 246, 247M
Rumania, 16, 36, 37, 116; and Russian war, 83, 84M, 85M, 87M, 116, 191, 192; Russian defeat of, 216, 216M, 221M; joins Allies, 217

RUMANIAN FORCES
see under German forces

Rundstedt, Field Marshal Gerd von, 12, 22; in Russia, 83, 85, 90; and Allied invasion of Europe, 226, 228, 233, 240
Russell Islands, 150, 151M1
Russia: annexation of Poland, 16, 17M; invasion of Finland, 18, 18M, 19M; German raiders sail round, 256, 256M; Germany prepares invasion of, 36, 37, 84–5, 84M, 85M; Germany invades, 82–3, 190, 253, 266; and Arctic

convoys, 266, 266M, 267M; counter-offensive against Germany, 190–223, 226; and choice of Second Front, 236; and division of Germany, 248, 248M; *and see* Russian forces

RUSSIAN FORCES
in Europe: 16–18, 17M–19M, 82, 84, 88; and choice of Second Front, 236; and invasion of Europe *see under* Russian forces in Russian campaign, *below*
in Russian campaign:
Army: strength of, 82–3, 84–5; and German invasion, 83, 86–8, 87M, 88M; and siege of Leningrad, 89, 89M, 191; and battle for Moscow, 90–3, 90M–3M, 190; counter-offensive of, 190, 192–5, 192M–5M; and Battle of Stalingrad, 196–200, 197M–200M, 202; advance of, 202–17, 204M–16M; invades Germany, 218–19, 218M, 219M, 220–1, 220M–1M captures Berlin, 222, 222M, 223M
Stavka (Soviet Supreme Command), 92
Fronts: 1 Belorussian, 212, 212M, 218, 218M, 219M; and capture of Berlin, 222, 222M, 223M
2 Belorussian, 218, 218M, 219M, 222, 223M
3 Belorussian, 215, 215M, 218M
1 Baltic, advance to Riga, 212, 215, 215M
2 Baltic: and relief of Leningrad, 209, 209M; in Estonia, 215, 215M
3 Baltic: in Estonia, 215, 215M
Bryansk, 91M, 92M, 93, 93M, 203, 203M, 205M, 206M
Central, 204, 205M, 206M
Don, 198, 198M; at Stalingrad, 200, 201M
Kalinin, 92, 92M, 93, 93M; and battle for Moscow, 91M, 92
Karelian: and defeat of Finland, 214, 214M
Leningrad: and relief of Leningrad, 208–9, 208M, 209M, 214M, 215, 215M3
South, 85M, 93M; and winter offensive, 192, 192M2,3; and Kharkov, 203, 203M
South West: and invasion of Russia, 85M, 86, 87M; and battle for Moscow, 91M, 92, 92M, 93M; and winter offensive, 192, 192M2,3, 195M; at Stalingrad, 198–200, 198M–200M; and Kharkov, 203, 203M, 205M, 206M
Stalingrad, 190, 195M, 198–200, 198M–200M, 202, 202M, 203
Steppe, 205, 205M, 206M
Trans-Caucasus, 195, 195M, 202, 202M
1 Ukrainian, 210, 211M, 212, 212M, 219M, 221, 221M; and capture of Berlin, 222, 222M, 223M
2 Ukrainian, 210, 211M, 216, 216M, 220, 220M, 221, 221M
3 Ukrainian, 210, 211M, 216–17, 216M, 220, 220M, 221, 221M
4 Ukrainian, 210, 211M, 212, 212M, 216–17, 216M, 221, 221M
Volkhov: and relief of Leningrad, 208–9, 208M, 209M
Voronezh, 195M, 203–5, 203M–6M

West: strength of, 84, 84M, 85M; and invasion of Russia, 87M, 91M, 92, 92M, 93M, 205, 206M
Armies: Second, 90, 90M
Fifth, 86, 87M
Sixth, 192, 192M2,3
Ninth, 90, 90M, 92, 92M, 192, 192M2,3
Fourteenth, 215, 215M2
Eighteenth, 90, 90M, 92M, 93
Nineteenth, 215, 215M3
Thirty-seventh, 86, 87M, 90, 90M
Fortieth, 203
Forty-seventh, 218, 218M
Fifty-first: at Stalingrad, 196, 197M1, 198M, 199M
Fifty-seventh, 192, 192M2,3
Sixty-second: and Stalingrad, 196, 197M1, 198M, 199M
First Shock: and battle for Moscow, 92, 92M
Third Shock: and battle for Moscow, 92M, 93
First Tank: and Stalingrad, 196, 197M1
Third Tank: takes Kharkov, 203, 203M
Fourth Tank: and Stalingrad, 196, 197M1
Corps: XIII Mechanized on Stalingrad Front, 190
Military Air Power: strength of, 82–3; in Russian campaign, 212

Ruweisat Ridge, 64, 65M
Ryuku Islands, 98M, 149, 166; *and see* Okinawa
Rzhev, 90, 91M, 92M, 93

Saar, and Allied invasion of Germany, 226, 241M, 243M
St Goar, 246, 247M
St Lô: US capture of, 233–5, 232M–1M, 238M
St Helena, 254, 255M, 257M
St Malo, 238M, 241M
St Matthias Islands, 150M1, 151
St Nazaire, 32; raid on, 272, 272M
St Valéry-en-Caux, 26, 27M, 241M
St Vith, 244, 245M, 247M
Saipan, 98M, 153, 154, 154M, 156M
Salamana, 147, 147M
Salla, 215, 215M
Salerno, Allied landings at, 117, 120–1, 120M, 121M
Salween, river, 112, 113M, 173M
Samar, 158M, 159; battle of, 161M, 163M
San Antonio, Luzón, 162M, 163
San Bernadino Strait, 159, 159M, 160, 161, 162M
Santa Cruz, battle of, 143, 143M4
Santa Rosa, Mount, 108, 108M
Sangro, river, 17, 120M, 121, 122M, 123
Sarawak, 98M, 110, 110M
Sardinia, 118, 118M, 119, 265M
Savo Island, battle of, 140, 140M, 142, 142M1, 144, 145M
Sbeitla, 74, 75M
Sbiba, 75M
Scapa Flow, 260M, 270
Scharnhorst, German battle-cruiser, 257, 257M, 262, 263M, 276; sunk, 269, 269M
Schelde, river, 12; Estuary, 240, 241M, 242, 243M
Schlieffen Plan (1914), 22, 22M
Schlüsselburg, capture of, 89, 89M
Schmidt, General, 153
Schörner, Field-Marshal, 191, 210, 221
Schweinfurt, US raid on, 277, 278, 279M
Scoone, General, 178
Scotland, 226
Scott, Rear-Adm., 142–3
Second Front: Allied choice of, 236; preparations for, 117, 118; air support for, 277; *and*

see Europe, Normandy, Operation Overlord
Sedan, 12, 22, 22M, 23M
Sedjenanane, 70, 71M
Seeckt, Gen. Hans von, 14
Seikpyu, 182, 182M
Seine, river: Germans cross, 26, 27M; bombing of, 277; and Allied invasion of Europe, 228, 228M, 229M, 236M, 238, 238M, 240
Sendai, Japanese cruiser, 144, 145M2
Sengmai, 181, 181M
Senio, river, 129, 129M3
Servia Pass, 42, 43M
Sevastopol, 83, 87M, 93M, 192, 192M; falls to Germans, 193, 193M, 206M, 207M; falls to Russians, 210, 211M
Seydlitz, German cruiser, 253
Sfakia, 44, 44M
Sfax, 76
Sheffield, British cruiser, 268, 268M, 269, 269M
Sherbrooke, Captain R., 268
Shibasaki, Rear-Adm., 153
Shima, Admiral, 160–1
Shoho, Japanese carrier, 136, 137M
Shokaku, Japanese carrier, 136, 137M, 142, 142M2, 143, 143M4, 156, 157M
Shuri Line, Okinawa, 166, 166M
Shwegu, 186, 186M
Sicily: Luftwaffe in, 37, 49, 70M, 265M; Allied landings in, 116, 118–20, 118M, 119M, 190, 206
Sidi Azeis, 58, 58M
Sidi Barrani, 50, 51M1, 54M, 73M
Sidi Bou Zid, 74, 75M
Sidi Hamza, 63, 63M1
Sidi Nsir, 70, 71M
Sidi Omar, 56M, 57, 57M, 59M4
Sidi Rezegh, 58, 58M, 59M2, 61M2
Sidra Ridge, 60, 61M2,3
Siegfried Line, 24M, 234; Allied advance to, 241M, 246, 247M
Silesia, fall of, 219, 219M
Simovitch, General, 37
Simpson, General, 242
Singapore Island, 98M, 102, 103M, 105, 105M, 110M
Singora, 102, 102M, 110M
Sino-Japanese War, 96, 99, 187, 187M
Sirte, 54, 54M, 72, 72M
Sittang, river, 173M: Battle of, 97, 112, 113M, 184, 185M
Sittaung, 179M, 182, 182M
Skopje, 40, 41M
Slim, Lieut.-Gen. Sir William, 97, 112, 173; in Burma, 178, 181, 182, 184
Slim, river, 102, 102M
Smolensk, 83, 84, 84M, 86, 87M; Russians take, 206–7, 206M, 207M, 212M, 213M
Smith, Maj.-Gen. 'Howling Mad', 152, 154
Smuts, General Jan C., 276
Sollum, 54M, 56, 56M, 57, 57M, 58M, 59M
Solomon Islands, 98M, 134, 135, 136, 137M, 140, 144; naval battles of, 140, 142–3, 142M1,2, 143M3,4; Allied victory in, 150–1, 150M, 151M
Somaliland, British, 52, 53M2,3
Somaliland, French, 52, 53M2
Somerville, Adm. Sir James, 252
Somme, river, defence of, 12, 26, 26M
Sortvala, 88, 88M
Soryu, Japanese carrier, 138, 138M2, 139
South America, 255M, 256M, 257M
South Dakota, US battleship, 144, 145M2

Souk el Arba, 70, 70M, 71M
Speer, Albert, 277
Sperrle, Field-Marshal, 276
Spitzbergen, 266M, 267M; Commando raid on, 270, 270M1
Sprague, Rear-Adm., 161
Spree, river, 222, 223M
Spruance, Vice-Adm., 134–5, 152
Stalin, Josef, 82, 83, 85, 92, 190, 196, 208, 236
Stalingrad, 49, 84M; German offensive against, 194–5, 194M2, 195M; battle of, 190, 196–202, 197M–201M
Stänge, Captain, 268–9
Starodub, 86, 87M
Stavanger, 20, 20M, 257M, 266M
Stettin, 253
Stilwell, Lieut.-Gen. Joseph W.: adviser to Chinese army, 187; and Burma campaigns, 172, 176, 178, 182, 186
Stopford, General, 180
Strasbourg, 241M, 243M, 246, 247M
Strasbourg, French battle-cruiser, 32
Strumica, 42, 43M
Student, General, 242
Suda Bay, 36, 43M, 44, 44M
Sudan: British forces in, 50, 52, 52M1, 53M
Sudetenland, annexation of, 14, 15M
Suez, 73M, 271; Canal, 44, 73M
Suffolk, British cruiser, 260
Sultan, Lieut.-Gen. D., 186
Sumatra, 98M; Japanese attack, 110, 110M
Suribachi, Iwo Jima, 164, 164M
Surigao Strait, 159, 159M, 160M1
Susuki, General, 158, 163
Swift, General, 162–3
Sword beach, Normandy, 231, 231M
Sydney, Australian cruiser, 256, 258
Syfret, Vice-Admiral E. N., 264, 271
Syracuse, Gulf of, 119, 119M
Syria, 32, 32M3

Taga, El, 66, 67M
Taganrog, 192, 192M1
Taiko, Japanese carrier, 156, 157M
Taivu, 140, 140M
Takanami, Japanese destroyer, 145, 145M3
Takagi, Vice-Admiral, 136
Taman peninsula, 202, 202M
Tanaka, Admiral, 135, 144–5
Tarakan, 110, 110M
Taranto, 120M, 121; Italian fleet attacked at, 258, 258M
Tarawa Atoll, 98M; battle of, 135, 152–3, 152M1,2
Tarhuna, 72, 72M
Tarnopol, 191, 210, 211M
Tassafaronga, 145, 145M3
Taungy, 112, 113M
Tavoy, 112, 113M
Tebaga Gap, 76, 77M
Tebéssa, 74, 74M, 75, 75M
Tell el Eisa, 64, 65M
Tenga airfield, 102, 103M
Tengeder, 54, 54M, 55
Termoli, 117, 120M, 121, 122M
Thabeikkyin, 182, 182M, 183M
Thailand, 98M; Japanese occupation of, 99, 102, 102M, 105M, 113M, 173M, 184
Thala, 75, 75M
Thazi, 183, 183M
Thebes, 42, 43M
Thermopylae, 42, 43M
Thessaloniki, 41M, 42, 43M
Thessaly, 36, 37M, 38
Thor, German raider, 256, 256M
Thorne, Lieut.-Gen. Sir A. F. A. N., 226
Thrace, 42, 43M
Tikhvin, 89, 89M

287

Timor, 98M; Japanese attack, 110, 110M
Tinian, 154, 154M, 156M
Tirpitz, German battleship, 266, 270
Tito, Marshal, 217
Tobruk: Allied capture of, 50, 51M2, 56, 58, 59M, 60, 60M, 61M2,3; Axis capture of, 48, 49, 62, 62M, 69, 72M
Tojo, General, 96
Tokyo, 98M, 138M1, 164; Doolittle Raids on, 136, 277
Tolbukhin, General, 216
Torgau, 222, 223M
Torun, 16, 16M, 17M; surrender of, 219, 219M
Tosno, 208M1, 209, 209M
Toulon, 32, 236M; Allies capture, 236, 237M
Treasury Island, 151, 151M1
Trenchard, Lord, 276
Trident Conference (1943), 228
Trigno, river, 120M, 122M, 123
Trigh el Abd, 60, 61M2,3
Trigh Capuzzo, 60, 61M2,3
Tripoli, 37, 48, 52M1, 54; Eighth Army enters, 72M
Trondheim, 20, 20M
Truk Island, 98M, 152, 156M
Truman, President H., and atomic bomb, 168
Truscott, Maj.-Gen. Lucius, 127, 129, 130
Tsirilyansky, 194, 195M
Tugegaroa, 106, 107M
Tula, 90, 91M
Tulagi, 134, 135, 136, 137M, 140, 140M
Tummar, 50, 51M1
Tunis, 70M, 71M; falls to Allies, 78, 79M, 118M, 190
Tunisia: Allied and German landings in, 70M, 71M; war in, 48, 49, 70–9, 72M–9M; Axis surrender of, 78–9, 79M, 116, 118, 118M
Turner, Rear-Admiral Richmond K., 140, 152, 153, 154
Tuslov, river, 90, 90M

Ugaki, Vice-Adm. Matome, 156
Ukraine, 83, 84M, 85M, 86, 87M, 90, 92, 190; battles in, 210, 211M, 212M
Uman, 86, 87M
United States of America: relations with Japan (1941), 96, 99; support of China, 99, 187; enters war, 96, 194; and Pacific War, 99, 134, 136; plans counter-offensive in Far East and Pacific, 149; and N. African campaign, 49; aid to Russia, 204; and Italian surrender, 117; and choice of Second Front, 236, 236M; and atomic bomb, 168; *and see* US Forces

UNITED STATES FORCES
in Burma: 172–3, 176–7, 177M
American Air Transport Command, 173
Northern Combat Command, 182, 186
5307 Provisional Regiment, 177, 177M
in China: US Fourteenth Air Force, 187
in Europe: qualities of, 227; and choice of Second Front, 236; and invasion of Germany, 221, 221M, 222, 223M, 226, 227
Army
Army Groups: Sixth (US Seventh and French First Armies: landings in France, 236, 237M; invasion of Germany, 242, 243M, 246, 247M
Twelfth (US First and Third Armies): and breakout from Normandy, 238, 238M; and invasion of Germany, 221, 221M, 227, 240–6, 241M–7M
Armies: First, Third and

Seventh *see above*; Ninth, in advance to Germany, 242, 243M, 244M
Corps: V, 238, 238M, 245M; VIII, 244, 244M, 245M; XVIII Airborne, 245M
Divisions: (3 and 45), in South of France, 236, 237M; (9, 80 and 87) cross Rhine, 246, 247M; Airborne, 236, 237M, 246, 247M; 82 Airborne, and Arnhem, 242, 242M; 101 Airborne, and Arnhem, 242, 242M; defence of Bastogne, 226, 244, 245M; 4 Armoured, 246, 247M; 7 Armoured, 244, 245M
Butler Task Force, in South of France, 236, 237M
US Army Air Force: Eighth Airforce and raids on Germany, 277, 278, 279M
and see US forces in Italy, US forces in Normandy
in Italy
Army: and campaign in Italy, 119–27, 119M–27M
Armies: Fifth (British X, US II and US VI Corps): landings, 120M, 121, 121M; offensives of, 123–30, 122M–31M
Seventh, 119, 119M
in Mediterranean:
Navy: and Malta convoys, 264, 265M
in Normandy:
Army
First Army Group (FUSAG, Phantom Army), 226
Twelfth Army Group: and Normandy landings, 234–5; reorganization of, 238
First Army: strength of, 228, 228M; and invasion of Normandy, 226, 230–8, 230M–9M
Corps: V, and invasion of Normandy, 228M, 230M, 231, 233, 238M; closing of Falaise Gap, 238, 239M; VII, 228M, 230M, 231, 232M, 233, 234M, 235, 238M; VIII, 232M, 234M, 235; XIX, 228M, 233, 234M, 235, 238M
Divisions: (4, 9 and 79), 232M, 233; Airborne, 228, 228M, 230; 82 Airborne, 228, 228M
Rangers, 226, 227
in North Africa:
First Army: and Allied victory in Tunisia, 49, 70, 70M, 71M, 74–5, 74M, 75M, 78–9, 79M
Corps: II, 75, 75M, 78–9, 79M
Divisions: (9), 78, 79M1; 1 Armoured, 74–5, 75M, 78–9, 79M
Centre and Western Task forces, landings of, 70, 70M
in Pacific:
strength of, 99; and Pearl Harbor, 100, 100M; and fall of Philippines, 96, 106–9, 107M–9M; and Pacific War, 134–68, 137M–69M
Armies: Sixth: and Leyte Gulf, 158–9, 158M; and Luzon Campaign, 162, 162M
Eighth: and Luzon Campaign, 162M, 163; and freeing of Philippines, 163, 163M
Tenth: and Battle of Okinawa, 135, 166, 166M
Fortieth: and battle for Solomons, 150M1, 151
Corps: I, and fall of Bataan, 108, 108M; in Luzon Campaign, 162–3, 162M
II, and fall of Bataan, 108, 108M
X, and Battle of Leyte Gulf, 158–9, 158M

XI, in Luzon Campaign, 162M, 163
XIV, and Guadalcanal, 141; in Luzon Campaign, 162, 162M, 163
XXIV, and Battle of Leyte Gulf, 158, 158M; and Okinawa, 166, 166M
Divisions: (25), attack on New Georgia, 150; (37 and 43) attack on New Georgia, 150, 150M2; (77), and capture of Guam, 154, 155M; 11 Airborne, and Luzon Campaign, 162, 162M, 163; 1 Cavalry, invasion of Los Negros, 151; 7, 8, 12 Cavalry, invasion of Los Negros, 151M4; 7 infantry, and clearing of Marshalls, 153, 153M4; 27 Infantry, attack on Saipan, 154, 154M
Regiments: 26 Cavalry, defence of Philippines, 106, 107M; 32, 106 and 184 Infantry, and clearing of Marshalls, 153, 153M4, 153M5; 164 Infantry, and Guadalcanal, 140; Paratroops, in New Guinea, 147, 147M
Army Air Force: USAFFE, and fall of Philippines, 99, 106–8, 107M–9M; 7th Army Air Force, and clearing of Marshalls, 152; bombers, and Iwo Jima, 164; Twentieth Air Force, and raids on Tokyo, 136, 277, 281M; Superfortress 'Enola Gay' drops atomic bomb, 168
Marine Corps:
Corps: III Amphibious, and Okinawa, 166, 166M; Wake Island Garrison, 97, 100
Divisions: in battle for New Georgia, 150, 150M2
(1), and Guadalcanal, 135, 140M, 143; on New Britain, 150M1, 151
(2), and Battle of Tarawa, 135, 152M2, 153, 153M3; attacks on Saipan and Tinian, 154, 154M
(3), in battle for Solomons, 151, 151M3; and capture of Guam, 154, 155M
(4), and clearing of Marshalls, 153, 153M4; attack on Saipan and Tinian, 154, 154M; and capture of Iwo Jima, 164, 164M
(5), and capture of Iwo Jima, 164, 164M
(7), and Guadalcanal, 140
Brigades: (1), and capture of Guam, 154, 155M
Regiments: (22, 23 and 24), and clearing of Marshalls, 153, 153M4,5
Fifth Amphibious Force: and clearing of Marshalls and Marianas, 152, 153, 154; and capture of Iwo Jima, 164, 164M
Dive-bombers, and battle of Eastern Solomons, 142, 142M2
Navy
Pacific Fleet, 96, 98M, 99, 110; and Pearl Harbor, 100, 100M; and Pacific War, 134–5
Fleets: Third: and clearing of Marshalls, and battle of Leyte Gulf, 159–61, 159M
Fifth: and clearing of Marshalls, 152–3
Seventh: and Battle of Leyte Gulf, 159M, 160–1; and Luzon Campaign, 162, 162M
Task Forces: (11), and Battle of Coral Sea, 136, 137M
(16), and Midway, 138M, 139; and Santa Cruz, 143, 143M4

(17), and Coral Sea, 134, 136–7, 137M; and Santa Cruz, 143, 143M4; and Battle of Midway, 134–5, 138M, 139
(38), and Battle of Leyte Gulf, 159M, 160, 161, 161M
(58), and Saipan, 154; and Battle of Philippine Sea, 156, 156M, 157M2,3
(61), and Battle of Eastern Solomons, 142, 142M2
(64), actions off Guadalcanal, 144, 145M2
(77), in Battle of Leyte Gulf, 160–1, 160M1,2
East Carrier, and clearing of Marshalls, 153

Uruguay, 254
Ushant, 262, 263M
Ushijima, Lieut.-Gen., 166
Utah beach, Normandy, 230M, 230–1, 232M

Vaagsö Island, 270, 270M3
Valmontone, 127, 127M
Valona, 37, 39M
Valiant, British battleship, 259, 259M
Valletta, 264, 265M
Vandergrift, Maj.-Gen., 140
Vasterival, 273, 273M
Vatutin, General, 198, 200
Veghel, 242, 242M
Veis Pass, 42, 43M
Vella Lavella, 150, 151M1
Velletri, 127, 127M
Venlo, 242, 243M
Versailles, Treaty of (1919), 14
Vian, Rear-Admiral P., 270
Vichy, government at, 26, 27M4; and occupation of Indo-China, 96; French Empire, of, 32, 32M, 270–2M, 271M
Victoria Point, 112, 113M
Vienna, falls to Russians, 220, 220M, 221
Vietinghoff, Gen. Heinrich von, 123, 130
Vigan airfield, 106, 107M
Viipuri, 88, 88M, 89M; Russian capture of, 214, 214M
Vilna, 16, 16M, 17M
Vilnyus, 215, 215M
Vis, Allied occupation of, 117
Visconti-Prasca, Gen. Sebastiano, 36–7
Vistula, river: battle of, 16, 17M3, 212, 212M, 213M, 218, 218M, 226
Vittorio Veneto, Italian battle-ship, 258M, 259, 259M
Volga canal, 90, 91M
Volga, river: German thrust to, 190, 194–6, 195M, 197M; in Russian counter-attack, 198, 198M, 200M, 201M
Volkhov, river, 89, 89M
Volturno, river, 120M, 121, 122M, 123
Voronezh, 194, 194M1,2, 195M
Vuosalmi, 88, 88M
Vyazma, 90, 91M, 92M, 93

Wace, New Guinea, 147, 147M
Wadi Akarit, 76, 77M
Wainwright, Lieut.-Gen. Jonathan, 96–7, 108
Wake Island, 96–7, 98M, 100
Walker, Captain E. J. 253
Warsaw: fall of, 16, 16M, 17M; Russians approach, 212, 212M, 213M; falls to Russians, 218, 218M
Washington, US battleship, 144, 145M2
Washington Conference (1922), 276
Wavell, Field-Marshal Sir Archibald: and defence of Balkans, 36, 37, 48, 82; commands ABDA, 110; in N. Africa, 48, 49, 50–8, and Burma campaign, 174, 176
West Africa, French, Vichy occupation of, 32, 32M
Wedmeyer, Maj.-Gen. A., 186

Wei Li-huang, General, 186
Weichs, General, 194, 198, 203
West Wall *see* Siegfried Line
Westenwald, German supply ship, 254
Westfjord, 270, 270M2
Western Dorsale, Tunisia, 74, 75, 75M
Western Front in First World War, 12
Western Front (1940), 22–4, 22M–5M
Weygand, General Maxime, 12, 26
Widder, German raider, 256, 256M
Wiesbaden, 247, 247M
Wiese, General, 236
Wilhelmshaven: bombing of, 254, 255M, 263M, 276
Wilson, Gen. Sir Henry Maitland, 50
Wingate, Brigadier Orde, 172, 176; death of, 177
Woodlark Island, 151
Worms, 246, 247M
Wright, Rear-Admiral, 145
Wungshigum, 181, 181M

Yamamoto, Admiral, 138, 139
Yamashiro, Japanese flagship, 160, 160M1
Yamashita, General, 102, 158, 162–3
Yeremenko, General, 199
Yorktown, US carrier, 134, 137, 137M, 138, 138M2, 139
Youks les Bains, 70, 70M
Yugoslavia: defence of, 36; coup in, 37, 38; German invasion of, 38, 40, 41M, 42; German army in, 216M, 217; partisans in, 117; and Russian advance, 216M; invasion of, 220M, 221

YUGOSLAV FORCES
Air Force, destruction of, 40
Army: in Balkan campaign, 36; and invasion of Yugoslavia, 40, 41M

Zaborie, 89, 89M
Zara, Italian cruiser, 258M, 259, 259M
Zhdanov, M., 208
Zhukov, Marshal G., 92, 212, 215, 216, 222
Zubza, 180, 180M
Zuiho, Japanese carrier, 143, 143M4, 161M
Zuikaku, Japanese carrier, 136, 137M, 142, 142M2, 143M4, 157M2,3, 161M

288